LEADERSHIP
IN TIMES OF CHANGE

A Handbook for Communication
and Media Administrators

LEA's COMMUNICATION SERIES
Jennings Bryant / Dolf Zillman, General Editors

Selected titles in media administration (William G. Christ, advisor) include:

Blanchard/Christ • *Media Education and the Liberal Arts: A Blueprint for the Profession*

Christ • *Media Education Assessment Handbook*

Christ • *Assessing Communication Education: A Handbook for Media, Speech, and Theatre Educators*

Christ • *Leadership in Times of Change: A Handbook for Communication and Media Administrators*

For a complete list of other titles in LEA's Communication Series, please contact Lawrence Erlbaum Associates, Publishers

LEADERSHIP
IN TIMES OF CHANGE

A Handbook for Communication and Media Administrators

Edited by

William G. Christ
Trinity University

NATIONAL COMMUNICATION ASSOCIATION
Annandale, Virginia

LAWRENCE ERLBAUM ASSOCIATES, PUBLISHERS
1999   Mahwah, New Jersey   London

Lawrence Erlbaum Associates, Inc., Publishers
10 Industrial Avenue
Mahwah, NJ 07430

Cover design by Kathryn Houghtaling Lacey

Library of Congress Cataloging-in-Publication Data

Leadership in times of change : a handbook for communication and
media administrators / edited by William G. Christ.
      p. cm.
    Includes bibliographical references and index.
    ISBN 0-8058-2698-X (cloth). — ISBN 0-8058-2911-3 (pbk.)
    1. Communication—Study and teaching (Higher)—Manage-
ment—Handbooks, manuals, etc. 2. Mass media—Study and
teaching (Higher)—Management—Handbooks, manuals, etc. I.
Christ, William G.
    P91.3.L39 1998
    302.2'071'173—dc21   98-35455
                                              CIP

Printed in the United States of America
10 9 8 7 6 5 4 3 2 1

This book is dedicated to
Robert O. Blanchard
colleague . . . mentor . . . friend

Contents

PART II: PROGRAMMATIC CHALLENGES

PART III: ADMINISTRATIVE CHALLENGES

Preface

Useful books on administration need to walk a tightrope between being too general and too specific. On one hand are the general platitudes about such things as leadership that provide the grist for inspirational speeches. On the other hand are the detailed, situation-specific case studies that seem to have little relevance beyond their limited sphere. This book tries to walk the tightrope by providing both broad principles and specifics, both theory and practice.

From federal mandates to fund raising; from leadership strategies to specifics about being an administrator in graduate education, distance learning or community colleges; from defining the field to acknowledging our social responsibility, the authors in this volume represent hundreds of years of combined administrative experience. This book is meant as a handbook for *potential* administrators trying to determine the challenges involved in administration; for *new* administrators who need to quickly learn about the multifaceted responsibilities of administration; and, for *seasoned* administrators who may want a quick reference guide to some of the "meatier" challenges of administration.

Part I of the book lays out a number of *background* issues facing administrators including accountability, defining the field, international linkages, and social responsibility. Part II presents broad *programmatic* challenges involved with being an administrator of hybrid (speech and media), community college, graduate, experiential learning, or distant education programs. Part III concentrates on *specific* challenges faced by most administrators including defining one's leadership style, fundraising, reacting to calls for downsizing and realign-

ment, dealing with intra-university competition and outside stakeholders, responding to student needs, gender issues, diversity and multiculturalism, promotion, tenure, and faculty evaluation, federal mandates,
self-studies, external reviews, and programmatic assessment.

It is hoped that the book will fill a gap in the literature by providing,
in one place, solutions and strategies for leadership in times of change.

ACKNOWLEDGMENTS

A book like this is truly a collaborative effort. First, there were those,
like professor Joe Foote (Southern Illinois University) who has champi-
oned the need to mentor young administrators in our field. His concern,
which he has addressed within a number of national associations,
provided an impetus for developing this book.

Second, there are the chapter authors. Time is perhaps the greatest
challenge of being an administrator. People and problems are pulling
at you in many different ways. I would like to formally thank the
authors in this volume for finding the time to share their ideas and
experience. Throughout the lengthy review process, these authors kept
their focus and senses of humor.

And, finally, there are the people behind the scenes. From Lawrence
Erlbaum Associates, I would like to thank Linda Bathgate who took this
project as it was just beginning and saw it through with grace. I would
also like to thank the best copy editor in the business, Teresa Horton,
and Debbie Ruel, senior production editor who helped keep me on
schedule. And, finally, I would like to thank Joe Petrowski who handled
the business side of the project, and Kathleen O'Malley who believed
enough in the project to do the initial signing.

From the National Communication Association, I would like to
thank Ann Nadjar, NCA Publications Manager, for her support in this
co-publication venture. I would also like to thank the NCA publication
board who believed in the importance of this project.

From Trinity University, I would like to thank my department for
their friendship. They are a terrific group of colleagues. I also would
like to thank President Ronald K. Calgaard, Vice President Edward C.
Roy, Jr., and Dean William O. Walker, Jr. Under their leadership Trinity
University has prospered. All three are leaving higher education administration. All three will be missed. I would especially like to thank

my colleague, mentor, and friend, Robert O. Blanchard, a consummate administrator.

On a more personal note, I would like to thank Nathan and Jonathan Christ who remind me always that we teach and lead through precept and example. And, thanks to my true friend, Judith Anne Christ, who makes all this possible.

Thank you one and all.

—William G. Christ
San Antonio, Texas

I

BACKGROUND

1

Introduction: Administration and Accountability

William G. Christ
Trinity University

> *Unless the higher education sector changes the way it operates by undergoing the kind of restructuring and streamlining that successful businesses have implemented, it will be difficult to garner the increases in public funding needed to meet future demands.*
>
> —Council for Aid to Education (1997, p. 3)

Higher education continues to be under the gun. Decreasing federal and state revenues and resources; increasing tuition costs; loss of access to schools by diverse class and racial groups; deferred building maintenance; increasing equipment and salary costs; faculty morale; lost public trust; disconnects between what is taught and what is learned; lack of clear focus and mission; and limited links between universities, their communities, business, and K–12 education are examples of the challenges facing administrators in higher education today. Administrators are being held accountable for decisions involving personnel, resources, funding, legal and political challenges, and student learning while trying to fulfill the mission of their units, colleges, and universities. The challenges are daunting.

The purpose of this chapter is, first, to identify key off-campus challenges impacting higher education and, second, to introduce the other chapters in the book.

INTRODUCTION

Blanchard and Christ (1993) identified three challenges facing communication and media educators in the late 1980s and early 1990s: calls for the reinvention of undergraduate education, the convergence of communication technologies, and the philosophical and theoretical ferment in the communication and media field. They suggested that the reinvention of undergraduate education called for a New Liberal Arts that combined elements from both traditional and newer fields and disciplines. They argued for a new commitment from programs to the nonmajor, general student. They called for the centrality of media studies in the common curriculum of all students.

Blanchard and Christ (1993) saw the convergence of communication technologies and the philosophical and theoretical ferment in the communication and media field leading to a New Professionalism that required students to become broad-based communication practitioners. They argued for a strong core of courses that would provide a foundation for all communication students and a flexible series of second-tier and elective classes that would allow students to build broad, personalized programs of study. Their call for a broad approach to communication and media education has been both praised and attacked (cf. Dickson, 1995; Duncan, Caywood, & Newsom, 1993; Medsger, 1996).

Christ and Blanchard (1994), building on their earlier argument, suggested a second aspect to the challenges facing undergraduate higher education, when they wrote that there are "at least two major interrelated forces impacting today on higher education: a re-emphasis on undergraduate education and a movement toward assessment" where "the concern about the first has lead to the second" (p. 32).

Two recent studies both confirm and extend the analyses done by Blanchard and Christ and suggest new areas that will have direct impact on communication and media administrators (Council for Aid to Education [CAE], 1997; Kellogg Commission on the Future of State and Land-Grant Universities, 1997). Like Blanchard and Christ, these new studies suggest the need to reinvent undergraduate education and respond to technological innovation. Moreover, and perhaps most importantly, one of the studies suggests the need to realign universities' missions and governance structure.

UNDERGRADUATE EDUCATION AND ACCOUNTABILITY

In the 1980s and early 1990s, the critiques of undergraduate education focused on "three, interrelated, broad criticisms: The first is that undergraduate education lacks integrity and purpose. The second is that its content, especially the liberal arts 'canon,' needs revitalization. The third is that it was too vocational, narrow and fragmented, and needs integration and unity of knowledge" (Blanchard & Christ, 1993, p. 4). These broad criticisms, along with other concerns, have encouraged calls for educational accountability.

Christ and Blanchard (1994) suggested that by stressing program outcomes, these three criticisms, and the calls for accountability, could be positively addressed. For example, outcomes help demonstrate that the so-called distinctions between professional and liberal education are not only no longer useful but also are ultimately self-defeating for the traditional liberal arts, "professional" education, and undergraduate education. Whether they are labeled "essential undergraduate experiences" (Boyer, 1987), or "capacities" (Association of American Colleges, 1985) or "professional preparation" ("Strengthening the ties," 1987), the ability to articulate what educators want their students to learn and the ability to measure that learning is important. This is evident in the kind of recommendations, now a decade old, that were made by the National Governors Association to state governors, state legislatures, state coordinating boards, and institutional governing boards:

1. Clearly define the role and mission of each institution of public higher education in their state. Governors should also encourage the governing board of each independent college to clearly define its mission.
2. Reemphasize the fundamental importance of undergraduate instruction—especially in universities that give high priorities to research and graduate instruction.
3. Adjust funding formulas for public colleges and universities to provide incentives for improving the learning of undergraduate students, based on the results of comprehensive assessment programs. Independent colleges and universities should be encouraged to do likewise.

4. Reaffirm their strong commitment to access to public higher education for students from all socioeconomic backgrounds.
5. Each college and university should implement systematic programs that use multiple measures to assess the learning of undergraduates. The information gained from such assessments should be used to evaluate the quality of the institution and of this program. Information about institutional and program quality should also be made available to the public.
6. The higher education accrediting community should require colleges and universities to collect and use information about student outcomes among undergraduates. Demonstrating levels of student learning and performance should be considered for institutional accreditation. (Ervin, 1988, pp. 19–23; order changed)

The call for accountability has been continued in the Kellogg report.

Kellogg Commission: Reinventing Higher Education

The Kellogg Commission on the Future of State and Land-Grant Universities (1997) released their first of several planned "open letters" entitled "Returning to Our Roots: The Student Experience," in April 1997. The Commission, comprised of 25 presidents and former presidents of state and land-grant universities and an advisory council, argued that "State and land-grant institutions must again become the transformational institutions they were intended to be" (Kellogg Commission, 1997). Although aimed at state and land-grant universities, what they said was in keeping with many other institutions of higher learning. The Commission suggested "three broad ideals."

(1) Our institutions must become *genuine learning communities*, supporting and inspiring faculty, staff, and learners of all kinds. (2) Our learning communities should be *student centered*, committed to excellence in teaching and to meeting the legitimate needs of learners, wherever they are, whatever they need, whenever they need it. (3) Our learning communities should emphasize the importance of *a healthy learning environment* that provides students, faculty, and staff with the facilities, support, and resources they need to make this vision a reality. (pp. v–vi)

The move from universities being conceptualized as *teaching* institutions to *learning* institutions requires a paradigm shift that has profound implications for higher education (cf. Christ, 1994, 1997). As universities become more focused on student learning than on teaching, more concerned with the outcomes of education than the "inputs" into education, then at least two things become evident. First, outcomes assessment of learning becomes critical and, second, the classroom is seen as only one part, and sometimes one small part, of the total learning environment.

The paradigm shift from teaching to learning communities, from teacher-centered to student-centered approaches to education, changes the role of the classroom teacher and the university administrator. If, as the Kellogg Commission (1997) suggested, that learning communities should be committed "to meeting the legitimate needs of learners, wherever they are, whatever they need, whenever they need it" (pp. v–vi), then it is clear that teaching and learning can no longer be confined to the classroom. And, as the costs of higher education have escalated, as more people lose access to traditional higher education opportunities (CAE, 1997), the idea of a 4-year residential university or college, where lectures are delivered in huge classrooms, will become an anachronism. In a student-centered approach, among all the other things that administrators are held accountable for, they will also be judged or rewarded on how well the students in their units learn or perform. This call for outcomes assessment linked to resource allocation is already taking place in a number of states and programs and should intensify as limited resources bump up against increasing costs. (For an overview of assessment in higher education, see Rosenbaum, 1994.)

Specifically, the Kellogg Commission (1997) suggested that state universities and land-grant colleges should:

- Revitalize partnerships with elementary and secondary schools.
- Reinforce commitment to undergraduate instruction, particularly in the first 2 years.
- Address the academic and personal development of students in a holistic way.
- Strengthen the link between education and career.
- Improve teaching and educational quality while keeping college affordable and accessible.
- Define educational objectives more clearly and improve our assessment of our success in meeting them.
- Strengthen the link between discovery and learning by providing more opportunities for hands-on learning, including undergraduate research. (pp. vi–vii)

TECHNOLOGY AND ACCOUNTABILITY

Blanchard and Christ (1993) suggested that the technological communication revolution including computers, fiber optics, satellites, and new uses for the telephone were changing how people and corporations communicated; how they received, processed, and used information. Long gone were the days when the city paper or the network affiliate held the privileged position as the only news, information, and advertising source in town; when interpersonal communication could be solely conceptualized as face-to-face communication without a mediating technology involved; when organizations could successfully function without understanding how technology impacted small group dynamics, organizational communication, and public relations. Blanchard and Christ suggested that communication educators needed to account for these changes by developing programs that were fundamental, flexible, and broad-based. They called this kind of integrative, broad-based approach the New Professionalism, suggesting that if nothing else, communication programs should be studying and teaching the impact of communication technology on such issues as culture, texts, politics, community, family, privacy, and identity.

With multimedia and the Internet, the whole mediated world can become a classroom. How will we use multimedia in our courses and how will multimedia transform the ability of colleges, universities and governments to deliver an educational experience to students? What will become the roles of the teacher and curriculum in a multimedia educational world? Multimedia will have a profound impact on how and what we teach and the perceived relevance of our profession (cf. Christ, 1998). Along with the Internet, multimedia promise to change the university learning experience itself in a number of ways. Kerr (1996), in discussing K–12 education, raised issues that also apply to higher education when he suggested that various types of technological impact would include

> the ways in which technology is typically used in schools (e.g., types of software employed); the effects those uses have on students' thinking (e.g., effects on learning and belief); our teachers' ways of interacting with students and other teachers, the ways they have of learning about new practices (such as the use of technology), and their images of their professional work (what it means to be a teacher); the organization and structure of education (including how administrative and management decisions are made when technology is employed, technology as a vehicle for public engagement). (pp. 8–9)

Furthermore, Kerr (1996) wrote:

Ultimately, though, there is some evidence that technology's most pronounced effects on education may be on organizational structures. There is widespread public sentiment that the present pattern of hierarchical bureaucracy that characterizes education in many Western countries is counterproductive and outmoded. For technology to break those patterns, support will be needed not only from educators but also from the public, legislative bodies, and the business community. (p. 16)

Kellogg Commission: Technology

What is clear from the foregoing is that technology is not only changing media, and how and what is studied at the unit level (Blanchard & Christ, 1993; Christ, 1995), but also how institutions deliver education and create learning communities. Although the educational promise of distant learning is not new, changes in telecommunications technology suggest radically new ways of delivering interactive learning experiences.

The Kellogg Commission (1997) identified five developments or initiatives linking education and the telecommunications revolution. First, "New York City's independent New School of Social Research . . . has always catered to adult learners and since 1994 it has provided courses to more than 1,500 students from 17 countries" (p. 5). Second, in 1994, 13 governors announced that they intended to "establish a Western Governors' University, a 'virtual university' offering college-level course work by employing the latest telecommunications capabilities" (p. 5). Third, the Kellogg Commission suggested that "corporate 'universities,' thought to number about 400 in 1989, are now estimated to total more than 1000" (p. 5). "Corporate training expenditures are booming, totaling about $52 billion in 1995 (a 15 percent increase from 1990) and involving 41 percent of employees (up from 36 percent a decade ago)" (p. 5). These competitors to institutions of higher learning are often better equipped and funded than some colleges and universities, or units. Administrators might expect changes that include a movement "from bricks and mortar to virtual distributed education" where faculty move "from tenure track" positions to being "hired guns" and where academic degrees have less importance than "demonstrated competencies" (Moore, 1997).

Fourth, "New institutions such as the University of Phoenix in Arizona (a publicly traded, accredited, for-profit institution of higher education) are beginning to appear. Phoenix provides distance-learning opportunities to more than 20,000 students annually" (p. 5). Finally, "about one home in four now possesses a personal computer (with one in three of them reporting they own more than one), many equipped with modems to access the information highway and CD-ROM players to take advantage of the latest educational software" (p. 5). The point is that technology will continue to transform how education is conceptualized and delivered.

Technology, however, is a two-edged sword. Anderson (1997) suggested that one of the greatest challenges facing administrators was "integrating new technology" (p. 18). He suggested:

> Journalism-mass communications administrators and their schools are confronted with technology-related challenges on three levels: first, finding funds to purchase and maintain needed equipment; second, determining the most appropriate ways to integrate it into the curriculum; and, three, devising ways to keep faculty members current in its use. (p. 19)

Even with the problems and challenges, the bottom line is that the new communication technologies give communication and media administrators the opportunity to take leadership roles in their colleges and universities.

UNIVERISITY GOVERNANCE AND ACCOUNTABILITY

In 1994, the Council for Aid to Education, a subsidiary of the Rand Corporation, created a Commission on National Investment in Higher Education to "examine the financial health of America's higher education sector" (CAE, 1997, p. 1). They argued that access to higher education was central to our democracy and our way of life. They suggested that by 2015 there will be a crisis in higher education due to increased pressures for classroom space and higher prices. The CAE report called

> for a two-pronged strategy: increased public investment in higher education and comprehensive reform of higher education institutions to lower the costs and improve services. The second of these, institutional reform, is in fact a prerequisite for increased public funding. Unless the higher education sector changes the way it operates by undergoing the kind of restructuring and streamlining that successful businesses have implemented, it will be difficult to garner the increases in public funding needed to meet future demands. (p. 3)

What the CAE (1997) was suggesting is a business model for higher education that would make administrators, colleges and universities more accountable (see the Appendix for the five recommendations):

> One of our strongest recommendations is that institutional restructuring, including mission differentiation, be made a national priority. Like the health care industry, the higher education sector must systematically address issues of cost, productivity, efficiency, and effectiveness as a prerequisite for increases in public sector investments. (p. 14)

Although the CAE call is not new, it clearly intensifies the drum beat of criticism aimed at higher education, and administrators should take heed. What makes the CAE call troublesome is its direct attack on faculty governance. In the dominant U.S. business model of the 1990s, workers might be considered partners in some companies, but the reality is that management calls the shots. Academic protections, like tenure, will be considered impediments to the streamlined, efficient university business model of the CAE. Free-standing colleges and schools with their own resources make little sense in this new model. As calls for accountability continue to grow, communication and media administrators need to be ready to act. This book is one attempt to help administrators be prepared.

BOOK CHAPTERS

This book is meant for three kinds of faculty: those who are thinking about becoming administrators and want to get some idea about the challenges of being an administrator, those who are new to administration, and those who have been administrators and are looking for new perspectives to old problems.

Part I

Part I of this volume presents a background to the area of communication and media education. Over the last 10 years, a number of programs have found themselves under attack and chapters 2 and 3 address the historical purposes of communication and media education. In chapter 2, Rubin and Daly argue that communication education has a vital role in higher education with its central focus of "teaching students how to send and receive messages, structure interaction, develop relationships, and cooperate with others" (p. 23). They identify five concerns facing administrators, including the reputation of departments on some campuses as being easy, burgeoning enrollments of students, disciplinary identity, departmental structure, and calls to link educators' work with social policy.

In chapter 3, Rowland identifies the problems of contemporary media education as being twofold: "the field's complex history," and "the field's frequent failures to recognize the strength of what it has to offer, the way its core elements and themes directly address many of the key criticisms of higher education" (p. 57). He identifies six common elements that cut across a number of media programs' missions and purposes and argues that these, if taken to heart and not simply used as a laundry list, might help establish the field's identity:

1. Teach the basic communications skills.
2. Encourage critical thinking.
3. Ground our curricula in the liberal arts.
4. Develop an understanding of the role and impact of the media in society.
5. Inculcate a sense of ethics.
6. Broaden the skills and understanding of the information technologies generally. (p. 51)

Beebe, in chapter 4, assists "communication administrators and faculty to establish and sustain international contacts that can enhance teaching, research and service" (p. 63). An "overview of the current status of the communication discipline in the world is presented" and "a rationale for developing international contacts is developed" with benefits that range from "faculty development, student enrichment, curriculum development and research enhancement" (pp. 63, 66).

In chapter 5, Rakow asks the question, "What should our collective mission be and what changes to academic programs might flow from this adoption?" (p. 86). She begins with an examination of the social context—including political and economic, technological, and epistemological changes—during the past century that have had an impact on society and all public institutions, including universities. Then some of the conflicting views of the role of the university are discussed. She suggests that, "the ability to articulate a new vision, mission, and unique role of the university as an institution should be the test of the next generation of university administrators" (p. 99).

Part II

The chapters in Part II of the book look at specific programmatic challenges including hybrid programs (chap. 6), community college programs (chap. 7), graduate communication programs (chap. 8), experiential learning programs (chap. 9), and distance education (chap. 10).

In chapter 6, Tan addresses the challenges of administrating programs that combine one or more areas in advertising, broadcasting, journalism, and public relations, with areas in "speech" communication like oral, interpersonal, small group, or organizational communication. As he writes, "Regardless of where one stands on the issue of consolidation (combining media and speech areas), the reality is that more and more mass and speech communication programs are being integrated into single administrative units" (p. 105). This chapter is aimed at those faced with integration.

Engleberg, in chapter 7, discusses the special challenges of administrating communication programs at community colleges. Community colleges now enroll the majority of the country's undergraduate student population. Although community college administrators have similar administrative challenges as other institutions of higher learning, they also have their own particular concerns. Engleberg's 19 recommendations provide a foundation for developing useful administrative strategies.

Bryant and Thompson remind us in chapter 8 that "communication programs have not always been embraced by the higher education establishment" (p. 135). They present a brief history of graduate education in the United States as an "'uneasy marriage of the British liberal arts college and the German university'" (p. 137). They then give a history of communication graduate education in the United States and provide a profile of contemporary graduate education. One of their interesting findings is that the "official history of graduate education in this area differs somewhat from 'common knowledge' and the reports of our fledgling professional associations" (pp. 143–144). Their history is followed by an outline of a graduate dean's and graduate director's activities, and issues facing communication graduate programs including recruiting and retention, multiculturalism and diversity, mentoring, placement, distance education, quality control, professional master's degrees, and continuing graduate education.

In chapter 9, Moore discusses the challenges of administering experiential learning programs. He provides a number of theories, models, and frameworks for conceptualizing experiential learning. His case study shows how theory and practice can be integrated over a 4-year program. As he suggests, "the administering of experiential learning programs goes far beyond various logistics of offering courses, learning activities, and internships" (p. 176).

Distance education is the topic of Krendl's chapter 10. She cites educational access, student expectations, and teaching–learning models as three goals for developing and implementing distance education. She provides seven steps to developing and maintaining distance education programs that challenge the distance education administrator: audience identification, academic support service, program marketing and promotion, faculty concerns, technological support and system maintenance, evaluation and assessment, and fiscal management. She suggests, "the challenge has been to articulate those steps [involved in administering traditional programs] as part of the broader discussion about profound changes in the educational landscape today—the need to serve a more diverse student population, adopt a more student-centered approach to teaching and learning, and respond to the high demand for education throughout the life cycle" (p. 195).

Part III

Chapters in Part III of the book deal with specific administrative challenges including leadership (chap. 11); fundraising (chap. 12); downsizing and realignment (chap. 13); intra-university competition and outside stakeholders (chap. 14); student occupational concerns in a liberal arts program (chap. 15); gender issues (chap. 16); diversity and multiculturalism (chap. 17); promotion, tenure, and faculty evaluation (chap. 18); federal mandates (chap. 19); and self-studies, external reviews, and programmatic assessment (chap. 20).

Hill, in chapter 11, reviews three contemporary perspectives on leadership—the trait, situational, and style approaches—before suggesting a number of reconceptualizations including differentiating among leadership, management, and administration. His alternative framework suggests that leadership "is a rare commodity," "a more circular, rather than linear, process," "defies neat categorization," and "is an art" (pp. 207, 208). He ends his chapter by articulating essential principles, strategic accommodations, and the selection of administrators. Through it all, Hill argues for "the centrality of communication to leadership" (p. 221).

Anderson (1997) reported that one of the most frequently mentioned challenges by journalism and mass communication administrators in his study was "raising private funds and fighting for fair internal allocations" (p. 18). Murphy and Shorrock, in chapter 12, lay out strategies for academic fundraising. In their chapter, they raise a number of questions that administrators who need to do fundraising must answer including: "Why would someone give to my educational institution?" "What is the need we want to meet?" "Who can help meet these needs?" and "How do I go about it?" They then describe how to develop a proposal and the work required after a submission is made.

There are a number of communication and media programs that have faced realignment or downsizing in the last few years. In chapter 13, Foote suggests that "communication's interdisciplinary nature makes it a first cousin to a number of fields, but leaves it without a clear birthright" (p. 242) and therefore open to a number of administrative configurations. He discusses preventative and reactive measures for those facing realignment or downsizing. Preventative measures include: understanding university policies, maintaining centrality, managing up the organization, and reaching out to external constituencies. Reactive measures include: "(a) Assess proposals for downsizing or realignment objectively; (b) present a realistic, positive alternative that is sensitive to the administration's concerns; (c) Build a coalition to support the alternative plan; and (d) implement an effective communication strategy for the plan" (p. 248). In conclusion, he agrees with Tip O'Neill's dictum that "all politics [including academic politics] is local" (p. 256).

McGregor and Alexander, in chapter 14, discuss the challenges of intra-university competition and the importance of outside stakeholders. Using a case study approach they argue that in terms of intra-university competition,

a department should be strategic in bolstering its image and protecting itself. These strategies include convincingly defining the mission of the department, protecting against core curricular encroachment, seeking alliances with other programs when appropriate and beneficial, demonstrating excellence, and developing a good relationship with the dean. (p. 263)

In terms of outside stakeholders they concentrate on alumni, parents, and industry connections. They build the case for administrators to make time for external constituencies.

In chapter 15, McCall addresses a concern facing those who administer and teach communication and media courses in a liberal arts setting: student occupational concerns. He argues that "a sensible academic program must not be sacrificed in the name of careerism" (p. 283). He provides strategies for providing career perspectives within a liberal arts context that include getting the right message to students, advising, exposure to industry professionals, internships, cocurricular opportunities, and career planning. He acknowledges that "students today are career-minded and it is fruitless to tell them they should not be. But they can be reassured by a direct message that solid, liberal-arts-based academic preparation is an appropriate and effective way to prepare for a career" (p. 292).

Gender, diversity, and multiculturalism are the important topics of chapters 16 and 17. Hynes, in chapter 16, writes that "gender issues continue to present significant challenges to our nation's willingness to offer genuinely equal opportunities to all its citizens" (p. 295). Hynes' overview "identifies and highlights a number of major, recurring gender issues that administrators need to be aware of and deal with if they wish to create an environment in which all faculty, staff, students, and other administrators can do their best" (p. 296). These gender issues include personnel recruitment and retention, salary equity, family-friendly workplaces, students, advisory boards/alumni/alumnae, curriculum, sexual harassment, and sexual orientation. She then identifies women's administrative experiences, including achieving a balance between professional and personal lives, stereotypes, and double binds. She concludes by suggesting that

> administrators who hope to lead and manage their units in an exemplary manner need to constantly monitor their environments and the scholarly and popular literature to assure that their knowledge of the issues is as current and complete as possible and that their behaviors, at a minimum, conform to legal and institutional standards and, optimally, are consistent with he goals of providing a supportive and inclusive environment for all. (p. 313)

Dates and Stroman, in chapter 17, address issues of diversity and multiculturalism. They argue that "diversity and multiculturalism are direct, hard-hitting challenges to White cultural hegemony. . . . issues of power and equity undergird any understanding of multicultural-ism" (p. 317). They provide recommendations to communication and media administrators in terms of philosophy, curriculum, students, faculty, and staff. They identify the characteristics of programs that have successfully met the challenge of diversity and multiculturalism with "perhaps, the most important attribute that a college or university can embody is that the president and the board of trustees embrace mul-ticulturalism and diversity and use their authority to provide an insti-tutionwide, integrated approach to enhancing diversity and multiculturalism" (p. 333).

One of the great challenges for administrators is personnel. In chap-ter 18, Witherspoon and Knapp address the promotion, tenure, and evaluation of faculty. They argue that important to the evaluation process are faculty participation, regular implementation, clear expec-tations, timely feedback, motivation to achieve, and fair application. They then lay out four stages in the evaluative process leading to the award of tenure: (a) collection of materials, (b) contact of outside reviewers, (c) preparation of the dossier, and (d) review of the dossier. Their chapter also includes sections on promotion to full professor, and what has become one of the more controversial issues facing higher education administrators and faculty: posttenure review. Fundamental to all evaluation, they argue is communication: "If faculty evaluation is to be regarded as the preeminent component of faculty development, communication administrators must implement this process, whatever its ultimate purpose, with the same commitment to communication they reflect in the classroom, the laboratory and the field" (p. 358).

Federal mandates is the topic of Weymuth's chapter 19. She writes:

Almost everyone in academia has heard of federal mandates like Title IX, Title VII, EEOC, 504, ADA and FERPA and can recall that they are associated with nondiscrimination, sexual harassment, persons with dis-abilities, and student privacy issues. Vague recollections, however, will not protect a department chair nor the faculty members. As a chair or director of an administrative unit, one must have a clear understanding of these federal mandates. (p. 361)

This chapter presents the reader with a clear understanding of a number of pertinent federal mandates and guidelines for meeting the mandate requirements. Weymuth's guidelines, which apply to administrators and faculty alike, are meant to meet both the letter and spirit of the mandates.

In chapter 20, Christ, Orlik, and Tucker address programmatic reviews that might include self-studies, external reviews, and assessment. They identify key parts of a self-study and suggest what both reviewers and those reviewed should be asking themselves. They provide a case study of an external review that was demanded by an administration after a mixed internal review of the department. They end by arguing that periodic self-reviews are essential to the overall well-being of the academic unit.

CONCLUSION

In summary, it is clear that administrators face overarching external and internal challenges like grappling with changes in technology; attacks on current governance structures; accountability; defining our field to ourselves and to other constituencies; developing mission statements that meaningfully link us to our field, schools, society, and international communities; grappling with gender, diversity, and multiculturalism issues that promise different kinds of people will become administrators; conceptualizing experiential and distance learning and liberal arts education so that higher education becomes more than a lockstep of lectures and regurgitated facts.

It is clear, also, there are other, more "specific" challenges, that impact the day-to-day operation of a program whether it be a community college, hybrid program, or a graduate program; challenges like leadership, fundraising, downsizing and realignment, intra-university competition and outside stakeholders, faculty evaluation, federal mandates, and program reviews. What is needed as we move into the 21st century are administrators who are willing to face the chaos, confusion, opportunities, and accountability of administration with vision and strength. We need leadership in times of change.

Appendix: Council for Aid in Education (1997) Recommendations (Abbreviated)

"**Recommendation 1:** *America's political leaders . . . should reallocate public resources to reflect the growing importance of education to the economic prosperity and social stability of the United States*" (p. 15).

"**Recommendation 2:** *Institutions of higher education should make major structural changes in their governance system so that decision makers can assess the relative value of departments, programs, and systems in order to reallocate scarce resources*" (p. 15) and therefore "must **1. Improve performance-based assessment.**" and "**2. Define and measure faculty productivity.**... The average teaching load in major research universities, for example, has been reduced from about eight courses a year to four or five.... No fundamental restructuring can occur until the current incentive system governing faculty behavior is changed." "**3. Improve internal accountability in financial management.**" (pp. 15–16)

"**Recommendation 3:** *As part of their overall restructuring, colleges and universities should pursue greater mission differentiation to streamline their services and better respond to the changing needs of their constituencies*" (p. 16). Specifically, "**1. Community colleges should take a leadership role in workforce preparation.** ... **2. State undergraduate institutions should take the lead in teacher training and areas related to regional economic development.** Eligibility for college will not improve among low-income socioeconomic groups unless K–12 school reform succeeds, and training of K–12 teachers is a prerequisite to that success. ... The independent college sector should focus on its comparative advantage: the liberal arts undergraduate mission. **3. The major research universities should focus on the promotion of research and graduate education.** To help maintain the critical funding needed to support research, a National Research University Act should be passed that allows federal investment in research to be concentrated in the nation's top-ranked research universities" (pp. 16–17).

"**Recommendation 4:** *Colleges and universities should develop sharing arrangements to improve productivity*" (p. 17). There were five subparts under this recommendation with the first dealing with alignment: This would include the "seamless alignment of undergraduate requirements, transfer requirements, and joint teaching and degree-producing arrangements between community colleges, state undergraduate universities, and public research universities" (p. 17). Second, "Departments and universities should collaborate to pool introductory courses and instructors as a way to save resources and provide the best instruction available in the subject. Use of the Internet may facilitate this task" (p. 17).

Third, "joint outsourcing of functions" (p. 18) is recommended. Fourth, "combining all or parts of physical plants of, say, state undergraduate universities and community colleges that serve the same geographical area could save considerable resources" (p. 18). And, fifth, "substantial savings and improved library services can be obtained by focusing on the software needed to place library resources on the Internet rather than continuing to support individual research library collections" (p. 20).

"**Recommendation 5:** *It is time to redefine the appropriate level of education for all American workers in the 21st century. All citizens planning to enter the workforce should be encouraged to pursue—as a minimum—some form of postsecondary education or training"* (p. 20).

REFERENCES

Anderson, D. A. (1997). *The leaders guiding journalism education into the 21st century.* San Francisco, CA: The Freedom Forum Pacific Coast Center.

Association of American Colleges. (1985, February). *Integrity in the college curriculum: A report to the acadmic community.* Washington, DC: Author.

Blanchard, R. O., & Christ, W. G. (1993). *Media education and the liberal arts: A blueprint for the new professionalism.* Hillsdale, NJ: Lawrence Erlbaum Associates.

Boyer, E. L. (1987). *College: The undergraduate experience in America.* New York: Harper & Row.

Christ, W. G. (Ed.). (1994). *Assessing communication education.* Hillsdale, NJ: Lawrence Erlbaum Associates.

Christ, W. G. (1995, Winter). J/MC agenda for the 90's . . . the role of journalism and mass communication in the university of the future. *Insights,* pp. 1–5.

Christ, W. G. (Ed.). (1997). *Media education assessment handbook.* Mahwah, NJ: Lawrence Erlbaum Associates.

Christ, W. G. (1998). Multimedia: Replacing the broadcast curriculum. *Feedback, 39*(1), pp. 1–6.

Christ, W. G., & Blanchard, R. O. (1994). Mission statements, outcomes and the new liberal arts. In W. G. Christ (Ed.), *Assessing communication education* (pp. 31–55). Hillsdale, NJ: Lawrence Erlbaum Associates.

Council for Aid to Education (CAE). (1997). *Breaking the social contract. The fiscal crisis in higher education.* Available http://www.rand.org/publicatins/CAE/CAE100/.

Dickson, T. (1995). *JMC education: Responding to the challenge of change. A report of the AEJMC Curriculum Task Force.* Columbia, SC: AEJMC.

Duncan, T., Caywood, C., & Newson, D. (1993). *Preparing advertising and public relations students for the communications industry in the 21st century: A report of the Task Force on Integrated Communications.* Columbia, SC: AEJMC.

Ervin, R. F. (1988). Outcomes assessment: The rationale and the implementation. In R. L. Hoskins (Ed.), *Insights* (pp. 19–23). Columbia, SC: ASJMC.

Kellogg Commission on the Future of State and Land-Grant Universities (1997). *Returning to our roots: The student experience.* Available http://www.intervisage.com/kellogg/state-ments/contents.html.

Kerr, S. T. (1996). Visions of sugarplums: the future of technology, education, and the schools. In S. T. Kerr (Ed.). *Technology and the future of schooling* (pp. 1–27). Chicago: The University of Chicago Press.

Medsger, B. (1996). *Winds of change: Challenges confronting journalism education.* Arlington, VA: The Freedom Forum.

Moore, T. E. (1997, March). The corporate university: Transforming management education, *Accounting Horizons,* pp. 77–85.

Rosenbaum, J. (1994). Assessment: An overview. In W. G. Christ (Ed.), *Assessing communication education: A handbook for media, speech, and theatre educators* (pp. 3–29). Hillsdale, NJ: Lawrence Erlbaum Associates.

Strengthening the ties that bind: Integrating undergraduate liberal and professional study (Report of the Professional Preparation Network). (1988). Ann Arbor: The Regents of the University of Michigan.

2

Communication Education

Rebecca B. Rubin
Kent State University

John A. Daly
University of Texas, Austin

Communication education programs, although they vary somewhat in size and content, have a central focus: teaching students how to send and receive messages, structure interaction, develop relationships, and cooperate with others. Higher education courses concentrate on increasing knowledge, motivation, and skill; they teach students how to act in ways that are socially appropriate for the context of interaction and those that are effective in bringing about desired outcomes.

Communication education serves a vital role in higher education. Classrooms are communication chambers and students with a poor understanding of the communication process and who lack essential speaking, listening, and relational skills have a fairly good chance at failing to obtain a good education. The speech communication discipline has focused on skill attainment, following principles set forth by the ancient Greek philosophers and later on the British and U.S. theorists (Cohen, 1994; Enos, 1985). These principles are centered on how to best present oneself in a public forum, especially in persuasive situations where one's credibility is involved.

WHERE WE'VE BEEN

As was the case with many journalism programs (Bochner & Eisenberg, 1985), most speech programs began in English departments (Friedrich, 1989; Mader, Rosenfield, & Mader, 1985). Some are still there! But in the early 1900s, public speaking faculty realized that written and oral styles differed (as listening and reading do also), so some faculty forged ahead to break from English and form their own departments, which reflected a strong humanistic, rhetorical tradition (Cohen, 1994; Enos, 1985). With this independence came research, and so a new national association formed in 1914 that focused on the theory and practice of oral discourse, The National Association of Academic Teachers of Public Speaking (Bochner & Eisenberg, 1985). Faculty in these departments researched public speaking style as well as some other performance issues of the time that were theater related (e.g., oral interpretation of literature).

From its roots in English to its tendency today to adopt freely ideas, methods, and research from other fields, communication has always been interdisciplinary in its interests. Social psychologists always had an interest in communication topics, but concentrated research efforts increased just before and during World War II. Psychologists were more interested in dyadic interaction, personality characteristics, and persua-sibility. Speech departments, up until the 1960s, focused almost exclu-sively on the history of rhetoric, pedagogy, debate, and public address (Enos, 1985). Scholars in the speech communication discipline became noticeably interested in psychological methods in the late 1950s and early 1960s. Today, a sizable chunk of the research and theory of-fered—on topics such as interpersonal communication, persuasion and social influence, small group interaction, and organizational communi-cation—draws from this social psychological tradition. Those who were more sociology oriented studied group interaction, roles, and organiza-tional structure. Although some scholars and teachers have adopted sociological approaches to communication, proportionately more have held to either psychological or rhetorical methods.

Interest in psychological and sociological approaches spawned a much broader definition of the discipline. Departments began to as-sume that course work in interpersonal communication, family com-munication, intercultural communication, gender communication, conflict management, and a host of other topics was necessary. The tradition of intellectual Catholicism continues today. Young scholars are carefully probing the opportunities that exist in cultural studies, socio-biology, linguistics, and subjects falling under the rubric of computing and artificial intelligence. Course work on topics related to these fields is just now becoming established in academic units.

WHERE WE ARE TODAY

Defining the Field and Its Mission

With such an array of courses, speech communication majors need to specialize. In addition to the traditional broad major, many programs offer such tracks as organizational or business communication, communication education, language and discourse, public communication, professional studies, and human relations. Communication majors become organizational trainers, clergy, salespeople, patient advocates, teachers, political speech writers, counselors, managers, and lawyers. Many students find the degree in speech communication a useful preprofessional degree, a collection of courses that will serve them well as they seek a law, MBA, or medical degree.

Although we realize that this is not always the case, we use *speech communication* in this chapter to refer to communication programs that do not include mass communication elements. Currently, many speech communication programs have adopted other names, such as Communication or Communication Studies, but still are not integrated with the more professional side of the field housed in Journalism and Mass Communication, Broadcasting, or Mass Media programs. We use *Communication* to refer to programs that include both speech and mass communication or to communication programs in general. We discuss this integration issue later on. In this section, however, we talk mainly about degree programs in speech communication.

Degree programs in speech communication are not solely directed to develop functional job skills. In many academic units, education includes training in rhetorical history and criticism, in cultural studies, in philosophical approaches to communication, and a wide collection of other important, but perhaps less immediately practical topics. Students often say that completing courses in communication offers them excellent "practical liberal arts" degrees. Given its broad appeal, it is not surprising that the speech communication major is one of the most popular on many campuses.

Communication's Centrality:
Research and Service

Since the 1970s, speech communication programs on many campuses have attained recognition not only for their academic course work but also for their scholarship. Even a cursory review of our major journals (e.g., *Communication Monographs, Journal of Communication, Quarterly Journal of Speech, Communication Education, Critical Studies in Mass Communication, Human Communication Research*) reveals the exceptional quality of current scholarship. These departments also have scholars publishing in the leading journals of other disciplines, producing books published by the best academic houses, and being cited in newspapers, television, and other media regularly. In 1997, the National Communication Association (NCA), which was formerly the Speech Communication Association (SCA), was admitted to the American Council of Learned Societies, a recognition that the scholarship of the discipline was on intellectual par with sister disciplines such as English, history, sociology, classics, and psychology.

Many programs also provide basic skills instruction for the university as well (under the label of *service courses*). Typically, speech communication departments offer a basic course that is either: (a) practical, focusing on public speaking performance; (b) theoretical, emphasizing an understanding of basic communication principles; or (c) hybrid, looking at communication in interpersonal, group, organizational, and mediated contexts. They also provide lower division courses (e.g., business and professional speaking, interpersonal communication, speech for teachers, oral interpretation, parliamentary procedure, group communication) that other departments require for their students. These courses provide students with training useful in their future careers. These service courses reflect a strong bias by many academic units on campus that oral communication skills are both substantively important and practically useful to students.

Service courses are a double-edged sword for communication educators. On the one hand they allow departments to have large enrollments, graduate assistantships, and recognition on campus for their contribution. On the other hand, the "tail" can often end up "wagging the dog" in that (a) other departments begin to shape the curricula; (b) graduate programs begin to offer assistantships on the basis of how many students are needed to teach the service courses; and (c) the status of the department, as an academic unit filled with scholars, is often sacrificed so that the reputation of the department lies with its basic courses. Moreover, many academic units are beginning to offer their own specialized communication courses.

Many speech communication programs also offer cocurricular programs in forensics and theater. Forensics programs, emphasizing debate and individual events (e.g., extemporaneous speaking, prose reading), have long been popular and have served as an introduction to the field for many people who later made marks in society. Theater-related activities generally fall under the rubric of oral interpretation or performance of literature and have offered many, many undergraduates experience in public performance.

However, speech communication programs provide more than this specialized training. Their basic skills and lower division courses are focused on developing the basis of life long skills. Basic courses in public speaking, interpersonal communication, argumentation, rhetorical criticism, and small group communication, for example, concentrate on essential knowledge and skills that citizens and future employees need before the development of more specialized and advanced skills. These basics allow students to make the most of their education and to identify skills that they will need in their future occupations.

Numerous studies demonstrate the centrality of communication in personal and professional lives. Work on intimate relationships (e.g., dating, families) clearly reveals how important communication is to life satisfaction. Studies in work settings consistently show that communication is one of the most important skills employers seek out and one of the best predictors of long-term success in virtually any profession. At the same time, when asked what the biggest weaknesses of employees are, executives will often cite poor communication skills (see, e.g., Curtis, Winsor, & Stephens, 1989). Clearly, many, if not most, occupations require oral communication on a daily basis. Moreover, success in those occupations is highly dependent on one's abilities as a communicator.

Skills Assessment

Media courses teach media majors specialized skills for journalism, advertising, public relations, and the electronic media. College instructors assume that these majors can, for example:

- Take a position and defend it.
- Tell as story from beginning to end.
- Persuade someone to buy something or believe differently.
- Relate to coworkers in effective and appropriate ways.

Basic communication classes provide both information and methods on how to accomplish these skills and the opportunity for educated feedback on skill attainment. In addition, communication classes help media majors become more comfortable in their interactions with others.

Skill Deficiency.   Some college students lack prior education and experience in communication. Unlike many academic specialties, communication courses are offered only selectively in elementary or secondary schools, so few students are exposed to it prior to college. Courses on speaking and listening skills are often not required at the high school level, resulting in college students with bad habits or practices that need alteration. College instructors often must teach all they know about basic skills in one course, but this is difficult to do. Because most nonmajors only take one or two courses in speech communication, rarely is there time to identify and train students in more advanced skills.

The NCA has provided leadership in determining basic skills for college students. In *Speaking, Listening, and Media Literacy Standards for K through 12 Education* (Speech Communication Association, 1996), communication specialists identified 23 essential skills for students. Jones (1994) asked groups of faculty, employers, and policymakers to agree on essential communication skills for students. By merging these two lists, we can see agreement on basic communication skills essential for college students (R. Rubin & Morreale, 1997). Some of those relevant for media majors are:

- Speaking clearly and expressively, using appropriate articulation, pronunciation, volume, rate, and intonation.
- Decoding verbal and nonverbal cues accurately.
- Being aware of language indicating bias regarding gender, age, ethnicity, or sexual or affectional orientation.
- Assessing the communication context and adapting the message to the audience.
- Presenting ideas in an organizational pattern that allows others to understand.
- Listening attentively.

- Conveying enthusiasm for one's topic.
- Defending a position with evidence and reasoning.
- Distinguishing fact from opinion.
- Giving information and supporting it with illustrations and examples.
- Asking clear questions.
- Asking for information.
- Identifying main points, understanding what is said, and remembering important points in others' messages.
- Summarizing messages for others.
- Describing and summarizing viewpoints different from one's own.
- Identifying conflict situations.
- Expressing feelings to others when appropriate.
- Performing social rituals (introductions, telephone answering, greetings, farewells, etc.).
- Working on collaborative projects in teams.
- Keeping group discussions relevant and focused.

Morreale and Rubin (Morreale & Rubin, 1997; R. Rubin & Morreale, 1996) have recently distinguished between these basic and advanced skills. Advanced skills (a) are blends of knowledge, skill, and attitude; (b) require greater levels of behavioral flexibility and adaptability; and (c) require reasoning and audience analysis. Here are some of the more advanced skills that are relevant for media majors, again supported by the survey of faculty, employers, and policymakers (Jones, 1994). Media majors should be able to:

- Incorporate language that captures and maintains audience interest.
- Demonstrate credibility.
- Demonstrate competence and comfort with information.
- Recognize time constraints of a communication situation and know how to operate within them.
- Manage multiple communication goals effectively.
- Demonstrate attentiveness through nonverbal and verbal behaviors.
- Adapt messages to the demands of the situation or context.
- Incorporate information from a variety of sources to support a message.
- Develop messages that influence attitudes, beliefs, and actions.
- Manage and resolve group conflicts effectively.

- Approach and engage in conversation with new people in new settings with confidence.
- Allow others to express different views and attempt to understand them.
- Be open-minded and receptive of another's point of view.
- Set and manage realistic agendas.
- Understand and adapt to people from other cultures, organizations, or groups.
- Identify important issues or problems, draw conclusions, and understand other group members.

These competencies represent only foundational elements. In upper level courses students come to discover, among other things, the critical skills necessary in understanding rhetoric, the methodological skills central to research, and the issues of cultural differences that shape communities in language use. Communication education programs, then, provide basic skill instruction as well as advanced skill training. A recent trend is to verify skill attainment through skill assessment programs.

Communication Apprehension.   Communication apprehension—along with reticence, unwillingness to communicate, and shyness—can be considered an example of a lack of motivation to communicate (Kelly, 1982). Students who avoid communication in dyadic, small group, large meeting, or public arenas often lack motivation to communicate. The apprehension they have about communication can profoundly and negatively affect their personal and professional lives (Daly, McCroskey, Ayres, Hopf, & Ayres, 1997).

Why the apprehension develops is still not clearly understood. Some research suggests genetic contributions; other scholarship finds the sorts of reinforcements (or lack thereof) people receive as children shape their apprehension. Whatever its etiology, communication apprehension affects a significant number of students in any communication classroom.

The recognition of the severity of the problem of communication apprehension has led scholars and teachers to explore methods for alleviating this malady. For many years, the presumption was that skills training in classrooms—teaching people how to give a speech more effectively, participate in an interview, or engage in group interactions—would significantly reduce the apprehension. However, that belief has been questioned in recent years. Some evidence indicates that for people with severe communication apprehension, skills training by itself will not reduce and in fact may actually increase anxiety. What appears to work better are more psychologically oriented procedures. One very common treatment procedure is called *systematic desensitization*. This technique, at its core, tries to get people to begin to associate relaxation, rather than nervousness, with the thought of communicating. Another common treatment, called *cognitive restructuring*, works with the unrealistic beliefs highly apprehensive individuals often have about communicating. Most recently, Ayres and his colleagues have found that for some students, *visualization* reduces anxiety (Ayres & Hopf, 1985, 1989, 1992).

Speech communication departments and classes often offer treatment for communication apprehension. Some departments integrate visualization techniques into the class structure. Others offer stand-alone systematic desensitization classes to alleviate anxiety. Still others offer skills training that focuses on goal setting. When media majors learn about the extent of communication required in their future profession, they turn to such classes to reduce whatever apprehension they might have.

Once students are motivated to communicate, they need to hone their skills and understand why and how to enact such behaviors. Naturally talented individuals might be able to communicate and not know why or how it works (R. Rubin, 1983), but these special people are few and far between. Students who understand why their behaviors work (or do not work) develop the basis for even further understanding. The presumption is that it is not sufficient for students to simply interact well; they must also understand the dynamics underlying those skills.

Assessment Programs.   One way to find out if students are attaining the knowledge, skill, and motivation to communicate better is through assessment. Another is to determine if the major makes a difference in students' lives. The former relies on assessment or testing of individual students' knowledge, skill, and motivation (see Daly, 1994). The latter hinges on program or outcomes assessment (see Christ, 1994). Prior to the 1980s, few data existed on outcomes assessment (Rosenbaum, 1994).

Several surveys have been taken to see how widespread assessment is on college campuses and results indicate a lack of such programs (see

Litterst, VanRheenen, & Casmir, 1994). Few example programs on knowledge or cognitive skills exist (R. Rubin, 1994), yet skill and attitudinal assessment programs are common (Hay, 1994).

Skill assessment instruments exist for public speaking (Morreale, 1994), interpersonal (Hay, 1994), small group (Beebe & Barge, 1994), organizational communication (Shockley-Zalabak & Hulbert-Johnson, 1994), and media education (Christ & McCall, 1994). Christ (1994) and Morreale and Backlund (1996) have provided collections of methods of ascertaining both skills and outcomes assessment in these areas as well. Assessment of affect or motivation has mainly been in the form of attitudes students have about communicating with others (McCroskey, 1994).

A national call for accountability has led to detailed outcomes assessment programs on college campuses. Many educational institutions have been asked to provide evidence that the resources invested in educating students resulted in learning (Rosenbaum, 1994). Some have relied on standardized tests such as the American College Testing (ACT) or Graduate Record Examination (GRE). Others have chosen either authentic methods (e.g., oral exams, performance appraisals, portfolios, self–evaluations), incorporated longitudinal research designs into classes, or assessed quality by asking students about their satisfaction (see Christ, 1994, 1997; R. Rubin, 1994). These methods, then, provide information on changes in skill, motivation, and knowledge.

THE FUTURE OF COMMUNICATION EDUCATION PROGRAMS

Even though they may be housed in different departments, mass and speech communication programs in the future will need to consider their complementary nature. Both will be concerned with both interpersonal and mediated channels and students need instruction in both. The recent development of new technologies only highlights current and future concerns.

New Technologies and Their Role in Instruction

With the advent of new technologies, communication skills will become even more important. Today, teleconferencing often requires basic group communication skills as well as knowledge of intercultural communication. Computer-mediated communication requires basic interpersonal and business communication skills, but often in written form; digital cameras will allow long-distance communication in real time.

In the best communication classrooms, students are grappling with new technologies every day. In presentation skills courses, they find themselves using computers for visual aids; in group communication courses, they discover the values and problems involved in group decision support systems. In a wide variety of courses, they grasp the importance of videoconferencing and they discover some of its inherent limitations. Computer literacy will be important for information gathering as well as presentation and interaction with others (A. Rubin & R. Rubin, 1997).

Communication education programs should continue the emphasis on basic skills, but realize that technology may enhance the efficiency of messages and interactions. Speech communication departments must keep up with technology and identify arenas for future instruction.

There is no question that technology will continue to have profound impacts on communication education. People who hire our students demand it. Today's graduate already is assumed to have mastery of many technologies that even one generation ago could not have been imagined. The rate of technological change will only increase and communication educators will need to not only keep up but take a leadership role in shaping it. Consider the area of videoconferencing. For most people, current technologies for video-conferencing are suitable for the exchange of basic information. However, for decision making, most people still prefer face-to-face interactions. Yet as the technology improves and people's familiarity with the techniques increases, perhaps the emphasis on face-to-face communication will wane. Perhaps not, as well, for historically, media have not generally replaced one another. Instead, new technologies add dimensions.

We must be aware of Internet communication arenas as well as face-to-face opportunities for communication. The wide array of information (e.g., statistics, speeches, government documents, databases, discussion groups) available on the Internet will change the entire nature of reporting, for instance. Phone calls to news sources are now replaced by visits to home pages, e-mail messages, and database searching. Media majors will need to know how to access and use more than just the mass media. Communication education programs can help with instruction on database searching, e-mail protocol, and computer mediated presentation techniques.

Communication educators are also just beginning to explore the potential of distance education. Currently there are masters degrees in communication available through distance education as well as numerous individual courses. Although it is difficult to imagine teaching public speaking over the Internet, it is being done in a few locations today. A wide variety of less skill-oriented courses on topics such as rhetorical history, persuasion, and organizational communication, are regularly offered over the Internet for both undergraduates and graduates. This is a burgeoning area in communication education and the issues involved are numerous.

Many communication programs are currently introducing applied masters degree programs. These degrees, mostly in "executive" formats are meeting the needs of people in the work world who feel a masters in communication, like an MBA, could significantly enhance their professional careers. Most of these programs have a strong organizational communication focus, although some incorporate many topics one typically finds in regular MA programs. Some specialized masters degree programs are also offered for particular client groups (e.g., teachers).

Courses offered in such programs, like Interpersonal Communication for Managers and Media in the Organization, reflect a growing trend of media and speech communication programs to support one another. Basic communication skills, for instance, are needed in media internships (Novak, 1986), just as interviewing skills are necessary for students learning reporting techniques. Likewise, public speaking students can use instruction in camera operation and editing (Dewis, 1992) for their presentations. Thompsen (1991) has argued that communication programs have been too medium specific (e.g., electronic vs. interpersonal) and that communication instruction should be more unified, focusing on communicating, not just mediated or face-to-face communicating. Courses in personal and mediated communication can show the commonalities these two areas have in theory and research (A. Rubin & R. Rubin, 1985).

Departments of the Future

Administratively, there are a few major issues communication departments are grappling with today. The first is a reputation problem on some campuses. Sometimes, a communication degree is seen as an "easy" one. It is, in some people's minds, not as intellectually rigorous as many other academic pursuits. Why this perception exists is an interesting question. Perhaps it is because most people only encounter our skill-focused courses; perhaps it is that we deal with a topic that is seemingly so obvious; perhaps it is that we have not been part of the academic conversation for as long as many disciplines; perhaps it is because we actually are easier. Whatever the reason, it is important for communication to bolster its campus reputation.

The second is the burgeoning enrollments of students in our degree programs. Although proving the field popular, high enrollments raise issues of responsibility. Can a large number of students find employment within the major when they graduate? In addition, can the subject matter offered in our departments be taught to large numbers of students at one time? Are resources (e.g., faculty, computer terminals) available for all students for adequate periods of time? Administrators from most state or federally funded colleges naturally favor high student enrollments, but often skills cannot be taught adequately in large classes. When students share a computer terminal, serve in limited capacity in student productions, or give only one or two speeches a semester, they are not receiving adequate hands-on or practical instruction.

The third concern is with disciplinary identity. What is the field of communication? In many of the nationally recognized ranking studies (e.g., *U.S. News & World Report*) speech communication is not included as a degree. Why? When queried, editors will say it is because they have great difficulty defining the discipline. Some departments contain theater programs, others do not. Some contain radio and television sequences, others do not. Some contain speech pathology and hearing sciences, others do not. The consequence of this is not only that academic units fail to gain the reputation advantage of those rankings, but also suffer from a deeper sense of academic integrity. What is core to the field is not yet clear.

A fourth issue relates to department structure. Early retirement programs and downsizing have too often resulted in clustering mass and speech communication programs. These forced linkages often are not preceded by discussions of issues important to each. For instance, mass communication departments are highly concerned with professional accreditation, whereas speech communication departments often value broad-based educational programs. Likewise, faculty values in terms of tenure, promotion, retention, and merit are not always congruent. Thus, forced linkages may result in battles over scarce resources (such as new positions, funding for conventions, and office and classroom space) and incongruent values.

A fifth concern is a perceived call to link our work with social policy. As we discussed earlier in this chapter, a concern for accountability has resulted in outcomes assessment programs. In addition, NCA has developed policies on several timely and important issues. For example, the NCA Legislative Council has endorsed policies advocating free and responsible use of electronic communication networks, free air time for televised political debates, and diversity in the workplace, and opposing campus speech codes, English as an official U.S. language, and California's Proposition 187, which prohibits social services and education for undocumented immigrants ("National Communication Association's Policy Platform," 1997). These positions are often controversial and often NCA members disagree, thus working against the intended goal of presenting a united front.

Working Together in the Future

Communication programs must learn to work together in the future. Media educators can expect speech communication programs to increase student competence to minimal levels of attainment. They can also ask for more and should help identify what advanced skill attainment means for their students. What entry-level work skills are needed and what does "advanced" mean?

Media educators can expect more eclectic instruction for their students. Classes once focused on face-to-face communication must necessarily be expanded to mediated environments. Public speaking is more often mediated than not. Instruction in database searching and the Internet will provide media students with alternative channels for information gathering. Classes melding interpersonal and media theory and research will help media students understand basic principles of interpersonal communication in mediated environments.

Support systems are already in place to help achieve these goals. For instance, the NCA has several groups working on skill identification and assessment. The NCA Communication Assessment Commission sponsors assessment projects on public speaking, small group, and interpersonal assessment. The NCA Committee on Assessment and Testing encourages research on assessment and its dissemination. Many of the projects sponsored by SCA and NCA over the years are referenced in this chapter. In addition, the NCA recently appointed a task force to examine the possibilities and limits of distance education to the field.

In a recent volume, Krendl, Warren, and Reid (1997) reviewed the possibilities of distance learning in media programs and identified important issues. Likewise, A. Rubin and R. Rubin (1997) looked at information-gathering skills important for students in both media and communication education programs. Christ, McCall, Rakow, and Blanchard (1997) discussed the benefits of integrated communication programs where channel-specific concerns are less important and pooling instructional resources benefits both the department and student learning alike. Current efforts seem to be pointed at showing how media and communication programs can work together (Christ, 1997). This is what media educators can expect in the future, and this is what communication education programs can expect as well.

REFERENCES

Ayres, J., & Hopf, T. S. (1985). Visualization: A means of reducing speech anxiety. *Communication Education, 34*, 318–323.

Ayres, J., & Hopf, T. S. (1989). Visualization: It is more than extra-attention? *Communication Education, 38*, 1–5.

Ayres, J., & Hopf, T. (1992). Visualization: Reducing speech anxiety and enhancing performance. *Communication Reports, 5*, 1–10.

Beebe, S. A., & Barge, J. K. (1994). Small group communication. In W. G. Christ (Ed.), *Assessing communication education: A handbook for media, speech & theatre educators* (pp. 257–290). Hillsdale, NJ: Lawrence Erlbaum Associates.

Bochner, A. P., & Eisenberg, E. M. (1985). Legitimizing speech communication: An examination of coherence and cohesion in the development of the discipline. In T. W. Benson (Ed.), *Speech communication in the 20th century* (pp. 299–321). Carbondale: Southern Illinois University Press.

Christ, W. G. (Ed.). (1994). *Assessing communication education: A handbook for media, speech & theatre educators.* Hillsdale, NJ: Lawrence Erlbaum Associates.

Christ, W. G. (Ed.). (1997). *Media education assessment handbook.* Mahwah, NJ: Lawrence Erlbaum Associates.

Christ, W. G., & McCall, J. M. (1994). Assessing "the what" of media education. In S. Morreale & M. Brooks (Eds.), *1994 SCA summer conference proceedings and prepared remarks: Assessing college student competency in speech communication* (pp. 477–493). Annandale, VA: Speech Communication Association.

Christ, W. G., McCall, J. M., Rakow, L., & Blanchard, R. O. (1997). Integrated communication programs. In W. G. Christ (Ed.), *Media education assessment handbook* (pp. 23–54). Mahwah, NJ: Lawrence Erlbaum Associates.

Cohen, H. (1994). *The history of speech communication: The emergence of a discipline, 1914–1945*. Annandale, VA: Speech Communication Association.

Curtis, D. B., Winsor, J. L., & Stephens, R. D. (1989). National preferences in business and communication education. *Communication Education, 38*, 6–14.

Daly, J. A. (1994). Assessing speaking and listening: Preliminary considerations for a national assessment. In S. Morreale & M. Brooks (Eds.), *1994 SCA summer conference proceedings and prepared remarks: Assessing college student competency in speech communication* (pp. 17–31). Annandale, VA: Speech Communication Association.

Daly, J. A., McCroskey, J. C., Ayres, J., Hopf, T. S., & Ayres, D. M. (1997). *Avoiding communication: Shyness, reticence and communication apprehension* (2nd ed.). Cresskill, NJ: Hampton Press.

Dewis, R. (1992, February). *Student–made PSAs: Teaching the motivated sequence design and other public speaking concepts with a camcorder.* Paper presented at the meeting of the Western States Communication Association, Boise., ID (ERIC Document Reproduction Service No. ED 347 601)

Enos, R. L. (1985). The history of rhetoric: The reconstruction of progress. In T. W. Benson (Ed.), *Speech communication in the 20th century* (pp. 28–40). Carbondale: Southern Illinois University Press.

Friedrich, G. W. (1989). A view from the office of the SCA president. *Communication Education, 38*, 297–302.

Hay, E. A. (1994). Interpersonal communication. In W. G. Christ (Ed.), *Assessing communication education: A handbook for media, speech & theatre educators* (pp. 237–256). Hillsdale, NJ: Lawrence Erlbaum Associates.

Jones, E. A. (1994). *Essential skills in writing, speech and listening, and critical thinking for college graduates: Perspectives of faculty, employers, and policymakers.* State College, PA: National Center for Teaching and Learning Assessment.

Kelly, L. (1982). A rose by any other name is still a rose: A comparative analysis of reticence, communication apprehension, unwillingness to communicate and shyness. *Human Communication Research, 8*, 99–113.

Krendl, K. A., Warren, R., & Reid, K. A. (1997). Distance learning. In W. G. Christ (Ed.), *Media education assessment handbook* (pp. 99–120). Mahwah, NJ: Lawrence Erlbaum Associates.

Litterst, J. K., VanRheenen, D. D., & Casmir, M. H. (1994). Practices in statewide oral communication assessment: 1981–1994. In S. Morreale & M. Brooks (Eds.), *1994 SCA summer conference proceedings and prepared remarks: Assessing college student competency in speech communication* (pp. 187–215). Annandale, VA: Speech Communication Association.

Mader, T. F., Rosenfield, L. W., & Mader, D. C. (1985). The rise and fall of departments. In T. W. Benson (Ed.), *Speech communication in the 20th century* (pp. 322–340). Carbondale: Southern Illinois University Press.

McCroskey, J. C. (1994). Assessment of affect toward communication and affect toward instruction in communication. In S. Morreale & M. Brooks (Eds.), *1994 SCA summer conference proceedings and prepared remarks: Assessing college student competency in speech communication* (pp. 55–71). Annandale, VA: Speech Communication Association.

Morreale, S. P. (1994). Public speaking. In W. G. Christ (Ed.), *Assessing communication education: A handbook for media, speech & theatre educators* (pp. 219–236). Hillsdale, NJ: Lawrence Erlbaum Associates.

Morreale, S. P., & Backlund, P. M. (Eds.). (1996). *Large scale assessment of oral communication: K–12 and higher education.* Annandale, VA: Speech Communication Association.

Morreale, S. P., & Rubin, R. B. (1997, April). *Setting expectations for speech communication and listening.* Paper presented at the meeting of the Eastern Communication Association, Baltimore, MD.

National Communication Association's policy platform. (1997, July). *Spectra, 33,* 4–5.

Novak, G. D. (1986, November). *Mass communication internships: Problems and misconceptions.* Paper presented at the meeting of the Speech Communication Association, Chicago. (ERIC Document Reproduction Service No. ED 301 899)

Rosenbaum, J. (1994). Assessment: An overview. In W. G. Christ (Ed.), *Assessing communication education: A handbook for media, speech & theatre educators* (pp. 3–30). Hillsdale, NJ: Lawrence Erlbaum Associates.

Rubin, A. M., & Rubin, R. B. (1985). Interface of personal and mediated communication: A research agenda. *Critical Studies in Mass Communication, 2,* 36–53.

Rubin, A. M., & Rubin, R. B. (1997). Information gathering. In W. G. Christ (Ed.), *Media education assessment handbook* (pp. 189–212). Mahwah, NJ: Lawrence Erlbaum Associates.

Rubin, R. B. (1983). Conclusions. In K. V. Lauridsen (Series Ed.) & R. B. Rubin (Vol. Ed.), *New directions for college learning assistance: No. 12. Improving speaking and listening skills* (pp. 95–100). San Francisco: Jossey–Bass.

Rubin, R. B. (1994). Assessment of the cognitive component of communication competence. In S. Morreale & M. Brooks (Eds.), *1994 SCA summer conference proceedings and prepared remarks: Assessing college student competency in speech communication* (pp. 73–86). Annandale, VA: Speech Communication Association.

Rubin, R. B., & Morreale, S. P. (1996). Setting expectations for speech communication and listening. In M. Kramer (Series Ed.) & E. A. Jones (Vol. Ed.), *New directions for higher education: No. 96. Preparing competent college graduates: Setting new and higher expectations for student learning* (pp. 19–30). San Francisco: Jossey-Bass.

Shockley-Zalabak, P., & Hulbert-Johnson, R. (1994). Organizational communication. In W. G. Christ (Ed.), *Assessing communication education: A handbook for media, speech & theatre educators* (pp. 291–310). Hillsdale, NJ: Lawrence Erlbaum Associates.

Speech Communication Association. (1996). *Speaking, listening, and media literacy standards for K through 12 education.* Annandale, VA: Author.

Thompsen, P. A. (1991, November). *Divvying up the discipline: On divorcing dame speech.* Paper presented at the meeting of the Speech Communication Association, Atlanta, GA. (ERIC Document Reproduction Service No. ED 339 056)

3

Media Education

Willard D. Rowland, Jr.
University of Colorado at Boulder

> *I know what a law school is, and the same goes for business, engineering, and medicine. Why then do I not know what journalism, speech, and communication programs are? You seem to be all over the map.*
> —Anonymous provost at a recent NASULGC meeting

THE UNCERTAINTY OF TERMS

The definition of media education varies widely in the U.S. academy. From university to university its very nomenclature suggests a welter of conflicting understandings about what constitutes the field. Programs titled *communication, mass communication, journalism, speech, speech communication, communication arts, broadcasting, film, telecommunications,* and *media studies* seldom have exactly the same meaning in different institutions. They might be entirely distinct from one another and vary to quite large degrees in some universities, yet elsewhere they might well overlap and be intertwined in another.

For instance, some *journalism* programs are tightly focused on conventional reporting and editing instruction, whereas others with that name are broader, encompassing a range of other communications professions and media study (e.g., broadcasting, advertising, public relations).[1] Many programs named *journalism and mass communication* (JMC) suggest all of the latter, yet some JMC units are even broader ranging, often featuring vigorous graduate research programs and doctoral education in communication research.

Many programs of *communication(s)* imply all of that, and yet many with that name are not even involved in media education, focusing more on traditional speech elements such as interpersonal or organizational communication. One clue to the differential meaning is whether the program is *communication* or *communications*. The absence of an "s" often, although not always, suggests speech, whereas its inclusion usually implies a wider ranging, media orientation typical of JMC units, although frequently with traditional speech emphases included. Another sometimes more telling clue is whether the program with the name *communication(s)* is a department, as in a college of arts and sciences, or a free-standing school or college in its own right. If the former, and especially without the "s," the program is likely to be a speech program without any media emphasis. If it has the "s," but is still a department, it is likely to be more broad ranging and include much of journalism and media study. If the program is free-standing, it almost certainly is broad ranging and includes all or more of the conventional JMC array. Indeed, most independent schools or colleges of communication(s) have strong journalism and JMC origins. The major differences among the free-standing schools or colleges usually are not in their core media orientation, but more in whether they include programs in speech, film, and doctoral-level communication research.

Advertising tends to be found predominantly in the JMC schools and those communication departments or schools with journalism origins (Ross & Johnson, 1993). The ties there, as with the later emergence of public relations programs, are to the writing and creative orientations of the journalism tradition, although a management emphasis is not uncommon. Advertising also exists in some business schools, as part of the growth there of marketing as a major subdiscipline and an interest in the management side of the industry.

Many *broadcasting* programs, particularly if production oriented, trace their origins to speech. Radio curricula developed in some speech

---

[1]Even among tightly focused news-oriented programs there will be differences of degree level; some will be undergraduate only, others graduate only, and yet others with both.

programs in the 1930s and 1940s, because at that time the new medium was seen as an extension of public speaking. Meanwhile instruction in radio, and then television, was emerging simultaneously in many journalism programs, but the emphasis there was initially less on speech performance and more on the news writing, reporting, and editing characteristics of the field. To this day broadcasting and the electronic media frequently remain split between what are at root journalism and speech programs.

In a similar fashion *telecommunications* varies considerably in its meaning and campus location. At some institutions telecommunications programs derive from, and are still largely, broadcasting departments. In such instances telecommunications units also trace their origins to speech or communication arts, and as with JMC programs they tend now to emphasize a wide range of media and social study based in communication research. At other institutions telecommunications is much more about telephony, common carrier communication networks, and applied technology with strong engineering and management orientations. There may be a certain policy character to such programs, but the overall approach is one of systems design and implementation; it is more about conduit and technical infrastructure and less about content and social impact.

Wherever they are located, *film* or *cinema studies* programs typically will have production components. Frequently they are units in arts and sciences colleges, reflecting roots in English, literature, or other aspects of the humanities, with a heavy emphasis on text (film as genre or art), and less on the social and institutional aspects of the motion picture industry more typical of communication research and media studies approaches. Occasionally film programs constitute an entire free-standing school themselves; or they may be part of larger schools or colleges of communication, either as a separate department or as part of a broadcasting program (e.g., *Radio–Television–Film*, or RTF). In the free-standing state they are likely to be more oriented toward traditions of literature and theater; in the RTF configuration they likely will be closer to the communication research and speech or JMC heritage of media study.

THE HISTORICAL ROOTS OF THE CONFUSION

This confusion of nomenclature is a reflection of several historical factors. First, there is the relative newness of the field. Until the rise of industrial mass communication in the late 19th century it was not possible to imagine, let alone create, a professional and academic study of media. The primary roots of journalism and speech developed separately in the first two decades of the 20th century, often as subemphases within English programs, breaking away more formally in the 1920s and 1930s. Journalism had some origins in the immediate post-Civil War period, but it did not become a widespread university phenomenon until after the turn of the century (Dressel, 1960, p. 21; Sloan, 1990, pp. 3–11). Speech had a much older, core canonical history, rising out of the ancient tradition of rhetoric, but it had been overshadowed by many newer disciplines by the end of the 19th century and internal struggles over the extent to which the rhetorical heritage implied both speaking and writing. As with journalism, it took another decade or two to find its new place in the modern academy.[2]

As the media grew in size and importance throughout the early 20th century, there emerged a felt need for professional training and academic inquiry about the meaning of these new institutions, both as powerful political and economic forces in modern society and as increasingly central cultural phenomena. Press and other media trade associations encouraged universities to develop journalism and communication programs that would provide entry-level training in the various media crafts and values. Then, as such curricula grew, typically within or close to the arts and sciences, journalism and speech faculties began to broaden the discourse, to raise more reflective questions about such things as media institutions and social impact; law, ethics, and policy; the entire process of human communication; and the role therein of contemporary media technologies. There had been fitful parallel movements toward creation of a study of communication in other fields, particularly under the umbrella of the Chicago school of social psychology (Delia, 1987), but it was not until media education emerged with the resources of a stronger professional purpose in the journalism and speech programs of midcentury that a superstructure of media theory could be constructed.

A second confounding factor is reflected in the different traditions of speech and journalism themselves and the attendant, essentially false impressions of a split over professional versus academic orientations. With its rhetorical origins, speech typically focused on the characteristics of individual and interpersonal communication, tending to see

---

[2]For the biography of one venerable speech program see Roach (1950); for more general reviews of the field's history see Cohen (1994) and Delia (1987).

the modern media technologies as extensions of the personal communications act. Many speech programs sought to distance themselves from any image of professional purpose, usually remaining in arts and sciences colleges and aspiring to various models of academic acceptability associated with the humanities or behavioral sciences, and often there were bitter struggles over just which of those should dominate (see, e.g., Fisher, 1981, p. 61).

Journalism programs were more overtly professional in their intentions, in the models of business, law, engineering, agriculture and medicine before them. In the midcentury academy they also frequently found it more comfortable to leave the arts and sciences nest to develop upper division and graduate curricula in the skills of newsgathering and other media crafts, nonetheless hewing to certain requirements of an interdisciplinary arts and sciences core. However, over time many such programs also began to develop a strong interdisciplinary, scholarly character themselves, providing JMC-core curricular elements in law, politics, history, and social theory as they all bore on the media. Indeed, it was in that tension between professional training and interdisciplinary theoretical debate rooted in the humanities and social sciences that much of contemporary communication research and media studies were forged (see, e.g., Rogers & Chaffee, 1994).

This duality was more characteristic of diverse arts and sciences disciplines, including speech, than was commonly acknowledged. So, for instance, with their roots in rhetoric and elocution, speech programs always had an applied heritage, as in training for public speaking, debate, dramatics, and speech disorders. By definition those more modern speech or communication programs with theater, broadcasting, and film emphases also have always had a clear professional purpose. Even those with more tightly focused interpersonal or organizational orientations have come to an overt position of preparing students for internal business communication, external public relations, and other industry, government, and mass communication employment (see Wolvin, 1981, pp. 42–45).

Meanwhile, very few of even the most craft-oriented journalism programs have ever been without roots in social, behavioral, or political theory. The syllabi and curricula of the vast majority of journalism programs have been much wider and deeper for far longer than is commonly acknowledged. Indeed, their definition of professionalism, as evidenced in their accrediting standards (Accrediting Council on

Education in Journalism and Mass Communications, 1996), has explicitly invoked theoretical and conceptual breadth. To varying degrees JMC and communications programs rooted in journalism have been loci of vigorous debate about the social implications of the media, and often of much more. Nonetheless, as the field emerged the false image of the distinction—of JMC as narrowly professional and of speech as intellectually richer—did much to confound the understanding of what constitutes media education and its various strengths and weaknesses.

A third factor in the confusion is that certain other logics associated with the emergence of various subaspects of the field no longer make as much sense as they originally might have. So, for instance, the split over broadcasting appears increasingly archaic. In a world of integrated, electronic, multimedia experience and interdisciplinary communication theory, the original oral versus print rationales for different approaches to radio and television education between speech and journalism have by now effectively ebbed. Whether it is the study of applied message creation and production or of more theoretical questions about institutional, textual, or social impact questions about the media, there remains little reason to divide the field along technological or industrial lines.

In a similar fashion, advertising's split history has added to misunderstandings about the field. Advertising programs usually began with a few courses in newspaper sales and economics, as a way of introducing journalists to the business side of publishing. Eventually, as advertising became a larger, more clearly identified industry with a central role in nearly all media, much of that education in the journalism context turned toward support of agencies and clients, losing most of its press orientation. Even then, though, the tendency was to stay within journalism and communication because of their emphases on writing and message design. Meanwhile many business programs had added advertising courses in association with their marketing interests, giving the field more of a management orientation, but confounding the question of where advertising is and should be in the academy. The more recent, largely graduate phenomenon of "marketing communication" reflects the management emphasis, explicitly seeking integration among advertising, public relations, marketing, and persuasion theory in both communication and business. Although the creative orientation in advertising tends to continue to reside in the JMC or communication context, it now appears that with the rise of commercial fine arts and more emphasis on multimedia design for all of the information industries there will be variations on the conventional model, of which marketing communications may be only one, adding further to the confusion.

Film's frequent associations with literature developed as the midcentury definition of text broadened and it became possible to consider film as a cultural form in the humanities' tradition. But the same thing has happened with television and all manner of popular culture. The locus of television explorations has been more in the JMC, speech, and communication research realms, often with a stronger interest in the social impact and economic and institutional issues associated with media study. Meanwhile, as film itself continues to move beyond silver-nitrate-on-celluloid, extending into the electronic video world, and as broadcasting programs also expand, becoming more a part of the integrating digital video and multimedia environment, the core instruction in writing, editing, directing, and production in both areas would appear to be increasingly similar.

However, distinct cultures of film and broadcasting or video persist, despite these overlappings. Although not as old or as widespread as journalism programs in the academy, film was more successful earlier in escaping the low culture opprobrium associated with journalism, broadcasting, and advertising studies. On the production side, film developed an image of being a fine art (along with painting, sculpture, music, dance, and theater), with a special set of aesthetics and techniques never quite claimed or accorded to television instruction. Similarly on the textual side, motion picture study quickly established itself as *film* or *cinema*, as an art form, never as the *movies*. In that guise it was suitable for treatment in the traditions of literary criticism (Rowland & Watkins, 1984, pp. 17–18). It took much longer for television and other media forms to be taken so seriously, and to a great extent, even with the rise of semiotics and interpretive media theory, television and video programs still struggle with a lower, popular culture image that film avoids, despite its own highly commercial, industrial, mass audience character.

The split between the JMC and communication research and electrical and computer engineering approaches to telecommunications has likewise confused the issue of the proper domain for study of the cable television, satellite, and information industries. Heretofore the telecommunications divide has been between instrumentalist, applied programs on the engineering side and sociocultural approaches in the media study world. The social study of communications technology has arisen more in the journalism and speech realms, due to their close associations with history, philosophy, ethics, social theory, and a long tradition of social responsibility approaches that have reserved for themselves the right of criticism of their constituent industries. But such matters are of more than a little concern in engineering, particularly in light of interests, even in applied science programs, in exploring such interdisciplinary realms as "science, technology and society" (see, e.g., Easton, 1997; Webster, 1991).[3]

Some of those developments in other fields suggest a fourth dimension to the confusion issue, namely the relatively recent emergence of competition over media education across the academy. Initially, as long as the media were seen by other faculties as somewhat dubious, low culture enterprises, the field was happily left to the newer and *lése-majesté* programs in journalism and speech. The canon of the early and mid-20th century did not include problems in the media and communication as central intellectual problems. The political and social effects of the media could be studied as behavioral science questions, particularly in the forms of the diffusion and persuasion models that dominated after World War II. However, it was not yet possible to see communication phenomena generally as core issues in individual and social life, let alone as defining characteristics of human civilization.

By the last quarter of the century, though, the situation had begun to change. To whatever levels of academic interest there had been in such media as the press, television, telephone, and film, there now was added the evidence of a steadily broadening range of change associated with the rise of cable television, satellite communication, and computerization. The integration, spread, and reconfigurations among traditional mass media and telecommunications brought the issues of communication technologies more directly to the forefront of the debates about society and culture at the dawn of a new millennium. Now, traditional disciplines in the social sciences and humanities, and even

---

[3]Indeed, as suggested already, throughout the academy the split between the so-called professional schools and the liberal arts are no longer as strict as they were once believed to have been. So, for instance, some research in such fields as electrical engineering and computer science can be found to bear directly on fundamental theory in quantum physics; an environmental engineer might be contributing to basic, formative research in chemistry; medical faculty might be dealing directly with issues in ethics; and some business faculty might be investigating the cultural forms and social impacts of marketing campaigns. Meanwhile, chemistry programs teach applied laboratory skills, psychology offers professionally oriented clinical programs, and the fine arts are training aspiring professional musicians, dancers, designers, and painters.

in other realms such as business and engineering, began to take notice. So, for instance, psychology and political science, which already had long-standing interests in the effects of the media on individual and political behavior, continued to extend those inquiries. Sociology and anthropology joined the debate more widely with interests in the role of the media as forces in the shaping of social order and culture. English and literature programs began to take seriously not only film, but also television and popular culture generally, expanding the range of interpretative and critical theory and staking a claim for a new "cultural studies." By definition computer science and electrical engineering were deeply involved in fundamental research into the design and application of the information technologies, and eventually some of those programs began to move more into the cognitive and social realms in association with their inquiries into such matters as artificial intelligence, human–machine interfaces, and public policy.

In field after field, awareness of the changing communications environment brought new questions to the fore with notable impact on research questions and curricula. None of the social sciences, humanities, or professional fields could ignore the media any longer, and communication issues were thoroughly implicated in all the late-20th century debates about power, ideology, interpretation, modernism, and the impact of technology and its significance in the emerging postindustrial, information society. What was not well understood was that most of these issues had long been part of the instructional mandate and research agendas of media and communication programs. The original communication fields such as journalism and speech had fostered a strong interdisciplinary discourse about the media, but the extent of those efforts, and due credit for the effective invention of a whole new field, were often overshadowed by the differing views and valuations of one another by the key media and communication programs themselves. Speech versus journalism, print versus broadcasting, behaviorism versus cultural studies, administrative versus critical research—all the tribalizing helped keep the field fractionalized and unable to seize the central mandate.

Meanwhile, many of the traditional disciplines were struggling for survival and new purchase in an otherwise rapidly changing academy, and in that posture they were beginning finally to see media and communication issues as no longer marginal to their own inquiries. The major fields that throughout the 20th century had constituted the core sciences, social sciences, and humanities, had been shaped in the mid- and late 19th century in a time of profound social, technological, and economic change. A century later a similar process was occurring around communication and the role of the media, and a key issue was how the academy would respond. Would it invest the newer communication fields with more authority at the heart of the canon's transformation, would it draw from those fields and reform the traditional disciplines, or would it effect some combination of the two? Whatever the process, these debates did much to vex the question of where and what media education was and should be.

CORE ELEMENTS OF MEDIA EDUCATION

In light of this history and the attendant internal and external confusion about themselves, what then can be said about the proper locus, content and contributions of media education? A major insight into such questions derives from the continuing efforts by the Association for Education in Journalism and Mass Communication (AEJMC), the Association of Schools of Journalism and Mass Communication (ASJMC), the Broadcast Education Association (BEA), the International Communication Association (ICA), the Speech Communication Association/National Communication Association (SCA/NCA), and other groups to better understand and define the field, and in the process to reorient and improve their curricula. Serious, systematic inquiry into these questions probably began in earnest with the Oregon Report, *Planning for Curricular Change* (1984). Thereafter, particularly throughout the 1990s, there was a series of studies, task forces, workshops, and conferences devoted to the identity question, some with strong foundation and industrial support. Many of these were quite specialized, as in the discussion of cultural diversity and internationalism (Carter, 1991), changing approaches to new technology instruction (Brooks & Ottaway, 1996), or the investigation of the proper training of broadcast journalists (Society of Professional Journalists, 1996). Some have been much more sweeping, as in proposals for whole new, integrated curricula (Blanchard & Christ, 1993; Brooks & Cohen, 1996) or in compilations of program missions and purposes (Christ & Hynes, 1996). Many issues of the ASJMC publication *Insights* (see, e.g., Autumn 1996, Winter 1995, Spring 1994, Winter 1993) have been devoted to questions about the identity and nature of the field.

In reviewing these many reports one can detect several major, frequently identified, specific characteristics of media education.[4]They are that our programs should (a) teach the basic communications skills, (b) encourage critical thinking, (c) ground our curricula in the liberal arts, (d) develop an understanding of the role and impact of the media in society, (e) inculcate a sense of ethics, and (f) broaden the skills and understanding of the information technologies generally. Few of the reports include all of these elements, but most of them contain several.

In many respects this list is not controversial, and most would seem to be perfectly appropriate at this point in the development of the field. However, simply to list them is insufficient for fully understanding what is meant by media and communication education. To illustrate the issue it might be useful to state a series of questions about each of these conventional definitional elements, taking up each in turn.

Skills

The first question in this regard, and one that applies to all of the following elements, is which skills exactly? Typically what is meant in the speech context is effective public speaking, the oral skills of presentation and argument. In journalism they are the basic skills of reporting, writing, editing, and equipment techniques necessary for the daily job of newsgathering. In broadcasting and film they also mean writing, editing, and oral presentation, but with an overlay of camera usage, directing, and general production. In advertising and public relations they involve copywriting, layout, and design. This list of craft skills would continue to expand as one went through all the media subspecialties.

But is that all we really mean by "skills"? What about basic intellectual skills such as the capacities of research, analysis, knowledgeable debate, insightful thinking, and widely informed understandings of the world? Media faculties would most likely all agree that we mean the latter as much as the former, but in reading many program mission statements and task force reports, and all too frequently in listening to conference debates, it is not at all clear that the field is as assiduous as it might be about those latter elements. There often is a tone that, although they are important, they are somehow someone else's responsibility, that they are not necessarily the core of the media part of their education.

---

[4]Much of the following is adapted from Rowland (1996).

If the latter concern is even partly true, then media education has remained too simplistic and too vocational in its own self-expectations. It needs an understanding of skills that goes beyond the mechanical, one that implies the skills of the mind as much as those of equipment and technique.

Critical Thinking

In the wake of the Mortimer (National Institute of Education, 1984) and Boyer reports (1987, 1990) and the Pew Roundtables (Institute for Research on Higher Education, 1996), "critical thinking" has become a fashionable buzzword in the contemporary academy, a mantra for all self-definitions of undergraduate education. However, although the term has been regularly invoked in the public debate about higher education, it is unclear that those calls extend to the normative implications of traditional criticism.

In the media realm the term typically means at least the skills of critiquing a story or the craft of a presentation. But, again, is that all that should be expected? In embracing critical thinking, media programs need to be dedicated to a classical sense of *kritikos*, of fostering a pattern of acute analysis and discerning judgment that is informed by deep and wide erudition and that springs from what are essentially moral sensibilities. In the deepest sense the call for critical thinking implies a full range of social and institutional criticism based in a set of ethical values. The point is important, because it relates directly to the following issues about the liberal arts and media in society.

Liberal Arts

What do media educators imagine the liberal arts to be? As reflected in many media curricula the term seems to suggest little more than a distribution of studies across whatever fields some faculty in a colossus college of arts and sciences say they are. As articulated in those statements and other documents, there also is a strong hint that media educators and leading media professionals, particularly in the accrediting process, seem to think that "the liberal arts" reflect something inherently broader, intellectually better, and less professional than media and communication education. The difficulty here is that the so-called liberal arts are now highly isolated from one another and unintegrated. The core curriculum requirements in too many universities are frequently little more than painting by the numbers, requiring only the taking of so many hours from Column A, so many from Column B and so on, without any clear sense of how those courses relate to one another, to integration among disciplines and to a rich sense of the educated person.

A major concern for media education is the frequent tendency to accept a mechanical definition of liberal education without any awareness of its shortcomings and without a proper understanding of the way in which media and communication study can help overcome them. Often forgotten is that at its very core media education teaches precisely the fundamental skills of liberal education (e.g., writing, disciplined thinking, concise public expression, and a range of interdisciplinary questions about politics, society, ideas, nature and culture).[5] Of course, there are significant contributions to the education of its students that media programs must expect from their colleagues throughout the academy. What is curious, though, is the way so much of media education abjectly defers to other fields and continues to compare itself so unfavorably to them.[6]

The media education posture also prevents itself from recognizing that many of the liberal arts are highly professionalized themselves. As argued earlier, there is an inherent duality of professional purpose and scholarly reflection in virtually all major fields, and the old distinctions between liberal arts and professional fields no longer are credible. Media educators need to be better students of the history of higher education and to see that this duality has always existed in the academy. They need to understand that in the socially constructed institution known as the university every academic generation creates invidious, protectionist distinctions between what is portrayed on the one hand as the timeless and essentially correct, the "liberal," and what is dismissed on the other as the new and "merely vocational" (Rowland, 1992).

The irony is that media studies and communication education have encouraged emergence of a whole new interdisciplinary paradigm (issues of meaning, interpreation, and symbol) that is part of a sweeping challenge to the canon of the past century. Yet, as all too tellingly revealed in Standard 3 of the Accrediting Council on Education in

---

[5]For an insight into the contributions of rhetoric and speech to this heritage see Hart (1981); pp. 40–41; for more on journalism's contribution, see Rowland (1992).

[6]For a classical yet still resonant examination of professional education as "liberal," see Dressel (1960), pp. 1–19.

Journalism and Mass Communications accrediting process, media educators would deny that contribution and shrink back from the wonderful opportunity it presents to help establish the new core curriculum, the liberal arts of the 21st century. Many leaders in media and communication study increasingly think of the field as being central to the academy and its own sense of purpose (Anderson, 1997), yet many others continue to think of their field as marginal, as a less worthy discourse.

Role of Media in Society

This function of media education is now generally accepted, although in some professional quarters that acceptance remains stubbornly grudging, even at this late stage of the field's development. Yet, although it would be appropriate to ignore such resistance as the reactionary response of those who would blame education for the failures of the practice of journalism and the media themselves, it also would be advisable to look more closely at the claim about instruction in the role of the media in society. It is important to ask: Which roles and which society? The underlying questions here are: What theories of society does media education bring to the classroom and lab, and how do these constructs inform our understandings of media and communication? Are they the images of journalism and the role of the media envisioned by, say, Walter Lippmann (1922), or are they the problems of communication posed by John Dewey (1927)? Surely all media students need to understand the differences, yet it is unclear that all media and communication programs actually provide such insight.

Many dismiss "theory" in journalism and communication education because such material is thought not to be practical. Much of the current hypertension about PhDs versus practitioners on faculties (Medsger, 1996) appears to be rooted in just such beliefs. For many the antitheory posture is an acceptable, if curmudgeonly realism that reflects the terms of doing business in the hard-bitten, cynical world of journalism and other media work. Yet the issue is serious, because it skates dangerously close to anti-intellectualism. Moreover, it reveals how the celebration of practice too frequently refuses to acknowledge that in any professional context there are very real theories of practice at work, whether spoken or not. Media, journalism, and communication education all fail utterly if they refuse to recognize that reality and at their very core to problematize the relevant social and ideological issues.

If it is truly committed to critical thinking and liberal learning, then media education is obliged to engage a broad-ranging, informed criticism of society and its institutions, including its media. If the field does not reserve that right and its attendant intellectual practices, then it is left to understand the media only in their own terms, in light largely of a corporate purpose and its comfort with fiscal and political power. Media education needs to recognize that some of the opposition to theory rests in a type of professionalism that resists fostering a critical sense of power, authority, class, and privilege. The danger of a largely vocational approach in professional education is that it often hints that faculties should hedge their bets, quietly suggesting to students that such forms of criticism are best checked at the door of their first internship.

Ethics

Media education should be justly proud of its heritage in this area. It began an explicit discourse about ethical issues considerably earlier than most other professional fields (see, e.g., O'Dell, 1935, pp. 61, 69, 84). Some of the early media law courses, for example, were as much about moral dilemmas and conscience as about the technical matters of legal interpretation and application. Those concerns typically were couched in the midcentury social responsibility tradition, which, for all its contradictions and unfulfilled promise, was a rich forum for questions not only about journalistic and media practice, but also about the entire framework of media in modern society (Commission on Freedom of the Press, 1947). Many aspects of contemporary critical theory were foreshadowed by that tradition.

Yet at times the field's approach to ethics can become quite mechanical, a debate not about the underlying moral issues, but about how to solve the immediate problem in the newsroom or agency, failing to recognize that a praxis of moral theory is usually made up through the repeated resolution of many such daily problems. In parallel with the resistance to theory, many media ethics courses are surprisingly disconnected from the deeper philosophical traditions of ethics, a debate in the academy, like that of criticism, that stretches back across the centuries and even millennia. So, as media education celebrates its tradition of ethical inquiry, it wants to be certain not to reduce that heritage to a cookbook approach, nor even to just a course. At its root, ethics speaks to a frame of mind that is critically self-aware and that is unafraid of engaging the broadly social and contradictory in media practices and institutions. Ethics and moral issues should be at the core of media education, but the approach must be transcendent, a pattern of inquiry across the curriculum. Also, in the end, the field needs to be clear on whose ethics it is that are being taught, those of, say, a Paulo Freire (1970), or those of the "Highwaymen" (Auletta, 1997).

Technology

As an explicit theme, technology is among the newest in media education statements of purpose. Teaching the skills of current media technology has always been an implicit part of media education, but the current process of rapid change in communications technology has clearly captured the field's curricular attention and self-reflection about what it does in unprecedented ways.

Now the field makes great haste to embrace the teaching of multimedia and the new technologies, but it needs to be cautious in such enthusiasm. The terms of this theme require careful articulation. An overly simplistic approach will lead programs to worry only about providing state-of-the-art hardware and software, to chase too exclusively after training in the latest techniques. This posture has been one of the great weaknesses of media and communication education. It is part of the concern about too narrow a definition of skills. It also has been associated with a celebratory vocationalism that too frequently focuses only on training for entry-level employment, rather than on the long-term implications for the ensuing career.

Such singular instrumentalism is, of course, insufficient in contemporary education, whether for the media or any other field. Indeed, one of the great, but little recognized, contributions of media research has been the study of technology in society, consideration of its history, its social origins, and the character of its impact. Media education, of all fields, should understand the current moment as another in what communication historians call the incunabula periods, when whole sets of social, political, religious, and economic order are in flux, in large part due to major changes in technological capacity. Few fields in the other professional domains, and few in the liberal arts, have this sort of understanding. Media education should proudly articulate its centrality to modern discourse about technology and culture, and it should be prepared to bring these debates to every table around which the new canon is being considered.

Summary

The problems of contemporary media education are twofold. First there is the field's complex history—its different and often contradictory roots and its internal tribalisms. Those factions and antagonisms seriously cloud the picture of the field held by others and they do much to inhibit it from taking a more coherent central place at the heart of the academy.

Second, there are the field's frequent failures to recognize the strength of what it has to offer, the way its core elements and themes directly address many of the key criticisms of higher education. However, the field needs to be certain that in each of its core elements there is an appreciation of their deeper meanings and potential contradictions. In the busy, harried pace of faculty and administrative life there is always the temptation to resort to slogans and symbols. A measure of media education's strength and of its enduring value to the academy will be its willingness to resist such tendencies and to be prepared to press the core issues as far as its intellectual imperatives dictate.

It has often been said that the best of media education is one of the finest preparations for citizenship. It would appear that the core elements of the field directly support just that goal. It is the continuing responsibility of media educators to keep their eyes on that longer term civic purpose and to continue to interrogate their own statements of intent and their actual curricula to be sure they express more than surface-level convictions.

REFERENCES

Accrediting Council on Education in Journalism and Mass Communications. (1996). *Accredited journalism and mass communications education, 1996–1997*. Lawrence, KS: Author.

Anderson, D. A. (1997, June). *The leaders: An exciting time for journalism education*. Presentation to Leadership Institute for Journalism Education Administrators, San Francisco, CA.

ASJMC Insights, (available from the Association of Schools of Journalism and Mass Communication, University of South Carolina, LeConte College, Room 121, Columbia, SC 29208–0251).

Auletta, K. (1997). *The highwaymen: Warriors of the information superhighway*. New York: Random House.

Blanchard, R. O., & Christ, W. G. (1993). *Media education and the liberal arts: A blueprint for the new professionalism*. Hillsdale, NJ: Lawrence Erlbaum Associates.

Boyer, E. L. (1987). *College: The undergraduate experience in America*. New York: Harper & Row.

Boyer, E. L. (1990). *Scholarship reconsidered: Priorities of the professoriate.* Princeton, NJ: Carnegie Foundation for the Advancement of Teaching.

Brooks, T., & Cohen, J. (1996, Autumn). Curriculum transformation and innovation in journalism and mass communication education: Four experiences. *ASJMC Insights,* (entire issue).

Brooks, T., & Ottaway, B. (1996, Autumn). New technology and curriculum: A survey of 26 JMC programs. *ASJMC Insights,* pp. 31–36.

Carter, S. S. (1991, Summer). ASJMC Roundtable No. 3: Administering J/MC units in the 1990s: Problem, issues and opportunities: First presentation. *ASJMC Insights,* pp. 2–3.

Christ, W. G., & Hynes. T. (1996). *Final report: Missions and purposes of journalism and mass communications education.* AEJMC–ASJMC Joint Missions and Purposes Committee. Paper presented at the AEJMC convention, Anaheim, CA.

Cohen, H. (1994). *The history of speech communication: The emergence of a discipline, 1914–1945.* Annandale, VA: Speech Communication Association.

Commission on Freedom of the Press. (1947). *A free and responsible press: A general report on mass communication: Newspapers, radio, motion pictures, magazines, and books* [Hutchins Commission report]. Chicago: University of Chicago Press.

Delia, J. G. (1987). Communication research: A history. In C. R. Berger & S. H. Chaffee (Eds.), *Handbook of communication science* (pp. 20–98). Newbury Park, CA: Sage.

Dewey, J. (1927). *The public and its problems.* New York: H. Holt.

Dressel, P. L. (1960). *Liberal education and journalism.* New York: Columbia University, Bureau of Publications, Teachers College.

Easton, T. A. (1997). *Taking sides: Clashing views on controversial issues in science, technology, and society* (2nd ed.). Guilford, CT: Dushkin.

Fisher, B. A. (1981). Communication theory. In G. W. Friedrich (Ed.), *Education in the 80's: Speech communication* (pp. 60–67). Washington, DC: National Education Association.

Freire, P. (1970). *Pedagogy of the oppressed.* New York: Seabury.

Hart, R. P. (1981). Speech communication as the new humanities. In G. W. Friedrich (Ed.), *Education in the 80's: Speech communication* (pp. 35–41). Washington, DC: National Education Association.

Institute for Research on Higher Education. (1996). The landscape: Leaving hats at the door: Themes from the Pew Campus Roundtables. *Change, 28,* 51–54.

Lippmann, W. (1922). *Public opinion.* New York: Harcourt.

Medsger, B. (1996). *Winds of change: Challenges confronting journalism education.* Arlington, VA: The Freedom Forum.

National Institute of Education Study Group on the Conditions of Excellence in American Higher Education. (1984). *Involvement in learning: Realizing the potential of American higher education* [Mortimer Report]. Washington, DC: Author.

O'Dell, D. F. (1935). *The history of journalism education in the United States.* New York: Columbia University Teachers College.

Planning for curricular change: A report of the Project on the Future of Journalism and Mass Communication Education. (1984). Eugene: University of Oregon, School of Journalism.

Roach, H. P. (1950). *History of speech education at Columbia College, 1754–1940*. New York: Columbia University, Bureau of Publications, Teachers College.

Rogers, E. M., & Chaffee, S. H. (1994). Communications and journalism from "Daddy" Bleyer to Wilbur Schramm: A palimpsest. *Journalism Monographs, 148*.

Ross, B. I., & Johnson, K. F. (1993). *Where shall I go to study advertising and public relations?* Baton Rouge, LA: Advertising Education Publications.

Rowland, W. D., Jr. (1992, Spring). The role of journalism and communications studies in the liberal arts: A place of honor. *ASJMC Insights*, pp. 1–9.

Rowland, W. D., Jr. (1996, August). *On enduring missions and purposes*. (Paper presented at AEJMC annual conference, Anaheim, CA.

Rowland, W. D., Jr., & Watkins, B. (Eds.). (1984). *Interpreting television: Current research perspectives*. Beverly Hills, CA: Sage.

Sloan, W. D. (Ed.). (1990). *Makers of the media mind: Journalism educators and their ideas*. Hillsdale, NJ: Lawrence Erlbaum Associates.

Society of Professional Journalists. (1996). *Tomorrow's broadcast journalists: A report and recommendations from the Jane Pauley Task Force on Mass Communication Education*. Greeencastle, IN: Author.

Webster, A. (1991). *Science, technology, and society: New directions*. New Brunswick, NJ: Rutgers University Press.

Wolvin, A. D. (1981). Speech communication in applied settings. In G. W. Friedrich (Ed.), *Education in the 80's: Speech communication* (pp. 42–50). Washington, DC: National Education Association.

International Communication Education

Steven A. Beebe
Southwest Texas State University

Educators trace the roots of the of the communication discipline to ancient Greece and before. The study of rhetoric—included in the trivium and quadrivium—has been a foundation of the educational curriculum of European universities for centuries. It is only during the past 100 years, however, that speech communication has become an entrenched discipline in higher education. In the early part of the 20th century, speech instruction as a distinct curricula was found almost exclusively in the United States, evolving from instruction in elocution and English (Cohen, 1994; Wallace, 1954). Notwithstanding its U.S. origin and evolution, several surveys document the expansion of speech communication instruction throughout the world. There is evidence that speech communication instruction is present in some form on every continent (Beebe, Kharcheva, & Kharcheva, 1996; Berry, 1961; Dewine, 1995; Ekachai, 1994; Engleberg, 1988; Flordo, 1989; Greenberg & Lau, 1990; Hadwiger, Smith & Geissner, 1972; Hewitt & Inghilleri, 1993; Irwin, 1992; Irwin, Galvin, & Nightingale, 1986; Jellicorse, 1994; James, 1990; Oliver, 1956a, 1956b; Rolls, 1992; Scarfe, 1962; UNESCO, 1989; Weitzel, 1990; Wise, 1963; Yonghua, 1988).

Given the development of communication instruction and research in other countries, there is increasing interest in U.S. schools and departments of communication to establish links with colleagues around the world. Communication administrators, faculty, and students see the benefits of learning about human communication in other cultural contexts. Communication studies plays an important role in helping to prepare students for a global marketplace. Increasingly, communication scholars recognize that the literature base of human communication is overly reliant on the proverbial college sophomore from the predominant U.S. culture. Given that most contemporary communication texts extrapolate principles from this literature, perhaps communication studies should be retitled "North American Communication," rather than "Human Communication." Consequently, because of the Western tilt to our research and the acknowledgment of multiple benefits that can occur when collaborating with international scholars, more colleges and universities are exploring ways to internationalize their curriculum through faculty and student exchanges, collaborative research programs, and curriculum development projects with international scholars.

The National Association of State Universities and Land Grant Colleges (1993) suggested that the impetus for internationalizing higher education in the United States occurred after World War II, following many Americans' wartime international military travel. Universities and colleges established area studies curricula and programs, notably in schools of business, that began to promote international education. Government support for international efforts through programs such as the Washington, DC-based International Research and Exchanges Board (IREX) and the Fulbright award also helped fuel the growing interest in international outreach. As more international students came to the United States in the 1970s and 1980s for advanced studies, universities provided additional support to integrate visiting students into the educational community and gained firsthand evidence of the value of gaining international perspectives in a variety of subjects, including communication. U.S. students also began to travel abroad in larger numbers than in the past. Drawing on the work of sociologists and cultural anthropologists, intercultural communication as a curricular entity also began to grow during the 1970s and 1980s (Beebe & Biggers, 1986). These initial exchanges and curricular innovations did not, however, seem to result in immediate significant changes in U.S.

educational programs. According to the National Association of State Universities and Land Grant Colleges (1993):

> Higher education made few curricula changes [in the 1970s] in response to these developments, and faculty did not gain a better knowledge of the world or increase their understanding of the cultures.
>
> In the late 1980s and early 1990s, many institutions began to explore more fully the potential for internationalizing the curriculum and broadening the sphere of their international activities. The task of infusing less traditional international disciplines and course offerings with an international component and expanding exchange and study abroad opportunities beyond the Western world challenged administrators and faculty alike. (p. 5)

Many academic disciplines have easily recognized academic counterparts in other countries; communication faculty have more difficulty identifying their academic colleagues because of the interdisciplinary nature of communication studies both in the United States and abroad. Students of the arts, linguistics, history, language, philosophy, and even more contemporary disciplines such as political science and sociology can readily identify equivalent academic departments, schools or faculty members at international institutions. Departments of speech communication exist with less frequency outside of the United States (Weitzel, 1990) than do many other academic programs. Although the internetting of academe makes it more likely for an exchange of information with our colleagues around the globe, scholars who study communication may be challenged to identify colleagues with similar interests. Yet as we appropriately focus our attention on studying and applying knowledge of human communication to other cultures, communication departments should be in the forefront to seek creative ways to initiate and sustain contacts with international scholars.

The purpose of this chapter is to assist communication administrators and faculty to establish and sustain international contacts that can enhance teaching, research, and service. Specifically, an overview of the current status of the communication discipline in the world is presented. A rationale for developing international contacts and strategies for establishing relationships is offered to help administrators make the case for initiating and sustaining international programs. Strategies for funding international initiatives are also offered, including an identification of sources to help bolster a rationale for embarking on internationalizing the communication curriculum. This chapter is written to help communication educators develop a strategic plan for developing international contacts that can enrich both the teaching and scholarship for the academic unit, as well as provide an important service to students and faculty, their institution, and the communication discipline. Although the primary focus of this chapter is speech communication, the virtues, obstacles to, and strategies of internationalizing speech communication instruction have application to the broader scope of communication studies, including journalism and mass communication.

COMMUNICATION STUDIES: AN INTERNATIONAL DISCIPLINE

Even though the stronghold of organized study and instruction in speech communication is in the United States, the communication discipline is evident in institutions of higher education worldwide. Oliver (1956a, 1956b, 1958) conducted one of the first systematic investigations seeking to identify the presence of speech education around the world. Focusing primarily on instruction in speech—as was the primary focus of our discipline in the mid-1950s—he found that speech instruction existed throughout much of the world, but was not as likely to be organized into a separate department or academic unit. Oliver (1956a) quoted one of his Italian respondent's observations about the process of searching for corollary academic disciplines abroad: "It is difficult, and possibly hopeless, to attempt to compare completely different systems of education" (p. 108). Despite the challenge of seeking comparisons among different educational systems, Oliver (1956a, 1956b) uncovered the presence of some degree of speech instruction in 27 countries. Speech instruction in the mid-1950s was most prominent in English-speaking countries. Almost half of Oliver's (1956a) sample included some instruction in public speaking and group discussion, which led him to conclude that there "exists a global fellowship within the theory of speech teaching Quintilian described so well" (p. 184). Oliver's advice as to how to build bridges with programs and colleagues in other countries is still well taken today. He suggested that we should: (a) send books, journals, and copies of syllabi to ministries of education, institutions, and individuals; (b) offer graduate assistantships and fellowships to international students; and (c) seek Fulbright appointments to help introduce and develop speech instruction at universities abroad.

Other scholars followed Oliver's pioneering work by reporting on the existence of country-specific speech instruction. Berry (1961) described the growth of speech communication education in Scandinavia. Wise (1963) traced the development of speech education in Great Britain. Hadwiger, Smith and Geissner (1972) reviewed the role the Speech Communication Association (SCA) played in helping to establish international outreach efforts in West Germany and other European and Pacific Rim countries. Hadwiger et al. (1972) suggested that the two reasons the Speech Association of America changed its name to the SCA in 1970 were to broaden the notion of the discipline of speech to include disciplines and interests embraced by the word communication, and to underscore SCA's commitment and intent to reach out to international colleagues. SCA's 1970 convention theme, "International–Intercultural Speech Communication," is evidence that the association was seeking to establish ties with international educators. In 1997, SCA membership approved changing the name of the association to the National Communication Association (NCA).

Other surveys and reviews of the internationalization of communication curricula as noted by Weitzel (1990) include the comprehensive study by Casmir and Harms (1970), *International Studies of National Speech Education Systems*, which provides a digest of several surveys and reports of international speech education programs. Other international investigations include Wiio's (1979) study that documented primarily mass communication instruction in Finland, Sweden, and Germany, as well as surveys by Trautman (1975) and Dyck and Jehn (1977) and McGuire and Berger (1979), which focused on the development of communication programs in Germany. Focusing primarily on journalism and mass communication instruction, Sala-Balust (1985) conducted a study for the *Federation International des Editeurs de Journaux* in France. Research by McPhaill and Larsen (1983) and Flordo (1988, 1989) summarized communication in higher education in Canada. Blythin (1990) reviewed the status of communication instruction in Mexico.

There is evidence that instruction in communication is now integrated into educational curricula on every continent and exists to some extent in most countries. With the establishment of the International Communication Association in 1948 came an organization whose purpose is to foster the development of communication throughout the world. The World Communication Association, established in 1968, is yet another organization that seeks to develop an international network of colleagues interested in communication studies.

How widespread is interest in studying communication in higher education throughout the world today? The most recent and perhaps the most comprehensive search for communication studies in higher education was conducted by Weitzel (1990). Using a data-gathering technique involving systematic referrals—called the *snowball technique*—Weitzel gathered data from approximately 250 respondents in Australia, Great Britain, Canada, New Zealand, Africa, Asia, Europe, and Latin America. He found, as had other researchers, that English-speaking regions are more likely to include communication instruction in higher education. Specifically, institutions in Australia and Great Britain had a well-developed curriculum in communication, perhaps most closely resembling U.S. curricula—especially in the polytechnics (now called universities) in Great Britain. Communication programs are least likely to occur in countries that have had or still have communist governments. In the late 1990s, however, there was growing interest in establishing communication programs in Russia (Beebe et al., 1996).

RATIONALE FOR INTERNATIONALIZING COMMUNICATION PROGRAMS

Why should communication faculty and administrators seek collaborations with scholars in other countries? One might argue that we have our hands full managing our programs and students without adding to the complexity of the administrative task by linking with international colleagues. There are several reasons why establishing contacts with international scholars can prove fruitful, including faculty development, student enrichment, program development, curriculum development, and research enhancement.

One of the obvious benefits of internationalizing the communication program is faculty development. Our students are much more likely to encounter colleagues from other cultures than were students of a generation ago. Even if our students do not travel the globe (yet many will), the contact they have with others is clearly evident. As Reed (1988) noted, North America is "a place where the cultures of the world crisscross. This is possible because the United States is unique in the world: The world is here" (p. 27). Because "the world is here," it is imperative our students are taught by faculty who understand the richness and subtleties of cultural differences and similarities. Having faculty who have developed ties with international scholars is a way to ensure such understanding. As Dewine (1995) noted in sharing the benefits of internationalizing the communication curriculum at Ohio University, "Until faculty members actually study and live in another culture they cannot acquire a deep understanding of the cultural differences of their students. Living in a country, rather than just visiting it, is ideal. To bring the rich experience into the classroom is very desirable" (p. 207).

One of the challenges administrators have is to identify faculty who would make a serious commitment to being involved in international education. Goodwin and Nacht (1991) identified a profile of faculty members who are most likely to sustain international outreach efforts. Relating their analysis to communication faculty members, good candidates for being involved in international efforts include:

1. Faculty who are already specialists in a particular area or region of the world— scholars who have an existing research program linked to a specific culture or geographic region.
2. Faculty members who teach intercultural or international communication.
3. Faculty members who have traveled in the past and seem interested in new experiences.
4. Faculty members who have existing international contacts.

According to Goodwin and Nacht (1991), faculty who tend to avoid international or intercultural experiences include:

1. Academic ethnocentrists—faculty who believe the most important work is conducted in the United States.
2. Faculty who are already involved in long-term, collaborative projects that currently do not include an international component.
3. Faculty who do not believe cultural variations need be factored in to developing principles or generalizations of human behavior.
4. Faculty who have a low tolerance for uncertainty; they tend to avoid new situations and are uncomfortable unless there is high structure and predictability.

In addition to faculty development, establishing international contacts with colleagues at other institutions can translate into direct benefits for students. Because, as noted previously, our students will compete in a global economy, they will need to be well versed in the role of culture in affecting communication and relationships with others. Although it is true that a student need not travel abroad to experience the benefits and challenges of interacting with other cultures, international experiences can broaden and enrich a student's *worldview* and diminish ethnocentric mind-sets. Ethnocentrism is more likely to occur when students have limited contact with people and values of cultures different from their own. International contact has the potential to diminish prejudice and increase tolerance and acceptance of cultural differences, especially if the international experiences (e.g., student exchanges, visiting international faculty) are coupled with instruction and discussion that present competencies of increasing intercultural awareness and sensitivity.

Besides benefits to students and faculty, benefits to the overall program, department, school, and university accrue from international outreach. International contacts help faculty to rethink and refine their teaching and research paradigms, which transcend the syllabus for an individual course. A department that has international contacts may develop a collective sense of pride and accomplishment in connecting to the world community of scholars. International outreach also holds the potential to garner recognition and increase prestige for the entire institution.

An additional benefit of internationalizing a communication program includes curriculum development. Our students, who will increasingly interact in a multicultural, global society, can benefit from learning principles and strategies that are relevant to a variety of cultures and traditions. Most of the communication journals and texts that fill our libraries purport to contain principles and theories of human communication, when, in reality, especially in data-based, social science research, the subjects are from the predominant U.S. culture. Although we have knowledge of North American and British rhetorical traditions, we have limited understanding of the rhetoric of other cultures. Our knowledge of what is truly human about human communication can be richly expanded by making contacts with scholars and teachers at other institutions to confirm or revise our understanding of human communication principles. Our students will be the beneficiaries of our efforts to learn more about how scholars throughout the world teach communication principles and skills.

In addition to enriching our curriculum, international linkages can also infuse our research with new perspectives and paradigms. As our communication texts and other pedagogical materials increasingly claim to teach students to adapt to cultural differences and live and interact in a diverse society, we often do not have substantive research to support our instructional observation prescriptions. In truth, our knowledge base of applying and developing principles of human communication is limited to predominant U.S. cultural perspectives. A scan of bibliographical references to cultural implications of communication in our introductory communication texts are few in number. Developing collaborative ties with other scholars throughout the world who are interested in studying human communication can help us develop research programs to test our assumptions of human communication in the context of a larger, international framework.

OBSTACLES TO INTERNATIONAL OUTREACH

Although the benefits have the potential to greatly enrich the program and advance program objectives, there are often several hurdles that should be addressed to achieve those benefits. Knowing what some of the typical obstacles are can help administrators advance a strategic plan to manage the challenges that accompany efforts to internationalize the program. McCarthy (1992) identified several potential problems that may dampen faculty efforts to seek and sustain international collaborations. Identifying obstacles and then seeking to circumvent them could serve as an action plan for changing a department or school culture to achieve the benefits of international outreach.

Lack of Faculty Identification With Overseas Activity

Many faculty have not associated international activities with their academic responsibilities (McCarthy, 1992). They may have a negative attitude toward the possibilities and advantages of international outreach or collaboration with international colleagues. Thus, one of the first tasks of an administrator is to develop a case for international efforts. The case must be clear first to faculty and second to central administration. Many may look at international travel as superfluous travel junkets that are doled out to reward faculty who wish to travel abroad. Integrating into the program's overall goals or strategic plan a clear rationale for internationalizing the curriculum is one way to

increase faculty identification with the benefits of international outreach efforts. For faculty to be solidly committed to international outreach, they must see tangible benefits that will occur to them, their
students, and the mission of the department, university, or discipline.

Lack of Time to Develop and Sustain
International Contacts

The typical U.S. university calendar corresponds to most international
institutions' calendars. Without a sabbatical or development leave,
faculty may find it difficult to spend a prolonged period of time at
international destinations. As noted by McCarthy (1992), "Family obligations (working spouses, school-age children), inflexible teaching
assignments on campus, ongoing research, and the scarcity of sabbatical or other paid leaves of absence all combine to virtually eliminate the
overseas semester or year for large numbers of faculty" (p. 5). Often
creative approaches to scheduling international travel need to occur to
permit faculty to meet their varied personal and professional obligations. Sabbatical and development leaves, spring break, summer, or the
end of the semester are blocks of time to consider scheduling international travel.

Lack of Financial Resources

Most faculty cannot afford to use their own resources to travel abroad.
Typically, university budgets do not include ample resources for international travel unless the travel is directly linked to an international
conference presentation or other "unusual" international imperative.
In addition, external funding for faculty international travel is also
scarce and highly competitive. Administrators, therefore, must be creative in seeking resources to support international outreach. Later in the
chapter we offer strategies for seeking external funding. Often the best
strategy for finding internal resources is to embark on collaborations
with other academic units seeking partial funding. A combination of
department, school, and university funds, augmented by some faculty
resources, has proved a useful approach for others.

Lack of Administrative Support

International outreach involves an investment of resources. Without
support from administration, it will be hard to secure resources, both

internally and externally. Administrators who may not yet have caught the vision of the benefits of internationalizing the curriculum may need evidence of the advantages of investing resources in faculty international travel. This obstacle may be exacerbated in state-supported institutions, where administrators may wonder whether the taxpayers will value international outreach efforts. Administrators must be able to articulate the answer to the question, "What is the value of international outreach in communication to the citizens of this state?" If students from the state find it challenging to attend the state institution, a strong rationale for assisting in student exchanges needs to be developed and disseminated. Developing a clear rationale for international outreach can serve a department or school well in overcoming the resistance external administrators have toward initiating international contacts.

Lack of Language Ability

Faculty may be appropriately concerned about establishing contacts with international colleagues if they have not mastered the host culture's language. Although this is certainly an obstacle that should be addressed, it need not be a debilitating roadblock to cooperation. Many more academicians abroad speak a second or third language (one of which is typically English); our international colleagues have usually invested more time in mastering English as a second language than many North Americans have spent in learning other tongues. Where there are language differences, most international universities are familiar with using translators to manage the language differences. Language barriers need not be an inherent obstacle to collaboration.

Lack of International Contacts

A department or school that has little experience in international outreach may be uncertain about how to begin establishing partnerships with colleagues at international institutions. Most universities, however, undoubtedly have departments that already have international contacts. Using the existing network of universities' contacts (e.g., the music department or foreign language program) can be a productive and efficient way to begin building bridges with international colleagues. International communication conferences (e.g., International Communication Association, World Communication Association) are also fruitful places to establish contacts. In addition, colleagues who study intercultural and international communication undoubtedly have established research partnerships or know of someone who has established such a collaboration. The key contacts that we have made at Southwest Texas State University have come through international conferences (e.g., the International Communication Association, the annual Intercultural Communication Conference at the University of Miami), our own office of international studies, and contacts made by performing arts programs, where language is less a barrier to developing international exchanges.

Conditions Abroad

The political and economic environment in many countries can be a barrier to collaboration. Our university's plans for collaboration with Russian institutions , for example, have had to be modified on more than one occasion due to political or health advisories posted by the U.S. Embassy. Despite the challenges, we have been able to safely and rationally pursue our goals with the Russian Federation, even in times of political and economic uncertainty. Being informed about world political conditions and responding prudently is perhaps the best approach to ensuring that collaborators are safe and the investment of time and money will not be thwarted by political uncertainties.

INTERNATIONAL OUTREACH AT SOUTHWEST TEXAS STATE UNIVERSITY: A CASE STUDY

In 1991 recently appointed Southwest Texas State University President Jereome Supple challenged the university to internationalize the curriculum. His rationale for encouraging the university to establish international contacts included benefits for faculty, students, the curriculum, and the university mission. As he noted in his inaugural address (Supple, 1991), "We have to ensure that our graduates are prepared to function in a global arena." He also called for "encouraging study overseas by faculty and students, expanded exchange with foreign universities, and bringing students and faculty from other countries to our campus." The Department of Speech Communication accepted the challenge and instituted several initiatives to internationalize our curricula. We added or increased the offerings of undergraduate and graduate courses in intercultural communication and sought contacts with international colleagues through an increased presence at international conferences. We also built on contacts made through our university office of international education. In addition, we have hosted international communication conferences on our campus. In the past few years faculty have given presentations, lectures, visited universities, or established research partnerships with colleagues in the Netherlands, England, Scotland, Denmark, Ireland, Poland, Hong Kong, Japan, Australia, Canada, Mexico, El Salvador, Venezuela, Guatamala, and Russia. These contacts have significantly enriched the curriculum, developed faculty, and spurred faculty grant activity.

Our most effective and sustained efforts have come from contacts made in Russia to introduce speech communication principles and skills to Russian educators. Our initial contacts with Russian educators came through initiatives inaugurated by the music department in two Russian institutes. From those connections came opportunities to visit Russia and establish contacts with institutions interested in communication. Initial travel was funded by a combination of faculty resources, department resources, and university resources. We have been able to secure some grant funding from the United States Information Agency and the United States Information Service. Our objective was to learn more about the status of communication in Russia and develop methods of providing meaningful exchanges. To achieve that objective, a survey was developed and distributed, with the help of the Sociological Research Institute of the Russian Federation, to 2,200 Russian educators (Beebe et al., 1996).

Our research sought to assess attitudes and perceptions Russian educators have toward the discipline of speech communication that has evolved in the United States. We also sought to identify the strategies Russian educators hold toward introducing speech communication to Russia. Because speech communication is not on the approved list of curriculum and has only recently been promoted by the State Committee on Higher Education of the Russian Federation, it was not surprising to find that Russian educators are unaware of the speech communication discipline as taught in the West. Lack of resources for higher education are also a major obstacle in developing any new curriculum in Russia. Because 78% of the sample are over 56 years old, the majority of them have many years of teaching in a variety of disciplines and do not see the relevance of speech communication instruction. Also, even though the investigators provided an introduction to the survey describing speech communication, most respondents (93%) had never attended classes in speech communication and virtually none of the respondents offered their own definition of speech communication. Yet there appeared to be interest in initiating speech communication instruction in Russia; half of the participants either agreed or strongly agreed that speech communication should be included in the curriculum.

Given the interest expressed by many Russian educators in speech communication, there are several pathways to forging Russian–American educational partnerships that could be emulated in establishing contact in other countries. First, faculty in departments of pedagogy, sociology, psychology, journalism, and philosophy could develop programs of curriculum exchange with U.S. colleagues in communication. Institutes and centers of research that focus on families, cultural values, teaching, philosophy, aesthetics, business, and education could incorporate theory and skills of communication inquiry and instruction. Partnerships with sponsoring businesses and grant support from foundations and government agencies are possible funding sources for future faculty collaboration.

Second, educators could explore establishing partnerships with English-language institutes and universities in Russia (e.g., Pyiatigorsk State Linguistic University). Again, this strategy could be used to establish collaborations with other English-language institutes in other non-English-speaking countries. Students study English worldwide; linking with linguistic institutes may be an avenue to integrate speech communication instruction with English as a second language (ESL) curriculum. For example, in Russia many students learn English in highly advanced institutes and universities. U.S. speech communication and English instructors could develop partnerships with instructors in Russia and other non-English-speaking countries to share curriculum development materials. Speech communication educators could suggest methods of teaching principles of communication while simultaneously teaching English. For example, we have taught Russian students principles and skills of giving a speech, working in small groups, and talking interpersonally as they learn English. Principles of rhetorical analysis, criticism, argumentation, and debate have also been incorporated into the English curriculum, helping Russian students to not only learn English language skills, but to develop competency in oral communication expression as taught in the West.

It is important to emphasize, however, that there are significant cultural differences in communication style and method between Russians and other Westerners. This same problem exists elsewhere. Teachers of communication and English in the United States would need to develop partnerships with Russian educators to adapt Western communication principles and skills to Russian cultural needs. Such partnerships could result in a collaborative curriculum that would enhance both Russian and U.S. communication.

The goal of establishing educational partnerships, however, should not be to promote a Western or U.S. research or educational agenda. If our aim is to proselytize our international colleagues so that they perceive our research traditions and knowledge as superior we will alienate our international colleagues and reinforce stereotypes of the "ugly American" abroad who judgmentally castigates those who do not share U.S. perspectives or traditions. The goal of international collaboration must be to promote mutual understanding and mutual benefits for all international partners.

Finally, another way to develop partnerships is to establish research consortiums for sharing communication research data and information. Comparative studies of human interaction in a variety of contexts, including family, organizations, media, and interpersonal relationships, can be developed in tandem with other universities seeking international outreach.

Communication scholars and educators need not wait until full funding is available before joint projects are conceived and implemented. Using low-cost technology such as the Internet, initial work can begin that will enrich our understanding of human communication in Russia, the United States, and throughout the world as we seek to develop peaceful methods of relating to others.

DEVELOPING A FUNDING STRATEGY

Relatively few foundations, government agencies or organizations make international outreach from academic institutions their highest priority. Consequently, to secure funding for international endeavors will necessitate developing a strong rationale for outreach activities. Gullong and Tomassi (1992) offered suggestions for developing arts exchanges that also have value for communication exchanges. They suggested administrators develop a fundraising strategy by: (a) working by country or region rather than taking a shotgun approach, (b) starting with government agencies rather than private foundation, and (c) using the traditional formula for proposal development that is expected of other traditional academic development projects.

To begin to develop a knowledge of funding source by country or region, *The Foundation Directory* (1997) is a good first place to start. Rather than looking in the index under "international," look for foundations that have ties to a specific country (Gullong & Tomassi, 1992). In developing a proposal, it is imperative that you already have existing contacts with a host institution. Most foundations will not be impressed with using their resources for an academic fishing expedition involving international travel for faculty just to explore contacts. Another source of funding is to look in the phone book for regional trade councils that may be interested in exploring contact with higher education; trade associations can provide information about U.S. corporations that do business in the host country and that could provide leads for foundation funding or collaborative educational, training, or research projects. Many organizations may be interested in communication faculty providing communication training and development for overseas employees.

Another source of contacts is the bi-national or national cultural agencies that are based in New York, Washington and other major U.S. cities. Your school's own development office is another good starting place for seeking contacts with foundations or organizations interested in international education initiatives. Personal contacts with individuals who already have a relationship established with a foundation are among the most fruitful entrees into understanding the interests of foundation funding.

In addition to private foundations, government agencies hold much promise for funding due to their specific requests for proposals and a more cogent set of guidelines to help a grant writer articulate a tightly focused argument for resources. Key government funding agencies include the United States Information Agency (USIA), International Research and Exchanges Board (IREX), the Fulbright Scholar Program, and for programs with a fine arts emphasis, the National Endowment for the Arts (NEA). As suggested by Gullong and Tomassi (1992):

> Make it your first step to present your project to government agencies, both U.S. and foreign. They might be able to give you advice about costs and special situations in the country. They might tell you about other programs that are going on. They might be able to suggest the best people

to work with and may propose possible sources of support. And they might even be able to support your project. (p. xvi)

Some of the specific agencies to contact include foreign consulates, embassies, or representatives of these agencies; write directly to a contact at one of these agencies. If you have a foreign colleague that you are working with, you could ask them to also seek support from their government's funding agencies.

The USIA is an agency within the executive branch of the United States government. This agency issues a request for proposals that fund both creative arts and communication-related programs. The University Affiliations program often seeks collaborations with programs in communication and journalism.

The IREX supports exchanges for U.S. specialists for the newly Independent States of Eurasia, Central and Eastern Europe, and Mongolia. They also are interested in training programs that help policy and academic specialists from this region become integrated into the global marketplace of ideas, and as stated in the IREX materials, "overcome a legacy of international isolation." They are specifically interested in helping emerging leaders develop skills in local governance, journalism, curriculum development, finance and entrepreneurship, parliamentary democracy, and ethnic-conflict resolution. IREX supports field research, international conferences and workshops, multistage training and research, international library and archival collaboration. It also promotes international networking among scholars and other professions via Internet technology. In most cases, applicants are required to have a full-time affiliation with a college or university and to be faculty members who are lacking only their dissertation or have a terminal degree.

One of the most promising government-supported programs for faculty exchange is the Fulbright Scholar Program administered by the Council for International Exchange of Scholars. Established in 1946 under legislation introduced by the late Senator J. William Fulbright of Arkansas, the program, according to Fulbright literature (1995), is designed "to increase mutual understanding between the people of the United States and the people of other counties" (p. 1). More than 64,000 U.S. scholars and 117,000 scholars from abroad have participated in the program since its inception. The Fulbright Scholar Program funds academic exchanges of U.S. and international faculty and professionals in a wide variety of academic disciplines including communication and journalism. Fulbright awards are administered by the Council for International Exchange of Scholars, a private, nonprofit organization.

The American Scholar Program is one of the most well-known programs sponsored by Fulbright legislation. An average of 1,000 faculty members and professionals travel abroad to lecture (for both graduate and undergraduate courses) or conduct research. A recent call for Fulbright proposals included under the heading of communications and journalism listed over 40 host countries seeking partnerships in such topics as health communication (Austria), conflict resolution (Cyprus), gender studies (Denmark), organizational communication (El Salvador), interpersonal communication (Hong Kong), communication theory (India), communication research (Indonesia), qualitative research methods (South Africa), and intercultural communication (Estonia). Besides looking for specific calls for proposals from institutions interested in communication studies, Fulbright scholars often first cultivate a relationship with a host institution and then the host institution makes the request for a scholar. The benefits of the Fulbright program mirror the benefits that can occur when departments seek to internationalize their program. As noted in the Fulbright descriptive materials provided by the Fulbright program (1995):

> A Fulbright provides a unique opportunity to gain a new perspective in how a discipline is perceived and taught abroad, and to develop skills in teaching courses from a comparative perspective. Fulbrights foster intellectual rejuvenation and act as a catalyst for scholarly activity; faculty pursue new research directions and scholarly interests, and bring back new areas of substantive knowledge. Changes in research paths never before contemplated often take place abroad. Fulbright scholars develop international contacts and participate in collaborative research, strengthen or develop foreign language skills, and experience the personal satisfaction of instituting new ideas and programs that mold the future. Cooperative relationships between scholars, laboratories, and institutions are established that can last for decades. (p. 6)

Eligibility requirements for Fulbrights include: (a) U.S. citizenship at the time of application, (b) a doctorate plus teaching or research experience, (c) foreign language proficiency if appropriate, and (d) medical clearance. Persons who have lived abroad for the full 10-year period immediately preceding the time of application are ineligible. A previous Fulbrighter is eligible for reconsideration after 3 years following the last award. August 1 is the application deadline for Fulbright research and lecturing awards and the Indo-American Fellowship Program. November 1 is the deadline for Fulbright German Studies Seminar and other selected exchanges, such as the U.S.–United Kingdom College/University Academic Administrators Program. January 1 is the deadline for NATO Advanced Research Fellowship and Institutional Grants. Each year about 3,200 Americans apply for the 1,000 announced awards.

The Fulbright Visiting Scholars Program brings over 1,100 visiting scholars to the United States each year from over 135 countries. There are two ways to sponsor a visiting scholar. The first is direct contact with the scholar through the United States Information Services program. The second approach, the Scholar-In-Residence Program, requires a different application process. Complete application materials for any Fulbright program may be obtained through Fulbright, Council for International Exchange of Scholars, 3007 Tilden Street, N.W., Suite 5M, Washington, DC 20008–3009.

Gullong and Tomassi (1992) also suggested that following the traditional approaches to any fundraising project can be fruitful in securing resources for international outreach. Those steps include:

1. Developing a strong case for the project. Why should the funding agency support your proposal for international outreach in communication? What will the agency gain? What specific and urgent need with the funding request fulfill?
2. Target prospects. Use the resources of your university development office or grants office. Conduct your own research by requesting annual reports from foundations that may have an interest in international educational outreach. The more you know about the funding agency—government or private—the greater your chances of success in securing funding.
3. Take risks. Just as salespersons make cold calls, consider making cold calls to funding agencies. The bulk of your research time should not be directed to long-shot efforts. Some risk taking, however, can pay off in developing future leads.
4. Diversify. Do not limit your fundraising efforts to only government agencies or private foundations.
5. Use your network. Some of the most fruitful contacts emerge from personal relationships that you have established or friends your colleagues have established. If you have a department or school advisory council, ask council members who they know and how their contact may help you.
6. Do not give up. As noted previously, resources to support international faculty travel are scarce and often difficult to locate and secure.

Gullong and Tomassi (1992) recommended persistence as one of the best strategies to ensure ultimate success: "Relentlessness is the fundraisers' best friend and is especially needed when mining new ground and persuading new sources. Do not be surprised if 99 percent of your requests end in refusals. Ask again in a few months and count on the 1 percent success rate to be all you need" (p. xvii).

The American Association of State Colleges and Universities (AASCU) may prove to be one of the most helpful organizations to assist in developing a rationale for international outreach or to provide resources that could help develop a funding strategy. The AASCU's address is One Dupont Circle, Suite 700, Washington DC 20036–1192. This organization offers a wide range of resources and information that can assist faculty and administrators in developing a strategic initiative for internationalizing the curriculum. The bibliography prepared by the AASCU in the Appendix is an excellent source of ideas and strategies for inaugurating or sustaining international educational initiatives.

SUMMARY AND CONCLUSION

Communication departments and schools have much to gain from embarking on collaborations with international educators. The communication discipline exists in institutions of higher education on every continent. Establishing contacts with international scholars can benefit students, faculty, and the entire college or university community. Benefits include faculty development, student enrichment, program development, curriculum development, and enhanced research. A strong rationale for embarking on or sustaining international outreach efforts should be developed and customized by each institution embarking on international education initiatives.

Obstacles to internationalizing the curriculum include faculty resistance, lack of time, lack of money, lack of administrative support, language barriers, lack of international contacts, and troubled economic and political conditions in host countries. Despite these obstacles, the benefits of preparing students for a global marketplace outweigh the challenges of mounting international collaborations.

Strategies for developing joint international outreach include identifying faculty and institutions eager for international exchanges. Exploring partnerships with English language instruction holds promise for communication educators. Establishing research consortiums and using the Internet are other strategies that can be used to sustain international collaborations.

One of the biggest obstacles to international exchanges is finding resources to finance faculty travel and underwrite program development costs. Developing a funding strategy through both private and government sources will be an important component of developing a strategic plan for internationalizing the curriculum. Despite the effort and cost, it is well worth investing creative energy to develop international contacts. Given the nature of our study of improving human communication, communication programs have a special obligation to build bridges with colleagues around the globe to enhance our understanding of human communication.

APPENDIX: AASCU SUGGESTED RESOURCES FOR INTERNATIONALIZING CURRICULA IN HIGHER EDUCATION

Davis, T. (Ed.). (1994). *Open doors 1993–1994: Report on International Educational Exchange.* New York, NY: Institute of International Education.

Educating for Global Competence: The Report of the Advisory Council for International Educational Exchange. (1988). New York: Council of International Educational Exchange.

Goodwin, C. D., & Nacht, M. (1991). *Missing the boat: The failure to internationalize American higher education.* Cambridge, UK: Cambridge University Press.

Guidelines for college and university linkages abroad. (1993). Washington, DC: American Council on Education.

Hoffa, W., Pearson, J., & Slind, M. (1993). *NAFSA's guide to education abroad for advisers and administrators.* Washington, DC: NASFA: Association of International Educators.

International activity on state college and university campuses. (1994). Washington, DC: American Association of State Colleges and Universities.

Internationalizing the Curriculum. (1988, Fall). *Phi Kappa Phi Journal, 68.*

Johnstone, J. S., & Edelstein, R. J. (1994). *Beyond Borders: Profiles in International Education.* Washington, DC: Association of American Colleges.

Klasek, C. B. (Ed.). (1992). *Bridges to the future: Strategies for internationalizing higher education.* Carbondale, IL: Association of International Education Administrators.

Lambert, R. (1989). *International studies and the undergraduate.* Washington, DC: American Council on Education.

Picket, S., & Turlington, B. (1992). *Internationalizing the undergraduate curriculum: A handbook for campus leaders.* Washington, DC: American Council on Education.

Scott, R. A. (1991, November). The trustees' role in the globalization of university programs. Paper presented at the Retreat of University Trustees, North Carolina

Agricultural and Technical University, Greensboro, NC. (ERIC Document Reproduction Service No. ED 343–479)

Study aboard: A handbook for advisers and administrators. (1992). Washington, DC: NAFSA Association of International Educators.

Uehling, B. (1993). "University policy and international education." *Higher Education Policy, 6.*

Directories

Burton, J. (Ed.). (1994). *International exchange locator.* Washington, DC: Alliance for International Educational and Cultural Exchange.

Directory of resources for international cultural and educational exchanges. (1994). Washington, DC: United States Information Agency.

Guide to funding for international and foreign programs. (1992). New York: The Foundation Center.

Gutierrez, G., & Morehouse, W. (1990). *International studies funding and resources book: The education interface guide to sources of support for international education.* New York: Apex Press.

Hoopes, D. S., & Hoopes, K. R. (Eds.). (1991). *Guide to international education in the United States.* Detroit, MI: Gale Research.

International exchange and training activities of the U.S. government. (1993). Washington, DC: United States Information Agency.

Schlachter, G. A. (1992). *Financial aid for study and training abroad, 1992–1994.* San Carlos, CA: Reference Service Press.

REFERENCES

Beebe, S. A., Kharcheva, M. & Kharcheva, V. (1996, July). *The status of speech communication instruction in Russia.* Paper presented at the Speech Communication Association International Research Symposium, Moscow, Russia.

Beebe, S. A., & Biggers, J. T. (1986). The status of instruction in intercultural communication. *Communication Education, 35,* 54–60.

Berry, M. E. (1961). Speech education in Scandinavia. *The Speech Teacher, 10,* 22–26.

Blythin, E. (1990). *Huel Tiatoani: The Mexican speaker.* Lanham, MD: University Press of America.

Casmir, F., & Harms, L. (Eds.). (1970). *International studies of national speech education systems.* Minneapolis, MN: Burgess.

Cohen, H. (1994). *Speech communication: The emergence of a discipline, 1914–1945.* Annandale, VA: Speech Communication Association.

Dewine, S. (1995). A new direction: Internationalizing communication programs. *Journal of the Association of Communication Administration, 3,* 204–210.

Dyck, J., & Jehn, P. (1977). Rhetorical studies in West Germany, 1974–1976: A bibliography and addenda. *Rhetoric Society Quarterly, 7,* 1–19.

Ekachai, D. (1994, November). *Public relations education and teaching in Thailand.* Paper presented at the annual meeting of the Speech Communication Association, New Orleans, LA.

Engleberg, I. N. (1988). *Listening in Australia: Lessons from down under*. Paper presented at the annual meeting of the Eastern Communication Association, Baltimore, MD.

Flordo, R. (1988). The marriage of Aristotle to IBM: Integrating speech and technology in the future. In J. Lehtonen (Ed.), *Speech in the future and the future of speech*. Jyvaskyla, Finland: University of Jyvaskyla.

Flordo, R. (1989, February). *The basic course in Canadian universities: A preliminary study limited*. Paper presented at the annual meeting of the Western Speech Communication Association, Spokane, WA.

The Foundation Directory. (1997). New York: The Foundation Center.

Fulbright Program Brochure. (1995). Washington, DC: Council for International Exchange of Scholars.

Goodwin, C., & Nacht, M. (1991). *Missing the boat: The failure to internationalize American higher education*. Cambridge, UK: Cambridge University Press.

Greenberg, B., & Lau, T. (1990). The revolution in journalism and communication education in the People's Republic of China. *Gazette, 45*, 19–31.

Gullong, J. M., & Tomassi, N. (1992). *Money for international exchange in the arts*. New York: Arts International Institute of International Education and Allworth Press.

Hadwiger, K. E., Smith, C. N., & Geissner, H. (1972). West German speech education and the SCA toward a truly international association. *The Speech Teacher, 21*, 15–21.

Hewitt, R., & Inghilleri, M. (1993). Orality in the classroom: Policy, pedagogy, and group oral work. *Anthropology and Education Quarterly, 24*, 308–317.

Irwin, H. (1992, June). *Australian communication scholarship: 1970–beyond 2000*. Paper presented at the annual meeting of the International Communication Association, Miami, FL.

Irwin, H., Galvin, M., & Nightingale, V. (1986). *Applied communication studies: A new undergraduate degree program for Western Sydney*. Paper presented at the meeting of the Australian Communication Association, Canberra.

James, S. (1990). *Unpublished report of research sponsored by the African Council for Communication Education*. Unpublished manuscript, The Center for the Study of Communication and the World Association for Christian Communication, London.

Jellicorse, J. L. (1994). Applying communication studies in Hong Kong. *Journal of the Association of Communication Administration, 1*, 41–46.

McCarthy, J. S. (1992). *Mobilizing faculty for international education: The mini exchange*. Council on International Education Exchange. (Erik Document Reporduction Servce No. ED 357 679).

McGuire, M., & Berger, L. (1979). Speech in the Marxist state. *Communication Education, 28*, 169–178.

McPhaill, T., & Larsen, R. (1983). An overview of the Canadian communication and journalism scene. *ACA Bulletin, 45*, 42–43.

National Association of State Universities and Land Grant Colleges. (1993). Internationalizing higher education through the faculty. Eric document ED 3604 169.

Oliver, R. T. (1956a). Speech teaching around the world: An initial survey. *The Speech Teacher, 5*, 102–108.

Oliver, R. T. (1956b). Speech teaching around the world II: A co-operative enterprise. *The Speech Teacher, 5*, 179–185.

Oliver, R. T. (1958). Teaching speech around the world III: Report on Australia. *The Speech Teacher, 7*, 121–126.

Reed, I. (1988). *The world is here. Writin' is fighting.* New York: Atheneum.

Rolls, J. A. (1992, November). *Experiential reaming as an adjunct to the basic course: Assessment of a pedagogical model.* Paper presented at the annual meeting of the Speech Communication Association, Chicago.

Sala-Balust, A. (1985). Journalists' training: A FIEJ survey. *FIEJ Bulletin, 144*, 9–12.

Scarfe, N. V. (1962). Speech education in Canada. *The Speech Teacher, 11*, 108–114.

Supple, J. (1991). *The involved university* (Inaugural address). San Marcos, TX: Southwest Texas State University.

Trautman, F. (1975). Rhetoric far and near: Lessons for Americans from German books. *Quarterly Journal of Speech, 61*, 328–336.

UNESCO. (1989). *World communication report.* Paris: Author.

Wallace, K. (1954). *The history of speech education in America.* New York: Appleton Century Crofts.

Weitzel, A. (1990). *Higher education communication curricula outside the U.S.: An inventory and data report.* (ERIC Document Reproduction Service ED 322 562).

Wiio, O. (Ed.). (1979). *Communication education in selected nations: A symposium of reviews and commentaries.* In D. Nimmo (Ed.), *Communication yearbook 3* (pp. 83–89). New Brunswick, NJ: Transaction Books.

Wise, A. (1963). Speech education in Great Britain. *The Speech Teacher, 12*, 285–288.

Yonghua, Z. (1988). Communication research and education in Australia. *Australian Communication Review, 9*, 65–75.

5

Beyond Teaching, Research, and Service

Lana F. Rakow
University of North Dakota

Few who have been watching the landscape of the U.S. university over the past decade could argue that the university as an institution is not in the midst of significant changes. These changes have originated from external publics, who are demanding that faculty teach more, conduct less "pure" research, and be evaluated by new and less secure standards of accountability. Central administrators, charged by regents and legislators with implementing shifts in faculty roles and rewards, with downsizing, and with collecting data to demonstrate accountability, have met with varying degrees of success, yet their collective efforts signal that plans are well underway for altering the university in fundamental ways. Are we sure that these changes are in the best interest of both the institution and society? (For a sample discussion of these changes, see Gioia & Thomas, 1996; Guskin, 1996; Sewall, 1996.)

Little public or academic debate has accompanied this alteration of how we do business. The name of the public is invoked, however, by regents and legislators as they demand streamlined organizations and cut budgets. It is difficult to argue against the changes because the purported goal is the improvement of undergraduate education. Some faculty find the goal an admirable one and support administrative mandates. The resistance of many faculty, on the other hand, is widely noted and often resented. Administrators view the resistance of faculty as a sign of faculty members' parochial and entrenched professional interests. (See Guskin, 1996, on administrator and faculty approaches to change.) The resistance, however, reflects an unease—even hostility—with the implications these changes have for the traditional role of the university. We should view faculty reaction as a signal that differing expectations of the university need to be held up for public and scholarly scrutiny. If we do not honestly acknowledge the real reasons behind mandates, if we do not clearly assess the social and political context driving changes, and if we do not identify all of the possible models for the role the university could play as an institution, the de facto result may be unsatisfactory or worse. The solution is to begin a discussion of the mission of the university, not as a particular organizational entity but as a social institution with a critical role to play. What is that role?

Most of us are accustomed to campus discussion of mission—of our own institution and of our own academic unit. These can be frustrating or rewarding activities, depending upon the seriousness of intent to fully involve the campus or academic unit in identifying common values and purposes and the earnestness of intent to adopt and follow a commonly held mission. However, these exercises in determining mission typically occur in a theoretical vacuum. The collective mission of the university as a social institution should be the starting point from which individual missions flow, or society may be the loser. Administrators have become so concerned about the survival of their particular institutions they may have missed the greater danger to the survival of universities in their capacity to play a unique and critical role in society.

What should our collective mission be and what changes to academic programs might flow from its adoption? To start the conversation, this chapter takes up the question of the mission of the university as an institution with implications for our academic programs of communication. It begins with an examination of the social context—including political and economic changes, technological changes, and epistemological changes—during the past century that have had an impact on society and all public institutions, including universities. Then some of the conflicting views of the role of the university as an institution are discussed. Finally, the chapter suggests implications for the ways in which our communication programs can lead the way in better linking the university to society to fulfill its unique role in creating, preserving, and critiquing knowledge.

POLITICAL AND ECONOMIC CHANGES

Recent calls for change in the university can be traced to a changing social context during the past decade, out of which grew both political and economic frustrations with universities around the country. Fear about the future of our society, a growing intolerance for the demands of women and racial and ethnic minorities, and frustration with such urban problems as crime and illegal drug trafficking and use fueled a political agenda for a change of public institutions and in social values. National elections and their aftermath during the past decade reveal a shifting U.S. interpretation of the trustworthiness and viability of most public institutions, including higher education.

The political and economic anxieties of the previous decade are not new ones to this country. Recall the social anxiety about the changing U.S. character and about urban decay and decadence at the end of the 19th century, a 100 years ago (Hofstadter, 1955; Quandt, 1970; Wiebe, 1967). We share with that time period the dislocations of immigration and migration, the influx of new cultural groups resulting in increased ethnic and racial intolerance, the decline of the community in favor of large urban (and now suburban) centers, and the fear of mob rule (which has now been converted into a fear of the public opinion poll). Progressives and social scientists wondered then how social order could be restored, resorting to a top–down model of decision making, a representative model of democracy, and industrial capitalism characterized by large and powerful industries growing under the watchful but generally tolerant eye of a growing government.

Whereas the social upheaval of the end of the 19th century led to a larger role for government and the tremendous growth of other institutions, the current response has been to scale back the size of institutions, ostensibly to make them better able to respond to a rapidly shifting economic landscape. Bigness is equated with the past: Government agencies, business and industry, education, and social service organizations must be lean enough to solve problems quickly and to shift their priorities to current social needs or economic opportunities. Deregulation and privatization produced a cut-throat competitive environment, where mergers and "outsourcing" have chopped organizations and put people out of jobs.

As private enterprise has taken on a new shape, universities have been soundly criticized for their unbusinesslike approach to financial and personnel management and their lack of a product and customer mentality, leading to business seminars for administrators, Total Quality Management programs on campus, and national discussions of new ways to finance higher education (see Mercer, 1997). The current generation of senior university administrators is comprised of many who have convinced boards of higher education that they bring a tough-mindedness to the task of running a university more leanly and efficiently, who can make the university into an entrepreneurial enterprise that takes its place among its partners in business and industry and gives undergraduates added value to each credit hour undertaken. Like their business partners, these new universities look for their unique marketing niche, "outsource" traditional services, and focus on profit centers. The full-service university may become a thing of the past in this new political and economic environment.

TECHNOLOGICAL CHANGE

The boutique or convenience store university is made feasible by the changes in technology widely embraced by most administrators and faculty leaders. Many see greater potential for higher education if it is no longer tied to a particular time and place, especially in cases where declining enrollments threaten the financial stability of the organization. The technological university could function with minimal faculty and facilities, allowing students—who, it is imagined, will be taking classes throughout their lifetime—to learn at their own pace in their own communities or neighborhoods. A more modest or perhaps more short-term vision has faculty and students using multimedia systems on traditional campuses to teach and learn, enabling instruction to be more individualized and specialized.

Embracing new technologies to solve problems is not an unusual response in this country, although it may be for the university. Technology over the past century has been heralded by many for its ability to revolutionize institutions and relationships, to provide greater access to more people over greater distances (Czitrom, 1982), and to "bring the world to our doorsteps." Ironically, at the beginning of the 20th century, when there were great fears about the changes taking place in the country, some had great hope that the new media of communication would tie the country together and create a new order that transcended geographic limitations by linking communities together across space. Promises that the media would be our salvation in the midst of social turmoil were not fulfilled, however. At that time, distrust of the rationality of the masses of immigrants, farmers, the working class, freed slaves, and women demanding the vote led to a model of communication that lingers with us today. Those with political and economic power never envisioned that these new media—from the telegraph to movies to radio to television—might be put to use by everyone. From the earliest days, media developers primarily saw them as instruments for making money, not for enabling people to participate in democracy nor for expanding our means to communicate with each other. The First Amendment consistently has been used to justify the rights of media owners to develop technologies for profit rather than to support the rights of citizens to have access to the means to communicate.

As a consequence, technologies are designed so that people can receive entertainment and information but cannot provide it, except on a one-to-one basis. This model for the media—of few transmitters, many receivers—gave us our current configuration of mass communication, communication to the masses, but not of or by them. Newly marketed technologies—cellular telephones, laptop computers, new software products and information services, and the like—seem to be moving us beyond mass communication, yet these products share the same feature of being designed for individuals for the individual's private (personal and/or professional) use rather than a public use. Both mass media and individualized communication technologies, it can be argued, have contributed to a decline in geographic communities rather than a renewal of them, as early 20th-century social observers and now current social observers have hoped.

Measured by growth of the self-help industry, psychotherapy, treatment for depression, and suicide, we might conclude that never have so many people felt so alone despite the fact that we have never had so many means available for communication. Measured by the feeling of disconnection by citizens from their government and by what seem to be unsolvable rural and urban problems of our country, we might also conclude that never have so many people felt so unable to affect the outcome of political processes despite the ubiquity of communication technology. It is not for want of technology, then, that we have reached what might be termed a crisis state of communication; it is for want of a model of communication that links people together in communities of public participation.

It seems clear that the technological revolution that is being marketed to us will only give us more of the same. We are promised freedom from the constraints of time and place with more and better technologies. What kind of connectedness will we have in this new world? What will be said? By whom and to whom for what purpose? Who will decide? Technologies do not come about by themselves. They must by produced and marketed. They must be given meaning and purpose. Their many possibilities must be narrowed to a routinized part of our daily lives. Decisions are being made without the participation of citizens, members of the academic community, or scholars of communication.

Will this newly envisioned technological university use technology differently, in a new model? Will broad participation make the determination? Unfortunately, we have little reason to suspect our own use of technology in the academy will break new ground (see, e.g., Brown & Duguid, 1996; Walz, 1996; Wulf, 1995). Administrators have responded to technological developments by scrambling to keep up with each other in obtaining state-of-the-art technologies for classrooms, labs, and offices. Universities are criticized—even ridiculed—for being latecomers to the integration of technologies into support functions and classrooms. Disturbingly, acquiring technologies has been put ahead of acquiring a critical perspective on technologies. The university has taken little leadership in discussing and enabling the public to participate in decision making about technological change. Students are taught to use, not think about, technology. Visions for a university that teaches across distances fail to take into account the role of the intellectual community of the university as a critical component of learning.

Programs of communication have been more than remiss in raising questions about the wholesale adoption of technologies inside and outside of the academy. We have been quick to align ourselves with media industries that want to use new technologies to make money, or with the concerned moralists, who want to know what media are doing to people. Even our more recent research approaches, which value the lived experiences of people by asking what people do with media, is limiting. It restricts our thinking to our current model, even as it recognizes the negotiated and creative responses of people to texts and technologies. Why not align ourselves with the public, which needs access to media? Why not ask what people could do with media? New technologies could be used to address our problems of communication, to make and remake community. Citizens could use technologies for discussion and debate.

Communication programs—faculty and students—should be posing questions of this sort, then leading a public discussion of them. Adding technology to the classroom or replacing on-site teaching with distance teaching via technology does not address what is missing in the university's performance as an institution in its primary role of preserving, producing, and critiquing knowledge. We should be concerned that not only have universities but also the discipline of communication been seen first and foremost as technological players rather than as thinkers about technology.

EPISTEMOLOGICAL CHANGE

In addition to technological changes, our social context is characterized by epistemological changes in how we know, what we know, who we know, and who knows us. If we are in any revolution, it is one of knowledge and knowing. This upheaval can be seen inside and outside of the university, from new paradigms in the hard sciences that refute the ability of science to discover the ultimate truth about nature to trends in corporate management that view organizations as conversations to a recognition among journalists that objectivity is, like everything else, a belief system with moral consequences. What we are witnessing is a dramatic shift away from a view of knowledge as static, objective, and universal to a cultural view of knowledge as relative to the knower (see, e.g., Foucault, 1982; Habermas, 1971). Finally, we may be coming to realize the truth about truth.

This revolution in epistemology did not occur overnight. A long revolution in knowledge began late in the 19th century, developing through the historic expansion of a voting citizenship, through the goal of universal literacy and education, and through increased access to information. The revolutionary continuum began when the country witnessed a shift in its definition of who needs to know. Expanding voting rights to non-property-owning White men, then African American men, then women and other racial and ethnic groups had as its ultimate logical conclusion the need for all persons in society to be knowledgeable. They needed to be literate and educated in order to exercise their democratic responsibilities of voting. They must have access to information to make informed choices.

Now we are in the part of the knowledge revolution where our notions of what and how we need to know have been challenged and, in some cases, revised. The most obvious and important source for this change has come from those groups—women and racial and ethnic minorities—who have successfully challenged what we know as a society, how we know it, and what is known about them as groups (Banks & Banks, 1989; Belenky, Clinchy, Goldberger, & Tarule, 1986; Kramarae & Spender, 1992; West, 1993). The success has come even though we who are scholars and activists on issues of race and gender are attacked for our ideas. For example, the term *sexual harassment* was virtually unknown only a few years ago. The experiences of girls and women in schools and in workplaces were not considered valuable knowledge. Thanks to feminism, women's truths are now being told. As the full weight of this epistemological shift sinks in at the workplace, men may be uneasy as they are confronted with the realization of the multiplicity of truths about a topic or experience, truths that are dependent on one's social and cultural standpoint.

Universities, fortunately, have been a place where this realization about the relativity of knowledge has been allowed to develop, although with varying degrees of support or hostility. Two decades' worth of attention to issues of diversity by managers in many kinds of organizations, prompted usually by pragmatic legal and economic imperatives, also has paved the way for recognizing the need to have knowledge of the standpoints of groups other than European American men. It is important that all institutions—from government to business and industry to universities to news media—fully accept that unless we hear from all perspectives and experiences our knowledge is incomplete and partial.

Another step in completing the knowledge revolution entails a new agreement about what we do with our knowledge. Signs that some people and organizations are recognizing the significance of knowledge in "doing the world" are apparent, most readily in the use of the term *information economy*. To many—too many, yet—this simply means that information, which they understand to be pieces of truth about the world, has replaced other pieces of the world as the primary outcome of our economic system of production and consumption. At a more profound level, others have observed that people and the organizations they work for are knowledge systems, making knowledge a competitive resource in addition to a competitive product.

Managerial gurus want to convince organizations to think of themselves as systems of knowledge dependent on the quality of knowledge produced by the knowledge workers they employ. Peter Senge (1994) called them "learning organizations" in *The Fifth Discipline: The Art and Practice of the Learning Organization*. A business editor observed, in a fashion similar to Senge, that "In the new economy, conversations are the most important form of work. Conversations are the way knowledge workers discover what they know, share it with their colleagues, and in the process create new knowledge for the organization" (Webber, 1993, p. 28).

How can we, in our universities, fail to see the implications for the university when the creation of knowledge is no longer one of our primary or unique functions? Public criticism of faculty research has gone hand-in-hand with reduced funding for research and heavier undergraduate teaching loads. Business organizations sell information; even university libraries have started to charge for such services as interlibrary loans. If the creation of knowledge becomes nothing more than a means to extract profit from organizational processes and knowledge is nothing more than a commodity, what is the function of the university? Who will need it? It is ironic, and perhaps tragic, that the university does not see itself as the original and most critical knowledge system of contemporary society. The new purpose and role of knowledge currently shaping organizational thinking should be a contestable assumption brought to light by the university in its role of challenging and questioning knowledge rather than accepting another taken for granted "fact" of modern life. Already too much of society remains taken for granted without the scrutiny of the one institution that should be responsible for contributing to the public good by critiquing and producing knowledge. Other institutions create information for their own purposes, much of which is proprietary and represents the goal of a particular organization to further its own interests. It is the challenge of the university of the future to improve its capacity to serve as society's knowledge institution and to ensure that society is the beneficiary.

MISSION OF THE UNIVERSITY

We have seen that major social changes are affecting the role of the contemporary U.S. university, changes that are political, economic, technological, and epistemological in nature. Viewing the university as an institution in the midst of a society in flux, we should be struck by the peculiar irrelevance of the university to these pressing social issues. The university certainly cannot be said to be taking a leadership role in a discussion, public or academic, of the effect of the changes on society or even on its own role. The changes appear to be impacting the future shape of the university rather than the university impacting the shape of the future.

The void created by our collective silence has been filled with criticism of us. Faculty, angry and on the defensive, are also puzzled by the reaction of the public, of parents, of donors, and of students to the university. Most faculty have assumed an implicit social contract between the university and society. The value of their work—teaching students and preserving the university as a haven for the discovery of truth and the discussion of ideas—has been assumed to be self-evident. We have advocated a lofty role for ourselves but in practice that role has been reduced to the presentation of our ideas within the confines of the classroom or behind the closed doors of our professional associations and publications.

The university is no stranger to these conflicts over its role. The history of the U.S. university shows a pattern of struggles over the definition of the university and purpose of higher education. Arguments have been made about vocational learning versus education for citizenry and about autonomy from powerful special interests versus the application of the resources of the university to the needs of society. For example, we may feel that "careerism" is an unfortunate or dangerous trend among our current students and their parents, but the concern was reflected in the works of Robert Hutchins (1936), who observed:

> There is a conflict between one aim of the university, the pursuit of truth for its own sake, and another which it professes too, the preparation of men and women for their life work. This is not a conflict between education and research. It is a conflict between two kinds of education. (p. 33)

To Hutchins, the university must be a place to search for the truth without the pressure of justifying its utility. In a similar vein, arguments about the relevance of the university to society were made decades ago by the students of the 1960s, leading to a rebuke by Kenneth Minogue (1973), who argued that the university has been attacked since the 17th century for its tradition of isolation but that a functionalist view of the university—responding to national needs—is a covert political doctrine about universities that could lead to their destruction.

These disagreements have never been resolved, leading to our current confusion. Now parents, students, donors, taxpayers, and legislators want more for their money, it is that simple. We are being held to the only productivity standard that the public has seen and knows it should benefit from, the education of undergraduates for their individual career aspirations. Of course the education of undergraduates is not unimportant but it is unfortunate to consider the education of undergraduates to be the goal of the university rather than a means to an end. We have never made the case, at least not convincingly, that the university could be of great benefit to society in other ways. Of course, students and parents will still want to get their money's worth, but donors and legislators may be more willing to fund an institution that seems to be solving the country's problems than, as they believe now, contributing to them.

A broader mission has never been widely shared nor understood outside the university, nor has it been properly carried out at the university. Until now, it has only been in the natural and physical sciences that the university's role as a producer of knowledge with a readily apparent social application has been nurtured and developed by government and industry in a direct relationship. Land grant universities were to make tangible the mission of applied service to society through extension and outreach to farmers and homemakers. Professional schools have served their professions and only indirectly the public, precluding some of the deep critique of social institutions and processes that we would hope to find in a university. Schools of journalism and mass communication, to hold up a mirror, have cultivated their relationships with media industries, concerned to provide an academic program that trains future employees, but seldom serving as a "fifth estate" as they should; as a consequence we have media critics pointing out that no one is watching the watchdog.

In short, the ways in which universities have addressed their service to society have been insufficient and inconsistent. We need to ask who, which groups in society, have benefitted from the knowledge of universities? Who has shaped its research, teaching, and service agenda because of the financial benefits to programs and individuals? The answers to these questions illuminate the reasons that most of the pressing social, economic, and political issues of our day have received so little sustained and collective attention. The university, while trying to make itself relevant to industries and institutions with political and economic power, has made itself irrelevant to the public's need for knowledge.

IRRELEVANCE OF THE UNIVERSITY

We perpetuate the university's unwillingness or inability to serve all of society and its need for knowledge by the very structure of our organizations and the reward system of the academy. These include the following.

Departmentalization

The division of universities into discrete and specialized departments, which link faculty to national and international disciplines of inquiry but not their local geographic communities, ensures a disjuncture between the academy and the rest of the world. The physical world, people, and their cultures and experiences, are not divided into boxes that neatly fit the boundaries of our departments and disciplines. Our scholarship and our teaching suffer because we do not see all of the context of what we are studying, we do not see the larger picture that requires us to bring together an understanding of economics, politics, the environment, culture, and history. As a consequence, linking up what goes on in the university with the public and its needs is difficult.

Individualism

The second reason that the university is disconnected from the needs of society for our intellectual resources lies in our individualistic model of the university as an aggregation of faculty, operating as independent contractors, who are expected as individuals to participate in teaching, research, and service. The knowledge that faculty produce is presumed to filter into society through teaching and through publication of books and scholarly articles, although some faculty engage in individual service projects in the local geographic community. Producing knowledge for ourselves is not only self-serving, but potentially dangerous. The country cannot afford—metaphorically as well as financially—to be deprived of our intellectual ideas.

Teaching undergraduates will not suffice as a mechanism to connect the knowledge produced in the university with the knowledge needs of society. Educate them in whose knowledge? Toward what end? We certainly have been educating individuals for a long time; our alumni are everywhere. It is sobering to consider that our state legislators, our boards of regents, Congress, state agencies, management of business and industry and the senior administrators of our universities are college graduates. They are somebody's former students. Can we truly say we believe we have done all that we can to ensure that society reaps the greatest benefits from the knowledge gained through time from all quarters of the human community?

Let us put the intellectual resources of the university at the disposal of the public, working with them as partners to address the public's need for knowledge. Teaching, research, and service are all, then, means to accomplish that larger social good. However, the concept of the public is a contentious one and we should be reminded of how careful we need to be in calling on it. We should not continue to put ourselves into the hands of the highest bidder, but neither should we have a naive notion that we can escape the rhetorical politics of invoking the name of the public. Nonetheless, if we do nothing else but put the debate about what serving the public means at the center of what we do, we will have made a tremendous contribution to focusing the debate about our mission.

We should not, along the way, fear that the truth will become contaminated by the needs of special interests, a criticism that university faculty interested in "pure" research and knowledge are known to make about what might seem to be an argument here for simply more applied research. We should be able to own up to the fact now that the truth is always contaminated: It always reflects the standpoint of the knower. Race studies and feminist studies have shown us the way to move from the pursuit of truth to the pursuit of understanding, from the bankruptcy of individualism and competition to the promise of community and cooperation, from the folly of the pursuit of learning for its own sake to the necessity for applying theory to action.

Lack of Means to Participate

In addition to departmentalization and individualism separating the university from society, we are hampered from fulfilling a larger mission in society by the lack of processes that would enable the public to participate in discussion, reflection, and decision making. Our failure as universities to engage in the public world reflects the inability of the public in general to do so. If we are to be a real democracy, citizens must have voice, the means and ability to have one's opinion matter in public discussion. If we are to be a real democracy, we must create healthy and egalitarian processes for knowing and being known,which are, ultimately, communication processes. A new model of communication and the university is needed to accomplish the goal of citizen discussion and participation. We have relied on the country's news media to provide information to citizens about the activities of its institutions but without providing the means for citizens to use the information in a meaningful way for decision making. This one-way, mass communication model excludes the knowledge of the university except by chance (when universities make news or a professor is used as a news source). An interactive, dialogic model of communication would establish the role of the university in providing the mechanism for sharing the knowledge it preserves and produces by facilitating and leading public discussion of matters of importance.

Implications for Communication Programs

Implications for our role in the field of communication and in our specific programs of this challenging social and university context should be clear. We need to understand how political and economic changes are driving changes in the university without adequate reflection on the mission of the university. We need to be leaders in the discussion of the potential benefits and losses that come with different uses of communication technologies, in society and within the university. We need to envision new communication processes inside and outside of the university that connect the university to society, enabling everyone to participate in the construction of a richer base of knowledge, taking into account all perspectives and experiences, and directed toward a constructive process of discussion and debate. We need to show the rest of the university how to redefine its institutional role by modeling the reforms that are needed.

To do so, those of us in the field of communication need to find our commonalities across sequences and specializations, because our curricula are as guilty of separating us from public life as are any department's. Reality, the sum total of our shared understandings about the world, is not divided into discrete categories of journalism, public relations, advertising, broadcasting, or speech. Training journalism or broadcasters or public relations practitioners or sales managers or personnel managers is an insufficient contribution to the public good. Who will raise the tough questions about technologies and media industries if we do not? Who will imagine how to create the means for citizens to participate in their own communities and government? We must reinvent our own mission, bigger, bolder, more noble than we have in the past. We must design our curricula to link us richly and effectively to the public and its needs for knowledge, not simply to media industries and their need for workers. (For a discussion of how this was done at the University of North Dakota School of Communication, see Rakow, 1995. The School uses three themes—community, information, and technology—rather than traditional career sequences to organize an integrated curriculum.) We should design our faculty responsibilities around the synergistic possibilities of our collective, integrated, and strategically planned teaching, research, and service contributions to society.

This chapter has identified some of the possible or likely models of the university of the future that are being forced upon us by the changing political, economic, technological, and epistemological changes occurring in society. These changes have been a long time in the making. Because the university has never had a clearly agreed upon mission in society, universities as individual and unique institutions have been left to adapt their own missions in response to external pressures. However, the greater, collective mission of the university as an institution remains unidentified. Calls for a new social contract between the university and society are a hopeful sign that we may be recognizing what is at stake (see Greer, 1993). Now the ability to articulate a new vision, mission, and unique role of the university as an institution should be the test of the next generation of university administrators.

REFERENCES

Banks, J. A., & Banks, C. A. McGee (Eds.). (1989). *Multicultural education: Issues and perspectives*. Boston: Allyn & Bacon.

Belenky, M. F., Clinchy, B. M., Goldberger, N. R., & Tarule, J. M. (1986). *Women's ways of knowing: The development of self, voice, and mind*. New York: Basic Books.

Brown, J. S., & Duguid, P. (1996, July–August). Universities in the digital age. *Change 28*(4), 10(10).

Czitrom, D. J. (1982). *Media and the American mind: From Morse to McLuhan*. Chapel Hill: University of North Carolina Press.

Foucault, M. (1982). *The archeology of knowledge*. New York: Pantheon.

Gioia, D. A., & Thomas, J. B. (1996, September). Identity, image, and issue interpretation: Sensemaking during strategic change in academia. *Administrative Science Quarterly, 41*(3), 370.

Greer, D. G. (1993, February). Vision and purpose: Foundations of higher education reform. *Policy Perspectives, 4*(4), 3B–4B.

Guskin, A. E. (1996, July–August). Facing the future: The change process in restructuring universities. *Change, 28*(6), 26.

Habermas, J. (1971). *Knowledge and human interests* (J. J. Shapiro, Trans.). Boston: Beacon Press.

Hofstadter, R. (1955). *The age of reform*. New York: Knopf.

Hutchins, R. M. (1936). *The higher learning in America*. New Haven, CT: Yale University Press.

Kramarae, C., & Spender, D. (Eds.). (1992). *The knowledge explosion: Generations of feminist scholarship*. New York: Teachers College Press.

Mercer, J. (1997, May 23). Academic administrators try to apply business principles to campus challenges. *Chronicle of Higher Education, 43*(37), p. A35.

Minogue, K. R. (1973). *The concept of a university*. Berkeley: University of California Press.

Quandt, J. (1970). *From the small town to the great community*. New Brunswick, NJ: Rutgers University Press.

Rakow, L. F. (1995). New curricular categories for the future: University of North Dakota School of Communication. *Journal of the Association for Communication Administration, 3*, 211–215.

Senge, P. (1994). *The fifth discipline: The art and practice of the learning organization*. New York: Doubleday.

Sewall, A. M. (1996, Spring). From the importance of education in the 80's to accountability in the 90's. *Education, 116*(3), 325.

Walz, M. (1996, October 14). Technologies reach beyond the campus. *MacWEEK, 10*(39), 23.

Webber, A. M. (1993, January/February). What's so new about the new economy? *Harvard Business Review, 71*(1), 24.

West, C. (1993). *Keeping faith: Philosophy and race in American*. New York: Routledge.

Wiebe, R. (1967). *The search for order: 1877–1920*. New York: Hill & Wang.

Wulf, W. A. (1995, Summer). Warning: Information technology will transform the university. *Issues in Science and Technology, 11*(4), 46.

II

PROGRAMMATIC CHALLENGES

6

The Hybrid Program

Alexis S. Tan
Washington State University

Most communication programs are either mass communication or speech communication. Mass Communication programs are often housed in units called Journalism and Mass Communications, whereas speech communication is often found in Speech Communication or Communication Arts units. However, some programs combine speech communication and mass communication in single administrative units. Whatever the reasons—budgetary or philosophical—such hybrid programs seem to be on the rise, and are receiving close scrutiny (Blanchard & Christ, 1993).

THE HYBRID COMMUNICATION PROGRAM

The typical mass communication program includes undergraduate sequences in one or more of the mass media professional fields—advertising, broadcasting, journalism and public relations. Accrediting standards require that the majority of courses should be in the liberal arts. Far from being vocational, many programs stress not only professional skills courses but also theory and research. However, the emphasis is on the mass media, and there is the explicit expectation that these programs are educating students for the mass media professions. This mission is stated by the Association for Education in Journalism and Mass Communication (AEJMC), the largest organization of mass communication faculty in the United States, as "to improve journalism and mass communication education in order to achieve better professional practice, a better-informed public, and wider human understanding" (AEJMC Constitution and ByLaws, n.d.).

Graduate education in mass communication programs continues the focus on the mass media, although there is more emphasis on theory and research. Some MA programs lead to terminal degrees, offering advanced professional courses and seminars on law and ethics. Other MA programs prepare students for PhD programs, most of which are interdisciplinary with cognate areas in other liberal arts departments. Much of the research in PhD programs addresses questions in mass communications, or communication mediated by the mass media.

Speech communication programs generally focus on interpersonal and small group communication, organizational communication, language systems, rhetoric, and public address at the undergraduate level. The same topics with the exception of public address are generally emphasized in MA and PhD programs, which are interdisciplinary. The mission of speech communication education is articulated by the National Communication Association (NCA; formerly the Speech Communication Association or SCA) as "to promote the study, criticism, research, teaching, and application of the artistic, humanistic, and scientific principles of communication" (SCA Constitution and By-Laws, 1995).

Both mass communication and speech communication programs deal with communication as the substantive area of teaching and research. However, by default or historical serendipity, the field has been divided into two distinct (although not mutually exclusive) areas: intra- and interpersonal communication for speech communication (Cohen, 1994; Work & Jeffrey, 1989) and mass or mediated communications for mass communication (Rogers & Chaffee, 1994).

To some central university administrators and many of our colleagues in other academic areas, the division of communication into separate speech and mass communication administrative units does not make sense. If indeed communication is a legitimate area of academic study, then there should be definable boundaries and one discipline housed in a single administrative unit. This is certainly true for psychology, sociology, political science, law, and medicine.

Adding to the confusion is the large number of names used by communication programs. For example, the 410 programs listed in the AEJMC directory use a total of 113 different names. For departments, the most frequently used, in order of frequency, are Communication or Communications, Journalism, and Mass Communication or Mass Communications. For colleges, the popular names are Communications or Communication and Journalism. Most schools are named Communication or Communications, Journalism, and Journalism and Mass Communications. (These figures are based on a study I did for this chapter.)

To many of our colleagues in mass communications and speech communications, separate academic units make a lot of sense. The most compelling reason is the different missions of the two fields. Mass communication education prepares students for professional careers in the mass media. Professional education is generally not of interest in speech communication programs. As a consequence, competency requirements for faculty are generally different. Professional experience—and the PhD—are valued in mass communication programs. Professional experience of faculty is not an issue in speech communication programs. Mass communication programs offer professional (skills) courses; speech communication programs offer courses in public address. Mass Communications programs have an influential, vocal constituency in the mass media professions; speech communications does not. These historical differences have led to specializations within each field that make integration into one academic unit, particularly when forced by central administration, difficult.

Regardless of where one stands on the issue of consolidation, the reality is that more and more mass and speech communication programs are being integrated into single administrative units. The most common combinations are speech and mass communications; some units include, in addition, theatre, speech pathology, fine arts, and graphic arts. Such combinations can work, and often work when certain conditions are met.

WHEN HYBRID PROGRAMS CAN WORK

How Do We Know It Works?

Measures of success of hybrid programs are the same as for any other program (Christ, 1994, 1997).

1. Students.

- Knowledge and appreciation of the field (as defined by the unit).
- Preparation for careers in communication and related fields.
- Satisfaction.
- "Good" citizenship.

2. Faculty.

- Effective teaching.
- Productive scholarship.
- Collegiality.
- Service to the discipline.
- Satisfaction.

3. The Unit.

- Support from central administration.
- Support from alumni and other external constituents.
- Recognition within the discipline as a quality program.
- Adequate resources.

Conditions for Success

Hybrid programs are more likely to work when only speech and mass communications are integrated into an academic unit, particularly if the unit is a department or school within a college of liberal arts. Speech and mass communications have more in common intellectually than speech pathology, fine arts, theatre, and graphic arts—other areas sometimes included in the mix. Most of my comments then are directed at the marriage of speech and mass communications in single administrative units.

Mission Statement, Strategic Plan, and the Curriculum. The first and most important requirement is faculty agreement on the mission of the unit. The unit's leaders should inform the appropriate central administrators of the project to write (or rewrite) the mission statement. Central administrators do not like to be surprised. They can also define the parameters within which the hybrid program can operate. For example, most traditional research universities will not be receptive to professional communication education; public land grant universities are more likely to embrace professional and theoretical programs. In forced mergers of speech and mass communication programs, the faculty will most likely be directed to write a mission statement within limits defined by central administrators.

Several options are possible for a hybrid program's mission (Christ & Blanchard, 1994; Christ & Hynes, 1997):

1. To offer professional education in mass communication.
2. To offer theoretical education in mass and speech communication.
3. To offer professional education in mass communication and theoretical education in mass and speech communication.

The first option generally will not be tenable because speech communication is not directly associated with an identifiable professional field, as is mass communications. Whether the second or third option is selected depends on the makeup of the faculty. Programs with a mix of professional (mass media) and research faculties will do well with the third option; if only scholars and researchers are in the faculty, the second option would be the choice.

The mission statement, then, should be based on existing faculty strengths. It should be articulated in a written strategic plan agreed on by the faculty that defines goals and objectives and identifies strengths, weaknesses, resources, opportunities, and strategies for attaining the unit's mission.

Implicit in the mission statement will be a definition of the discipline (speech and mass communication) and identification of its boundaries. The mission statement should specify which areas within mass and speech communication will be included in the unit. For example, a broad-based unit could include all the mass media areas (print journalism, broadcasting, advertising, and public relations) and rhetorical, interpersonal, and organizational communication. A narrower focus could include only print journalism and rhetoric. Faculty agreement on the definition and boundaries will help establish the unit's identity for external and internal constituents.

Definitions of the discipline by hybrid programs will by necessity be more general than "pure" programs in speech or mass communications. One possible approach is to examine the definitions implied in the mission statements of our research journals. Here are some examples:

- *Journalism & Mass Communication Quarterly*: "Should provide leadership in developing theory and introducing new concepts.... Because communications is a diverse field, articles should address questions using a variety of methods and theoretical perspectives.... Should challenge the boundaries of communication research."
- *Communication Monographs*: "Has reported original research grounded in theory dealing with processes of human symbolic exchange in varying social contexts."
- *Human Communication Research*: "Is devoted to advancing knowledge about human symbolic activities."

These research journals offer general definitions of communication as human symbolic activities, which would be appropriate for most hybrid programs. Symbolic activities include intra-, inter-, and mediated (mass) communication processes, topics of concern to speech and mass communications scholars.

We can also look at the mission statements of the three largest academic organizations in our field for definitions of the discipline:

- NCA: "To promote study, criticism, research, teaching, and application of the artistic, humanistic, and scientific principles of communication" (SCA Constitution and ByLaws, 1995).
- International Communication Association (ICA): "To promote the systematic study of communication theories, processes and skills."
- AEJMC: "To improve journalism and mass communication education in order to achieve better professional practice, a better-informed public, and wider human understanding."

NCA and ICA use the more generic *communication* to describe their activities; AEJMC specifies education and professional practice in *journalism and mass communication*. It is fine to have a general definition of communication but as a practical matter, a hybrid program cannot excel (or even be functional) unless it narrows its focus. A look at the organizational structures of NCA, AEJMC, and ICA reveals a large number of divisions and interest groups that define the teaching and research activities of the memberships. Here are some common divisions and interest groups:

1. Mass Communications (ICA and NCA), Mass Communication and Society (AEJMC).
2. Intercultural and Development Communication (ICA), International and Intercultural Communication (NCA), International Communication (AEJMC), Minorities and Communication (AEJMC).
3. Organizational Communication (ICA, NCA); Media Management and Economics (AEJMC).
4. Public Relations (AEJMC, NCA, ICA).
5. Law (AEJMC), Communication and Law (NCA), Communication Law and Policy (ICA).

These divisions common to NCA, ICA, and AEJMC could be the starting points for determining programs to be included in a hybrid program because they indicate existing overlaps in faculty teaching and research interests in the associations. Further refinements can be made, considering the interests and competencies of faculty in the hybrid unit and opportunities for developing specific areas with new hires or replacement of retiring faculty. Of course, strengths of existing faculty should be utilized, even if those strengths do not fall in any of the areas just mentioned. Interpersonal and small group communication are not necessarily represented in the divisional structures of the associations, but they permeate most of the other divisions.

The program's curriculum should reflect the hybrid nature of the unit as articulated in its mission statement and strategic plan. For most hybrid programs, the starting point could be a core of courses required of all majors and to include foundation courses in speech and mass communications. Which courses deliver the fundamental knowledge considered by the faculty to be essential in each field? Some likely candidates are mass communication theories, speech communication theories, writing, and oral communications. After completing the core courses, students could then specialize in the traditional speech and mass communications sequences. The core and sequence courses required would depend on faculty strengths and competencies. Few programs can be effective emphasizing all possible areas in speech and mass communications. The program should concentrate resources on those areas in which some degree of excellence and recognition is possible.

To recap, hybrid programs should have a clear mission statement and strategic plan that define the unit and that reflect faculty strengths and opportunities for growth. A curriculum should be designed to support the program's mission. The mission statement, strategic plan, and accompanying curriculum should be generated and approved by the faculty. Central administrators should be informed of the process before it starts. (Mission statements from over 120 journalism and mass communication programs are available from the Executive Director, AEJMC, University of South Carolina, Columbia, SC 29208–0251; see Christ & Hynes, 1997. For guidelines and examples of strategic plans, see Cope, 1981; Kaiser, 1993).

Support From Constituents.   The second requirement for a successful hybrid program is support from its internal and external constituents. Among important internal constituents are students, colleagues in other academic departments, and central administrators. Important external constituents are alumni, allied professional groups (e.g., media professionals), and donors.

Students are often overlooked in the planning process until it is too late—the plan is leaked, someone does not like it and objections are raised publicly (e.g., in the student newspaper) or with central administrators even before the plan is formally submitted. Whether it is revising an existing mission statement, strategic plan, and curriculum, or starting from scratch, it is a good idea to involve students at the beginning, particularly for a potentially volatile issue such as hybrid communication programs. Students have a right to ask how they will be affected by the change—will they get a good education, will they graduate on time, will they be able to pursue their career interests? I believe that the faculty should generate and write the mission statement, strategic plan and curriculum. However, I recommend that a draft of the resulting document should be circulated among undergraduate and graduate students (or their leaderships). Open hearings should be held and appropriate revisions made.

The heads of other academic departments in the humanities and social sciences should also be given the opportunity to comment on the hybrid program's mission statement, strategic plan, and curriculum. This is an opportunity to build alliances and to prepare for any serious objections.

Although students and academic colleagues give comments and information, central administrators give approval. Formal endorsement of the hybrid program's plan should be obtained from the appropriate dean (if applicable), the provost, or the academic vice president.

External constituents—key alumni, allied professional groups, and donors—should also be consulted. Approval of the plan should not be sought from these groups because their many and varied interests and agendas would preclude agreement with the total plan. However, they should be given the opportunity to make suggestions; and those suggestions should be considered when making revisions. It should be made clear to them that the faculty has the final say on curricular and related matters.

One key to making a hybrid program work is obtaining endorsements from all the important constituent groups. Consensus will not be reached, but each group will have been consulted, and they will have some ownership of the program, which could translate into tangible support.

Establishing the "Centrality" of the Hybrid Program.   Communication programs in general are not considered as central to the missions of their universities as the more traditional humanities and social science departments. This is indeed ironic, considering the growing importance of communication in the information age. Hybrid communication programs have the unique opportunity to promote communication courses as general education requirements (GERs) to be taken by all university students. Consolidation of speech and mass communications into one unit reinforces the argument that there is a discipline of communication. The question is: In which bodies of knowledge within the discipline should all students be educated? Two courses come to mind. Countless surveys indicate that one characteristic employers look for in new hires is the ability to communicate ideas—orally and in writing—clearly, concisely, and effectively. Writing courses are often offered by English departments as GERs. Similarly, communication programs should be offering oral communication courses (public speaking) as communication proficiency GERs. These courses can be designed with a theoretical foundation to support the practical component to make it more acceptable to curriculum committees within the university approval structure.

Another course that hybrid communication programs can offer as a GER is Communication, Technology and Society. Before new communication and computer technologies, this course was often called Mass Communication and Society. How individuals and societies are affected by the new communication technologies should be of concern to all students. If qualified faculty are available, then the hybrid communication program should push this course as a GER. At the very least, a Communication and Society (with less emphasis on technology) should be submitted as a GER.

Most communication programs will face resistance within their universities in obtaining approval for their GER courses. A case will have to be made for the validity and utility of these courses as "core knowledge" areas in a university education and for the ability of the faculty to teach them effectively. If communication GER courses are approved, the hybrid communication program will have established some degree of centrality. This should help the program obtain its share of resources, thereby ensuring stability, if not growth.

Obtaining and Allocating Resources. Success begets success in the academy. Academic programs with national reputations for their faculty, professional programs, or research programs and those considered to be central to the university mission will obtain their share of resources. Those struggling with their identity and mission or with a mismatch between unit and university missions will be vulnerable to budget cuts.

Communication programs, in general, and hybrid programs in particular will have to be aggressive in informing the university community about successes and opportunities. Most colleagues in other departments and many administrators need to be informed about what it is that hybrid programs do, and about those things that the programs do particularly well. A newsletter distributed to department heads and central administrators can be an effective promotional vehicle, provided it is brief, attractive, and covers only those items our academic colleagues would likely be interested in—such as teaching and research programs, external support, grants, and in some cases, professional programs. This should not be the alumni newsletter, becuase much of the material of interest to alumni will not be of interest to our academic colleagues. Faculty of hybrid programs should be visible in the academic community. Whether it is serving on university committees, participation in campus colloquia, or winning teaching or research awards, visibility helps build the case for the program.

Although all these promotional strategies are important, the program will receive its fair share of resources only if there is a clear connection between the unit's mission, strategic plan, and the budget request. Central administrators are interested in cost efficiencies and outcomes. Therefore, the hybrid program will have to make its case on the basis of increased enrollments (if that is a university goal), quality, enhancement of the university's missions, national prestige, or other criteria important to the university.

A hybrid program's budget should reflect the priorities set by the faculty and should not be an issue of which area (e.g., mass or speech communications) gets the most dollars. It is easy for faculty in a hybrid program to get into this rut—us versus them. One way of avoiding this is to look at missions, goals, objectives, and strategic plans from the perspective of one program. Common areas of interests, strengths, and opportunities should be identified, and resources allocated accordingly. Within limits defined by central administration, the faculty should set the criteria for allocating resources. Examples are enrollment growth, intradisciplinary collaboration (areas integrating mass and speech communication) or program quality (areas that can attain regional or national prominence).

A CASE STUDY

The Edward R. Murrow School of Communication at Washington State University has had its ups and downs as a hybrid program. The school has experienced a metamorphosis in recent years that has allowed it to meet most criteria for a hybrid program that works.

The Murrow School Today

The school is the largest single academic unit at Washington State University, a land grant university with an enrollment of 17,000 in Pullman, with a population of 24,000. The school offers undergraduate specializations in advertising, broadcasting, journalism, public relations and speech communication. An MA degree in communication, with tracks in mass media, rhetoric, and organizational communication, is also offered. The school participates in an interdisciplinary PhD program with communication as a major area of emphasis and including cognate areas in the humanities and social sciences. The school is in a college of liberal arts.

Undergraduate enrollments total 750 majors (juniors and seniors) and 650 premajors (freshmen and sophomores), There are 75 MA and 18 PhD students. Broadcasting has the largest undergraduate enrollment, followed, in order, by advertising, public relations, journalism, and speech communication. At the MA and PhD levels, there are more speech communication than mass communication majors. Requirements for certification are a 2.7 GPA for premajor communication classes, a 2.5 overall GPA, "passing" a writing test, and a grade of C or better in a mass media writing class. Approximately 60% of students who apply for certification are accepted each year.

Of 26 full-time faculty, 6 are in speech communication. In addition, five temporary faculty teach professional courses in mass communications. There are 38 teaching assistants, mostly in speech communications.

Approximately 80% of the school's graduates find employment in a communication-related job within 2 years of graduation, or they enter graduate school.

The school has done reasonably well in national rankings. (Although these rankings have their shortcomings, they can be taken to be indexes of some recognition, and are useful in boosting faculty morale and promoting the program with internal and external constituents.) A 1997 survey by the Radio and Television News Directors Association placed the school's television news academic program fourth nationally (Stone, 1997). The School's MA program has been ranked in the top 25 nationally based on the quantity of articles published in 10 national and regional research journals, and in the top seven for overall quality (out of 27 programs) in the Western region (Trout, Barker, & Barker, 1988). Another survey ranked the school 11th in the nation based on number of telecommunications articles published in research journals (Atkin, 1996).

The School's instructional budget has increased over 35% in the last 7 years. Private support has increased over 300% in the same period.

More important than rankings and funding is the collegiality among the school's faculty. Speech and mass communications faculty are mutually supportive of each other, collaborate in teaching and research, and, simply get along. The school has had no difficulty in recruiting faculty from major communication doctoral programs.

So, by most measures, this hybrid program seems to work. However, major problems had to be surmounted to get to this stage and there are new challenges arising from its hybrid nature.

Problems

The first problem was to establish an identity consistent with the university. A Department of Communications had been established in 1976 by combining journalism (an existing department) and speech communication (which was in a department of speech, speech pathology, and theatre arts.) The new hybrid department had strong undergraduate professional programs and consequently struggled with an image of being only a professional department. The task was to establish programs that would gain respect within a research university, preserve the undergraduate professional programs, and integrate faculty strengths in speech and mass communication. From 1976 to 1986, the department developed, obtained approval for, and implemented an MA in Communication that included tracks in mass and speech communication. In 1986, the Dean of the College of Liberal Arts told the faculty and new chair that the department had a lot of potential, but that additional resources would be allocated only when research was added to the unit's mission.

The faculty met throughout 1986 to establish a mission statement and a strategic plan. Working drafts were shared with the dean and central administrators. Input was also obtained from students. The final document approved by the university included the following provisions.

1. The mission of the department is to educate students in the profession, art, and science of communication, while maintaining a strong liberal arts foundation.

2. Undergraduate sequences would be maintained in the professional areas of mass communications and speech communication. The MA program combined the mass media areas into one (mass communications), and focused on organizational communication and rhetoric as the speech communication areas. The interdisciplinary PhD program would not make a distinction between "speech" and "mass" communications.

3. Making use of existing faculty strengths, and new and replacement hires, the department would focus on the following areas of scholarship and teaching. The speech communication area is mentioned first, followed by the mass communication area. These areas were chosen because they provide the greatest opportunities for integration of speech and mass communication interests: (a) organizational communication and media management; (b) public discourse, rhetoric, and media effects; and (c) intercultural communications and minorities and the media. The department would phase out oral interpretation and debate.

4. The department would change unit designation to "School," still under Liberal Arts, and name the school after Edward R. Murrow, a 1930 graduate in speech communication (approved in 1988).

5. The department would implement a core undergraduate curriculum including speech and mass communication courses, and to be required for certification as a major in communication (now in place): Writing for the Media, Communication Theories, Public Speaking, Language and Human Behavior, Mass Communication and Society.

Also, some speech and mass communication courses would be cross-listed in sequence (major) requirements. Examples are Law, Ethics, Persuasion, and Organizational Communications.

6. The department would institute a PhD program in Communication integrating study and research in speech and mass communication (proposal in final stages of approval).

7. A Communication Professional Advisory Board would be created with members from practicing speech and mass communication professionals (Limburg, 1994). (The board now has 30 members.)

8. The department would establish two tracks for faculty appointments—a tenure track for research faculty and a professional track for faculty teaching professional media courses. The department had several professional faculty, but they were on yearly renewable appointments.

The system now in place appoints professional faculty to renewable 4 year contracts. They are not required to do research, but teach more (5 courses per academic year). Tenure-track faculty teach four courses per academic year. Salaries for the two appointment tracks are comparable. Some tenure-track faculty also teach "skills" courses. This system allows the unit to maintain both the professional and theory and research components of the undergraduate curriculum. The ideal faculty member should be able to teach both professional and theory and research classes. However, it is difficult to find faculty who can do both well, so we look for the best person for the specific job.

9. The department would increase the number of enrollments in GERs in communication.

Today the school has 3 GERs: Public Speaking (3,000 students per year), Mass Media and Society (700–1,000 students per year) and Intercultural Communication (80 students per year.) The programs in our school are still being fine tuned. A curriculum committee continues to reexamine the core requirements to make sure they keep up with technological, professional, and theoretical developments in the field. For example, the school is considering the addition of a course on ethics to the core.

The school continues to consider additional courses for GERs. The latest proposals are for courses on media ethics and new communication technologies.

The school has obtained preliminary approval for a PhD in Communication to replace the interdisciplinary PhD. The new degree will be intradisciplinary (speech and mass communication) but will still include cognate areas in the humanities and social sciences.

CHALLENGES

The major challenge to hybrid programs is in making sure that our definition of the field, curriculum, and research keep up with rapidly developing communication technologies. How should we define communication when the boundaries of human symbolic exchange are being redefined by computer technology? Is mass communication still a viable concept, with interactive technology, increasing choices of information, and more audience freedom to make those choices? What is speech communication, with virtual interaction becoming more common via e-mail and other vehicles? In this new communication environment, what careers are we preparing our students for? Will the traditional subdivisions according to media (for mass communications) still hold? Answers to these questions will determine the substance and structure of communication programs in the future.

REFERENCES

AEJMC constitution and bylaws. (n.d.). Columbia, SC: AEJMC.

Atkin, D. (1996). Telecommunications research article productivity in the U.S.: 1985–1993. *Journal of the Association for Communication Administration, 1*, 1–11.

Blanchard, R. O., & Christ, W. G. (1993). *Media education and the liberal arts: A blueprint for the new professionalism.* Hillsdale, NJ: Lawrence Erlbaum Associates.

Christ, W. G. (1994). *Assessing communication education: A handbook for media, speech and theatre educators.* Hillsdale, NJ: Lawrence Erlbaum Associates.

Christ, W. G. (1997). *Media education assessment handbook.* Mahwah, NJ: Lawrence Erlbaum Associates.

Christ, W. G., & Blanchard, R. (1994). Mission statement, outcomes and the new liberal arts. In W. G. Christ (Ed.), *Assessing communication education: A handbook for media, speech and theatre educators* (pp. 31–56). Hillsdale, NJ: Lawrence Erlbaum Associates.

Christ, W. G., & Hynes, T. (1997). The missions and purposes of journalism and mass communications education. *Journalism and Mass Communication Educator*, *52*(2), 73–100.

Cohen, H. (1994). *The history of speech communication: The emergence of a discipline, 1914–1945*. Annandale, VA: Speech Communication Association.

Cope, R. G. (1981). *Strategic planning management, and decision making*. Washington, DC: American Association for Higher Education.

Kaiser, J. S. (1993). *Educational administration* [Computer disk]. Mequon, WI: Stylex.

Limburg, V. (1994). Internships, exit interviews, and advisory boards. In W. G. Christ (Ed.), *Assessing communication education: A handbook for media, speech and theatre educators* (pp. 181– 200). Hillsdale, NJ: Lawrence Erlbaum Associates.

Rogers, E., & Chaffee, S. (1994). Communication and journalism from "daddy" Bleyer to Wilbur Schramm. *Journalism Monographs, 148*, 1–50.

SCA Constitution and ByLaws. (1995). Annandale, VA: Speech Communication Association.

Stone, V. (1997). News directors favor hands-on schools. Columbia: Missouri School of Journalism.

Trout, D., Barker, D., & Barker, L. (1988). Evaluation of Masters programs in the speech communication discipline: 1988. *Communcation Education, 37*, 257–262

Work, W., & Jeffrey, R. (1989). The past is prologue: A 75th anniversary history of SCA. Annandale, VA: Speech Communication Association.

7

Community Colleges

Isa N. Engleberg
Prince George's Community College

The 1,473 community colleges in the United States (i.e., 2-year colleges offering associate degrees) represent 39% of all institutions of higher education and enroll 53% of the country's undergraduate student population (*1997 Higher Education Directory*, 1997; American Association of Community Colleges, 1995). The academic curricula at these 2-year colleges range from traditional liberal arts study for students intending to pursue baccalaureate degrees to technical and career programs designed to prepare students for immediate employment in the workplace. Moreover, as local institutions, community colleges are often the first choice of residents seeking to upgrade job skills or pursue lifelong learning goals.

Community colleges are highly diverse institutions—from small, rural colleges enrolling as few as 200 students to the giant Miami–Dade Community College where over 50,000 students take courses annually. Despite such diversity in mission, locale, and size, administrators responsible for instruction in communication and media studies face unique challenges. Recommending common strategies for the community college administrator, therefore, should take into account the differences among community colleges as well as the ways in which community colleges differ from 4-year colleges and universities. To that end, input was sought through a questionnaire sent to communication and media administrators at selected community colleges throughout the country in order to help shape the claims and recommendations presented in this chapter. Although the phrase *communication and media* is used to describe community college programs, it should be noted that many such programs also include theater courses within the purview of speech communication.

THE NATURE OF COMMUNITY COLLEGE PROGRAMS

Programs in communication and/or media may be more diverse in community colleges than in any other type of educational institution. An English teacher commandeered to teach public speaking may be the only evidence of a communication program at one community college, whereas at another a broadcast management and technology degree program may be placing successful graduates in media outlets throughout the country. At some community colleges, speech courses may be housed in a division of social science, humanities, fine arts, business, or English, whereas at another community college a communication department—particularly if it includes speech communication, theater, and media—may constitute one of the largest departments in the college.

Those who administer programs in communication and/or media at community colleges may be consummate professionals in the communication field or foster parents whose backgrounds and interests are remote from or even unfriendly to the discipline. Few communication departments in 4-year colleges operate under the aegis of a teacher or administrator with a master's degree in Spanish, agriculture, or remedial reading. Yet such is the case in some community colleges, where communication programs may not be large enough or valued enough to find a more legitimate academic home. Most community colleges do not offer associate (2-year) degrees in communication or media. There are, however, a few noteworthy and highly sophisticated 2-year media degree programs that rival baccalaureate degrees at major universities. These 2-year programs in media studies have varied titles (e.g., broadcast management and technology, radio–TV–film, communication technology, broadcasting, mass communication) and offer associate degrees for students seeking immediate employment as well as students intending to transfer to 4-year colleges. In some of these degree programs, dozens of courses are offered in a variety of media areas (e.g., TV production, audio production, management and sales, multitrack recording, advanced photography, television newsgathering, public relations, computer animation, multimedia authoring and design, writing for radio–TV–film). In some locales, the media degree program at a community college may be more extensive and sophisticated than those offered at nearby 4-year colleges and universities.

Despite the many differences among community college programs, there are issues that challenge administrators regardless of their training or predilections. Certainly, administrators in communication and media programs at community colleges have a great deal in common with administrative colleagues at all levels of higher education. Issues related to funding levels, the recruitment of students and faculty, and the respect accorded the discipline are virtually universal concerns. Rather than focusing on the issues that most administrators have in common, regardless of institutional setting, this chapter concentrates on those issues unique and critical to community college administration in communication and media programs.

ADMINISTRATIVE ISSUES AND STRATEGIES

The unique nature of community college education accentuates certain administrative responsibilities. There are many issues facing the community college administrator, but three appear to be consistent across institutions of different sizes and orientations. The following section describes these issues and offers suggestions for effectively meeting the challenges posed by these concerns. Central to effective administration, however, is an overriding challenge: the need for and commitment to a clear and appropriate mission statement for communication and/or media programs. The first recommendation in this chapter is the most basic and important:

- Communication administrators should, in conjunction with their faculty, develop a clear purpose statement that is consistent with the mission of the community college and clearly understood by those inside and outside the program.

The basis for a well-defined purpose statement has been set forth by the Association for Communication Administration (ACA, 1997) in *Communication Program Review Standards*. In this document, the standards related to program administration and resources, faculty and staff, curriculum, instruction, faculty service and scholarship, and diversity issues are all linked to a program purpose statement. Communication administrators who use such standards as guidelines and success indicators are, in essence, making a commitment to the development of an exemplary program. The purpose statement is the foundation on which all other program initiatives are built and maintained.

Once a communication and/or media program has a clear set of goals, other administrative issues can be addressed more efficiently and effectively. Amidst the dozens of issues facing most community college administrators, the central challenges revolve around three issues: the quality of instruction, the maintenance of a speech communication requirement, and the transferability of course credits to 4-year colleges and universities. Interestingly, these issues begin with an internal focus on the program itself (quality of instruction), move to a consideration of the program's status on campus (collegewide speech requirement), and culminate in the program's external relationship with other institutions of higher education (transferability). Figure 7.1 emphasizes how each of these challenges is dependent on the one that precedes it. Accordingly, with a clear purpose statement as a foundation, administrators must ensure the quality of instruction before promoting program benefits to others on and off campus.

Quality of Instruction

Two concerns dominate the core issue of instructional quality—full-time to part-time faculty ratios and the need for continued faculty development.

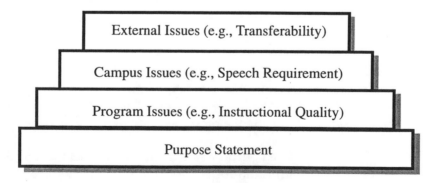

FIG. 7.1. Administrative challenges.

The increasing reliance on part-time faculty has led to concerns about the quality of instruction in community colleges. Communication administrators have expressed their frustration with this imbalance in the full-time to part-time faculty ratio as follows: "We hover at about 50% of our sections taught by adjunct faculty." "It's become routine to be hiring (part-time) faculty the day classes start which means we're hiring sight unseen." "We can't hire good part-time faculty because neighboring universities pay twice as much for the same course."

Approximately two-thirds of the teaching faculty at community colleges are part-time. At 4-year colleges and universities, approximately one-third of the teaching faculty are part-time. In some urban community colleges, 70% to 80% of the teaching faculty may be adjuncts (Gadberry, 1996; National Center for Education Statistics, 1996). In a survey of 100 community college chief executive officers, more than half of the respondents indicated that the percentage of classes taught by part-time teachers in their own institutions is too high. "When the volume of part-time faculty rises, the supervision requirement increases, but increased resources for that purpose are seldom provided" (McCabe, 1993, p. 4).

At first, the reliance on part-time faculty may appear justified and nonproblematic. After all, adjuncts only teach basic courses—the same courses taught by inexperienced teaching assistants at the closest university. Such a perspective ignores or is insensitive to the critical role of basic courses in a community college. The basic course is more than the bread-and-butter course in a community college; it is often the *raison d'etre*. The basic course in a community college is not necessarily a way to attract majors or to make sure that the department has a strong enough financial base to permit senior faculty to teach upper level courses. At many 2-year colleges, the basic speech communication course is why there is a speech program. The exception to this rule may be in community colleges that offer media degrees. In such departments, student graduation and employment are shared goals. Yet, in all of these situations, the quality and dedication of instructors are critical to the program's success.

The administrator responsible for a communication and/or media program may be powerless to direct a college's financial resources or policies for hiring adjunct faculty. Instead, the administrator must develop strategies that ensure the sufficiency and quality of part-time faculty. Roueche, Roueche, and Milliron (1996) described how difficult this challenge can be:

> New community college part-time faculty are often shocked by the diversity of the students, the times of the classes, and the amount of support afforded to students by community colleges. Exacerbating this situation are the graduate schools from which they came, schools that are rarely ideal preparatory institutions for those who will face the challenges of community college instruction. (p. 5)

In speech communication programs, the problem is even more serious given the erroneous but all-too-pervasive belief that "anyone can teach speech." Applications from high school English teachers, local ministers, government administrators, and office managers may outnumber applicants with as few as 18 graduate hours in communication. In fact, at some community colleges, 18 graduate hours in a teaching area is the minimum qualification for both full-time and adjunct instructors.

The following recommendations can help an administrator enhance and capitalize on the contributions of adjunct faculty:

• Adjunct faculty orientation should be mandatory or professionally expected and should include a detailed introduction to the community college environment and the requirements of the communication and/or media program.

• A flexible but detailed master syllabus as well as an instructor's handbook (either department produced or a textbook's instructor's manual) should be provided to each faculty member. All adjunct faculty members should submit their syllabi and course requirements to the program administrator in the second week of class for review and, if necessary, revision.

• Each adjunct faculty member should be assigned a full-time faculty member as a mentor. In large departments, a full-time faculty member may be given released time to supervise and mentor adjunct faculty members.

• Adjunct faculty members should be strongly encouraged to attend department meetings and participate in faculty development programs within the program and college. Incentives for such involvement could include teaching schedule preferences and conference travel support.

• Communication programs should capitalize on the potential contributions of adjunct faculty. At community colleges, qualified high school speech teachers often teach several courses. Not only are these faculty members pleased to teach a college-level course, they also can become recruiters-without-portfolios. Lawyers, government officials, broadcasters, and business leaders from the community may have degrees in the field. With a master's degree they also can become adjunct faculty members who extend the reputation and credibility of a program beyond campus boundaries.

The issue of part-time faculty has become so critical in community colleges that the journal *Academic Leadership* ("Part-time faculty," 1996) devoted an entire issue to and has publicized seminars dealing with the processes and procedures for recruitment, orientation, professional development, and evaluation of community college adjunct faculty. Adjunct faculty can be an administrator's biggest headache or a program's most valuable resource. Well-selected adjunct faculty members can enrich a program by bringing exceptional backgrounds, skills, and community sensitivities to a program. Even if (as is the case in some community colleges) the ratio of full-time to part-time faculty is as much as seven to one, the necessity for direct involvement with adjuncts is critical if a department or program is to maintain standards and achieve its mission.

The second major consideration under instructional quality also revolves around the qualifications and development of faculty members. Even with an experienced, full-time faculty, the challenge of promoting and continuing faculty development is critical to effective instruction. The following comments represent this concern as expressed by community college administrators: "Very few of our applicants have degrees in speech communication." "We need a larger pool of qualified teachers with work experience in radio, TV, and film." "How do we keep up in the field when there's no money for faculty development and no support or respect from our closest university?" "We know how to teach diverse students with many needs but we need more discipline-based faculty development (i.e., *what* to teach)."

Regardless of whether instructors are full-time and tenured or part-time and inexperienced, faculty development is critical to program success. Although the same can be said of 4-year college faculty members, the issue is, again, different at a community college. These differences go beyond degree preparation and professional goals. At community colleges, faculty members often rate themselves as teachers first and members of a discipline second. "They tend to be modestly connected with their academic field, and the longer they stay in the (community) colleges, the weaker that connection becomes" (Cohen & Brawer, 1987, p. 75). On average, most full-time community college instructors teach five basic-level classes per semester. Promotion and tenure decisions are based on the quality of teaching and college service; publications and traditional scholarship are not as critical. As a result, community college faculty members may be less familiar with the scholarship and advances in their discipline. Very often, their knowledge of the field comes from reviewing new textbooks or from gleaning a few ideas from colleagues who have been lucky enough to attend a state or regional meeting of their professional association. The professional journals in the field often seem unconnected to the primary interests of a community college instructor.

The importance of campuswide and program-based professional development may be more critical for community college faculty than for their counterparts at 4-year colleges. The following recommendations range from home-based, professional development strategies to ventures beyond the campus:

• Administrators should, at the very least, subscribe to the practitioner-focused journals of their professional organizations and share relevant materials with all faculty members. Publications such as the National Communication Association's (NCA) *The Speech Communication Teacher* and *Communication Education*, the Broadcast Education Association's *Feedback*, or the *Journal of the Association for Communication Administration* can provide administrative advice, pedagogical strategies, curriculum ideas, and collegial contacts for faculty members and administrators who feel cut off from their discipline and colleagues.

• Community college programs should plan faculty development workshops dealing with issues related to pedagogy and scholarship.

• Community college programs should seek or pool professional development resources in order to send at least one member of the faculty to specialized faculty development institutes or to an annual professional conference. In addition to state, regional, and national conventions of professional organizations, there are special institutes that may be of equal or greater value depending on a program's need for professional development. Two national examples are the master teachers retreats held at various institutions throughout the country and the community college administrative workshops and conferences for chairpersons sponsored by The Chair Academy headquartered at Maricopa Community College in Arizona. Senior academic administrators receive regular announcements from such groups. Of special interest in communication studies are the summer conferences sponsored by the NCA and the summer Institute for Faculty Development at Hope College in Holland, Michigan, at which nationally recognized scholars in communication studies spend time in residence with communication instructors discussing the current theory, research, and pedagogy in specific topic areas (e.g., communication theory, rhetorical theory, intercultural communication, media, small group communication).

In terms of professional development, many community college faculty members are more active at a local level than their university counterparts. According to Cohen and Brawer (1987), fewer than half of all community college faculty members are members of disciplinary associations; around 15% present papers. In such a localized atmosphere, the continued professional development of faculty members is essential to program quality.

MAINTAINING OR SECURING
A SPEECH REQUIREMENT

At many 4-year colleges, the number of majors and graduates are more critical to program survival than the maintenance of a speech requirement. At many community colleges, however, securing and maintaining a speech requirement spells the difference between program survival and termination. Community college administrators understand how critical this issue is to their programs: "Maintaining the speech requirement is a life and death issue for our department." "How can we justify a speech requirement when the state university won't require it and doesn't even consider it a humanities course?" "Employers want graduates to have communication skills but our academic colleagues don't see the need."

Certainly, there are community colleges in which a speech communication course is not required for graduation or as a general education requirement. At some 2-year colleges, the success and integrity of a media program is measured by the number of majors and subsequent job placements. Yet, there is little doubt that many speech communication, theater, and media programs depend on a speech requirement to support a department and enable faculty to teach sophomore-level courses.

Although securing, maintaining, and expanding a speech requirement are different tasks, there are common strategies that can help support this important effort as illustrated in the following recommendations:

• Administrators should initiate and develop closer ties with communication and/or media colleagues at nearby colleges and universities in the interest of presenting a united front on issues related to including speech communication as a graduation or general education requirement.

• Administrators should collect business and educational research that supports the need for oral communication skills. Surveys of major corporations and personnel directors continually point to the need for communication skills in the areas of interpersonal communication, small group communication, intercultural communication, and public speaking. National databases such as DACUM (community college curricula based on structured group interviews with employees) can provide a justification for communication instruction (Engleberg & Wynn, 1995).

• Administrators should obtain the documents and services available from the NCA that justify the speech communication requirement. The following documents and services are provided to NCA members: *The Rationale Kit: Information Supporting the Speech Communication Discipline and its Programs*, the resolution on the role of communication courses in general education approved as part of the NCA policy platform, the names of community college administrators who can provide advice regarding the maintenance of the speech requirement, and the programs and publications of NCA interest groups such as the Basic Course Commission, the Educational Policies Board, the Instructional Development Division, and the Community College Section.

• In addition to faculty involvement in cocurricular activities (e.g., forensics, theater productions, student radio stations, television productions), administrators should encourage faculty members to become involved in campuswide projects and programs that demonstrate the importance of communication study and skills (e.g., directing a Communication Across the Curriculum program, serving as a speechwriter for administrators, volunteering to facilitate campuswide meetings, serving as a parliamentarian at faculty senate meetings, training speakers' bureau volunteers).

By building a strong case that relies on outside research and inside achievements, a program is in a stronger position to argue for a collegewide speech requirement. That, in addition to a program that has a reputation for instructional quality, can provide a strong foundation for securing a speech requirement and an equally strong infrastructure for maintaining such a requirement.

TRANSFERABILITY OF COMMUNITY COLLEGE COURSES

One of the thorniest problems facing community colleges is the difficulty in guaranteeing the transferability of credits to 4-year colleges and universities. Community college administrators have expressed their frustration as follows: "Our biggest problem is the lack of articulation agreements with other colleges." "Transfer is a problem, especially when we offer more advanced media courses than many 4-year institutions." "When our students transfer to_____, they don't accept our research methods or communication theory courses." "We teach the same courses using many of the same textbooks but (they) still don't want to accept our credits."

The reasons for refusing community college transfer credits range from questions about the quality of community college instruction to an opinion that community colleges have no right to teach anything beyond the basic course areas. In some states the problem of transferability has been solved by adopting statewide course numbering systems, statewide course competencies, and mandatory transfer regulations. In other states, the transfer of courses operates on something akin to a lottery system; students take their chances depending on who is evaluating their record at a particular institution. As elected officials and students demand more accountability and value for their public support and tuition dollars, the issue of transferability may be taken out of the hands of educators and placed in the hands of legislators. Thus, it behooves administrators at both the community college and 4-year college level to ensure the smooth transfer of courses between institutions. The following recommendations depend on the cooperation and professional respect between 2- and 4-year colleges for their effectiveness:

• Administrators should develop a system that tracks transfer problems in order to identify institutions and programs that will not accept or give proper credit to courses transferred from the community college. Program administrators should document cases and collect statistical data regarding transfer problems.

• Administrators should work with local colleges and universities when developing new courses, revising a curriculum, or seeking a new associate degree in communication and/or media to help ensure transferability.

• Administrators should obtain copies of master syllabi, course descriptions, and program descriptions from local colleges and universities to be used as the basis for comparing community college and 4-year college courses.

• Administrators, in conjunction with their college's senior administrators, should be willing to make transferability a political issue.

State and county legislators rarely look with favor on senior college programs that refuse to accept bona fide courses from a publicly funded community college in their voting districts. Although an appeal to elected officials may be a last resort, it may be the only recourse when community college administrators have made every effort to negotiate reasonable transfer agreements with their counterparts at 4-year colleges.

CONCLUSION

This chapter has highlighted three of the major challenges facing community college administrators in speech communication, theater, and media (see the appendix). There are many more including equipment and technical staff support, cocurricular program support, student recruitment and retention, program development, class size, funding, and the community college image. For a sophisticated media program, the need for state-of-the-art equipment and technical staff support may supersede all other issues. In a communication department that was built on the success of a cocurricular forensics or theater program, the funding of that program may be the most important issue. In those few, unfortunate programs where skills-based communication courses enroll as many as 50 students in a section, class size becomes the most critical challenge facing a program and its faculty.

In looking for a common thread amidst the many challenges facing community college administrators in communication and/or media, one issue emerges as central: the relationship between community college administrators and faculty and their counterparts in 4-year colleges. Unfortunately, many community college administrators describe their relationships with local colleges and universities in negative terms. Although community colleges rely on graduate schools to provide full-time and part-time faculty members, they have not been very successful in convincing graduate schools to produce "generalists" who can teach basic courses. When community college administrators are asked whether graduate schools are preparing communication and/or media applicants for community college teaching positions, most do not give graduate programs, particularly in the area of speech communication, high marks. When asked how graduate schools can improve their programs to better prepare instructors, community college administrators advocate that students interested in community college teaching should (a) do internships or part-time teaching at local community colleges, (b) be taught how to work with a diverse student population, (c) have a thorough understanding of and experience teaching the basic course areas, (d) be encouraged to do instructional communication and communication education research, and (e) be treated with as much professional respect as other graduate students.

In addition to developing better relationships with 4-year colleges, there is also a need for community college administrators to develop and maintain an active 2-year college network. To that end, the community college sections, interest groups, and committees in various professional organizations should be joined and used as a source of information and support. Membership or participation in the activities of organizations such as the ACA, the NCA, and the Broadcast Education Association can help focus articles, research, and seminars on the unique needs of community college administrators.

If there is a bottom line strategy in community college administration, it is the need to be political—to develop campus-based strategies that ensure survival and growth. Despite lofty purpose statements, well-qualified faculty, and model curricula, "the day is often won by those who understand and can navigate the political geography" (Engleberg, 1996, p. 145). As a political agent, a community college administrator should employ twin strategies that have applicability for all programs regardless of size or orientation:

- Avoid isolation. Never let a program become an island unto itself. Build bridges across the college and into the community served by the college.
- Pursue political positioning. Certain collegewide offices, committees, and special assignments have the potential to produce political payoffs. Whether you are the only communication instructor or the chair of a large division, political positioning requires a well-planned strategy that puts faculty members in the right place at the right political time.

A successful community college administrator should develop a strong sense of cohesiveness, vigilance, and vision for a program based on a clear purpose statement. If a program avoids isolation and pursues political positioning, cohesiveness, vigilance, and a shared vision are the natural outcomes. Cohesiveness provides a united front of colleagues, vigilance provides the wariness necessary to detect and deflect potential problems, and vision sustains program achievement and pride.

APPENDIX:
SUMMARY OF RECOMMENDATIONS
FOR COMMUNITY COLLEGE
ADMINISTRATORS

1. Develop a clear purpose statement that is consistent with the mission of the community college and clearly understood by those inside and outside the program.
2. Require orientation for all adjunct faculty.
3. Provide all faculty members a flexible but detailed master syllabus as well as an instructor's handbook for each course.
4. Assign a full-time faculty mentor to each adjunct faculty member.
5. Encourage adjunct faculty members to attend department meetings and participate in faculty development programs.
6. Capitalize on the potential contributions of adjunct faculty.
7. Subscribe to practitioner-focused communication journals and share relevant materials with all faculty members.
8. Plan faculty development workshops dealing with issues related to pedagogy and communication scholarship.
9. Send faculty to specialized faculty development institutes or to an annual professional conference at the state, regional, or national level.

10. Initiate and develop closer contacts with colleagues at nearby colleges and universities.
11. Collect and share business and educational research that supports the need for speech communication skills.
12. Obtain documents and services available from the NCA that support the program or the speech communication requirement.
13. Encourage faculty members to become involved in campuswide projects and programs that demonstrate the importance of communication study and skills.
14. Track transfer problems in order to identify institutions and programs that will not accept courses transferred from the community college.
15. Collaborate with local colleges and universities when developing new courses, revising a curriculum, or seeking a new associate degree to ensure transferability.
16. Obtain copies of master syllabi, catalogs, and program descriptions from local colleges and universities as the basis for comparing community college and 4-year college courses.
17. Be willing to make transferability a political issue.
18. Avoid isolation by building bridges across the college and into the community.
19. Pursue political goals by placing faculty in key positions.

REFERENCES

1997 Higher Education Directory. (1997). Falls Church, VA: Higher Education Publications.

American Association of Community Colleges. (1995). *National profile of community colleges: Trends and statistics, 1995–1996*. Washington, DC: Author.

Association for Communication Administration. (1997). *Communication program review standards*. Annandale, VA: Author.

Cohen, A. M., & Brawer, F. B. (1987). *The collegiate function of community colleges*. San Francisco: Jossey-Bass.

Engleberg, I. N. (1996). Let's get political: Strategies for departmental survival and growth. *Journal of the Association for Communication Administration, 2*, 143–149.

Engleberg, I. N., & Wynn, D. R. (1995). DACUM: A national database justifying the study of speech communication. *Journal of the Association for Communication Administration, 1*, 28–37.

Gadberry, J. L. (1996). The adjunct faculty instructor facilitator. *Academic Leadership, 4*, 10–12.

McCabe, R. H. (1993, June 3). The status of community college educational programs: The views of 100 CEOs. *Community College Week*, pp. 4–5.

National Center for Education Statistics. (1996). *Institutional policies and practices regarding faculty in higher education* (NCES Rep. No. 97-080). Washington, DC: U.S. Department of Education.

Part-time faculty: Contributions of excellence in community colleges. (1996). *Academic Leadership: Journal of the Chair Academy, 4*(2) [Special issue].

Roueche, J. E., Roueche, S. D., & Milliron, M. D. (1996). A part-time faculty support system that makes sense. *Academic Leadership, 4,* 3–7.

8

Graduate Communication Programs

Jennings Bryant
Susan Thompson
The University of Alabama

> He [Harvard University President Abraham Flexner] would also have banished
> all Schools of Journalism and Home Economics, football, correspondence courses,
> and much else.
>
> —Kerr (1963, p. 5)

Communication programs have not always been embraced by the higher education establishment. In the early years especially, many scholars held condescending attitudes toward professional studies such as journalism. They believed such programs did not belong in the elite reaches of the academy.

Despite initial misgivings, communication programs burgeoned as the discipline matured, with a rate of growth that can only be described as phenomenal. Although the first communication graduate programs appeared less than a century ago, thousands of students are pursuing graduate degrees in various aspects of communication study—advertising, journalism, broadcast journalism, public relations, organizational communication, speech, rhetoric, radio and television, interpersonal communication, and mass communication, among many others. In 1994, more than 5,000 communication students received master's degrees, and 337 were awarded PhD degrees (National Center for Education Statistics, 1996). Such rapid growth is a credit to the efforts of both past and present administrators and teachers, and to the viability of the communication discipline.

As a matter of necessity, the process of graduate program administration in communication evolved at light-year speed and for this reason, it may seem ironic that many of the same issues that confronted the early administrators remain to this day. Academicians continue to disagree on fundamental elements such as the ratio of professional training to liberal arts instruction, and many of the tensions that initially arose between undergraduate and graduate communication education continue to persist.

With so many modern-day concerns rooted in the past, a brief examination of the history of graduate education in general, and graduate education in communication in particular, is warranted. A profile of contemporary graduate communication education follows, accompanied by illustrative normative data. Outlines of the process of administering graduate programs are offered, followed by a discussion of several of the key issues facing today's graduate communication administrators. Many of these other issues—recruitment, retention, multiculturalism, job placement, and so forth—are the direct result of more recent developments and trends. These issues are not so firmly entrenched in the past; instead, they are the sprouting offshoots of a rapidly changing educational and social milieu.

A BRIEF HISTORY OF GRADUATE EDUCATION IN THE UNITED STATES

If we grant that "universities, like cathedrals and parliaments, are a product of the Middle Ages" (Haskins, 1940, p. 3) and trace their origins to the time of the earliest conferring of degrees or licenses at the University of Bologna and the University of Paris in the 12th century (Wieruszowski, 1966), it soon becomes obvious that graduate education is a quite recent development in the life span of higher education. As Fig. 8.1, which plots graduate enrollment in U.S. universities (*American Universities and Colleges*, 1992) reveals, only in the middle portion of the 20th century did the numbers rise significantly.

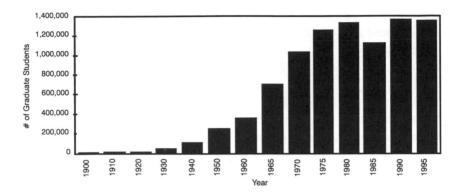

FIG. 8.1. Graduate student enrollment by year.

Historians frequently stress the bifurcated roots of U.S. graduate education. Arlt (1971) described U.S. graduate schools as the progeny of "the uneasy marriage of the British liberal arts college and the German university" (p. 267), and Spurr (1971) called them "the result of the grafting of the German concept of postgraduate study upon collegiate institutions which evolved from the English model and whose course of study traditionally ended with the A.B." (p. 251). The explicit or implied tension involved in these parturition metaphors foreshadows much of the angst that characterizes contemporary debates about the place of research versus teaching in the academy. "Whereas the English liberal arts model emphasized teaching, the Germanic model brought emancipation from formal teaching, scientific and philological approach to research, scholarly thoroughness—in short, the ingredients of professionalism" (Arlt, 1971, p. 268).

Proposals for curriculum reform to include the onset of graduate education were common in U.S. colleges during the years 1825 to 1860, but the conservative forces at Harvard, Yale, William and Mary, Princeton, and the like consistently defeated these "grand plans for the establishment of a comprehensive graduate school" (Arlt, 1971, p. 269). Finally, after much deliberation, the Yale Corporation approved a PhD program in 1860—and three students received their doctorates from Yale only 1 year later. Presumably, these students were already in queue, anticipating approval of the doctoral degree!

In 1876 Johns Hopkins University established the first graduate school based on the German model. This was followed rapidly by approval and formation of graduate initiatives at Clark University in

1888 and the University of Chicago in 1890 (Spurr, 1971). In fact, all three of these institutions were established with "the inspired vision of a strictly graduate university" (Arlt, 1971, p. 271). Fiscal realities were ultimately to dictate the addition of undergraduate colleges at all three institutions, however.

The distinction between professional training and graduate education, a distinction that would cause numerous difficulties for the field of communication, first occurred in the late 19th century. For the most part, professional education (e.g., law, medicine, and theology) "is distinguished from graduate academic study in that it emphasizes skills for the practice of a profession and leads to a professional degree" (*American Universities and Colleges*, 1992, p. 21). Graduate education, in contrast, "refers to programs conducted beyond the level of the bachelor's or first-professional degree for the primary purpose of training research scholars and teachers. Such programs typically lead to the master's degree or the PhD" (p. 21).

Initially, the colleges of arts and sciences at the major U.S. universities were the only units authorized to grant doctoral degrees. Most organized graduate councils to supervise postbaccalaureate degree programs, with the administrative officer for the council typically being a faculty member who was recognized as an associate dean of the arts and sciences college. Eventually, these councils separated from the faculty of arts and sciences to become separate entities—graduate schools that represented the entire university (Spurr, 1971).

A series of developments shifted the perspectives of graduate education from elitism to populism. First the land-grant movement, "the antithesis of elitism" (LaPidus, 1988, p. 4), made university education available to the children of middle-class workers and farmers (Kerr, 1963). With this movement, graduate programs expanded to include applied research as well as service. A second major influence in expanding graduate education was World War II. With the exception of agriculture, federal involvement with higher education prior to World War II had been minimal. This changed dramatically during the war years, when academicians were asked to direct their research toward military objectives, and after the war, when the G.I. Bill enabled thousands of veterans to attend college (LaPidus, 1988).

The result was the complex new hybrid social institution. Growth has been qualitative as well as quantitative, as is reflected in the words of Jules LaPidus (1988), longtime President of the Council of Graduate Schools:

It has grown, in terms of the number and kind of degrees it offers, and the number of people it serves, into something quite different from that envisioned by its founders, who saw it mainly in terms of doctoral study and basic research. Much of the research done in our graduate schools today is very applied and there are pressures to make it even more so. Much of the graduate study being carried out is at the master's level, and most of that is in non-thesis programs directed toward preparing people for professional careers. This is all consistent with the idea of the university responding to the needs and expectations of society, but graduate educators continue to raise the same questions they have been raising for 100 years. Is this what we should be doing? How far do we go in being responsive? What should we expect of graduate education? The answers are far from clear. (pp. 7–8)

THE ORIGINS OF GRADUATE EDUCATION IN COMMUNICATION

Speech

The systematic study of rhetoric is commonly traced back to antiquity—from Plato and Aristotle through Cicero and Quintilian (e.g., Howell, 1954); however, formal departments of speech are of relatively recent lineage, beginning with speech instruction at Hamilton College in 1841, the School of Speech at Boston University in 1873, and the "first" Department of Speech, established at the University of Michigan in 1892 (Gray, 1949).

Graduate degrees in speech are entirely a 20th-century phenomenon. Contrary to the general historical model of the evolution of graduate education, the awarding of master's degrees in speech preceded the awarding of doctoral degrees. In 1902 the University of Iowa awarded the first master's degree in speech to H. S. Buffum, whose thesis was titled "The Influence of the Puritan Minister in the Making of New England" (Knower, 1935). Two decades passed before a department of speech awarded the first Doctor of Philosophy degree. The University of Wisconsin conferred the honor upon Sarah Stinchfield, whose dissertation was titled "The Formulation and Standardization of a Series of Graded Speech Tests" (Knower, 1935).

For those who might think that the bipartite humanities versus scientific division in the communication discipline is something new, it might be noted that "two of the first four dissertations accepted for Ph.D. degrees in speech were studies in experimental phonetics" (Curtis, 1954, p. 348)—one from the University of Wisconsin, the other from the University of Iowa. The other two (one from Cornell University and the other from the University of Wisconsin) were clearly in the tradition of the humanities.

Smith (1954) provided a wonderfully succinct quantitative summary of the origins of graduate education in speech:

> The decade before 1910 saw seven M.A. degrees carried out under "an adviser in a department of speech." Three of these were granted at Iowa, in 1902, 1903, and 1904; three at Utah in 1906, 1907, and 1909; and one at Ohio Wesleyan University in 1908. There were three graduate degrees in speech given in 1918, but the real development of graduate study came after 1920. Wisconsin, which had had its master's program approved in 1915, gave its first M.A. in 1920, and the first Ph.D. degree to be given in the field of speech in 1922. Cornell, which had begun its graduate instruction in 1916 was to award its first M.A. in 1922, and its first Ph.D. in 1926, in which year Iowa also granted its first Ph.D. degree. The first M.A. at Southern California was given in 1924, and Teachers College granted two Ph.D. degrees in speech in 1928. By 1936, Michigan, Iowa, Wisconsin, Northwestern, Teachers College of Columbia, Cornell, and Southern California had given 92 per cent of the graduate degrees awarded in speech to that date. By 1936, also, Stanford and Louisiana State offered graduate study in speech, and had granted the Ph.D. degree. (pp. 466–467)

As early as 1949 speech scholars were already calling for the systematic study of *communication administration*. Gray (1949), one of those first four individuals to receive a doctorate in speech, wrote in *Speech Monographs* that "the administrative aspects of the teaching of speech should be thoroughly explored" (p. 160). A 50-year lag time between that call for research and this book seems to be about par for the course!

Journalism and Mass Communication

The origins of journalism training in the United States are often traced to an 1869 proposal by General Robert E. Lee that journalistic training should be offered at Washington College (now Washington and Lee University; e.g., Baker, 1954; E. M. Rogers, 1994). General Lee, as president of Washington College, established a number of scholarships "for training boys as editor-printers" (Baker, 1954, p. 8), apparently motivated by a desire to assist Southern reconstruction.

Grand proposals for more systematic and professional university education in journalism became common in the 1870s. For example,

John Jay (grandson of the early U.S. statesperson of the same name) addressed the Columbia Trustees:

> This broad foundation presents advantages to a step which would certainly have the most important results, were Columbia to become the Alma Mater not alone of the coming editors of this section, but of the teachers and professors, who, in the academies and colleges of the republic, may hereafter assist in training accomplished conductors of the American press. (Baker, 1954, p. 17)

The campus newspaper, the *Acta Columbiana*, expressed hope "that the Trustees will approve and establish a school of journalism" ("Trustees Consider," 1877, p. 40).

Not everyone concurred with these proposals for university-based journalism education. Henry Watterson of the Louisville *Courier–Journal* adamantly declared that "there is but one school of journalism and that's a well-conducted newspaper office" (Schramm, 1996, p. 129). Many editors agreed. Tom Wallace of the *Louisville Times* echoed with the folk wisdom that "for proper preparation to become an editor, a course of study taking ninety-seven years is essential, and should be topped off with three years of foreign travel" (*Report of the Committee*, 1930, p. 143).

Nevertheless, progress toward journalism education in the academy continued. As E. M. Rogers (1994) noted, "Several universities lay claim to founding the teaching of journalism" (p. 18). The University of Missouri offered a journalism history and resources course in 1878 (Schramm, 1996). In 1903, the University of Kansas offered a journalism course that remains in their curriculum today (E. M. Rogers, 1994). A major step toward more formal journalism education was taken at a place that might strike some as unusual—the Wharton School of Business of the University of Pennsylvania. The Wharton School explicitly opened its doors to would-be journalists in 1893, making "the first effort to lead a would-be newspaperman through the whole discipline of mind and technique toward his professional goal" (Baker, 1954, p. 9). That program remained active until 1901 (Schramm, 1996).

Among the critical early visionaries were Joseph Pulitzer, Willard G. "Daddy" Bleyer, and Walter Williams. Pulitzer eloquently articulated the need for journalism education and proposed endowments for schools at Harvard and, later, at Columbia. The program ultimately established at Columbia reflected much of Pulitzer's professional philosophy. At the University of Wisconsin, Bleyer taught and inspired many individuals who later became leaders of journalism schools that would blend teaching with research. Williams, who founded the University of Missouri School of Journalism in 1907, stressed professionalism and career education, although he himself held only a high school diploma (Baker, 1954).

Once spawned, journalism education programs in colleges and universities flourished. "In 1910, there was only one school, at Missouri, and four departments. In 1917, 84 institutions were offering work in journalism. In 1934, there were 455 institutions and about 812 teachers" (Schramm, 1996, p. 129).

The origins of formal *graduate* education programs in journalism and mass communication are difficult to pinpoint. According to many reports from professional journalism associations, which relied heavily on informal surveys of the early journalism programs, growth in graduate journalism education occurred rapidly during the 1920s. For example, a 1926 report in *The Journalism Bulletin* (currently *Journalism & Mass Communication Quarterly*) stated the following:

> Graduate study in preparation for journalism, done in connection with schools and departments of journalism, shows a total of 122 students enrolled during the past year. Of this number 37 were holders of a general bachelor's degree who were seeking a professional bachelor's degree in journalism. Eighty-two were studying for the master's degree with emphasis on journalistic and supporting courses or a journalistic thesis. Three were studying for the doctor's degree combining advanced work in journalism with advanced work in other departments. ("Journalistic Education," 1926, p. 4)

That report also profiled the "approximately 450 persons teaching journalism in the colleges and universities of the United States" in 1926 (p. 4). In professional schools of journalism, the average teacher had 6 years of newspaper experience, 8 years of classroom experience, and only 1½ years of graduate school. The average amount of graduate study of those teachers was 1½ years. Of the teachers in professional journalism schools profiled,

> Nine have earned Ph.D. degrees, five have honorary doctor's degrees in letters, literature or laws, and 17 have the master's degree. Sixty are enrolled in the graduate schools for part time work for credit toward advanced degrees. In the non-professional schools the average length of newspaper experience represented by the full and part-time teachers is

less than six months; the average length of teaching experience with classes in journalism is less than two years . . . the average amount of graduate work is about six months; the minimum is no graduate work and in a few cases persons are teaching who do not hold a bachelor's degree. (pp. 7–8)

The problem with these association reports is that they frequently contradict official records. For example, the aforementioned report indicated that Columbia University's School of Journalism had awarded 31 master's degrees in 1926 ("Journalistic Education," 1926). A later professional association report indicated that Columbia University had 12 candidates for the master's degree in 1927 (Bleyer, 1928)—remarkable shrinkage in a 1-year period. More critically, according to their authorized history, the Graduate School of Journalism was not even approved at Columbia University until 1935 (Baker, 1954).

Another case may help explain the cause of these inaccuracies in reporting early graduate statistics. Many scholars give substantial credit to the development of early graduate education in journalism (prior to 1950) to Daddy Bleyer of the University of Wisconsin (Bronstein & Vaughn, 1998) and to our knowledge, no one doubts his importance in this regard. For example, Medsger (1996) wrote the following:

Bleyer pioneered graduate-school journalism education. He stressed that research about journalism should be as important a part of journalism education as preparing students to enter the professions. The two scholarly functions would coexist side by side and enrich each other, as Bleyer saw it; teaching the skills of journalism, and, additionally, studying journalism as an institution—its history, how it is practiced, its impact. Many of the people who earned doctoral degrees in his program later became the heads of journalism programs elsewhere. (p. 54)

Unfortunately, *The College Blue Book*, which is considered by most scholars to be the definitive source on degrees granted, does not list any official graduate degree in journalism or mass communication at the University of Wisconsin until after 1950. The problem rests in the official titling of the degree. Although Bleyer was officially a professor of journalism (Sloan, 1990), it appears that early journalism students at Wisconsin were officially receiving their degrees in political science, economics, sociology, psychology, and the like, while taking a minor in journalism (E. M. Rogers, 1994). Therefore, the official history of graduate education in this area differs somewhat from "common knowledge" and the reports of our fledgling professional organizations. Obviously, at least one doctoral dissertation in journalism history is needed to clarify our disciplinary heritage.

By 1950, according to conservative official sources, such as *The College Blue Book*, several institutions had joined Columbia University in offering officially approved graduate degrees in journalism. Among them were Indiana, Iowa, Kansas State, Louisiana State, Michigan, Minnesota, Missouri, Northwestern, Oklahoma, Oregon, Stanford, Syracuse, Texas, and Wisconsin. There is also consensus that the first doctoral degree in journalism was offered by the University of Missouri at Columbia (Sutton, 1945).

Graduate education in mass communication generally traces its origins to Wilbur Schramm, who, in 1943, created the first PhD in mass communication in the School of Journalism at the University of Iowa. "Schramm was not at heart a journalism professor, and he did not teach courses in writing and editing skills at any time during his career. He was pursuing a broader vision of communication study" (p. 16). Schramm (1996) himself noted "stirrings of change in curricula" (p. 129) by the 1940s, as kindred social scientific disciplines found application in the advancing field of communication studies.

Communication research institutes appeared at universities with major graduate programs in mass communication—The University of Minnesota, the University of Iowa, the University of Illinois, the University of Wisconsin, Stanford University, and Michigan State University. E. M. Rogers (1994) offered an explanation for this development: "A research institute can be more flexible than a university department. It is easier to launch than is a department, and it can facilitate interdisciplinary collaboration" (pp. 27–28).

Other Communication Degrees

The 1965 edition of *The College Blue Book* was the first to offer information about graduate programs in advertising and public relations, but courses in advertising had emerged in journalism and business schools (and public relations in journalism schools only) many years earlier. As in other areas of communication study, developers of early programs stressed the importance of a strong liberal arts emphasis in addition to skills orientations (Applegate, 1997).

In 1965, of the 46 graduate programs in *advertising* listed, eight offered the doctorate. A doctoral degree in advertising design was available only from Harvard University, and seven other universities offered more general advertising programs. In *public relations*, five universities offered master's degrees. The University of Wisconsin and Iowa State University offered master's degrees in *agricultural journalism*. Twenty-three doctoral programs were listed in television and/or radio (Burckel, 1965).

In the 1970s, several major universities began offering graduate programs that integrated the disciplines of public relations and advertising. Northwestern University, the College of St. Thomas in Minneapolis, the University of Colorado at Boulder, and the University of Alabama created such programs. Northwestern University merged separate graduate programs in corporate public relations, advertising, and direct marketing into "an integrated marketing communications program" (Applegate, 1997, p. 333).

By the 1970s, graduate degrees were available in every conceivable permutation and combination of communication—more than 60 different indicators between 1972 and 1981—from photojournalism to communication to communications and public address (*The College Blue Book*, 1972, 1975, 1981, 1995; see Table 8.1). This lack of consistency in program designations among colleges and universities poses a problem in that much "communication" information ends up being relegated to "other" categories, leading to underreporting of statistical indicators relative to our discipline. Some standardization would bring greater name recognition to the field and might enhance our image in the academic community.

CONTEMPORARY GRADUATE EDUCATION IN COMMUNICATION

A statistical profile of graduate education in communication is published regularly by the National Center for Education Statistics (1996). More detailed information on trends in graduate education in journalism and mass communication has been provided via informative studies by Becker and Kosicki (1995; Kosicki & Becker, 1996).

TABLE 8.1

Graduate Program Designations and Number of Graduate and Doctoral Programs Per Year

Designation	1972		1975		1981		1995	
	Grad	Doc Only	Grad	Doc Only	Grad	Doc Only	Grad	Doc Only
Advertising	7	0	7	0	3	0	8	1
Advertising & editorial art	1	0	1	0	0	0	0	0
Advertising & journalism	0	0	0	0	0	0	1	0
Advertising & public relations	0	0	0	0	1	0	2	0
Advertising art & design	0	0	0	0	4	0	3	0
Advertising design	6	0	6	0	0	0	3	0
Agricultural journalism	3	0	3	0	2	1	1	1
Broadcast journalism	0	0	0	0	0	0	3	0
Broadcast & film communication	1	0	1	0	1	0	0	0
Broadcasting	10	0	11	0	7	0	7	0
Broadcasting & film	1	0	1	0	1	0	1	0
Communication	1	1	1	0	18	6	56	16
Communication: rhetoric & communication	0	0	0	0	0	0	2	2
Communication & drama	0	0	0	0	1	0	1	0
Communication & media arts	0	0	0	0	2	0	2	0
Communication & theater arts	0	0	0	0	0	0	4	0
Communication arts	0	0	1	0	7	1	15	2
Communication arts & sciences	0	0	0	0	2	1	0	0
Communication, media studies	0	0	0	0	1	0	2	0
Communication sciences	0	0	0	0	0	0	8	5
Communication studies	0	0	0	0	3	0	17	2
Communication & rhetoric	2	1	2	1	1	1	0	0

Communication engineering	1	1	0	0	0	0	0	0
Communication research	1	0	1	0	1	0	0	0
Communication systems	1	1	1	1	0	0	0	0
Communication theory & methodology	1	0	1	0	2	1	4	2
Communication theory & processes	1	1	1	1	1	1	0	0
Communications	49	21	53	20	40	12	48	10
Communications & public address	1	1	1	1	0	0	0	0
Communications & theater	1	0	1	0	0	0	0	0
Journalism	62	9	64	8	52	7	53	5
Journalism & mass communication	0	0	1	0	1	0	0	0
Journalism & mass communications	1	0	1	0	2	0	11	2
Journalism advertising	1	0	1	0	1	0	0	0
Mass communications	0	0	0	0	13	3	31	8
Media studies	0	0	0	0	3	0	3	0
News & editorial journalism	1	0	1	0	1	0	0	0
Photojournalism	1	0	1	0	3	0	1	0
Public address	6	1	5	1	1	1	2	0
Public communication	0	0	0	0	0	0	4	1
Public relations journalism	2	0	2	0	0	0	0	0
Public relations	2	0	2	0	4	0	13	0
Public relations & communications	1	0	1	0	1	0	0	0
Public speaking & discussion	1	1	0	0	0	0	0	0
Radio & television	17	6	18	7	9	2	15	2
Radio & television broadcasting	1	0	1	0	5	1	0	0
Radio, television & film	8	3	8	3	4	1	4	2
Radio, television, & telecommunications	0	0	0	0	0	0	1	0

(continues)

147

TABLE 8.1 (continued)

Graduate Program Designations and Number of Graduate and Doctoral Programs Per Year

Designation	1972		1975		1981		1995	
	Grad	Doc Only	Grad	Doc Only	Grad	Doc Only	Grad	Doc Only
Rhetoric	0	0	0	0	1	0	9	7
Rhetoric & public address	7	2	5	1	4	1	2	1
Rhetoric & technical communications	0	0	0	0	0	0	3	3
Speech	147	41	137	40	84	19	35	4
Speech arts	0	0	1	0	1	1	1	1
Speech & theater	9	1	16	3	13	1	4	0
Speech & theater arts	0	0	2	0	0	0	0	0
Speech & drama	0	0	1	0	8	1	0	0
Speech & dramatic arts	0	0	0	0	3	1	2	0
Speech & language	0	0	0	0	0	0	3	1
Speech communication	2	0	5	2	12	3	41	12
Speech communication & theater	0	0	0	0	0	0	1	0
Speech communications	0	0	0	0	12	4	0	0
Speech communication & theater arts	0	0	0	0	1	0	0	0
Speech communication studies	0	0	0	0	1	0	0	0
Technical communications	0	0	0	0	0	0	5	0
Telecommunications	0	0	0	0	1	0	2	0
Television	2	0	2	0	1	0	1	0
Television & radio	1	1	0	0	0	0	0	0

Communication: General

As can be seen from Fig 8.2 and Fig 8.3, the number of master's and doctor's degrees in communication awarded between 1970–1971 and 1993–1994—the latest year for which published data are currently available—has been steadily increasing (National Center for Education Statistics, 1996). In 1993–1994, 5,005 individuals received master's degrees in the global "Communications/Total" category—1,870 (37.4%) of these degrees were awarded to men, 3,135 (62.6%) to women. During that same time period, 337 individuals were awarded PhD degrees in communication. The doctoral degree recipients were remarkably

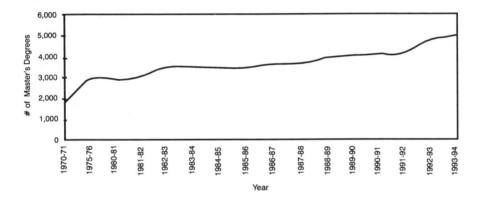

FIG. 8.2. Master's degrees conferred in communication
1970–1971 to 1993–1994.

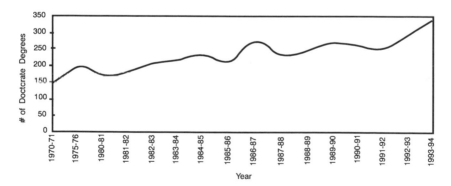

FIG. 8.3. Doctor's degrees conferred in communication
1970–1971 to 1993–1994.

evenly divided by gender: 172 men (51%) and 165 women (49%).

These data from the National Center for Education Statistics are further divided into subcategories: communications/general (which includes speech and interpersonal communication, but not organizational communication), advertising, journalism, broadcast journalism, public relations and organizational communication, radio and television, and communications/other. The totals for those subcategories are presented inTable 8.2.

Journalism and Mass Communication

According to Becker and Kosicki (1995), graduate enrollment in journalism and mass communication continues to increase at a rate higher than that for graduate enrollments overall. The period of growth began in 1990, the year after undergraduate enrollments peaked at 145,781. PhD enrollments reached their pinnacle in 1994. The next year they declined 22.8%. Fall enrollments for the period 1992 through 1994 showed a 23.3% increase in the number of doctoral students and a 3% increase in master's students during the period. "While journalism and mass communication remains a field dominated by undergraduate instruction, there is a gradual and steady change toward more graduate instruction over time" (Becker & Kosicki, 1995, p. 64).

TABLE 8.2
Number of Graduate Degrees by Area and Gender, 1993–1994

Communication Area	Master's Degrees			Doctor's Degrees		
	Total	Men	Women	Total	Men	Women
Communication/ general	1,822	636	1,186	215	108	107
Advertising	256	90	166	4	2	2
Journalism	1,432	517	915	28	19	9
Broadcast journalism	16	7	9	0	0	0
PR & organizational	240	58	182	0	0	0
Radio & television	383	183	200	10	6	4
Communication/ other	856	379	477	80	37	43
Communication/ total	5,005	1,870	3,135	337	172	165

The number of master's and doctoral (total graduate) journalism and mass communication *degrees awarded* increased significantly—23.1%—between the 1992–1993 and the 1993–1994 school year. According to Becker and Kosicki (1995):

> It may simply be a sign of the maturing of the field that growth at present is—in terms of percentage of change—concentrated at the graduate level. Restricting undergraduate enrollments may have the effect of driving up the quality of the graduates and it may allow for investment of resources in increasingly sought-out graduate education. (p. 70)

The number of women studying for doctoral degrees in mass communication declined significantly in 1995, after several years of growth. According to Kosicki and Becker (1996), in 1995 the percentage of women doctoral students enrolled in communication programs declined to 38.1% of the mix, compared with a more balanced 50.5% the year before. Kosicki and Becker viewed the decline in female enrollment as "a significant setback in terms of the long-term goal of recruiting female faculty" (p. 4). A year earlier, they had described the situation with optimism:

> If the majority of the women earning doctoral degrees take academic jobs, as seems likely, the current imbalance between the sex of the faculty and the sex of the students studying for degrees in journalism and mass communication should change. Women have made up a majority of students enrolled in journalism and mass communication programs since the late 1970s, but they made up less than a third of the faculty as recently as 1992. (Becker & Kosicki, 1995, p. 68)

AN OUTLINE OF GRADUATE ADMINISTRATION: GRADUATE SCHOOLS AND COMMUNICATION

In addition to reviewing literature on communication administration, we interviewed a dozen or so directors of graduate programs in communication and the dean of our graduate school in order to learn more about program administration and to identify significant issues. Our convenience sample included eight directors of large, established programs, seven of which offer doctoral degrees, and four directors of newer programs, all but one of which offer master's degrees only. In exchange for absolute candor, we offered anonymity and confidentiality.

What we learned is that the administration of graduate programs in communication is a complicated and often undervalued "calling." The successful execution of this process requires the ability to manage a lot of relationships, often with minimal "position power" or line authority. This typically includes direct coordination with the following: a graduate dean and the associated officers and staff of a graduate school; a dean, director, or chair; one or more graduate committees (often at universitywide, collegewide, and departmental levels); a wide range of graduate faculty and would-be graduate faculty (temporary and permanent); staff; potential employers; and, of course, our clients—potential and actual graduate students.

The duties of a graduate director are myriad, multilayered, beleaguered by deadlines, and often thankless. To put the process in perspective, Table 8.3 presents an outline of the typical activities of the dean of a graduate school at a midsize university (Rogers, 1997).

Administrators of graduate programs in communication colleges, schools, or departments perform many of these same functions and activities, albeit at a more parochial level. A partial listing of the activities of the directors of communication graduate programs we interviewed is given in Table 8.4.

All this, and the vast majority of graduate program directors with whom we spoke are expected to set the standard in teaching and research for their academic units. Dare we include "walk on water" as a criterion for appointment as a graduate director?

ISSUES IN ADMINISTERING GRADUATE PROGRAMS IN COMMUNICATION

Dean Ron Rogers at The University of Alabama Graduate School provided valuable insights that guided our interviews of administrators of graduate programs in communication. In the course of these interviews, we found that today's administrators of communication graduate programs are confronted with a wide range of issues. Profiled are some of those most commonly mentioned.

Recruiting and Retention

In recent years, considerable attention has been paid to the problem of recruiting and maintaining quality faculty members in communication (e.g., DeFleur, 1993; Ryan & Martinson, 1996). Among the problems

TABLE 8.3

TABLE 8.3
An Outline of a Graduate Dean's Activities

I. Academic Programs
    1. Review of existing programs.
    2. Assist in the development of new programs.

II. Academic Policies
    1. Admissions requirements.
    2. Degree requirements.
    3. GPA requirements.
    4. Transfer credit.
    5. Minimum registration requirements.
    6. Withdrawal.
    7. Residency requirements.
    8. Time limits.

III. Students
    1. Recruitment.
    2. Admissions.
    3. Fellowships and financial aid.
    4. Teaching and research assistants.
    5. Monitoring student progress.
    6. Appointment faculty committees.
    7. Maintain records and degree verification.
    8. Thesis and dissertation approval.
    9. Student support services.
    10. Liaison with administrative offices.
    11. Grievance procedures.
    12. Interdisciplinary PhD degrees.

IV. Faculty
    1. Appointment of graduate faculty.
    2. Recommendations to deans about selection of department chairpersons.
    3. Recommendations to academic vice president about promotion and tenure decisions.
    4. Recommendations to academic vice president about sabbaticals.

V. Administrative support
    1. Data collection & dissemination
    2. Liaison with the university attorneys, housing, financial aid, health services, computer services, student affairs, etc.

VI. Universitywide activities
    1. Central administration decision making.
    2. Ex-officio member of numerous standing university committees.

VII. External relations
    1. State commission on higher education, regents, and so on.
    2. Conference of regional graduate schools.
    3. Council of graduate schools.

TABLE 8.4

An Outline of a Communication Graduate Director's Activities

I.   Promotion and recruitment
    1. Develop program brochures and advertisements.
    2. Host receptions for potential graduate students at conferences.
    3. Organize and host campus visits for prospective graduate students.
    4. Provide information to alumni publications.
    5. Provide information and stories for university, college, school, or department newsletters.

II. Student activities
    1. Supervise admissions.
    2. Supervise transfer credits.
    3. Organize and conduct orientation and mentoring sessions.
    4. Prepare advising booklets and/or brochures and conduct initial advising sessions.
    5. Assist with the formation of advisory committees.
    6. Monitor student progress toward graduation requirements.
    7. Monitor registration, drop/add, late admissions, withdrawals, class size, residency requirements, statute of limitations, and so on.
    8. Handle a variety of grievance procedures.
    9. Appoint teaching and research assistants.
    10. Organize and/or conduct teacher and researcher training sessions.
    11. Supervise qualifying examinations.
    12. Assist with the formation of thesis and dissertation committees.
    13. Provide quality control and approval of classes, examinations, theses, and dissertations.
    14. Serve as career counselor and advisor on a variety of personal and professional matters.
    15. Organize student presentations to faculty and other graduate students.
    16. Assist in development of resumes and job applications.

III. Faculty
    1. Make and review appointments of graduate faculty.
    2. Appoint and monitor graduate admissions committees.
    3. Appoint and monitor graduate advisory committees.
    4. Appoint and monitor comprehensive examination committees.
    5. Provide appraisals of contributions to graduate programs for personnel actions.
    6. Solicit and screen for teaching of graduate classes.
    7. Maintaining files of faculty Full Time Equivalency contribution to graduate program.
    8. Help determine faculty teaching load reports and course reductions.

IV. Administrative liaison
    1. Coordinate with graduate dean.
    2. Coordinate with dean, director, or chair.

3. Coordinate with university graduate council.
4. Coordinate with graduate student council as well as college, school, or departmental graduate student officer(s), councils, or organizations.
5. Coordinate with college, school, or department graduate committee(s).
6. Coordinate with department graduate coordinators (for graduate directors of larger schools and colleges).
7. Coordinate with housing, computer services, student affairs, international programs, and so on.

V. Administrative support
1. Data collection, report writing, and so on.
2. Provide information and reports to various institutional officials (e.g., provost, graduate dean).

VI. External relations, fundraising, and placement
1. Give lectures and addresses to varied internal and external publics.
2. Arrange guest lecture series for graduate students and faculty.
3. Organize "brown bag" seminars.
4. Write letters of recommendation and/or call on behalf of candidates.
5. Constantly "network" for the benefit of the graduate program.

mentioned by those concerned with this topic are that "today's doctoral training and the tools it provides are not really up to the task expected by administrators" (Dennis, quoted in DeFleur, 1993, p. 1). Closely related to this is the projected forthcoming shortage in communication of faculty members who hold doctorates, resulting in what is perceived to be too few qualified faculty members (DeFleur, 1993). From the point of view of media professionals, the perceived dearth of well-qualified master's graduates is an equally critical issue (e.g., Medgser, 1996). Obviously, for the long-range success of our discipline, the recruiting and maintaining of quality graduate students is of vital importance and should be addressed by our professional associations.

The graduate program directors interviewed indicated a range of problems associated with *recruiting* graduate students. Many identified a scarcity of qualified candidates as the overarching issue. Common subsidiary issues were applications from candidates who would be better served by other programs—or the inverse of that, too few appropriate candidates for their type of programmatic emphases. Other frequently mentioned problems regarding recruiting were applications from students with serious writing deficiencies, the perceived lack of predictive validity of Graduate Record Exam scores, too many or too few international students, and the lack of compatibility of methods and theory courses from students matriculating from other universities.

Issues that drew top billing involving *retention* were as follows: students leaving after completing their course work but prior to completing dissertations, problems with the quality of annual reviews of graduate student performance, inadequately defined or inappropriate graduate school retention policies, lack of concordance between performance in courses and success in passing qualifying examinations, lack of funding for qualified teaching and research assistants, spiraling costs of graduate education, and lack of a supportive graduate school culture.

Multiculturalism and Diversity

If we define multiculturalism as including "people of color, ethnic minorities, gender distinctions, religious beliefs, and other attributes that distinguish one identifiable set of people from another" (Cohen, Lombard, & Pierson, 1992, p. 7), the vast majority of the graduate administrators we interviewed talked about issues of multiculturalism and diversity. However, the various dimensions of the issue on which they focused were quite diverse. Some are partially covered by the previous topic of recruiting and retention—how to attract and retain qualified minority faculty members and minority graduate students. Other graduate program directors emphasized the difficulty of adjusting the culture of their graduate programs so as to be more supportive of diversity (e.g., Rawitch, 1996). Others mentioned the need for infusing multicultural dimensions into their curricula, even if they were unable to attract faculty members or graduate students who are racial and ethnic minorities (e.g., Dickson, 1995). Also mentioned were "town versus gown" issues regarding multiculturalism (e.g., the university desired racial and ethnic diversity, but the community culture outside the university was less than hospitable toward minorities). Frequently mentioned were Accrediting Council on Education in Journalism and Mass Communication "Standard 12" issues—that is, were their programs doing enough to "prepare students to understand and relate to a multi-cultural, multi-ethnic, multi-racial and otherwise diverse society?" (Dickson, 1995, p. 43).

It might be noted that although most of the administrators interviewed identified this as a problem, no one thought that they had derived an acceptable solution to the problem. Among those partial solutions mentioned were "grow your own" programs (i.e., programs that identify interested and talented minorities while they are very young, bring them to campus during the summers, and gain and maintain their interest in communication as a career), special diversity and multiculturalism workshops for graduate faculty and graduate students, "target of opportunity" money to provide stipends to graduate students of color, and a program developed collaboratively with a historically Black college from which one university had successfully recruited several African American graduate students.

Mentoring

Another hot topic among those administrators interviewed was mentoring (e.g., Fedler, 1996; Lindlof & Boyd, 1997). It appeared to us that several different dimensions of this concept were being emphasized, including the following: establishing a durable relationship between advisors and students; developing closer links between professionals and students; teaching graduate students the "unwritten rules" of how to succeed in the program, get a desirable job, and launch a successful career; and teaching graduate students how to teach (e.g., Cohen, 1997; Lambert & Tice, 1993). One graduate administrator emphasized the emerging multidimensionality of the mentoring concept by indicating that her college had launched a program for "mentoring by advisors, peer mentoring, and postdoctoral mentoring." Whatever the dimensions of the concepts, it is clear that administrators of graduate programs in communication think this is an area in which improvement is vital.

Placement

Several of the graduate directors interviewed indicated that they spent a great deal of time attempting to ensure that their graduate students achieved desirable entry (or reentry) positions; other graduate administrators indicated that they did not see this as part of their "job description"—which may be an issue in and of itself. Many decried what they perceived as having been a tight job market for PhD students in premiere research universities during the past half-decade, although others indicated that they were taking a proactive stance on this issue by attempting to let their graduate students know that community colleges were desirable teaching locales. Related to this, three graduate administrators said that during the past few years, some of their best doctoral students had been going into industry research positions rather than enter what they perceived to be a "tight" academic job market. After entering the job market in the media industries, some of these same students had complained that their doctorates had not prepared them adequately for industry jobs. Under consideration at one of the programs was some sort of dual track system, with one option emphasizing industry research methods and the like.

Distance Education

Some of the graduate directors reported that their programs were being affected in some way by distance education ventures. This included a range of issues from being asked to offer graduate courses at remote sites, to the difficulties of trying to launch Internet-based graduate courses in communication (e.g., Bailey & Cotlar, 1994), to concerns about the need to standardize and even accredit distance education graduate programs in journalism. It was obvious from the degree of uncertainty that undergirded these discussions that this is an issue that has just emerged on the horizon, but one that may raise a number of questions for graduate directors of communication programs.

Quality Control

Quality control was the toughest and most thankless part of their job for quite a few of the graduate program directors, and our questions in this regard engendered a number of highly similar horror stories. Most related to the issue of what happened when the director was unwilling to rubber stamp a thesis or dissertation that a committee had approved but that had obvious deficiencies in the mind of the graduate program director. One interviewee—the former editor of a major communication journal—said that he had lost more friends by being a conscientious graduate program director than by being a rigorous journal editor! Other horror stories related to fallout from denying full graduate status to underachieving faculty members. One of the individuals who had identified this as an issue indicated that the only solution to the quality control issue is to "surround yourself with peers who are at least as 'high minded' as you are."

Professional Master's Degrees
and Continuing Graduate Education

When graduate administrators were asked what the biggest changes currently taking place in their programs were, two items that emerged were the granting of professional master's degrees and continuing graduate education. Two of the interviewees said that their professional (MS) master's programs were now much larger than their traditional (MA) programs—one described his program as "the tail that wags the dog," the other as her "new 600-pound gorilla." Both emphasized that they were having trouble ensuring quality, because courses were being offered off campus, no theses were required, and the like, and both were doubtful that sufficient critical thinking was infused into the curriculum. Despite their criticism, market demand was extremely high for both programs, so resources were being subtly shifted in that direction.

Another graduate director reported that she was facing considerable pressure from alumni to offer graduate-level continuing education—actually, her term was "continuous education"—courses, as the information age is causing "old knowledge" and old mind-sets to become obsolete so quickly. The primary measure of concern expressed was what should be included in such a curriculum.

Conclusion

A plethora of other issues emerged in our conversations with graduate program directors: accommodating interactive media into graduate education and other dimensions of the "technological challenge," funding and resource management, using publicly funded research assistants to conduct proprietary research, modernizing curricula without losing disciplinary heritage, balancing graduate and undergraduate education, methodological pluralism, epistemological warfare, and the like.

All of these issues reinforce the conclusion that we are indeed blessed and cursed by living in interesting times. To direct a graduate communication program in the information age clearly locates one in the center of the maelstrom.

REFERENCES

American universities and colleges (14th ed.). (1992). New York: Walter de Gruyter.

Applegate, E. (1997). Advertising. In W. G. Christ (Ed.), *Media education assessment handbook* (pp. 319–339). Mahwah, NJ: Lawrence Erlbaum Associates.

Arlt, G. O. (1971). Purifying the Pierian Spring. *The Graduate Journal, 8,* 267–276.

Bailey, E. K., & Cotlar, M. (1994). Teaching via the Internet. *Communication Education, 43,* 184–193.

Baker, R. T. (1954). *A history of The Graduate School of Journalism, Columbia University.* New York: Columbia University Press.

Becker, L. B., & Kosicki, G. M. (1995). Graduate degrees increase 23%, but bachelor numbers decline. *Journalism & Mass Communication Educator, 50,* 61–70.

Bleyer, W. G. (1928). A survey of instruction in journalism. *The Journalism Quarterly, 6,* 14–17.

Bronstein, C., & Vaughn, S. (1998). Willard G. Bleyer and the relevance of journalism education. *Journalism Monographs, 166.*

Burckel, C. E. (1965). *The college blue book* (11th ed.). Lutherville–Timonium, MD: Universal Lithographers.

Cohen, J. (1997). Learning the scholarship of teaching in doctorate-granting institutions. *Journalism & Mass Communication Educator, 53,* 27–38.

Cohen, J., Lombard, M., & Pierson, R. (1992). Developing a multicultural mass communication course. *Journalism Educator, 47,* 3–12.

The College Blue Book (14th ed.). (1972). New York: CCM Information.

The College Blue Book (15th ed.). (1975). New York: Macmillan.

The College Blue Book (17th ed.). (1981). New York: Mamillan.

The College Blue Book (25th ed.). (1995). New York: Macmillan.

Curtis, J. F. (1954). The rise of experimental phonetics. In K. R. Wallace (Ed.), *History of speech education in America: Background studies* (pp. 348–369). New York: Appleton-Century-Crofts.

DeFleur, M. L. (1993). *The forthcoming shortage of communications Ph.D.s.* New York: Freedom Forum Media Studies Center.

Dickson, T. (1995). Assessing education's response to multicultural issues. *Journalism & Mass Communication Educator, 50,* 41–51.

Fedler, F. (1996). Mentoring manual for teaching the culture of the field. *Journalism & Mass Communication Educator, 51,* 74–80.

Gray, G. W. (1949). Research on the history of speech education. *The Quarterly Journal of Speech, 35,* 156–163.

Haskins, C. H. (1940). *The rise of universities.* New York: Peter Smith.

Howell, W. S. (1954). English backgrounds of rhetoric. In K. R. Wallace (Ed.), *History of speech education in America: Background studies* (pp. 3–47). New York: Appleton-Century-Crofts.

Journalistic education in the United States. (1926). *The Journalism Bulletin, 3,* 1–11.

Kerr, C. (1963). *The uses of the university.* Cambridge, MA: Harvard University Press.

Knower, F. H. (1935). An index to graduate work in the field of speech, 1902–1934. *Speech Monographs, II,* 1–49.

Kosicki, G. M., & Becker, L. B. (1996). Annual survey of enrollment and degrees awarded. *Journalism & Mass Communication Educator, 51,* 4–14.

Lambert, L. M., & Tice, S. L. (Eds.). (1993). *Preparing graduate students to teach.* Washington, DC: American Association for Higher Education.

LaPidus, J. B. (1988, March 14). *Great expectations: The role of the American university in the 21st century.* Paper presented at the New Mexico State University Centennial Lecture, Las Cruces, NM.

Lindlof, T. R., & Boyd, D. A. (1997). Mentoring untenured communication faculty at research institutions. *Feedback, 38,* 16–25.

Medsger, B. (1996). *Winds of change: Challenges confronting journalism education.* New York: Freedom Forum.

National Center for Education Statistics. (1996). *Digest of education statistics 1996.* Washington, DC: U.S. Department of Education.

Rawitch, C. Z. (1996). Designing a model program for minority students. *Journalism & Mass Communication Educator, 51,* 13–24.

The report of the Committee on Schools of Journalism to the A.S.N.E. (1930). *Journalism Quarterly, 7,* 142–153.

Rogers, E. M. (1994). *A history of communication study: A biographical approach.* New York: The Free Press.

Rogers, R. (1997). *An outline of a graduate dean's activities* [Handout]. Tuscaloosa, AL: Author.

Ryan, M., & Martinson, D. L. (1996). An analysis of faculty recruiting in schools and departments. *Journalism & Mass Communication Educator, 50,* 4–12.

Schramm, W. (1996). The master teachers. In E. E. Dennis & E. Wartella (Eds.), *American communication research: The remembered history* (pp. 123–133). Mahwah, NJ: Lawrence Erlbaum Associates.

Sloan, W. D. (1990). Willard Bleyer and propriety. In W. D. Sloan (Ed.), *Makers of the media mind: Journalism educators and their ideas* (pp. 76–82). Hillsdale, NJ: Lawrence Erlbaum Associates.

Smith, D. K. (1954). Origin and development of departments of speech. In K. R. Wallace (Ed.), *History of speech education in America: Background studies* (pp. 447–470). New York: Appleton-Century-Crofts.

Spurr, S. H. (1971). The American graduate school. *The Graduate Journal, 2,* 250–265.

Sutton, A. A. (1945). *Education for journalism in the United States from beginning to 1940.* Evanston, IL: Northwestern University Press.

Trustees consider journalism school. (1877, November 20). *Acta Columbiana, 5,* 40.

Wieruszowski, H. (1966). *The medieval university: Masters, students, learning.* New York: Van Nostrand Reinhold.

Experiential Learning Programs

Robert C. Moore
Elizabethtown College

The arguments for experiential education are rooted in a concern for the total development of young people—social, psychological, and intellectual. This development is seen as jeopardized by a social milieu that increasingly isolates young people from the kinds of experiences, encounters, and challenges that form the basis for healthy development and that add purpose and meaning to formal education.

—Conrad and Heden (1995, p. 382)

THE FOUNDATION
OF EXPERIENTIAL LEARNING

Experiential learning has been often thought of as activity-based learning or even internships—practical experience. However, the philosophical foundations on which it has been based go far beyond active learning. Popularly labeled as *theory into practice*, experiential learning is more appropriately characterized as praxis.

Praxis translated into English means practice, but the philosophical concept does not deal with mundane experience or activity. Aristotle intended praxis to include the study and application of theory and of knowledge to life.

163

Sartre built on this integrated focus of learning by advancing consciousness as a key element of praxis. "To be a consciousness ... is to make choices.... In making such choices we are choosing what we are to become.... We make these choices reflectively ... or prereflectively ... but we are always choosing and thereby always acting" (Bernstein, 1971, p. 141).

These visions provided for Dewey's theory of education "a sense of life, process, and the concreteness of experience itself" (Bernstein, 1971, p. 167). Dewey believed that experience was founded in knowledge—"an affair of the intercourse of a living being with its physical and social environment" (Bernstein, 1971, p. 203). Whereas many philosophers have seen theory as separate and apart from experience, Dewey saw theory as integral to experience and, as a result, experience as a key factor in knowing and rethinking theory (see Dewey, 1938).

Based on Dewey' s assimilation of philosophical views on learning and experience, his own theory of education was one of a continual process of reconstruction in which a learner' s experience is guided and systematic. Experience creates a situation in which the student makes a "connection" between himself or herself and the subject. Dewey believed that the student was to be

> equipped with both "critical consciousness" of themselves and their place in society and the tools, knowledge, motivation, and roles with which to effectively participate in the world and improve it ... linking theory and practice through field experience and critical reflection was the only means for effective, progressive education. (Stanton, 1995, p. 144)

> Students who use information they are trying to learn, who challenge and grapple with their new knowledge, or who use it to solve new problems, tend to learn more effectively than students who passively read, memorize, or merely absorb that to which they have been exposed. (Jernstedt, 1995, p. 358)

Joplin (1995) said, "that anytime a person learns, he must 'experience' the subject—significantly identify with, seriously interact with, form a personal relationship with, (the subject)" (p. 15). She "connects" with Dewey in that learning can be generally successful when a learner is actively involved in the experience.

An experiential learning program can be described as an integrated and purposeful effort to manage experiences, make it more likely that learners will make connections, and to provide for ongoing curricular experiences to make the overall learning experience more meaningful and valuable in career preparation.

EXPERIENCE CAN BE A TOOL FOR LEARNING

In communication and media education programs, internships have been most often associated with experiential learning where students pursuing professional preparation have been passively indoctrinated that these opportunities are an important part of their education. By and large, these opportunities have been seen as jobs, experiences, field placements, or mentoring that is ancillary to a student' s curriculum of study. This perceived market need on the part of academé has resulted in a trend to incorporate experiential education as fashionable, yet isolated, internships into the curriculum. This trend has often made professional programs appear as technical, nonintellectual, or vocational in nature.

A well-designed professional curriculum provides a sound foundation in the liberal arts with critical thinking and problem-solving attributes, along with internships and other experiential opportunities. The issue of importance here is that experiential education must be integrated as a key component of the intellectual learning process across the curriculum. Such a sophisticated approach to learning serves the academy and its various constituencies better than a narrow technical of vocational curriculum.

Bell (1995) said that the theory of what experience does is more important than the actual experience: "Experience, according to Dewey, is ... a social relationship. He sees experience as a relationship between the individual and their environment, a replicable interaction in which meanings are found" (p. 11). Furthermore, Dewey believed that learning is evolutionary. For experiential learning, that means a process one may go through. The emphasis here may be on one and on process. Experiential learning is an individually significant event—a personal connection. The experiences one is exposed to may be group efforts, but the merit of the experience is grounded in intrapersonal value or significance to the learner. Beyond active learning, most valuable is the reflective process that should be built into an experiential education program.

Druian, Owens, and Owen (1995) cited six common elements of a learning sequence at the root of experience. They were application and

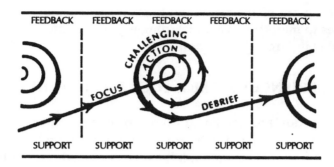

FIG. 9.1. The five-stage model (for experiential program design). Joplin, Laura. *The Theory of Experiential Education.* ©1995 by The Association for Experiential Education. Reprinted by permission of Kendall/Hunt Publishing Company.

generalization, sharing and publishing, reflecting and evaluating, engaging and experiencing, negotiation and planning, and assessment and goal setting. Expanding on the reflective stage, the authors indicated its importance to learning as "transforming the raw material of the experience in a form that can be shared by others" (p. 21). Joplin (1995) concurred, noting that reflection is the mechanism that directly and consciously connects the experience to the student's learning.

Joplin (1995) developed a five-stage model that attempts to conceptualize this need for a reflective process (see Fig. 9.1). Essentially providing a schematic for experiential planning, Joplin focused on a "central ... challenging action preceded by a focus and followed by a debrief. Encompassing all is the environment of support and feedback" (p. 16).

There is an inherent need in experiential education for the learner to be assisted prior to, during, and after the experience so that efforts are not wasted; to try and ensure that success is eventual and meaningful. Reflection, or debrief, is the conception and articulation of meaning; the recognition of learning from the experience—Dewey's connection.

EXPERIENTIAL LEARNING
IN PROFESSIONAL EDUCATION

Long a hallmark of higher education, the Socratic method—a teacher-centered structure of instruction—negates the philosophical basis of a learner-centered paradigm. Often, professional programs, especially those utilizing technology, offer as their alternative to the lecture educational "activities" that more often than not are adjunct to the learning process—not integrated into the process.

A curriculum integrating experience actively engages learners in well-designed problem-solving situations in which they draw on knowledge and truth. Chapman, McPhee, and Proudman (1995) outlined a methodology of the development of experiential education to include:

> mixture of content and process, absence of excessive teacher judgement, engaged in purposeful endeavors, encouraging the big picture perspective, teaching with multiple learning styles, (integrating) the role of reflection, creating emotional investment, re-examination of values, presence of meaningful relationships, (and) learning outside of one' s perceived comfort zone. (p. 246)

The important aspects of learner-centered experiential education, valuable to fulfilling the goals of the academy, include providing a foundation of knowledge and information that may be evaluated, analyzed, and validated by the learner through his or her experiences. "Wagner described such a program that effectively integrated three traditions of experiential education—group process, simulations, and field experience" (Stanton, 1995, p. 145). These traditions can be manipulated to occur in a variety of learning situations in and out of the classroom.

These categories of learner-centered experiences build on a focus on critical thinking. A student is placed in a challenging environment in which he or she can assess and solve a problem by engaging that knowledge actively to create a solution that has value to the learner. Activities are never designed to be the last step of the process. It is imperative to provide for criticism, judgment, and reflection on the learner's performance in applying knowledge and skills. Experience is a step in the process of learning itself. Faculty are encouraged to incorporate learning experiences into the classroom, leading to more competence in learning and ability. As confidence grows, students are then able to progress to a new level of more independent learning involving more sophisticated activity and assessment, often out of the classroom. Williamson (1995), in "Designing Experiential Curricula," provided a model similar to the preceeding conceptualization of what a curriculum should do (see Fig. 9.2).

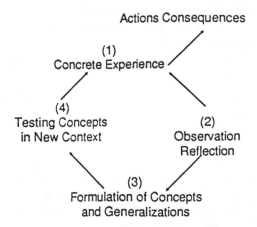

FIG. 9.2. Framework for experiential learning. Williamson, Jed. *Experiential Learning in Schools and Higher Education.* ©1995 by The Association for Experiential Education. Reprinted by permission of Kendall/Hunt Publishing Company.

A good experiential curriculum design concept goes far beyond that of "experience" often cited by professionals and academics in debating curricular needs responsive to an industry. Rather than "separate or isolated components, [it is] a holistic experience" (Moore, 1992, p. 15); it represents an integration of liberal and professional study.

DESIGN OF AN EXPERIENTIAL LEARNING PROGRAM

Stark and Lowther (1988) characterized competent professionals by "their ability to link technical knowledge with appropriate values and attitudes when making complex judgements" (p. 1). "Building from this understanding of the profession and the discipline, a student is ... able to develop three other essential professional competencies: technical, integrative (melding theory, practice, and setting), and marketability" (Moore, 1992, p. 15). Toffler (1981) described such a person as a "new worker ... (they) accept responsibility ... understand how their work dovetails with that of others, who can handle even larger tasks, who adapt swiftly to changed circumstances, and who are sensitively tuned into people around them" (p. 385). Kendall, Duley, Little, Permaul, and Rubin (1986) cited the challenge to education in *A Nation at*

Risk: Another View, as providing both general competence and specific job skills that may not be of immediate use but will allow professionals to meet the changing needs and new skills of the future workplace.

Jernstedt (1995) characterized such programs as "meld(ing) the structures of knowledge with the process of using knowledge" (p. 359). A basis for this approach is that students will use their knowledge and the information gathered to plan, design, and produce original projects that integrate various types of expression learned and mastered in the courses taken throughout the curriculum. For communication and media programs, this means a general professional program designed to educate a "compleat communicator (who) must be able to write well, speak and listen intelligently, communicate through media, develop a sense of aesthetics, and demonstrate creative expression" (Moore, 1994, p. 162).

A sequential and integrated experiential learning program seemed to be an effective way to reach these goals (Moore, 1985a, 1985b). Characteristics of such an approach to learning include: the faculty member as a coach, mentor, and observer; application of knowledge and skills, experimentation, and assessment that requires that the learner be permitted to make mistakes or to conceive of alternate approaches to problems or situations; and a final assessment made to determine the level of acquired knowledge, mastery of skills, and the ability to problem solve with original and creative solutions. The professional communicator of tomorrow will be someone who is cross-trained through a flexible, fundamental and integrated media education program (Blanchard & Christ, 1993).

In developing programs that integrate experiential learning into the curriculum, several underlying assumptions would need to be made explicit:

1. Experiential education was to be integrated across the communications curriculum.
2. Skill sets incorporated into courses were to be practiced with theory and knowledge as a basis.
3. Courses were to extend the hypothetical into real-world situations.
4. Faculty were to assess, guide, and promote proficiency.
5. Throughout the curriculum, experiential learning would be incremental and progressive, as would the intellectual and professional

development of the student. Both curricular aspects, theory and practice, would be linked along the way by increasing expectations.

6. In assessing the curricular outcomes, a final course would present learners with an opportunity to demonstrate a mastery of knowledge, professional values and standards, and technical acumen as transitional professionals (see Moore, 1994).

THE ELIZABETHTOWN COLLEGE COMMUNICATIONS MODEL OF INTEGRATED EXPERIENTIAL LEARNING

This model, first developed in 1985, evolved to incorporate a hierarchical approach to providing experiential learning opportunities. Goals of such a program included both intellectual and social and professional development. The learning increased in quantity, quality, and expectations of students progressing through the many levels of the experiential curriculum as they amassed additional knowledge. Experiential opportunities were not merely available, but a priority of most faculty and most required in the curriculum.

Garvey and Vorsteg (1995) presented a stage theory approach to learning that helped to explain the model. Based on many and varied theories of social scientists, they indicated that:

> Human behavior and development (occurs) through ... a progressive series of levels, which are often clearly recognizable, one from the other.... (This) is not intended to be a rigid, formal progression of concrete levels of understanding, but rather a possible recognizable pattern.... (p. 299)

Their four phases of theory integration, moving from theory into practice, were related to students studying experiential education applying classroom learning to actual leadership positions. The four phases were exhilaration, rejection, integration, and transformation. The phase theory is applicable to experiential education in general and useful in describing how students might move through the Elizabethtown model. Incremental and progressive intellectual and experiential development is important to student learning. Hierarchical and sequential processes not only allowed for the phases mentioned, but also enabled individual intellectual and experiential growth as a maturing process critical in learning.

In the first stage, exhilaration, students were introduced to the field and its various theories and practices, as well as enticed into initial application of skills, whetting their appetite as a communications professional. In a somewhat managed environment, students experienced general application of elementary skills.

Based on applying these skills as a result of specific theory, often students agitate for more advanced work and more obvious relevance to specific career desires. The second phase of the theory follows—rejection. Students sometimes experience frustration and may conclude that their learning was not directly relevant to those reasons they chose this facet of career education or preparation.

Yet, as Garvey and Vorsteg (1995) pointed out, the students were able to recognize that many of the techniques and aspects of their learning had relevance. On reexamining their learning of theories and practice, students move to the third stage—integration. It was at this point in their learning that students merged their knowledge and experiences with developmental opportunities to form a connection or link between themselves and their performance.

In the last stage, transformation, students begin to move from a learner mode to more professional behavior. At this level, which was characterized by advanced experiential opportunities and upperclass status, students should emerge as *compleat* communicators. Students "use their knowledge and the information gathered to plan, design and produce original projects ... as solutions to problems ... for real-world clients" (Moore, 1994, p. 162). These key opportunities for transformation of learning and the self occur for students in internships and are assessed in a capstone course experience (see Moore, 1994).

The four-phase theory of integration was generally descriptive of the foundational philosophy of the Elizabethtown College Department of Communications model of integrated experiential education, which is made up of five hierarchical stages of theory and practice.

This model (see Fig. 9.3) was represented by an inverted superimposed triangle over another triangle. The inverted triangle was designed to show the progression of learning cognitive and affective material from a very basic introduction to the discipline and profession to a more broad-based knowledge at the end of studies. The second vertical triangle displays a student's exposure to varied learning experiences that become progressively more focused and proficient as they proceed in their studies. These various experiential components pro-

Integrated Experiential Learning

Intellectual Development
Content

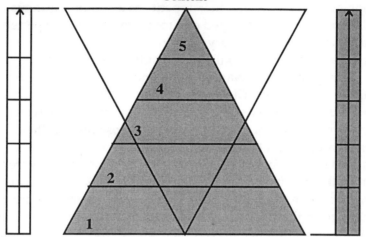

Experiential Development
Process

Mastery of Knowledge (Year 4) 5 Marketability
- Capstone Course   • Professional Transformation
- Applied Research
- Client Project

Synthesis (Year 3–4) 4 Professional Practice
- Internship   • Behavioral Development
- Practica
- Social, Attitudinal, Personal
  Development

Analysis (Year 3–4) 3 Integration
- Advanced Courses   • Skill Integration
- Problem Solving Focus   • Client Project
                                 • Proficiency

Application (Year 2–3) 2 Application
- Applied Communication/   • Skill Focus and Competence
  Media Requirements   • Adoption of New Skills
- Secondary Courses

Knowledge (Year 1) 1 Technical
- Introductory Courses   • Broad Skill Sets
                                 • Course Activities

FIG. 9.3.   Elizabethtown College Department of Communications
hierarchical model of integrated experiential learning.
(Copyright © Robert C. Moore, 1985, 1996)

vide for "direct participation in events ... knowledge, skill, or practice derived from direct observation of or participation in events ... something personally encountered, undergone, or lived through" (*Webster's New Collegiate Dictionary*, 1975, quoted in Jernstedt, 1995, p. 359). The experiences were either part of a course, a component of the program, or an experiential course itself.

With the progression of students through sequentially organized opportunities and courses, new learning experiences were added to the increasing expectations of their professors. In the introductory and first-year courses (Stage 1), students were presented with elementary skill sets unique to the courses in which the learner was enrolled. Expectations of students included classroom-based individual and group activities and the development of assessment abilities to evaluate their performance. A focus included students working in cooperative teams, exposure to role responsibilities, and development of elementary professional standards.

Stage 2 of the model was labeled "applied communication." Primarily organized around four media activity requirements, students continued to practice past skill sets along with acquiring new and relevant experiences in a public arena (radio, television, print media, or forensics) while adopting more professional standards and attitudes for their performances. A primary focus at this level was service to a particular media or communications group and segment of the community. These requirements were designed to be second- and third-year-level expectations.

As the student approached the third year of studies, advanced courses incorporated more focused experiential learning opportunities (Stage 3). These generally were client projects requiring an out-of-class, off-campus, professional contact for which real problems were assessed and knowledge and abilities applied as a solution to them. Basic skill sets were developed in the freshman and sophomore years; proficiency was now the focus. The faculty member functioned as a guide, consultant, and mentor. The projects were generally short term and had focused expectations for satisfactory performance in the class and for the client.

In the third year of study, a student who reached a level of proficiency was able to elect experiential opportunities with a more professional focus (Stage 4). These out-of-class experiences, practica, and internships were related but had differing purposes. Enrolling in a practica removed the learner from the actual classroom and placed them with a professional client as a member of their staff. Here they accepted responsibilities on a

part-time basis, performing alongside a professional mentor. Typical
guidelines require a minimum of 10 hours of active engagement with
the sponsoring organization every week for a full semester.

Those students who truly excelled and met other qualifying criteria like
an above-average grade point average, may elect an internship. Expectations for active commitment included a full-time position for an entire
semester. Here, it was expected that the students assume a position with
regular duties mentored by a professional.

In both of these instances, practica and internships, a faculty member
was assigned to the student. The faculty member's duties were to monitor
performance, assess activities, and integrate reflection and meaning to the
experience as a learning tool and not as simply an activity.

Performance was monitored with telephone calls to the student's supervisor, at least one (but usually two) site visits, and weekly submission
of a journal by the student. This journal, not to be confused with a log of
activities, had as its primary function an assessment of the week's responsibilities. It was a retrospective analysis of key perceptions of duties,
events, issues, and people encountered. Students were asked to place the
analysis in the context of past learning and career development.

Activities were assessed through routine visits and by midterm and
final evaluations conducted with the supervisor and student. However,
monthly on-campus seminars focused on a discussion and evaluation
of experiences by all students with the faculty member. The focus of the
sessions was to reflect and give meaning to the experience.

Finally, as summative reflective assessments, the student completed
an ethnographic study of the field setting including its culture and staff
behaviors. A research project accompanied the study analyzing the
theories encountered, evaluating the operation and goals of a typical
site as it compares to the ethnographic study, and assessing the value
of prior learning in the student' s normal course of study to the
experience.

Other exercises designed to bring meaning to the experience included literature summaries of articles directly related to issues, duties,
or responsibilities encountered; a final project as an expression of the
learning experience; and a final evaluation report assessing the overall
experience.

All students completing their BA in Communications enroll in the
capstone course, communications seminar, Stage 5 of the model. Functioning as an instrument to summarize and integrate the previous

seven semesters of learning, the course requirements incorporated expectations that the students demonstrate satisfactory completion of all of the curricular goals and objectives. The seminar takes the form of an independent student learning experience, and the faculty member guides and mentors the student in the preparation of a portfolio, senior applied research thesis and oral defense, and the production of a substantial and fully research-related senior project. Course expectations and requirements were structured so that in completing the course satisfactorily, the learner met all of the expected outcomes of the curriculum and was able to be awarded the degree (see Moore, 1994).

THE EFFECTIVENESS
OF EXPERIENTIAL LEARNING

Conrad and Heden (1995) undertook the evaluation of an experiential education project to assess the various claims of experiential educators and to determine if the touted benefits to students did, in fact, happen. The study focused on secondary school students, but the variables measured (psychological, social, and intellectual development) were the same elements on which experiential programs in higher education are based. It may be possible to extend the results of this study to postsecondary education. However, a definitive study is needed at that level.

Conrad and Heden (1995) reported the following findings. Experiential education programs did have a positive impact on the psychological, social, and intellectual development of the student participants.

Psychological Development

Experiential education programs do lead to personal and psychological growth more so than only formal study. Test results showed significant gains in moral reasoning and increased self-esteem (particularly for those entering career programs).

Social Development

Experienced-based programs helped students develop more responsible attitudes and behaviors. Improved were attitudes toward adults, toward others with whom they interacted, and toward the community in accepting responsibilities in the future.

Intellectual Development

Seventy-three percent of the students reported learning more or much more in experiential programs. Although problem-solving abilities were not significantly different, experiential program students moved more toward a complex pattern of thought with a focus on relational concerns.

In finding the correlates of effectiveness in the study, Conrad and Heden (1995) examined program features, student characteristics, and characteristics of individual experiences. Although clear patterns were found, no clear practice guaranteed effectiveness.

Program Features

Service programs appeared to do better than others, particularly in social and intellectual development. The presence of a formal seminar seemed to be the strongest factor in explaining student change. Length of experience was consistently related to positive student change; intensity was a positive factor to a lesser degree.

Student Characteristics

Only age was a positive indicator of effectiveness. Older students performed better as did more mature students.

Characteristics of Experience

Students rated experiential programs highly and reported social and personal development gains when experiences were interesting, they were shown appreciation for their effort, and they sensed personal gain when given some autonomy.

The results of the study show experiential programs as a "powerful educational vehicle for promoting personal and intellectual development and can do so more effectively than classroom instruction" (Conrad & Heden, 1995, p. 398).

CONCLUSION

The administration of experiential learning programs goes far beyond various logistics of offering courses, learning activities, and internships. Although such administrivia has a place of importance in operation, the issues surrounding the management of programs are far more complex.

The administrator is a curriculum developer. As such, knowledge is integrated with a wide variety of progressive learning experiences that make it likely that a student will make personal and professional connections between knowledge and skills. Little is accomplished if such experiences are isolated events separated from actual learning. Additionally, without serious reflection, experience seldom provides an interactive or significant relation to the individual.

Integrated experiential learning programs join liberal studies and professional education as holistic experiences. Cognitive, attitudinal, and psychomotor development occur hand in hand, leading to proficiency and marketability of the student. Without such a vision, experience seldom prepares a student beyond skills for today. Yet, in an ever-changing world, more integrative learning enables a broader range of problem solving and applicability of skills for new demands to be placed on professionals in the future.

Successful experiential programs, like that at Elizabethtown, require complete support and participation of faculty, involvement of nearly all courses, incremental and progressive building of knowledge and skills, and a method of culminating demonstration, evaluation, and reflection.

Actual administrative structures for these programs can vary from fully institutionally centered to a departmental structure like the one at Elizabethtown. Perhaps the most beneficial structure is a hybrid that allows for a coordination of efforts from both levels. Institutional advantages include central efficiency, joint management of resources, and institutional advocacy. Departmental advantages give the program academic integrity, a discipline focus, and management and interaction by regular faculty seeking to make the experiences more a part of learning. Excellent sources of information, program models, and professional or scholarly interaction in this field are the Association for Experiential Education and the National Society for Experiential Eduaction (see the appendix).

Experiential learning programs are an opportunity for individuals to demonstrate and apply what they have learned. When a program is properly constructed, broad-based skill sets are able to be integrated and advanced to a level of proficiency as applied to increasingly complex problems as knowledge or intellectual ability develops. Ultimately, cognitive, attitudinal, and psychomotor learning converge in the compleat communicator—the new professional.

APPENDIX: EXPERIENTIAL EDUCATION
PROFESSIONAL ASSOCIATIONS

Association for Experiential Education (AEE)
2305 Canyon Boulevard, Suite #100
Boulder, CO 80302
Telephone: 303-440-8844
FAX: 303-440-9581
E-mail: info@aee.org
Website: http: //www.princeton.edu/rcurtis/aee.html

National Society for Experiential Education (NSEE)
3509 Haworth Drive, Suite 207
Raleigh, NC 27609–7229
Telephone: 919-787-3263
FAX: 919-787-3381
E-mail: nsee@datasolv.com
Website: http://www.tripod.com/nsee/

REFERENCES

Bell, M. (1995). What constitutes experience? In R. J. Kraft & J. Kielsmeier (Eds.), *Rethinking theoretical assumptions in experiential learning in schools and higher education* (pp. 9–16). Dubuque, IA: Kendall/Hunt.

Bernstein, R. J. (1971). *Praxis and action: Contemporary philosophies of human activity.* Philadelphia: University of Pennsylvania Press.

Blanchard, R. O., & Christ, W. G. (1993). *Media education and the liberal arts.* Hillsdale, NJ: Lawrence Erlbaum Associates.

Chapman, S., McPhee, P., & Proudman, B. (1995). What is experiential education? In K. Warren, M. Sakofs, & J. Hunt, Jr. (Eds.), *The theory of experiential education* (pp. 235–247). Dubuque, IA: Kendall/Hunt.

Conrad, D., & Heden, D. (1995). National assessment of experiential education: Summary and implications. In R. J. Kraft & J. Kielsmeier (Eds.), *Experiential learning in schools and higher education* (pp. 382–403). Dubuque, IA: Kendall/Hunt.

Dewey, J. (1938). *Experience and education.* New York: Collier.

Druian, G., Owens, T., & Owen, S. (1995). Experiential education: A search for common roots. In R. J. Kraft & J. Kielsmeier (Eds.), *Experiential learning in schools and higher education* (pp. 17–25). Dubuque, IA: Kendall/Hunt.

Garvey, D., & Vorsteg, A. C. (1995). From theory to practice for college student interns: A stage theory approach. In K. Warren, M. Sakofs, & J. Hunt, Jr. (Eds.), *The theory of experiential education* (pp. 297–303). Dubuque, IA : Kendall/Hunt.

Jernstedt, G. C. (1995). Experiential components in academic courses. In R. J. Kraft & J. Kielsmeier (Eds.), *Experiential learning in schools and higher education* (pp. 357–371). Dubuque, IA: Kendall/Hunt.

Joplin, L. (1995). On defining experiential education. In K. Warren, M. Sakofs, & J. Hunt, Jr. (Eds.), *The theory of experiential education* (pp. 15–22). Dubuque, IA: Kendall/Hunt.

Kendall, J. C., Duley, J. S., Little, T. C., Permaul, J. S., & Rubin, S. (1986). *Strengthening experiential education within your institution*. Raleigh, NC: NSIEE.

Moore, R. C. (1985a, October). *Designing change: An undergraduate media specialist program*. Paper presented to the National Society for Internships and Experiential Education, Pittsburgh, PA.

Moore, R. C. (1985b, October). *Internships: An academic experience in the real world*. Paper presented to the National Society for Internships and Experiential Education, Pittsburgh, PA.

Moore, R. C. (1992). Let's retain the undergraduate core. *Feedback, 33*, 15.

Moore, R. C. (1994). The capstone course. In W. G. Christ (Ed.), *Assessing communication education: A handbook for media, speech, and theater educators* (pp. 155–179). Hillsdale, NJ: Lawrence Erlbaum Associates.

Stanton, T. (1995). Internship education: Past achievements/future challenges. In R. J. Kraft & J. Kielsmeier (Eds.), *Experiential learning in schools and higher education* (pp. 142–151). Dubuque, IA: Kendall/Hunt.

Stark, J. S., & Lowther, M. A. (1988). *Strengthening the ties that bind* (The Professional Preparation Network). Ann Arbor: The University of Michigan.

Toffler, A. (1981). *The third wave*. New York: Bantam.

Williamson, J. (1995). Designing experiential curricula. In R. J. Kraft & J. Kielsmeier (Eds.), *Experiential learning in schools and higher education* (pp. 26–31). Dubuque, IA: Kendall/Hunt.

10

Distance Education

Kathy A. Krendl
Ohio University

The term *distance education* can be used to describe many different types of education. For example, correspondence study, the earliest form of distance education, has been in existence for generations, relying on the postal system as its primary distribution system to overcome the distance that separates the student from the instructor (Keegan, 1988). Contemporary use of the term, however, is typically applied to educational contexts in which students and instructors are separated physically but linked electronically using technologies that support high levels of interaction. Often the linkages between students and instructors use a wide array of technologies putting together combinations of media—voice mail, fax, e-mail, Internet, computer conferencing, videoconferencing, and so on. That is, the distinguishing characteristics of distance education as it is used today focus on the use of instructional technology to overcome the boundaries of time and space that separate instructors and students and to enable either real-time or asynchronous interaction between and among instructors and students. The term itself describes many different types of linkages and interactions that can occur between students and instructors (see, e.g., Keegan, 1988; Smith, 1988).

PROGRAMMATIC GOALS

The discussion of distance education is intended to focus this chapter on particular types of technology-based programs and the importance of effective administration in launching and maintaining them successfully. The first rule in distance education administration is the necessity of a clear and demonstrable linkage between the unit mission and goals and the technology application. Any effort to launch and/or administer distance education programs must follow directly from the goals and objectives of the unit or institution. In the absence of clear goals and objectives that are directly served by the program, distance education initiatives are likely to fail in spite of effective administration. Thus, distance education efforts should emerge from an academic unit's strategic planning processes and should contribute in significant ways to fulfilling its mission and objectives. Provided that there is consensus on programmatic goals and principles and agreement that distance education efforts are an appropriate means to fulfill the unit's mission (Christ & Hynes, 1997), distance education can be highly successful both in terms of attracting students (traditional and nontraditional) and in enhancing teaching–learning effectiveness in higher education.

Educational Access

Three goals are typically cited in developing and implementing distance education efforts. The first and most frequently noted is *access*. Educators and policy makers discuss the importance of distance education programs in terms of enhancing access to educational opportunities. Educational access has become increasingly important because of the necessity of lifelong learning for maintaining successful careers in the contemporary workplace. Results of a recent survey suggested that adult respondents across the country reported that lifelong learning has become a necessity for their jobs (Dillman, Christenson, Salant, & Warner, 1995). This national study concluded, "The attitudes and behaviors of people from all age groups, income levels and backgrounds indicate that a large majority of adults recognize the value of lifelong education and training. Getting educated once is not enough in our knowledge-based economy" (Dillman et al., 1995, p. 12). This finding, coupled with recent statistics from the Bureau of Labor Statistics on increasing expenditures by industry in training the U.S. workforce—in 1995, $55.3 billion (Bassi, Gallagher, & Schroer,

1996)—suggest that ongoing training and professional development activities are, indeed, a reality in the contemporary workplace and represent a significant opportunity for higher education institutions.

There is clear evidence that the profile of those seeking higher education is, in fact, changing. Nontraditional students in higher education now outnumber traditional students (Rogers, 1990). Most nontraditional students enroll in higher education courses on a part-time basis. Often the nontraditional student continues to work on a full-time basis and continues to devote time and energy to family life and fulfill other demands while going to school.

The appeal of technology-based instruction for such students is obvious. Distance education technologies provide institutions with the ability to meet increasing demand for higher education using distribution systems that allow the student to participate asynchronously from a distance—in times and places that are convenient for them rather than according to a fixed schedule of time and place. In addition, recent advances in instructional technologies permit the distant student to interact with the instructor, as well as with other students, in flexible and convenient ways regardless of location or time.

Thus, for the nontraditional student, the ability to participate in higher education by means of convenient and flexible technology rather than by commuting to a campus or learning center at a particular time and place after working a full shift and tending to family and community demands is both efficient and appealing. Thus, increasing educational access by creating an educational environment that is responsive to the needs of the part-time, nontraditional student has become a central goal in the discussion of objectives for implementing distance education.

Student Expectations

A second goal for implementing distance education focuses on appealing to the more traditional audience, 18- to 22-year-old college students, and their changing expectations regarding the use of technology in educational settings. Unlike previous generations, these students consider instructional technology to be a natural part of both their educational and entertainment environments. Although the flexibility and convenience offered by instructional technologies are highly desirable characteristics for this audience as well as for nontraditional students, younger students have interests in and expectations of technology that go well beyond these basic traits. These students bring with them to the higher education context significant depth and breadth of technology experience, and, as a result, they have formulated different assumptions about the role of technology in their lives. They assume that technology is designed to help them meet their own unique interests and needs. Today's traditional students have spent many hours performing a variety of instructional tasks in computer labs at school, played hour after hour of video games in video arcades, searched multiple databases in libraries, scanned the endless shelves of video stores in an effort to locate a particular movie that will complement their mood at a particular point in time, and surfed the Internet at all hours in search of information and entertainment. This user-centered, goal-driven approach to technology is quite different from that of earlier generations who consumed mass media content as part of a large, undifferentiated, aggregate audience. Increasingly institutions of higher education are responding to traditional students' expectations by investing heavily in instructional technology and integrating technology-based approaches into instruction.

Teaching–Learning Models

A third goal for integrating technology into instruction through distance education programs focuses on the capabilities of interactive instructional technologies to enhance the teaching–learning process. Many scholars have suggested that one of the most important benefits that both instructors and students gain in a distance education context is the ability to move from an instructor-centered *teaching* model to a student-centered *learning* model (for review, see Krendl, Warren, & Reid, 1996). Using this model, researchers assessing learning outcomes focus on the extent to which students become engaged in learning and create their own understanding of the material rather than measuring the extent to which the student reproduces the material presented by the instructor. Discussions of the differences in student-centered learning and instructor-centered teaching have become prominent in the literature. This learning model, typically associated with constructivism, assumes that learning requires active processing of information that leads to the construction of understanding rather than the acquisition of knowledge (Duffy & Cunningham, 1996).

A number of other goals could be linked to the implementation of distance learning programs such as applying information technology as an instructional tool in teaching students who are preparing for careers that require high levels of sophistication in the use of such tools (e.g., library science or telecommunications). This hands-on approach, requiring students to become familiar and adept with the tools of their trade, has proven to be very effective in evaluation studies of distance education applications (Yoakam, 1997). Regardless of the application being considered, the program administrator must recognize the "goodness of fit" between the initiative being discussed and the anticipated outcomes. That is, the application must represent a reasonable and appropriate means to fulfill the goals and objectives of the program.

PROGRAM DEVELOPMENT
AND MAINTENANCE

Beyond the necessary attention to the relation between the distance education initiative and the intended goals of the program, administrators must consider a series of other concerns in order to launch successful technology-based efforts. The second rule of program administration in distance education begins by recognizing that administering successful distance education programs is directly parallel to administering traditional face-to-face programs. Thinking through the processes and steps that build a strong foundation for a traditional program will be the best preparation for developing and maintaining distance education programs. These include the following steps:

- Audience identification.
- Academic support service.
- Program marketing and promotion.
- Faculty concerns.
- Technical support and system maintenance.
- Evaluation and assessment.
- Fiscal management.

The mechanisms used in identifying, promoting, and distributing traditional programs are seldom analyzed in determining their role in offering effective programs. Imagine, for example, not having a course schedule that is widely distributed to prospective students, scheduling class meetings in rooms that remained locked during class times, or offering classes with extensive required readings that students were expected to locate on their own. In traditional programs, support structures to address such problems are already in place. In distance education environments, they must be addressed in new ways.

Audience Identification

Because distance education opportunities are not bound by geography, students from diverse backgrounds and experiences often come together in these learning environments. Such students often have distinct expectations of particular classes or programs. Thus, significant effort must be invested in identifying the appropriate audience for a given program and communicating clearly with the intended audience the programmatic goals and expectations. These two steps—identifying the audience and the program—are directly linked.

Program Identification

Academic programs emerge for a variety of reasons and in a variety of ways. However, there has not been a strong tradition in most academic fields for ongoing, systematic needs assessment; that is, instituting processes that keep the institution well informed about the emerging educational needs among the population and appropriate mechanisms for responding to those needs. In some cases a full-blown, credit-bearing curriculum may be the solution. In others the answer may be a 1-day, intensive professional development workshop. Appropriate mechanisms for assessing such needs and selecting alternative program strategies are not in place at many institutions. The solution is an ongoing commitment of resources and personnel to conducting needs assessment as a fundamental aspect of program administration.

Academic Support Systems

Effective distance education programs must be administered in such a way that the student can easily access institutional resources, (e.g., registration, financial aid and student advising) and instructional resources (readings, journals, etc.) from a distance. Most institutions have traditionally required students to access such support services by coming to the campus at designated times and specific locations. Such an approach will not work in a distance education context. Students will continue to require support services, but they will expect them to be delivered to them in flexible and convenient ways. Institutions are beginning to experiment with innovative solutions to these problems. Online advising systems, Internet-based resources on (and online applications for) financial aid, telephone registration systems, and online library resources are now in place at many institutions.

Program Marketing and Promotion

Most academic administrators expend little attention or time on marketing and promotion efforts for their programs. However, in the distance education context this nonissue will quickly become an issue of prime importance for the successful administrator. Higher education has become increasingly competitive, and much of the competition revolves around outreach and distance education programs. The notion of an institution having a particular service region with identifiable physical boundaries is in direct contradiction to technology systems that enable an institution to market and distribute its programs globally. The challenge to administrators will be to identify appropriate and effective marketing tools for promoting distance education programs to target audiences.

Faculty Concerns

Course and Program Development. Traditional procedures have been established to define faculty rights and responsibilities in defining curriculum, developing courses and programs, and teaching them in formats that instructors consider appropriate. Policies and practices must be developed to facilitate these processes in distance education. Again, we can use the model of the necessary steps for developing traditional courses as the template for considering necessary processes for technology-based programs.

We have already noted that curriculum for distance education applications will, to a much greater extent, be dependent on student needs to be identified through ongoing needs assessment rather than exclusively on faculty initiative. These needs will then be considered by faculty as opportunities for curricular development. Faculty will also require more information about prospective students, their technical capabilities, access to technology, and their specific needs and interests in the program (e.g., is it a requirement for professional certification) in order to make informed decisions regarding appropriate technology platforms and appropriate formats (e.g., credit or noncredit) to be used for delivering the program.

Course and program development will also represent new challenges for faculty accustomed to teaching in traditional formats and classrooms. Just as technology becomes more central to the distribution process in distance education, it will become much more central in the presentation of content, as well as the structure of the class. Instructors in most cases do not have the technical or design expertise to take full advantage of the possibilities offered by distance education technologies.

Team Orientation. As a result, many successful distance education programs have adopted a production team orientation to course and program development. The instructor serves as the content expert, with instructional design and technology experts also sitting at the planning table, working together to create effective course materials that realize the benefits of a wide range of content, design, and distribution expertise. This model, often used in producing curricular-based television content, has altered the role of the instructor. The instructor's content expertise is central to the program planning process. However, the instructor is no longer the distribution vehicle as well as the content provider. Because the primary interface with students will now be technology driven rather than face to face, instructional design expertise also becomes very important in preparing materials. The presentation of visual materials, the application of graphic design principles, and the preparation of online instructional resources that can be accessed asynchronously and repeatedly to meet students' needs all benefit from the presence of an instructional designer on the production team.

In some cases a librarian or instructional resource expert may also be included on the production team. This individual's role is to work with the instructor to explore how students will get access to required materials, how to make readings and research material available online, how students at a distance will learn to conduct information searches, and so on.

This team approach can be very successful in taking full advantage of the planning process and exploring creative alternatives to traditional face-to-face instruction. However, working as part of a team in preparing a class or program is a foreign process to many faculty. This change in the faculty member's role is directly related to the fact that distance education typically adopts a strong student orientation. We discussed the student-centered learning model earlier as one of the central goals of implementing distance education and instructional technology programs. Focusing the role of the faculty member on content expertise and placing significant emphasis on planning to produce effective course materials and to facilitate ease of access to materials is a direct result of a student-centered orientation typical of distance education programs.

Faculty Development. Clearly faculty roles and responsibilities will change with the implementation of distance education programs. As a result, one of the most valuable investments program administrators can make is a serious commitment to ongoing faculty development. In many institutions there has been a tradition of very modest resource allocation faculty development. Yet as faculty roles change and new opportunities emerge, institutions are obligated to help instructors make the transition to fulfilling new roles within the organization. A strong emphasis on an aggressive and highly visible faculty development program that outlines exciting opportunities for faculty and assists them in developing new skills and tools to realize these opportunities will serve the institution, the administrator, the faculty, the program, and the students well.

Rewards and Incentives. Program administrators must also give careful consideration to rewards and incentives for faculty participation in distance education development. Because new skills and approaches are required in teaching via distance education, faculty need to receive a clear message about the importance of developing programs and materials to serve new audiences in new ways. Basic issues include whether or not teaching distance education courses count as part of an instructor's regular teaching load, or is it treated as an overload; whether or not distance education program development and curriculum innovation count toward tenure and promotion deliberations; and if the new program is not successful, whether or not faculty involved in the program are considered to be responsible for the failure. These are difficult issues that need to be addressed by the administrator, and the answers to such questions will inform faculty about the importance of the initiative and its centrality to the unit's goals. Distance education efforts will seldom be successful without strong administrative support and attention. Providing clear incentives and rewards for faculty involved in developing such programs is a simple and direct way of demonstrating support. This is especially true in determining the value of such contributions in tenure and promotion deliberations. Unless the faculty member's activities in distance education programs are included in these deliberations—indicating that they are highly valued by the unit, the administrator, and the institution—it is unlikely that faculty will give serious consideration to such ventures.

Changing Roles.   Visionaries discuss changes in faculty roles that will emerge as technology becomes a more integral part of education and learning not as an incremental process but rather as a revolutionary one. As institutions work individually and as members of consortia to create new structures and procedures, they begin by articulating a new vision for higher education. One example comes from a consortium of large (Big 10) public institutions in the Midwest. The consortium's Learning Technology Task Force issued a position paper that began with its vision for the institutions:

> We envision a future in which the CIC [Big 10] universities are leaders in a transformation of undergraduate and graduate learning made possible by the ubiquitous availability and coordinated use of advanced technologies. The cooperative development and use of these technologies will enable our faculties to provide superior learning experiences and opportunities more efficiently to more students where and when they need them. The CIC universities will realize both academic and economic benefits through consortia mechanisms for sharing technological platforms, teaching resources, library materials, faculty, courses, and even degree programs. Through their commitment to work together to realize this vision—collaborating and sharing resources, ideas, and directions—the CIC universities will continue to lead higher education in meeting the educational and research needs of the United States. (CIC Learning Technology Task Force, 1996, p. 2)

At the state level, policymakers have weighed in as well, appointing study groups and task forces and issuing reports that outline new visions for higher education. One such report, *Technology in the Learning Communities of Tomorrow: Beginning the Transformation*, discussed the role of faculty as follows:

> The approaches educators choose in integrating technology with the curriculum and in using technology to transform their own roles will be the critical element in the successful creation of learning communities .
> The learning communities of the future will be built by educators who unlock the potential of technology as a tool for accessing learning opportunities that once would have been inaccessible and doing things that

once would have been impossible. (Ohio Technology in Education Steering Committee, 1996, p. 13)

Intellectual Property.   Lively debate has focused on a final aspect of the instructor's role in distance education programs: Who owns the intellectual property rights associated with materials developed using a team approach with faculty members as content experts, technical and support staff as technical consultants, librarians as instructional resource staff, and instructional designers as experts in the design and presentation of the material? Several institutions have been experimenting with policies related to intellectual property concerns. Increasingly the program administrator must be aware of and protective of institutional investments in distance education program materials and products. The textbook model in which the publisher agrees to publish and promote the text and the author receives royalties generated by the sale of the book does not apply to distance education products. The institution, as well as the instructor, has invested significantly in the creation of the product. Although the instructor has provided content expertise, other staff within the institution have provided expertise as well. In addition, the institution's investment in the technology infrastructure that supports the development of technology-based programs represents a significant contribution to the resulting product.

Thus, administrators must protect institutional interest in product development and revenue sharing at the outset of the project. The instructor and all other staff involved in the project must understand from the very beginning what their interests and ownership rights will be in the final product. Typical questions that arise include:

- Can other faculty use the materials to teach the class?
- How will revenues generated by the sale of the materials be split?
- If the faculty member leaves the institution, does the material remain with the institution to support the course, or depart with the faculty member?

Administrators must be prepared to answer such questions before they arise and should deal with them at the outset of any project.

Technical Support and System Maintenance

Despite the very best and most ambitious faculty development, instructors will never achieve the level of expertise necessary to support and maintain the new instructional technologies that will be applied in distance education programs. Instructors will grow in their level of understanding the capabilities of technology, and they will continue to experiment with emerging technologies that develop. However, their role as content experts will focus their energy on remaining current and comprehensive in their knowledge base and on facilitating student-centered learning.

A critical measure of the success of any distance education program is the skill level and response time of its technical support staff. The level of necessary training and sophistication in managing technology systems will continue to increase. Skilled technical experts are already necessary to support and maintain distance education systems. Thus, the program administrator must commit significant resources to staffing and supporting the technical aspects of distance education systems.

Suggestions for how to structure an efficient and effective distance education maintenance operation were outlined in a recent paper (Yoakam, 1997). According to Yoakam:

> Technical management of a distance learning system entails effective utilization of personnel and equipment resources in supporting day-to-day operations, troubleshooting and problem resolution, ongoing maintenance, and change management for expansion and upgrades to systems. Personnel involved in technical support must be sufficiently trained on the equipment they will be expected to support and must have easy access to detailed documentation about system operation and problem–resolution procedure. (p. 3)

He pointed out that in selecting technical support staff, administrators should give careful consideration to their responsibilities for long-term technology planning, as well as to short-term troubleshooting.

Evaluation and Assessment

We mentioned earlier the importance of ongoing needs assessment to maintain a dynamic inventory of student needs and interests. A similar approach should be adopted in considering how to conduct evaluations and assessments of distance education; that is, evaluation and assessment should be ongoing dynamic processes rather than summative conclusions about program or course effectiveness.

Typically, evaluation is used to discuss the effectiveness of the total program, whereas assessment refers to mastery of material related to specific courses (Warren, Reid, & Krendl, 1996). First, consider the goal of evaluation of the program as a whole. Program evaluation should begin by reviewing the unit's goals and objectives in designing and implementing distance education. As mentioned earlier, those goals may include increasing educational access, reaching out to new audiences, adopting student-centered learning models, or other programmatic goals. The strategies used and the issues addressed in program evaluation should be directly related to these goals. The overriding question in program evaluation should be: To what extent were the unit's programmatic goals and objectives realized in the distance education program? Such an all-encompassing question will involve consideration of many dimensions of program performance.

For example, in distance education programs the student support services often become as important as or perhaps more important than the course and materials themselves. If a student is unable to register for a course, obtain academic advising, or arrange for financial aid from a distance, the learning process that emerges from enrolling in a course may never begin for that student. Thus, services that provide necessary support for the program are central in determining the extent to which the program achieved the programmatic goals identified at the outset and therefore must be addressed in the evaluation plan. Typically, program evaluation emphasizes the extent to which the student-centered orientation at the core of most distance education programs is successful in delivering quality educational opportunities that are highly accessible to participants.

Similarly, in considering strategies for assessing learning outcomes and mastery of course material, administrators must, again, identify appropriate strategies. The emphasis in traditional course assessment is on instructor performance—were the lectures clear, were the tests fair, was the instructor prepared for class, and so on. However, as discussed earlier, the role of the instructor in the distance education course changes dramatically. The instructor is part of a team that includes instructional designers, technical experts, and instructional resource experts, as well as support staff on a day-to-day basis. Thus, the instructor's role should be assessed as part of a much larger instructional delivery and learning process. Assessments of learning in distance education programs reflect the dominance of the student-centered orientation and the emphasis on student learning.

The most comprehensive assessment and evaluation programs adopt multiple methods in their research strategies. The focus of the process should remain on the extent to which the programmatic goals were achieved, but evaluators rely on a wide array of analytic tools in reaching conclusions. One researcher suggested the use of an evaluation matrix, which includes diverse research tools and methods to explore evaluation and assessment issues (Thompson, 1996). He advocated the use of anecdotal records, expert review checklists, focus group discussions, formative review logs, implementation logs, personal interviews, survey instruments, and user interface ratings in analyzing program effectiveness and preparing evaluation reports.

Fiscal Management

For the most part, studies of the cost-effectiveness of distance education programs have emerged from commercial applications of technology systems in delivering training to employees. However, administrators in higher education are now being asked to account for the return on the significant technology investments necessary to make distance education work effectively.

We have identified the additional staffing and training needs for distance education in previous sections. However, distance education systems also require huge capital investments at the outset. Administrators are accustomed to dealing with capital projects that result in bricks and mortar in the shape of classroom buildings; now they must become accustomed to capital projects that build the necessary technology infrastructure for delivering distance education programs. Like the classroom buildings, there will also be ongoing support and maintenance costs associated with the use of the technology infrastructure; that is, equipment will fail, parts will be replaced, and new components and upgrades will be added. Line charges for system operation will also be incurred and should be included in any calculation of costs associated with implementing distance education programs. If we include resources in the form of incentives and rewards to encourage faculty to make the transition from the instructor-centered teaching model to the student-centered learning model, even more costs will be realized.

Clearly, program administrators must attend to the full range of costs associated with distance education program implementation, and they must include them in calculations of program cost-effectiveness. In doing so, however, they should also attend to the full range of costs associated with traditional, face-to-face education. Campus infrastructure is hardly free—buildings, utilities, offices, and real estate all cost real dollars. Yet many prospective students are unable to benefit from the physical investments in the campus environment. Increasing educational access and attracting new audiences to higher education are compelling goals for infrastructure investment and for launching distance education programs.

CONCLUSION

The approach adopted in this chapter is to suggest that, for the most part, administering distance education programs is very similar to administering traditional academic programs. A logical outline of the steps involved in developing traditional programs provides a reasonable template for doing so in a distance education context. The challenge has been to articulate those steps as part of the broader discussion about profound changes in the educational landscape today—the need to serve a more diverse student population, adopt a more student-centered approach to teaching and learning, and respond to the high demand for education throughout the life cycle. However, the same issues and problems that have challenged administrators in traditional, face-to-face instructional contexts in the past resource limitations, faculty concerns, infrastructure support and maintenance, and so on—are now emerging in discussion of implementing distance education programs. The goal of this chapter has been to articulate the necessary steps for successful administration of any program with special attention to the distance education context. This "cookbook" approach is intended to assist administrators in the successful integration of distance education programs into their units.

REFERENCES

Bassi, L. J., Gallagher, A. L., & Schroer, E. P. (1996). *American Society for Training and Development Data Book.* Alexandria, VA: American Society for Training and Development.

Christ, W. G., & Hynes, T. (1997). Missions and purposes of journalism and mass communication: An AEJMC–ASJMC Joint Committee Report. *Journalism and Mass Communication Educator, 52*(2), 73–100.

CIC Learning Technology Task Force. (1996). *Report to the CIC Provosts.* Champaign, IL: Author.

Dillman, D. A., Christenson, J. A., Salant, P. & Warner, P. D. (1995). *What the public wants from higher education* (Tech. Rep. No. 95–52). Pullman: Social and Economic Sciences Research Center, Washington State University.

Duffy, T. M., & Cunningham, D. J. (1996). Constructivism: Implications for the design and delivery of instruction. In D. A. Jonassen (Ed.), *Handbook of research for educational communications and technology* (pp. 170–198). New York: Macmillan.

Keegan, D. (1988). Theories of distance education: Introduction. In D. Sewart, D. Keegan, & B. Holmberg (Eds.), *Distance education: International perspectives* (pp. 63–67). London: Routledge.

Krendl, K. A., Warren, R., & Reid, K. A. (1997). Distance learning. In W. G. Christ (Ed.), *Media education assessment handbook* (pp. 99–122). Mahwah, NJ: Lawrence Erlbaum Associates.

Rogers, S. M. (1990, Summer). Educational applications of the NREN. *EDUCOM Review*, pp. 25–29.

Smith, J. K. (1988). The evaluation/researcher as person vs. the person as evaluator/researcher. *Educational Researcher, 17*(2), 18–23.

Ohio Technology in Education Steering Committee. (1996). *Technology in the learning communities of tomorrow: Beginning the transformation*. Columbus, OH: Author.

Thompson, C. (1996). *Evaluation tools*. Atlanta: Georgia Technical Research Institute.

Warren, R. G., Reid, K. A., & Krendl, K. A. (1996). *Building communication environments in distance education*. Paper presented at the annual meeting of the Speech Communication Association, San Diego, CA.

Yoakam, M. (1997). *Technical support: A model for multi-site interactive distance learning*. Bloomington: Indiana University.

III

ADMINISTRATIVE CHALLENGES

11

Leadership

L. Brooks Hill
Trinity University

The urgency of effective leadership, both its practice and its study, is well documented in the early literature of Eastern and Western civilizations, and probably was a serious consideration in all civilizations if we could reconstruct their discussions. In Eastern civilization, for example, the Chinese provided extensive advice for military leaders (Sun-tzu, 1993), and the current value of this advice is manifest in the extensive use of such Chinese classics in all military academies of the United States and elsewhere throughout the world (Ames, 1993). Interestingly, these books dealt with psychological warfare and essential communication aspects of such strategies and tactics. In Western civilization the ancient Greeks and Romans from Homer and Hesiod onward struggled with the qualities of the hero and whether those qualities could be taught or were gifts of the gods. Ultimately accepting the promise of instruction, they began to develop prescriptive guidelines and principles of effective leadership in government and the military. Here again, communication was an essential component as Homer depicted the hero as a speaker of words and a doer of deeds. In both civilizations the tradition of *imitatio* or imitation, modeling, and mentoring was never replaced by instruction alone (Clark, 1957), and often the lessons of leadership emerged in historical and biographical commentaries about prominent leaders.

From these powerful roots have emerged significant traditions regarding leadership, and for well over two millenia scholars and practitioners have wrestled with the principles and guidelines of effective leadership and the appropriate preparation of leaders. Accordingly, the purpose of this chapter is to distill from this history a framework for effective leadership in the modern academic environment. Building on these vast and diverse resources, this chapter primarily relies on more recent interpretations, but not simply to endorse these positions because of their modernity, but rather to challenge them in terms of some lessons from the ancient sources that may have fallen through the cracks of our social scientific approach to modern leadership. Those of us in the United States should never forget that our modern, technologically trained forces in Vietnam were overcome by leadership operating consistently with the Chinese classics written over 2,000 years before and modestly adapted by Mao Tse-Tung. Within this somewhat unusual perspective, several years of departmental leadership will guide the assessment of current traditions, the development of an alternative framework, and the formulation of some indispensable principles for effectiveness of leaders in the academy.

CONTEMPORARY PERSPECTIVES

An overview of modern literature reveals three traditional approaches and multiple adaptations of these approaches for the study of leadership (Northouse, 1997):

1. A trait approach emphasizes the qualities or traits of effective leaders, how these qualities are variously manifest, and the techniques for the cultivation of these qualities.
2. A situational approach suggests that effective leaders address the functional demands of any situation. Attention focuses on the identification of these functions, the adaptation to meet these expectations, and the sharing of leadership responsibilities.
3. The styles approach attempts to classify the diverse leadership styles, to help students identify their patterned tendencies, and to depict the adjustment of style to unique demands of any situation.
4. Crossing the prior alternatives are attempts to reconceptualize leadership as a distinct set of activities separate from management and administration, and to develop other variations of the more traditional approaches.

In perspective, all of these positions are insightful and helpful in dealing with the very complex subject of leadership, and extensive scholarship variously supports or rejects them (Hunt, 1991; Northouse, 1997). Each of these positions, however, is alone insufficient to capture the art of leadership. What follows is a brief explanation of the strengths and weaknesses of the more traditional, first three approaches, and of the reconceptualization and selected hybrids. From this consideration should emerge the justification for an alternative framework that accentuates both the social scientific and humanistic and artistic contributions to this area of study.

Trait Approach

Simply stated, this approach suffers from the difficulties (a) of specifying the traits that constitute effective leadership and (b) of explaining how much of each trait one needs in order to cope best in different situations. Similar to difficulties in personality research, these problems complicate enormously social scientific research about the usefulness of this approach. Despite these scholarly problems, the trait approach remains prominent in conventional wisdom, and nearly anyone "on the street" can tell us who is and is not a good leader and why. If we scholars will listen, and possibly even use the techniques of analytic philosophy and ethnomethodology, these same folks will further identify the presence or absence of essential qualities for leadership. This conventional wisdom is further reinforced by biographies and media that often build arguments about the success or failure of a leader around the presence or absence of certain leadership qualities. Simply because we cannot define and measure the variables scientifically should not exclude them from our consideration (Maccoby, 1981).

The scholarly unpopularity of the trait approach is not, however, exclusively a consequence of social science, but may also stem from our broader social and political environment. The apparent shortcomings of this approach, especially within an egalitarian worldview, may obscure its widespread influence on nearly any consideration of leadership. In earlier periods of history those people expected to assume positions of leadership were smaller in number and prepared in rather predictable patterns to assume such positions. They were, in turn, assessed as good, bad, or indifferent leaders dependent on how well they met those preconceived notions of leadership. On the more contemporary scene, with vast numbers of potential leaders prepared in a wide diversity of circumstances, the notions of leadership are so different that anyone may uniquely demonstrate leadership potential with or without any predictable set of traits. Contrary, however, to this professed egalitarianism in which nearly anyone can become a leader is the presence in nearly all personal evaluation schemes of reoccuring traits or qualities that are used to determine the outcome of an evaluation (Hill, 1984). Expressed another way, with more restricted paths of leadership positions, people could spell out the traits that served as criteria for assessing their leaders, but with expanded prospects the traits are ostensibly diffused to permit greater opportunity. In reality, these traits reappear as insidious criteria in our evaluations of each other's performance (Hill, 1984). Despite the problems with the trait approach, we may need to recognize its prominent role in our thinking and treat it more explicitly in a framework for effective leadership.

Situational Approach

Essentially, this approach assumes that the functional requirements for successful group work in our complex society are so diverse that one person can rarely meet the needs. Instead, leadership is a shared phenomenon that emerges from group behavior as the situation may demand. Even though one or another person may serve as a designated leader, the more objective leadership functions are shared by many, and the successful designated leader is the one who can wisely coordinate the collective efforts in the achievement of group goals and objectives. In a pluralistic, egalitarian society that prides itself on individual achievement, this approach is very attractive as more individuals can participate in group leadership, thus enhancing group cohesion, satisfaction, and commitment, as well as reinforcing our individualism and presumed objectivity. Because our society involves such widespread dependence on group work but often lacks a genuine commitment to the group over individual achievement, this approach is confounded over conflicting leadership functions, who should perform which ones in terms of situational needs, and how one might coordinate the results. As anyone who has taught small group communication can attest, groups often fail because they flounder with uncertainty about who should do what to whom in what situations with what preferred effects. In other words, the essential assumption of this approach may be correct about the inadequacy of one person, but the solution suggested by this approach is often weak.

From another angle, the problems of this approach are merely the other side of its strengths. The literature has carefully identified and classified the many leadership functions needed by groups (Gulley, 1968). From this accomplishment any approach to leadership can benefit. However, the infinite variation of situational demands accentuates the inherent problems of any such classification system. In a fashion parallel to the trait approach, what are the functions and, more importantly, which ones in what combinations are most important in any given situation? The illusions of success from this approach derive from its application in contexts of predictable constraints. If, for example, we can spell out the limitations of a situation, we may better identify the instrumental needs to achieve the broader goals of the group, and we can then train people to work within this presumed framework. However, what we ignore is the entrenchment of myopic vision as we simultaneously restrict creative potential. To be sure we can train people to lead effectively within carefully defined circumstances, but what happens when the group needs deviance from the entrenched patterns to address unusual and unpredicted contingencies? This line of reasoning underscores the troublesome efforts of so much U.S. industry when confronted by intense competition from foreign groups with more vital alternatives. On the one hand, we know a lot about situational needs for leadership as a result of this approach, but, on the other hand, it has created a seriously restricted delusion of effectiveness. To an artist, this approach is somewhat like painting by the numbers. Its real value may ultimately result from its integration in a more comprehensive framework.

Styles Approach

If we dig past the layers of trainer jargon and nifty gridworks, the styles approach is little more than an adaptation of the much maligned trait approach with accommodations to situational demands. This hybrid attempts to categorize leader qualities into patterns or styles that can then be measured and characterized for examination of necessary adjustments to address the diverse needs of varied situations. One of the more popular versions, for example, uses a square divided into quadrants and locates one's style based on self-assessed placement on continua with such anchors as task and people orientation (Blake &

Mouton, 1964, 1985). Additional criteria and continua reflect the ever-increasing imagination of management trainers who are continuously creating new approaches to describe our patterned tendencies and how they may need adjustment for different corporate tasks. If we continue to peel the layers of this onion, we repeatedly encounter the problems of any such system. Despite the remarkable creativity manifest in some of these packages, they are little more than reclustering of personality tendencies within a set of more or less explicit assumptions about situational needs. The resulting problems are, therefore, similar to those already addressed, but the creative personalization and accentuated situational accommodation may mislead us to imagine this approach as more effective than it can be. Like a sailboat, the inherent limitations of design constrain its maximum potential.

Outside the context of management training are other variations on the leadership styles approach. Although less explicitly developed around personal characteristics, these approaches still attempt to categorize sets of personal tendencies and then profile these categories as styles. Examination of these approaches reveals additional problems. Less obvious is the recurrent tendency to array styles on a continuum based on relative degrees of control. For example, the typical continuum might anchor one end with the authoritarian style and the other end with a laissez-faire style (Barnlund & Haiman, 1960). Between the anchors are other styles with varied amounts of control. Presentation of this type of approach often includes ingenious labels for the variations on the continuum, such as gamesman, artist, and other labels that accentuate the values of the middle zone of the continuum and of maximum flexibility (Tucker, 1984). Despite the attractiveness of these characterizations, they are undermined by questionable assumptions: Nearly all of these systems presume a democratic framework and a linear progression of styles. Despite our cultural commitment to democracy, much organizational behavior is undemocratic, and linearity restricts our understanding of the interrelations among these styles and the potential for greater latitudes of flexibility.

Reconceptualization and Other Variations

Perceived and actual shortcomings of the preceding approaches have encouraged people to reexamine the concept of leadership. Perhaps, they argue, we have overextended the concept to cover the enormous complexity of our current social system, thereby rendering the idea of leadership useless. To correct this overextension and yet salvage the essence of a deeply entrenched concept, one reconceptualization differentiates among leadership, management, and administration (Zaleznik, 1977). In some ways this is a good idea. It fits the egalitarian, democratic, individualistic features of our cultural worldview, as it sets leadership aside to embrace the more subjective, artistic, creative, visionary aspects and relegates to management and administration the more pedestrian functions of daily organizational life. Furthermore, this reconceptualization certainly reinforces the situational and styles approaches. Within this position we can presumably objectify what needs to be done and specify the adjustments of our style to meet these expectations. Unfortunately, this reconceptualization begs the issues by overlooking the problematic assumptions involved: Do we really enhance the potential to perform our position of leadership by defining the creative (i.e., leadership function) out of consideration and focusing our attention on the more pedestrian (i.e., administrative and management functions)? Regardless of desirability, this often results from an emphasis on management and administrative responsibilities. Curiously enough, recent fads in "adventure learning" or "survivalist" management training illustrate the wild attempts to escape the pedestrian aspects of positions of leadership and reemphasize the development of personal and social qualities so crucial for increasingly competitive situations that demand leadership.

Unlike the more traditional positions, efforts to reconceptualize leadership do not represent a coherent approach. Instead what one finds is discussion of reconceptualization as a prerequisite for the defense of some variations on the other approaches. In other words, redefinition of leadership precedes hybrid positions and training programs built on the perceived inadequacies of existing approaches. Consistent with Hunt's (1991) multilevel approach, for example, leadership training with middle-level management in the federal government can potentially create disastrous results because the bureaucracy may not require leaders, but needs instead administrators and managers who can allocate resources and execute highly restrictive sets of rules. A better approach might be to calculate just how much the trainees can handle at each level and carefully adapt to the situations they must address (Hunt, 1991). With extensive background in government training and consulting, I can confirm the intense frustration of employees and the dangers to their workplace from excessive information and inspiration about leadership. Yet to admit this problem undercuts our wholesale endorsement of the egalitarian, everyone-as-potential-leader, democratic mythology replacing it with skillful manipulation from above. It may seem to be cultural heresy, but the manipulative actions of those senior officials may represent good examples of effective leadership. The best advice for senior administrators is to beware the external trainer who lacks sensitivity to organizational realities.

Other variations have grown from these efforts to reconceptualize leadership and/or to synthesize ideas from the three traditional approaches. Whatever their origins, these positions represent creative efforts to overcome perceived shortcomings of what is available. Among these variations are three conceptions especially useful for the alternative developed later. First, Fiedler's (1967) extensive work on leadership led him to a contingency model that draws particularly on the strengths of the situational and styles approaches. A distinctive advantage of this conception is attention to the flexible adaptation for essential situational demands. Second, drawing on the need to revitalize the creative and visionary aspects of leadership, the concept of transformational leadership has inspired extensive research by several other scholars (Burns, 1978; Tichy & Devanna, 1986). Essential to this position is the integration of features from all three of the traditional approaches. The position accentuates qualities of transformational leaders that differentiate them from their lesser counterparts; stylistic patterns of creative, imaginative, and innovative concerns; and a strong value-driven energy for the implementation of a new vision for the group. A final variation seems to have spun away from the situational approach to emphasize the democratic potential of emergent leadership and the ultimate effectiveness of a designated leader who can discern and coordinate this creative potential that derives from the social energy of the group (Bormann, 1990). From these ingenious extensions and variations of traditional approaches emerges an alternative uniquely appropriate for the academy.

TOWARD AN ALTERNATIVE FRAMEWORK

From the preceding overview of contemporary perspectives derives a set of assumptions about leadership, both its practice and study, which creates the foundation for an alternative model. These assumptions fall into two groups. The first addresses some general aspects of leadership that frame any approach and that stem from ancient lessons current research sometimes ignores. The second group identifies salient aspects of the traditional approaches and hybrid variations particularly useful for an alternative. Following a consideration of these assumptions will come an alternative model and an explanation of its dynamic integration of the assumptions and of its relative advantages.

Ancient Lessons

Throughout ancient literature, the fascination with heroes, both mythical and real, suggests an assumption of great importance for all ages: *Leadership is a rare commodity.* The significance of this assumption grows out of its several implications. People are rarely leaders on a routine and daily basis. If we expect ourselves or anyone else to perform according to some ideal conception of leadership on a regular basis, then we will be plagued by frustrations and disappointments. Instead, leadership is episodic and manifest when someone brings insightful understanding to bear on a situation that permits remarkable accomplishment. So, whoever may be the designated leaders, they may or may not have the opportunity to lead or have situations that invite leadership. Most people in positions of leadership must on a daily basis perform rather pedestrian tasks and activities. Their leadership potential can and will emerge only as situations permit. Many people in these positions of leadership may never provide leadership themselves, but they may create situations in which other members of their group may effectively lead on one or another occasion. One of the semantic beauties of the phrase "position of leadership" is that it does not necessarily require a person in that position to perform the leadership activities. Insofar as a person can create situations in which others can excel, we may accurately assign credit to the designated leader for fulfilling leadership responsibilities. Rather than forcing people to become what they cannot become, maybe we need to concentrate more on helping people realize what needs to be done and achieving those goals.

Not only the ancient literature, but a lot of contemporary thinking as well, has attacked the sequential, linear approach to complicated phenomena. Thus, from a more Eastern perspective comes the second assumption: *Leadership is a more circular, rather than linear, process.* Any group of communication scholars can readily indict a linear model, even though the language we use to discuss our processes tends to emphasize sequential linearity. In stark contrast, Asian philosophers tend to address processes more holistically and use circles, rather than straight lines, to capture process dynamics. The Chinese fretted balls, an art form of carving balls within balls, provides a metaphorical vehicle for addressing leadership. What are the central, distinctive features of the persons in positions of leadership? What are the emergent styles of various leaders who might differently address the surrounding tasks? What situational demands generate group goals and set the course of leadership? In other words, the prominent sets of variables identified by the three traditional approaches to leadership are actually spheres within spheres with virtually unlimited combinations of leadership potential.

Consistent with the two preceding lessons from antiquity comes a third assumption: *Leadership defies neat categorization*. At any given time, nearly any person with a widely varied set of characteristics might emerge as uniquely capable of dealing with any possible situation. With that sort of unlimited variation, efforts to capture leadership in neat categories are seriously restrained. This does not mean, however, that we should not classify styles, categorize traits, or otherwise define circumstances. Instead, this assumption warns us to be more wary of the deception of our category system. Obviously we need to categorize for pedagogical purposes, but how we manage this material will dictate the learning and leadership potential we can generate. This assumption also implies a lesson for followers. Those who are not designated leaders must understand how our behavior can restrain the potential for leadership to emerge. Often these restraints grow out of a mindless imposition of unrealistic or inappropriate categories we create and reinforce. If we could simply remember the rich potential of a kaleidoscopic approach, perhaps we would realize the advantages of more effective leadership.

The final ancient lesson for treatment here is a reasonable extension and outgrowth of the preceding three: *Leadership is an art*. Despite the foundational value of our social scientific research, leadership represents a wonderful combination of the predictable and the unpredictable. In fact, some of the most exciting historical episodes of brilliant leadership built on the irrational or at least on such a radical departure from the currently predictable as to redefine the framework of rationality covering the situation involved. For centuries writers have spoken of the beauty of effective leadership, implicitly recognizing the creativity, imagination, and visionary aspects. Our social scientific reduction of this art and our consequent efforts to prescribe the ways to achieve leadership have eroded our recognition of the artistry involved. Perhaps one finds here a motivating idea behind the emergence of humanistic social sciences that argue for more holistic, and in many ways artistic, treatments of human behavior. As we scholars and teachers attempt to understand and to prescribe, we often inhibit the dynamics of the humane arts we circumscribe. In no place is this truer than for the art of leadership. Fortunately, on the current scene we are restoring the mentoring activities of the age-old apprenticeships as a way of teaching about the holistic dimensions of this art. Lest we compromise our potential, more needs be done.

Recent Lessons

From the situational approach comes extensive and convincing literature about the centrality, as well as diversity, of situational requirements. This lesson generates an essential assumption: *Central to effective leadership is successful completion of situational demands.* Nearly anyone will confirm that "getting the job done" is a critical aspect of leadership. However, this line of thought subtly shifts attention to three interrelated questions: What are the situational demands? What constitutes successful completion of them? Who must actually do the work involved? Many, if not most, situations provide an array of expectations. The effective leader can identify those tasks, order them according to relative importance, and communicate the importance of that hierarchy. Only with agreement and consent of those being led will this definition of situational demands permit the exercise of leadership. From the definition of the situation should also emerge the criteria of successful completion. Without this potential for closure, groups become aimlessly constrained by process and frustrated by what they perceive as endless meetings and wasted time. Because of the many demands, skillful leaders will recognize self-limitations and relegate responsibility to the lowest level of potential completion of tasks. Effective relegation, coordination, and communication of results and credit for achievement translate as prudent fulfillment of situational demands.

People who work in complex organizations intuitively recognize the value of separating leadership from management and administration, but they also have many examples of the inseparability of these three sets. From this lesson comes another critical assumption: *The inextricable, interdependent functions of leadership, management, and administration encompass the situational demands.* To this stage in the chapter, I have deliberately avoided definitions, but have tried instead to insinuate functional distinctions. Restated, leadership tends to embrace the creative, imaginative, and visionary aspects; management tends to involve the allocation and coordination of available resources: and administration tends to include the translation and implementation of institutional and unit rules and procedures. To keep these definitions loose fits the concept of the inextricability and interdependence of these three function clusters. To separate them more definitely restrains the potential of realizing their interdependence. Most departmental chairpersons, for example, live in a world of administrative constraint, modest management opportunities, and rare leadership prospects. If acknowledged by the chair and colleagues, this more realistic perspective could enable more chairs to fit comfortably in the position of leadership they hold.

The concept of leadership styles is deeply entrenched as a pedagogical vehicle for self-inventories and self-development. Whatever the labels used to identify the various styles, control of prejudicial treatment of any style is difficult. Even when we use objective labels, the guidelines offered for effective adaptation to situational demands reflect inherent bias. The lesson attached to this useful concept and its problems creates our next assumption: *A wide diversity of styles may successfully and variously meet situational demands.* Crucial to the development and application of this idea are four guidelines: The styles identified must be treated objectively so as to acknowledge the potential of any style at any time emerging as effective. The styles must not become cages of constraint, but rather serve as touchstones of possibility. Treatments of styles, like horoscopes, should acknowledge compatibilities and incompatibilities. Finally, we need to recognize the potential for change without creating an illusion of evolution toward some fantastic ideal. Collectively these guidelines suggest that styles are not fixed; are not necessarily good or bad, but are instead situationally effectual or not; and are differently related to other styles. Potential leaders need to identify their styles in relation to other styles so they can knowingly adjust to meet more effectively the demands of whatever their position of leadership.

Regardless of how sophisticated the approach, we simply cannot escape who we are as a person and the unique character demands of any situational contingency. This lesson of conventional wisdom and of selected lines of scholarship leads to a final assumption: *We cannot ignore personality and leadership traits.* Each of us has a personality profile of qualities, and that profile operates within latitudes of potential. Although one may occasionally escape the persona, the basic profile will most likely resurface. One must be further cautious not to equate the persona with a leadership style, because the latter is an a priori categorization of many personal profiles and the former is unique to the person. Although some patterns may surface, many different personal profiles may fit within a particular leadership style. So, to make the leadership style literature fit one must first understand the persona in the "role" of a leadership style. Just as one's personality profile has a loose relation with leadership style, the traits of leadership are only loosely correlated with situational demands and personal qualities. Whatever the leadership traits appropriate for certain contexts, personal characteristics may uniquely combine to meet the demands, or someone in a position of leadership may perceive the combination required and create a responsive environment of people and their reactions to deal successfully with the tasks involved.

A Multidimensional Model

From the overview and the assumptions it spawned emerges an alternative model, graphically depicted in Figs. 11.1 through 11.4. Capturing this multidimensional model in a two-dimensional graphic requires some explanation. Imagine, if you will, three spheres related as the Chinese fretted balls with each free to move independent of the others. Each of these spheres is bounded by permeable lines inviting the easy movement of external and internal influences in and out of the sphere. These spheres represent the essentials identified in the three traditional approaches with personality and leadership traits at the core, surrounded by the equally permeable styles; these personal dimensions are, in turn, encompassed by situational demands that are ordered loosely by leadership, management, and administrative functions. These spheres are finally suspended in a social and cultural context within which numerous other people and situations give meaning to whatever occurs in our own circumstance. Even though the spheres may move in relation to each other, they are like the rest of our reality and subject to the gravitational pull that tends to have them rest off-center from the weight of their components until they are shocked or dislodged into further movement by the situational demands of social or cultural context.

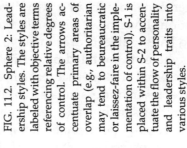

FIG. 11.4. Composite leadership model.

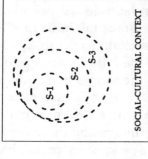

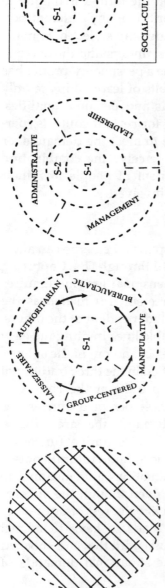

FIG. 11.3. Sphere 3: Situational demands. Remember, this is a sphere and the leadership, management, and administrative aspects of situational demands all surround the internal spheres. The leadership, management, and administrative aspects overlap and are permeable to reciprocal influence. S-1 and S-2 are placed within to accentuate the flow of personality and leadership traits as clustered in styles to align with the varied situational features.

FIG. 11.2. Sphere 2: Leadership styles. The styles are labeled with objective terms referencing relative degrees of control. The arrows accentuate primary areas of overlap (e.g., authoritarian may tend to beureaucratic or laissez-faire in the implementation of control). S-1 is placed within S-2 to accentuate the flow of personality and leadership traits into various styles.

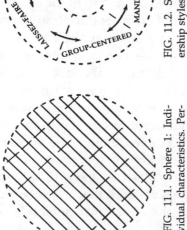

FIG. 11.1. Sphere 1: Individual characteristics. Personality traits are represented by solid lines and leadership traits by broken lines. The smaller number of leadership lines suggest that not all personality traits may contribute to leadership potential.

The dynamics of this model underscore its relative advantages over other models: The person who serves as designated leader in a position of leadership (POL) is central to the proper alignment of the other spheres for situational accommodation. The personality features of the one in the POL are within the same sphere (S-1) as the traits of leadership and may variously combine to create a style. Which style (S-2) may also be a matter of temporary alignment with the outer sphere (S-3). The situational demands encompass and influence, but do not necessarily control, the alignment of the internal spheres, which may get totally out of synchrony or achieve remarkable synchronization. All three spheres move within the broader constraints of larger, social–cultural circumstances that may directly alter situational demands and how easily or unevenly the spheres may move in relation to each other. The movement of the spheres, any one or combination of them, is realistically imperfect and will load up or become off-centered by the weight and distribution of its components. So, certain combinations of traits could restrict the movement of the core sphere and generate a weighted style that may, in turn, be more or less inclined to certain situational requirements. The person at the core may also create movement that forces realignment for better or worse.

Perhaps the most exciting feature of this abstraction is its emphasis on the kaleidoscopic prospects of the leadership art. Theoretically any possible combination or alignment could produce effective and challenging results. On a parallel with mathematics, this approach "fuzzies up" some concepts that have become too stale and fixed. When management training programs place senior executives in wilderness games, we should realize our professional desperation in grappling with leadership. Rather than wallowing in the mud with our colleagues, maybe what we need is reasonable dialogue about the artistry of strategic and tactical alignment of our goals and objectives within the constraints of personal and situational conditions. This model attempts to shake up our categories, to acknowledge the incredible variability involved with effective leadership, to build on the strengths of traditional approaches and their ancient predecessors, and to accentuate the need for more creative consideration of a topic that experts in communication should increasingly recognize as a test of our ideas and theories. Consistent with this line of reasoning, the final section extends this framework with several useful guidelines that grow out of its possibilities.

GUIDELINES FOR ACADEMIC LEADERSHIP

The preceding assumptions and model helped to organize this final section into a hierarchy of three overlapping sets of suggestions. After sorting through the lessons learned during many years of leadership responsibility, I settled on a relatively small number of essential principles, some strategic accommodations, and a lengthy list of complementary considerations and issues. Before turning to these particulars, I must confess a strong bias: Having spent most of my professional career in communication administration, I have a strong belief that leadership is primarily a set of communication behaviors that collectively deal with the development, adaptation, and transmission of ideas. Within this bias, I also believe that professional communicators too often presume uncritically their effectiveness in a way similar to physicians imagining themselves to be above illness. So, the task of advising our professional colleagues becomes somewhat problematic. We all know so much about communication processes that we presume ourselves above the interactional problems that comprise a large part of our turf. Until this attitude is overcome, no one can reasonably disrupt the inertia and set the spheres of our model into productive realignment. Perhaps the following can at least generate some dissonance about our presumed effectiveness.

Essential Principles

Consistent with our model, the essential principles address its component parts: First and through one of several possible ways, any person in a position of leadership must conduct a self-inventory of personal and leadership traits. None of us should forget that the self is central to any success or failure in human interaction. Thus the better we can know ourselves, the better we will be able to adapt and adjust to contingencies encountered. Several personality and leadership style tests are available (Tucker, 1984), but honest and systematic self-confrontation is certainly more accessible, portable, and adaptable. As one engages this first step, recognize the dangers of selective perceptions and self-deceit. Remember, one is sizing themselves to determine goodness of fit and not to reject individual potential or the new role. The remarkable success of programs to train university administrators through special seminars or mentoring projects at other universities is probably traceable to the opportunities provided by these situations for extensive and intensive self-reflection and self-examination.

At a broader level, the next principle advises the careful study of one's institutional circumstances, this is to say, examination of the box in our model that surrounds the person in a POL. The more one can know about the institution, the better able they are to relate to it and explain it to others. Acquiring this knowledge requires careful consideration of the institutional rhetoric or what they say they are trying to do, how they imagine themselves to be doing these things, and how they actually operate. Listen carefully when other chairs and deans speak about institutional history, mission, and operations. Especially learn how people outside your unit perceive it and how they define your successful integration within the institution. Finally, learn how bureaucratic tasks are best done and how the results of these bureaucratic efforts will affect your unit and its people. Sizing up the context is indispensable in learning the rules, especially the more informal social norms, before setting any unrealistic and misunderstandable goals. Whether one is new to administration or not, never neglect the importance of such information to the success of the unit.

The third principle is to define one's situation by working with colleagues in the formulation of a set of shared goals. Two ways of generating shared goals are readily available. Initially employ individual consultations whereby you escape the bias of group power structure and allow equal access to your thinking by the new and older members of the unit. With this information in mind, engage the group in regular meetings or, depending on how much needs to be done, special sessions such as retreats. Older faculty sometimes perceive special sessions as unnecessary, but their motivations are often questionable. So, gently persuade them for the good of the group to share their insights and participate. Pay careful attention to both what is said in these group efforts and the group dynamics. In this fashion, sensitize yourself to conflicts, the power structure, and the diverse agendas presented. Hold your commitment to any position until you have heard from your colleagues and had time to relate the individual and group results. Later organize the input, separate the real from the ideal, and plan courses of action to help achieve some short-time results. By all means, generate criteria for determining when goals are met and relate collective progress toward successful conclusions. Try to involve as many people as possible in manageable tasks and regularly relate their work to goal achievement. In these ways you are defining situational demands, learning what is expected, and discovering who can help best with what tasks and in what ways.

As one enters the goal-setting stages, communication effectiveness becomes a pervasive concern. The communication tasks seem twofold: On the one hand, the leader must convey ideas and information efficiently and prudently to colleagues. By efficient is meant timely and briefly; by prudent is meant effectively adapted in quality and quantity. Some leaders do not want to share information, and others want to share nearly everything; the most prudent course lies somewhere in between those extremes. On the other hand, the leader must also create a communicative environment in which people are willing and motivated to communicate with each other. This is often possible through social events that foster openness, but must be sustained through genuine interest and attention on a regular basis on the job. With both of these communication concerns, the designated leader is crucial for the creation of an environment in which colleagues can become more satisfied, energized, and committed to the fulfillment of group objectives. Through all of these efforts never neglect the value of personal reinforcement and public assignment of credit for individual and group achievements. Collectively, these communication tasks and opportunities are the primary ways the designated leader can adjust personal and leadership traits and styles to the constantly evolving situational demands.

A final essential principle concerns the need to maximize the potential of everyone involved. This idea directs attention to the generation of emergent leadership potential. To implement this principle requires knowledge of everyone in the unit, careful attention to their needs and desires, and skillful integration of their contributions into alignment with group goals and objectives. The problems here often concern the dejected or burned-out on the lower end, and the "prima donnas" on the other end. For either person or group, their "care and feeding" becomes a litmus test of one's leadership potential as most colleagues know these people and are carefully watching how well you can deal with them. Despite the trying demands of integrating these folks, the rewards of patient nurture can stimulate the unit and reenergize everyone. Recognize, however, that dealing with the difficult may require a skillful blending of kindness, genuine interest, and occasional use of strong force. By no means allow the recalcitrant to undermine your leadership or contaminate the unit morale; do not neglect these problems. Rarely will they simply go away. With the promise of 5-year, posttenure reviews, some of these problems may diminish. Meanwhile, spread your attention evenly, cultivate the potential of everyone, and relegate responsibility as circumstances permit. Reward achievement and keep collective attention focused on shared group objectives.

Strategic Accommodations

The idea of strategic accommodation calls our attention to a set of guidelines that collectively assist implementation of the essential principles. Of major significance are institutional and professional networks and networking. Effective leaders are usually well connected to achieve instrumental goals on a predictable and dependable basis. As students of human communication we acknowledge the value of this approach, but on a daily basis we sometimes neglect its development and maintenance. Especially critical are those people "in the trenches" who actually accomplish so many bureaucratic chores. We must learn who they are and variously reinforce their attention and support of our unit needs, and we must be well prepared to reciprocate when they need help. Similarly, we need to network professionally. As the recent Speech Communication Association Task Force Report on the Advancement of the Discipline (1996) underscored, the viability of a communication unit may ultimately depend on the assistance from colleagues at other universities. Even at much lower levels of significance, we need each other to help with innumerable tasks such as external tenure reviews, course development and curricular guidance, and assistance with convention presentations and publications. Becoming networked, both institutionally and professionally, is virtually a prerequisite for one's effectiveness in academic administration.

Once networked, the leader is better positioned to protect the people in the unit. Central to this strategic concern are three general guidelines: First, most people will have undulating patterns of commitment, motivation, and productivity. Teachers predictably experience burnout, research projects often flounder, and nearly everyone has personal problems. The effective leader is sensitive to those ups and downs and tries to help with opportunities to rejuvenate. Second, the leader must provide some sort of safety net for creative exertions that fall short. One's colleagues quickly discern whether to take risks or not, and providing support when people stumble will convey a strong message to others. Third, all members of the unit must help the leader create the safety net. Essential to this task is treating internal problems within the unit. Do not "air your laundry" publicly or you will invite intrusion and rumor development. By handling problems internally, you project to the outsiders that your group has their situation under control and to the insiders that we deserve our self-confidence and that we can mutually protect each other from institutional dangers. Protection of your colleagues, therefore, has many positive outcomes, but most importantly it can create a far better communication environment for teamwork.

Another strategic consideration involves the relative maturity and other developmental aspects of the unit. In his theory of departmental development, Murray (1964) characterized the evolutionary stages of department maturation and general accommodations necessary. Obviously one will operate differently in a well-established, heavily tenured, mature program than in a struggling, immature program with untenured faculty. Here again, however, the tendency to stereotype programs invites danger. Leaders should never forget to particularize individuals and situations, and they should vary techniques accordingly. For an administrator new to an institution, this set of variables may seriously constrain one's timetable and compel uncomfortable alignments within the spheres of our model, but in time the situation will become more comfortable as alliances form around task achievement and mutual respect develops. Be prepared for the varied patterns of dependence and emergent expectations so that you keep your workload manageable.

Through thick and thin, the designated leader must model good citizenship and personally reflect the criteria of effectiveness established by the unit. How involved one can be in professional organizations and university committees will impact on how much time one can devote to the individuals in the unit, to one's own teaching and advising, and to one's own research agenda. Good advice is to select very carefully what you will do and balance your commitments. For example, if the unit has several untenured faculty, try to get onto the promotion and tenure committee in order to learn from the inside how things are best done. If you have curricular changes to make, get onto the university's curricular committee. Be very cautious about extensive involvement in the more politically sensitive groups that may threaten indirectly your unit's success. Whatever you choose, make informed choices in terms of your unit's needs. Convey this line of thought to your colleagues, share what you learn in your activities, and advise them to follow a similar course of carefully considered involvement. Unless the leader sets a good example, the opportunity to instill good citizenship patterns is compromised.

At every institution of higher education, the balance among teaching, research, and service is a crucial concern. Unless this balance is wisely addressed, your colleagues may not succeed with their career development, the image of your unit may suffer, and internecine conflicts may consume your unit. Obviously, this balance will vary widely among schools, and it is often a hot political item. The effective leader must first learn the position of the central administration and especially those faculty groups who advise about rewards such as tenure, promotion, and leaves. This will constitute a framework within which you must operate. Then one must learn the unit and individual relation to this institutional position. Within this set of constraints the effective leader must determine how to encourage and discourage individual patterns of achievement. Networking can help one learn these important chunks of information and consequent strategies. Sufficient to say, how well a chair can guide the unit membership to respectability and excellence will often become a measure of academic success.

A final suggestion about strategic accommodations is closely related to modeling good citizenship, protecting your colleagues, and balancing your workload. No one in a POL can neglect the administrative dimension of their job. One must complete the bureaucratic tasks efficiently and effectively. Many of these tasks are loathsome chores, but they are a significant expectation of the central administration, and how timely and carefully you complete this work will reflect on you and your unit. It will further set an example for the members of your unit as they synchronize their behavior with yours. Prudence suggests caution against the fashionable criticism of bureaucratic expectations. Your casual comments may discourage needed compliance within your unit and render your job more difficult. Try insofar as possible to represent these onerous tasks positively. Such action may create an environment in which people willingly meet these more pedestrian requirements and, in turn, create better institutional sensitivity and understanding.

Complementary Considerations and Issues

From years of experience and many convention war stories, the preceding sections abstracted some essential principles and strategic accommodations. There remains a myriad of particulars for sorting and learning the tactics of academic leadership. Elsewhere in this anthology many of the current issues and problems are considered, and from these analyses one can learn about adaptations of the principles and strategies suggested here. Whether you are confronted by forced combination of academic programs, morale decline from downsizing, the integration of part-time faculty, or reduction of budgets, the general principles and strategic guides provided here are sound. The tactics necessary for successful engagement of these pressing issues should become the next stage of one's growth as a leader, because any one of these problem areas may create circumstances for the realization of one's leadership. As General George Patton so vividly reminded us, how can one realize their genuine potential as a leader without the opportunity to participate in important circumstances? Rather than attempt to itemize these unlimited tactics, this consideration concludes with two aspects of leadership potential that are separate from the POL, but predetermine the potential of anyone in that position.

Books could and should be written about the selection of administrators for positions of leadership. Unfortunately, this literature is weak, groups continue to make poor choices, and individuals find themselves in devastating situations. A few guidelines may assist this difficult task: When an opening occurs, the people involved need to study carefully their needs and expectations. Too often we rely on formulaic job descriptions and delay consideration of needs and goals until we are assessing the finalists or after we have hired the new administrator. These are dangerous prospects that invite confusion during on-campus interviews and during the later socialization of the person hired. Only after the group has reasonably considered what it wants and expects can a well-synchronized interview develop, and proper expectations become established for the candidates. Groups also create incredible expectations when they seek a superhuman type who will help them advance their research profile, cope with an amazing variety of management and administrative problems, and generate visionary leadership. We must recognize the reality of reasonable expectations, formulate them collectively, and present them clearly. In this fashion more groups might hire more fitting administrators who may or may not have great leadership potential, but who can successfully fulfill their position of leadership.

Advice about the selection process invites the final guideline for members of the unit. Good followers make for successful leadership (Townsend, Gebhardt, & Austin, 1997). As individuals within a unit, we need to adapt former President Kennedy's inaugural admonition: Ask not what our leader can do for me, but what I can do to achieve effective leadership. In fact, one can reasonably argue that the more followers understand about leadership, the better they can help with its attainment. Too often, individuals become so self-serving and create such excessive expectations that they limit the potential for anyone to lead well. As good followers, we need to take a self-inventory and determine how and to what extent we can and will help. We need to let our colleagues and the designated leader know about our potential to help, and then we need to follow up on our commitments. Followers must truly understand the concept of shared leadership before they can create a situation of effective leadership. Perhaps we simply know too much about the processes to see how we frequently wound ourselves. Until we are able to place ourselves, our unit needs, and our designated leader in perspective, we will be unable to help create an environment conducive to collective prosperity. Becoming a good follower is everyone's contribution to effective leadership.

CONCLUSION AND PROJECTION

This chapter began with explicit recognition of the history of leadership and the incredible complexity of the subject. More implicitly, the chapter presumed some inadequacies of modern, Western approaches and suggested that the adoption of some Eastern and some more ancient ideas could be fruitful. From this unusual vantage point, the chapter then assessed contemporary perspectives in the study of leadership, provided an alternative model built on two central sets of ancient and recent assumptions, and projected some essential, strategic, and complementary principles for leadership effectiveness in the academic world. From this consideration comes a final projection of special significance for this anthology.

The more I study leadership and the more positions of leadership I assume, the more I realize the centrality of communication to leadership. Whether we are administrators in positions of leadership or not, our concern for communication should invite and challenge us to address this subject area from our distinctive perspective. Perhaps more than most topics, this one urges us to examine how rhetorical and communication studies merge in the domain of political realities. Drawing an analogy with Aristotle's position about rhetoric as the counterpart of dialectic in the world of politics, perhaps we should conclude that the art of communication is the counterpart of the social science of communication in the world of leadership studies and practice. As this chapter accentuates, understanding leadership necessitates the synthesis of communication and other traditions rather than the constraining limitations of a singular, myopic perspective.

ACKNOWLEDGMENTS

I express my appreciation to Dr. Moya Ball and Dr. Robert Blanchard of Trinity University for their advice and guidance.

REFERENCES

Ames, R. T. (Trans.). (1993). Introduction and commentary. In *Sun-tzu: The art of warfare: The first English translation incorporating the recently discovered Yin-Ch'ueh-Shan texts.* New York: Ballantine.

Barnlund, D. C., & Haiman, F. S. (1960). *The dynamics of discussion.* Boston: Houghton Mifflin.

Blake, R. R., & Mouton, J. S. (1964). *The managerial grid.* Houston, TX: Gulf.

Blake, R. R., & Mouton, J. S. (1985). *The managerial grid III: The key to leadership excellence.* Houston, TX: Gulf.

Bormann, E. G. (1990). *Small group communication: Theory and practice* (3rd ed.). New York: Harper & Row.

Burns, J. M. (1978). *Leadership.* New York: Knopf.

Clark, D. L. (1957). *Rhetoric in Greco–Roman education.* New York: Columbia University Press.

Fiedler, F. E. (1967). *A theory of leadership effectiveness.* New York: McGraw-Hill.

Gulley, H. E. (1968). *Discussion, conference, and group process* (2nd ed.). New York: Holt, Rinehart & Winston.

Hill, L. B. (1984). *The military officer's guide to better communication.* Glenview, IL: Scott, Foresman.

Hunt, J. G. (1991). *Leadership: A new synthesis.* Thousand Oaks, CA: Sage.

Maccoby, M. (1981). *The leader: A new face for American management.* New York: Simon & Schuster.

Murray, R. K. (1964). On departmental development: A theory. *The Journal of General Education, 16,* 227–236.

Northouse, P. G. (1997). *Leadership: Theory and practice.* Thousand Oaks, CA: Sage.

Speech Communication Association Task Force on Disciplinary Advancement. (1996, December). Report submitted to the Administrative Committee of the Speech Communication Association, Annandale, VA: SCA.

Sun-tzu. (1993). *Sun-tzu: The art of warfare* (R. T. Ames, Trans.). New York: Ballantine.

Tichy, N. M., & Devanna, M. A. (1986). *The transformational leader.* New York: Wiley.

Townsend, P. L., Gebhardt, J. E., & Austin, N. K. (1997). *Five-star leadership: The art and strategy of creating leaders at every level.* New York: Wiley.

Tucker, A. (1984). *Chairing the academic department: Leadership among peers* (2nd ed.). New York: Macmillan.

Zaleznik, A. (1977). Managers and leaders: Are they different? *Harvard Business Review, 15,* 67–80.

12

Fundraising

Sharon Murphy
John Shorrock
Bradley University

An increasingly important role of academic administrative leaders is
that of developing external resource support for the programs they lead.
The role might be described as friend-raising and fundraising. It involves thoughtful and sustained cultivation. Whereas university presidents and provosts focus on the goals for their entire institutions, it is
deans and faculty who develop and focus on the visions and goals of
their individual colleges and programs. They build relationships, day
in and day out. They, by and large, deliver on the promises made by
institutional development officers. The quality of their product and the
promise of continued and ever greater quality are what benefactors
judge in committing their resources.

Deans and program heads also have the responsibility of establishing
in their colleges and departments a climate for scholarship and creative
productivity. To do so often demands resources beyond the unit's
existing budget. Therefore deans and department chairs need to develop processes for mentoring faculty members through the search for
support of their individual research and academic initiatives.

225

INTRODUCTION TO THE PROCESS

This chapter is designed for deans, directors, and chairpersons as they begin or continue cooperative work with both the development office and the office of research and sponsored programs, however titled on individual campuses. The chapter focuses both on institutional development and on the context for research and sponsored programs within which individual deans and faculties work.

It should go without saying that externally funded initiatives can benefit not only the applicant unit but also the college or university as a whole. Also, beyond individual campuses, well-presented proposals and well-executed projects often tell higher education's story very effectively among important constituency groups.

Institutions, public and private, whose members embrace the challenge of developing friends and finding funding support for important priorities are increasingly recognized as targets of opportunity. They are seen as places where exciting things are happening, where the significant ideas are emerging, where people are determined enough and creative enough to find ways to make happen the things that shape the future. Put another way, winners beget winning. Winning institutions attract winning students and graduate winning alumni. The accomplishments of those students and alumni attract public attention, appreciation and, often, support. It is indeed a virtuous circle.

Several key questions, some general and some more program specific, come to mind as college or university administrative officers plan their work for development. Giving these questions careful attention at the outset can help put the work into context and can provide powerful motivation for sustained and consistent effort, as well as for finding ways to involve a variety of individuals across the college or school.

Why Would Someone Give to My Educational Institution?

Somebody Asks. Americans have been supporting institutions of higher education with personal and corporate gifts for more than three and a half centuries (Curti & Nash, 1965). Therefore, it is no coincidence that the oldest, for the most part, are also among the wealthiest. It is not their longevity that accounts for their material success; it is their mission and their inherent quality that has attracted support. However, gift support did not just happen. It occurred because it was requested; motivated agents in the earliest days invited others to help further education in this country by underwriting with financial support the goals and objectives of the institutions they represented. The process has continued without interruption to the present day.

The private educational institutions with which the process began now share the resource development stage with a host of public entities. That support of higher education has lasted so long and has grown so great is ample evidence of the value with which higher education is held and the breadth of support it enjoys, but the process of establishing support must be an institutional priority. No one is going to do it for you, particularly in the philanthropic marketplace. Having established a viable climate for advancement to succeed, it is incumbent on those who must generate philanthropic support to request contributions.

Worth Is Established. The factors motivating individuals, corporations, foundations, and even governments to support higher education are many and varied. A host of human factors come into play: belief in the mission and goals of higher education, its perceived worth and quality, association with others, gratitude for service received, opportunity for recognition, influence of others, well-being of humanity, national security, civic pride, successful athletics, and tax benefits (Seymour, 1988). Whatever the reason or combination of reasons that results in support of higher education, that support comes from individuals and organizations motivated to give. The motivation results largely from a deliberate cultivation process that brings about meaningful relationships between the college or university and potential donors.

Cultivation is a simple process of identification, information, interest, involvement, and investment. It is a never-ending continuum of building relationships with current and potential donors that assures their interest in higher education and their ongoing financial support (Murphy, 1992). It is educational and incremental. It incorporates personal contacts, special events, publications and public relations. Approaches taken vary with the institution as well as with the target audience and the purpose for which support is sought (Schumacher, 1992).

Constituencies Are Key. Virtually every college or university engaged in resource development receives support from a variety of constituencies, including alumni and other individual friends; corporations and foundations; certain organizations; and federal, state, and local government agencies. In this global age, support is sought and received internationally as well from foreign governments and corporations sponsoring targeted campus programs and initiatives.

Those colleges and universities receiving the broadest and deepest levels of support have well-defined resource development programs that involve in the fundraising process a broadly based constituency of gift seekers. These include volunteers, professional resource development staff, presidents, trustees, provosts, academic deans, and faculty and staff. Success helps stimulate a culture where institutional advancement (i.e., fundraising, recruitment, alumni relations, and public relations) in the broadest sense can succeed.

Priorities Lead.   The key is to stimulate campus culture in which institutional advancement can succeed. For maximum effectiveness, that culture must mirror the institution's own strategic plan and priorities with the fundraising objectives designed to help the institution accomplish its immediate and long-range objectives (Murphy, 1992). The institution's priorities must be endorsed by key internal constituencies starting at the top with the governing board and president and including the academic and nonacademic leadership. Anything short of internal consensus will undermine the process of building the case for support that will appeal to the institution's donors and prospective donors from all constituencies. Indeed, the best and most compelling cases for support will speak with one voice in a way that interested donor and potential donor constituencies will know that the institution has done its due diligence and that donated resources will be well managed and well spent toward accomplishing clearly defined goals and objectives.

In responding to requests for support, individuals and agencies want to see that key institutional goals and objectives are clear, consistent, and widely embraced. So, for example, all public relations and publications sponsored by the institution must be used to tell the institutional story and deliver the message in ways that will cause others to be knowledgeable and supportive. Messages must touch them and help them to understand and develop confidence. Thus, especially in times of scarce resources, budgets available to promote public image must be used prudently through key publications to advance the institutional mission and to build the case for support.

The Match Is Right.   Solicitation of gift support is neither an art nor a science. It is a process that usually begins with the identification of the prospective client, the involvement of the client with the institution, and eventually the solicitation of the client for the right program at the right time for the right amount. Knowing and understanding these variables of solicitation is the essence of the gift-asking process and applies equally to individuals, corporations, foundations, organizations, and government agencies. Donors need to know why gift support is needed and how it will be used, but the process will not come full circle unless a gift is requested.

Institutional representatives meeting with prospective donors to request support drive the philanthropic process in higher education. For as many individuals who feel great comfort with the solicitation process, there are equal numbers who do not. This does not mean the latter are ineffectual; they are only human. Some of the most successful are never comfortable with direct solicitation, and some of the most confident turn out to be the least effective.

The key to success is the rock-solid conviction that the institution deserves the support being requested and that the outcome will validate the donor's motivation to provide that support. The balance of the process focuses on matching donor-driven motivations with institutional goals and objectives. If the institutional climate for advancement is in place and functioning, philanthropic support and government grants and contracts will be sought and found to help underwrite annual operations as well as intermediate and long-term institutional goals and objectives.

What Is the Need We Want to Meet?

Some needs are best met via long-term support. Some are research and programmatic in nature, and are more appropriately supported by one-time grants and/or contracts. Each has its peculiar opportunities and approaches. Both share some general demands. But developing, understanding, and committing to a focus is the first step on the road to funding success.

Developing a New Program or Project.   It is often easier to get this kind of support because the well-presented proposal suggests an opportunity for involvement in the bold and creative initiation of something in which the grantor can be proud to have had a hand. This is particularly true when the emerging priority matches the interests of targeted grantors.

Responding to an Announcement of Funding Opportunities. An invitation to apply for funds, published widely or made to limited constituents, is just that, an invitation. In such a case, particularly, note the expressed interests of the agency, along with any stated geographic preferences and limitations, and take these seriously. Do not waste the agency's time or yours with ill-fitting proposals. If it is worth asking for, it is worth asking appropriately.

Meeting Emergency Situations. In this case the prospective grantor needs assurance that the emergency is legitimate, not a product of mismanagement or worse. Be alert that grantors are less likely to give to causes that are desperate than to those that are proven winners, so the appearance of desperation should be avoided. A dean might be tempted to declare that "Unless we can generate (a given amount) we will have to close down the program." However, that stance can be an invitation to reject or at least mistrust the leader's ability to succeed regardless of largesse. At the same time, prospective donors know that fires occur. Student individual emergencies call for special responses. Legislative sea changes can wreak havoc on already strained budgets. Unexpected disasters, large and small, strike even the best organized colleges and universities. It is in the presentation, and in the tone of the presentation, that the case can be made or lost.

Support for Continuing Operations. Sustaining support is less exciting and it is important to look creatively at the program or unit, identifying the elements that specifically meet a prospective donor's focus, or that could be packaged creatively. Annual support, for example, for computer labs might seem prosaic. However, offering the opportunity to name facilities, even individual study stations after individuals, or proposing a named workshop series to develop computer graphic skills for advertising majors or a named yearly competition or award might have genuine appeal. Alumni anniversary classes often look for projects that carry both lasting value and lasting commemorative opportunities.

Whatever the Needs. The literature regarding funding programs and timetables should be studied carefully. Information comes to every campus in a variety of ways and on an almost daily basis. Good ideas are often generated in reading through the published requests for proposals (RFPs), and in reviewing foundation annual reports. Be sure you are on the regular routing lists, and get into the habit of reviewing and discussing opportunities with the appropriate campus agencies, as well as with the faculty in your college and departments.

Who Can Help Meet Those Needs?

Review the information on funders whose goals match yours. A review of directories and listings can indicate many opportunities. Involve the research staff of the development office or the office of research and sponsored programs (ORSP) with your search for funding agencies. If and when you contact an agency representative, be clear about how your project matches agency interest. Be sure that the title and need statement demonstrate the match, and that you can indicate awareness of the agency's history and current focus as indicated via annual reports and grant prospectuses. If your university, school, or college has received funds from that agency in the past, be conversant with the basic concepts of the grant and the successes reported about it.

Go beyond the first logical list of targets. Beyond media and communication programming and instruction, for example, what outcomes, even secondary or tertiary, are you after? Community literacy improvements via media usage, for example? Enhanced quality of incoming students as result of enhanced quality of work in the schools? When working to develop gifts and foundation support it can be helpful to review the membership lists of boards and councils at your institution to see if anyone is able to establish contacts for you. Remember also that some individuals and agencies are especially open to contacts by well-placed alumni who can offer the best testimony of the quality of your work. If a conversation with such an individual can precede your call or letter it can help direct your conversation. This contact should be pursued and should be considered the opening for relationship development beyond the single proposal. In no case, however, should the making of contacts circumvent procedures established within the funding agency or within your institution.

How Do I Go About It?

Campus processes call, in most cases, for some reviews and required approvals by deans and vice presidents. It is good to allow plenty of time for consultation, revision, and final approvals in advance of published deadlines. Especially if there are likely to be several or competing proposals emanating from the campus to the same agency, beginning conversations with university coordinating agencies early in the fund-seeking process can prevent conflicts. The bottom line here is fundamental: Make certain your prospect has been "cleared" for solicitation or approach and is an appropriate resource.

Development Strategies.   Institutional planning for gifts and endowments, coordinated through the development office, is based on case statements and identification of long-term and short-term institutional priorities. It often sets parameters within which individual units can approach external funding agencies or approach alumni and friends. (Worth, 1993).

Institutions seek both "annual" support and special support through capital campaigns. The latter are intensive efforts for specific lengths of time with targeted fund raising objectives including endowment, facilities, equipment or instrumentation, and operating support if the campaign is comprehensive. Through annual support, on the other hand, gifts are given year in and year out by alumni, other individual friends, corporations, and foundations.

Whether seeking annual gifts or capital gifts, the key ingredient to success is the willingness to both state the academic need and to ask convincingly for support (Golden, 1997). Direct mail and telephone solicitations are frequently used in asking for smaller annual gifts. Funding at higher levels requires personal solicitation, involving deans or department heads meeting with prospective donors and requesting support.

Virtually all major gifts require one-on-one solicitation, coordinated by a development professional working with a specific college or department. Remember that 95% of any fundraising goal will come from less than 10% of the donor constituency. Academic leaders are well advised to keep the sights high and focus on potential donors who have the ability to make major gifts. It is the development professional's responsibility to keep academic leaders focused on major gifts; it is the academic leaders' responsibility to follow through with targeted solicitations. Those who ask receive!

Research Grants.   Preparation of research and program grant proposals, on the other hand, benefits from close coordination with the institution's ORSP, staffed by individuals selected for their skill in such review and cognizant of institution policies and practices. Their interest is in helping faculty identify opportunities and prepare winning proposals. On some campuses, regularly scheduled workshop sessions conducted by the ORSP often help to initiate new faculty to the research-funding process and highlight the successes of more senior faculty (Bauer, 1995; Coley & Scheinberg, 1990).

Reading the funded research grant proposals generated on your campus can be instructive. So can invitations to the successful writers to visit with your faculty. Knowing that the proposal-writing process takes time and effort, and that not all proposals can succeed given the competitive nature of most opportunities, it is good to be able to identify and make available to colleagues people whose time and effort have been rewarded with positive response. It is a good idea to include among the mix proposal writers whose success came after second or third attempts, because a first-time rejection can discourage further efforts. Contact with colleagues at other institutions who have received proposal funding can also be helpful.

Most agencies have at least some restrictions on their grants. They want to make particular, targeted impacts and they realize that directing their grant making is both necessary and effective. Read the information and guidelines, in whatever form. Attend the workshops or public meetings the agency may sponsor. In many instances, the agency invites prospective funding applicants with unanswered questions to call, or write, or both. Prepare carefully and then call the individuals or offices indicated in announcement materials. Your goal is to engage the agency as much as possible in helping you to understand the opportunity and decide if it fits your needs and interests.

Keep the grantor's priorities in mind (Ries & Leukefeld, 1995). The proposal, or the preproposal letter, needs to indicate understanding of what the grantor is trying to do and demonstrate that what is proposed supports those priorities and that mission. Above all, be honest with your hoped-for grantor and with yourself regarding what you want to do and what you are prepared to do. Do not give the impression that needs have been created to fit grantors' priorities. It might be tempting to create a need that matches the interesting RFP. It might be fun to launch a whole new project. But the temptation needs to be weighed: Beyond the grant dollars, other hidden and not-so-hidden costs and personnel demands can easily distract from key college or department—or individual—programmatic and research priorities. In short, it is best to find grantors with priorities that fit your needs.

Explore avenues for access to the decision-making members of the granting agency: Sometimes, not always, it is who you know that counts here. So the role of college advisory boards and councils in making contacts should not be overlooked as such boards and councils are established and their members selected.

Developing the Proposal

A certain amount of thoughtful work should precede the initial contact, whether letter or information-seeking telephone call, and the process of developing the proposal. Guidelines and RFPs often outline priorities, grants made previously, and special directives. Formats may vary, but there are some generally expected elements. Key ingredients in the package include the statement of need, background on the institution and key project participants, the target audience, the expected outcomes, the evaluative process, the timetable, and the budget.

Background: Spotlight on the Institution.   Be prepared to describe your university, your college, and your department. Work with the materials used across campus, as well as with statements crafted about your specific unit. Grantors want to know why they should support your project, at your institution, in your college or department, in your geographic area, and within your time frame.

Think carefully about what your institution or your unit has to offer to prospective grant-making partners that is unique and promising. Your vision and mission statements, which help direct long-term and short-term decisions regarding curriculum, can also help as you focus the attention of funders on ways to realize that vision and mission. Think about what you have done or are doing that demonstrates your ability to produce the results you want to achieve with the funds you are requesting.

Statement of Need.   Having developed a clear, concise statement of the need and the opportunity, narrow the statement to as attractive and unforgettable a title as you can. Remember that, as with any communication opportunity, you need to make contact, generate interest, and tell your story. Be sure that you are able to keep the summary statement and title in focus throughout your conversation and throughout your planning and writing process. Be sure, also, that you are able to identify just what it will take to do what needs to be done: personnel, work hours, funds, overhead, facilities and equipment, and contextual elements.

Participants.   Identify the key players and their credentials, including previous related projects they have completed. Decide whether the project is a single-agent effort or whether it will involve collaboration among departments, colleges, universities, or campus and community. Keep in mind that such collaborative approaches are often appreciated by funding agencies as indicators of strength and promise of accomplishment. Deans and chairpersons who have established advisory councils will find these bodies very helpful in reviewing proposed projects. Their insights and suggestions can enrich the planning process. In addition, they can often assist in identifying potential funders and, by their questions, help eliminate ambiguities in the proposals.

Target Audience.   Indicate who the project is intended to benefit and how wide the impact is expected to be. This could include numbers of students involved, geographical area impacted, specific target groups, national or international processes that can realistically be predicted to be influenced. Remember that such influence can come through, among other ways, direct participation, access to published or broadcast work, and the likelihood of prototypes being replicated or improved on.

Budget.   The project's financial plan and timetable are key indicators of how well thought out the proposal is. The budget should be clear, simple, logical, and internally consistent, reflecting the things you say you want to do, and the numbers of people you say you want to serve. It should account for everything that needs to be done, providing for appropriate support to allow the project a reasonable likelihood of success. If matching or in-kind funding is required, negotiate the sources well in advance of submission deadlines.

The budget should indicate that you have planned appropriately for personnel costs, supplies and equipment, facilities, travel, telephone, and other essentials, which should be included in the line-item budget you supply with your narrative. Note that some RFPs are specific on what will and will not be funded. Follow these specifications. At the same time, where something not fundable is clearly needed, indicate how it will be provided. As a rule of thumb, ask yourself, "If this were my personal project and my personal paycheck, what would I honestly plan to spend?" Readers and reviewers bring some of these same questions to their consideration of proposals.

Other Sources of Funding.   Agencies are interested in whether you are seeking or have secured other funding sources and what kinds of institutional resources you can commit. Your case is strengthened with evidence that someone else believes enough in this opportunity to commit money to it. Remember, also, that many agencies like to view their awards as seed money toward larger and longer lasting projects or problem solutions. So be prepared to indicate how the program, if it is to be continuing, will be supported when external funding ends.

Timetable for Action.   In preparing the proposal, allot sufficient time to accomplish what you say you will do. Take into account such factors as agency timing of award decisions and any funding beginning and ending dates. Given academic calendars, some of these dates will demand creative implementation as well as some forms of interim financing. These elements should be worked through with appropriate offices well in advance of submission deadlines.

Anticipated Outcomes.   Explain who will benefit, how you will know if the project is a success, and the kinds of benchmarks you have designed as indicators, and devices for measuring effectiveness. Indicate vehicles, such as forums, newsletters, journal articles, and online services by which you can share your findings and broaden the applicability of your innovation. Include the opportunities for acknowledging the supporting role of the agency. Here again, collaborative conversations early in the planning stage can greatly enhance both the project and its likelihood of success.

Follow-Up and Continuity.   In some instances of multiyear projects, the agencies support acts as seed money. Indicate your plan for sustainability. In a single, finite project, show how it fits into the long-term mission of the department, college, or university. For example, it may be an opportunity to measure a curricular process, improve a program, or complete a building project.

Postsubmission Work

This phase is often as important as the preparatory work (Golden, 1997). As stressed earlier, ongoing success in developing external support is a matter of consistency and quality of approach.

Rewrite and Resubmission.   If rewrite is requested do it carefully and address all the questions and problems. Show your commitment to the project, a commitment that will continue even after the funding cycle ends. If phone call and conversation are required, be prepared and be cooperative. Remember that the reviewers are considering many worthy proposals, each of which probably means as much to its writer as yours does to you.

Sometimes representatives of the foundation or agency want to visit the institution to assess for themselves the character and quality of your program and of the individuals likely to be conducting the project or leading the curricular innovation. They would like to see the campus, get a feel for the faculty and the student body, and get a sense of how the prospective partnership would function. These visits are best coordinated with the development office and ORSP, so that all players know what each is doing.

Agency Visit.   At other times grant seekers are invited or can request to visit to the agency itself for a brief opportunity to present the proposal. A visit to a potential funding agency or even to a potential individual donor should be planned well in advance. Your personal presence will reinforce what has been presented formally in the written proposal and will either strengthen or detract from what has been proposed. Therefore, a neat, professional appearance is mandatory, and a polite, professional "can-do" attitude will reinforce the strength of your written presentation. Be prepared to answer thoughtful and penetrating questions about the proposal. Program officers who host client interviews are knowledgeable and well prepared themselves, and their questions will normally probe beyond what they have seen on the printed pages. The ability to discuss your institution in the broadest sense will be very helpful, as will a knowledge of your institution's track record with other similar programs, especially any supported by the agency being visited.

Be prepared to discuss the work of your closest colleagues and how you plan to respond to any agency guidelines for reporting results of the program. Know your institution's procedures for managing grant resources and rates of overhead. Do not be timid about requesting from the funding agency permission to invite along another institutional representative to answer agency questions about which you are unsure, such as matters of budget and other fiduciary responsibilities. Keep in mind always that the funding agency is looking for evidence that the program for which you are requesting funding is going to be professionally managed, is going to begin and end on time and within budget, and will be sustained or followed up in the manner proposed (Murphy,

1989). In this regard, do not fail to invite the host agency to campus for a site visit.

Finally, remember throughout that your agency hosts are busy people and that their time is valuable. Come to the point, present the key ideas, make the case. Afterward, thank the hosts in writing for their interest and handle in a timely manner any requested follow-up. Your ability to respond efficiently and effectively will strengthen your request for funding.

Success—and Beyond

On learning that the proposal has succeeded, be sure to acknowledge receipt of that information and work with the agency in any guidelines it may have regarding public announcements. Provide the agency with advance drafts of any news releases for review and approval.

Stewardship. Agencies and individual donors expect a certain amount of stewardship of the resources they share. The timeliness and thoroughness of any required periodic or concluding reports should be considered opportunities for cultivating the agency or donor for continuing support. Copies of unit or institutional annual reports or other materials that acknowledge the grant and describe the work it supports should be sent to the grantor as a matter of course. Also consider inviting the grantor or a representative for any special event planned as part of the program or project.

Grants are made in the interests of longer and larger goals and visions, and your ability to share the realization of those goals and visions will be important. Thus, if changes must be made in the project or key personnel, they should be communicated about with the agency in advance and forthrightly. In most cases, the logic or urgency of the situation will be recognized by the agency and the proposed changes will be endorsed. In other cases it may be necessary to return funds if the project cannot be completed, or if the needed changes will somehow conflict with agency guidelines. However, operating in good faith and with a commitment to responsible stewardship is always the best policy.

Next Approaches. When a successful project is nearing completion, it is time to launch your next efforts. A review of the outcomes, letters of endorsement and testimonials from individuals who benefited, and published and pictorial documentation all can be compelling evidence of the good work you do with funds given you. Plan to gather this evidence, and be disciplined in doing so. The results can be most rewarding.

REFERENCES

Bauer, D. G. (1995). The *"how to" grants manual: Successful grantseeking techniques for obtaining public and private grants*. (3rd ed.). Phoenix, AZ: Oryx.

Coley, S. M., & Scheinberg, C. A. (1990). *Proposal writing* (Sage Human Services Guides, Vol. 63). Newbury Park, CA: Sage.

Curti, M., & Nash, R. (1965). *Philanthropy in the shaping of American higher education*. New Brunswick, NJ: Rutgers University Press.

Golden, S. L. (1997). *Secrets of successful grantsmanship: A guerilla guide to raising money*. San Francisco: Jossey-Bass.

Murphy, M. K. (Ed.). (1989). *Cultivating foundation support for education*. Washington, DC: Council for Advancement and Support of Education.

Murphy, M. K. (Ed.). (1992). *Building bridges: fund raising for deans, faculty, and development officers*. Washington, DC: Council for Advancement and Support of Education.

Ries, J. B., & Leukefeld, C. G. (1995). *Applying for research funding*. Thousand Oaks, CA.: Sage.

Schumacher, D. (1992). *Get funded!* Newbury Park, CA: Sage.

Seymour, H. J. (1988). *Designs for fund raising* (2nd ed.). Rockville, MD: Fund Raising Institute.

Worth, M. J. (1993). *Educational fund raising principles and practice* (American Council on Education Series on Higher Education). Phoenix, AZ: Oryx.

13

Facing Realignment and Downsizing

Joe S. Foote
Southern Illinois University

During the 1990s, universities have experimented with a variety of new internal configurations to cut costs, balance supply and demand, and create synergy among units. Communication programs have been particularly vulnerable in these realignment struggles partly because they come in so many disparate configurations. Communication can be found in colleges of agriculture and departments of English and range from being an independent free-standing college or school to being just one among many departments in an arts and sciences colleges. Nelson (1995) of Ohio University found 19 different names of communications departments in Alabama. He also reported that telecommunications might mean radio–TV or voice and data and that speech communication might mean as many as seven different specialties. Given the confusing and inconsistent breadth and diversity of its homelands, communication units are hard-pressed to make a compelling case for unambiguous placement.

Communication's interdisciplinary nature makes it a first cousin to a number of fields, but leaves it without a clear birthright. Established disciplines like chemistry, physics, English, or classics know where they belong, having claimed their territory within the university long ago. Communication, meanwhile, has often found a home for reasons of expediency rather than philosophy. Because communication's biggest surge accompanied higher education's baby boom dynamism, the problem of ambiguous placement was exacerbated. Built on such a shaky foundation, it is no wonder that communication is among the first targets to appear on administrators' radar screens.

Downsizing and realignment became urgent issues in the field when a wide range and quality of programs were targeted. Within the last few years, programs at Arizona, Iowa State, Maine, Maryland, Nebraska, North Carolina, Ohio State, Oregon State, San Diego State, Southern Illinois, and Washington have all been affected. The scare was so great at one point that an Association for Education in Journalism and Mass Communication panel entitled "Endangered Species" played to an overflow audience in Atlanta. The endangered species cry turned out to be premature, but it sensitized administrators to the realities of modern higher education administration.

As Becker (1995) wrote, "We have left the period of growth and expansion. We are now in a period of redefinition, consolidation, and retrenchment" (p. 157). There are few programs where downsizing and realignment are not at least possibilities. This chapter discusses how communication units can meet the challenges of downsizing and re-alignment by discovering clues to their vulnerability and by developing positive strategies for responding to forced change.

In nearly every case where communication units have been threatened, warning signs have foreshadowed their vulnerability. In some cases, units have been unwilling or unable to assess their position accurately within the university. In others, communication study's broad-based image problem has made units particularly vulnerable.

UNDERSTANDING UNIVERSITY PRIORITIES

In an era of limited resources, many universities find themselves with too many programs and too little money to fund them. This situation naturally leads to an assessment of priorities and a discrimination among the many fields of study offered. In finding candidates for downsizing and realignment, administrators consider objective criteria like cost per credit hour, number of majors, test scores of majors, job placement, cost per faculty member, and faculty–student ratios, but they also examine more qualitative factors like national or regional standing, student achievement, and faculty research visibility. In the end, the "doability" factor also plays a part, as does the political environment on campus. Some units appear to be easier targets than others regardless of their academic quality; likewise, administrators are reluctant to attack units with strong internal and external constituencies.

Some universities are very clear and specific about the priorities of their units, but most are quite ambiguous. A few schools explicitly name the departments that are (a) slated for regional or national excellence, (b) expected to serve their regional coverage area at a quality level, (c) needed to service the rest of the university, and (d) those that are of marginal quality. The advantage of these delineations is that every unit knows where it stands at all times despite the initial pain of the process.

In most institutions, administrators send conflicting messages about academic quality. Every unit is good at something so there is always a modicum of good news and rarely a discrimination based on quality until the ax is about to fall. In this unsure environment, unit heads will often misread the intelligence coming from higher administration and be lulled into a sense of complacency.

Ideally, a program should look good on the institution's cost studies, have a distinctive quality of excellence in some area of its operation, and be seen to fill a major occupational need in society. Because there is always a tendency for faculty within a unit to place a higher value on their strengths than the administration does, external validation of quality and centrality may be necessary. Units that have a clear sense of their own worth and a vision for the future are less likely to be surprised by downsizing and realignment.

There is evidence to suggest that communication units carry an inherent vulnerability because of their unstable placement within universities and because of their consistently low standing within larger arts-and-sciences-type colleges. Except for the basic speech course, communication units provide neither a service function needed for the core curriculum to operate, nor a vital research link. Furthermore, it is one of the easiest units to shuffle because of its interdisciplinary nature.

Communication achieves a degree of protection when it is housed within a communication college because its battle for legitimacy has already been fought, it is likely to have a higher standing when a separate college has been designated, and deans coming directly from the field are able to make a stronger, more focused argument to higher administration. With a seat at the leadership council equal to all other colleges within the university, communication deans have a disproportionate opportunity to advocate their causes. Assuming that all colleges get a finite number of requests granted, this reality favors small colleges.

A disadvantage of the small communication college is its vulnerability in decentralized budget systems. More and more campuses are distributing the bulk of funds to colleges and expecting them to pay their way within the university. This system favors large colleges that generate huge amounts of general education hours, have significant outside grants and contracts, and have considerable budgeting flexibility. There is question whether small communication colleges can survive without subsidies in this type of responsibility-centered management environment. Communication colleges must argue that their critical mass goes far beyond their own boundaries to valuable, integrated relationships that serve the entire university.

Regardless of their configuration, communication units have the opportunity to gain strength by (a) using their interdisciplinary nature to become more central within the university, (b) developing leadership that can position them more favorably, and (c) building strong relationships externally with a variety of constituencies. (For more suggestions on how to avoid downsizing, see Nelson, 1995, and Long, 1993.)

MAINTAINING CENTRALITY

It is the interdisciplinary nature of communication that offers the greatest opportunity in the digital age to become more central to the mission of the university. Increasingly, governing boards are becoming more concerned about the centrality of academic units. The Illinois Board of Higher Education already reports on what percentage of credit hours are generated by students outside of a department, graduate as well as undergraduate. Other measures of centrality are the formal relations between units and the number of interdisciplinary research and service enterprises.

It is not necessary to have grand plans or new resources to build relationships. Simple initiatives like extending invitations to professors to become adjunct or cross-listed faculty, initiating cross-listed courses, or jointly sponsoring symposia or workshops can lay the groundwork for building strong alliances. Administrators need to be sensitive to and supportive of even modest faculty initiatives that have the potential to widen the scope and expertise of the unit. It is not always easy to see the rewards from collaborative relationships, but patience is usually rewarded. The key to success is to have an outward-thinking and creative faculty and be known on campus as a good partner who will be open-minded to innovative ideas and perform in good faith.

A careful reading of the university's goal statement should provide clues to the institution's priorities. Units that align their own goals with the goals of the university can build allies within the administration and lessen their chances for downsizing and realignment. Because the purview of communication is so wide, finding an intersection with the university's goals should not be difficult.

Communication units can gain strength from the dynamism in the information industries. Each year, the field becomes more relevant to the economic productivity of the United States. The rise of computers integrates our field with a variety of allied disciplines that are on the forefront of industrial and cultural change. Increasingly, the engines of communication are perceived to be at the vortex of creative thought and expression. With some of the fastest growing new job tracks being within the purview of communications, administrators can make a strong case based solely on international occupational and technological trends.

As technology changes in the field, programs can be positioned more centrally to gain a higher status in the academic hierarchy. A window is opening to use our application of technology to broaden the student base, to connect communication to disciplines previously alien to our interests, and to achieve upward mobility within the university structure.

MANAGING UP THE ORGANIZATION

A major part of assessing a unit's strengths and weaknesses is the quality of its leadership and its relationship with upper administration. Yet, we have not taken full advantage of opportunities to represent ourselves successfully to the persons who make the programmatic and financial decisions within the university.

Too many times, communication units circle the wagons and look inward, seeing the administration as an intrusive threat rather than as a friend and ally. Provosts and presidents will support programs where they have confidence in the leadership and when they are well informed about the unit's promise. The frontline administrator is the only person who can perform that function consistently.

A major element of success in building better relationships with administrators is consistency. Hale and Redmond (1995) explained that four different persons as chair in four different years at Iowa State "prevented the development of credible and forceful influence with College and University administrators" (p. 174) during their struggle with realignment. Many downsizing and realignment initiatives have no doubt begun when the unit is in leadership transition.

As a dean, my highest priority is to communicate with the provost, the chancellor, the system president, and the board of trustees. Much of the success my college has had over the past few years can be traced to the productivity of those relationships. The better administrators understand the substance of my college and the more time they devote to it, the better chances there are for productive partnerships to develop.

Communication colleges have a special advantage because their deans have immediate, direct access to the upper administration without a filter in between. Having a seat at the main table can be a singularly powerful tool in working a college's will. It automatically puts the field in an elite group of less than a dozen management centers within the university. Within larger arts and sciences colleges, department communication with not only the dean, but with higher level administrators, is essential. Department chairs who do not utilize access to provosts, presidents, and governing boards are missing significant opportunities.

Because of the obvious penalties for doing end runs around deans, department heads must use creative but acceptable ways to increase their visibility with upper administration. Inviting administrators to departmental ceremonies and social occasions, providing individualized demonstrations and tours for new administrators, and seizing opportunities to make presentations before governing boards can all build important relationships and help educate administrators on the department's appeal. We have made it a practice to invite at least one administrator each month to our college either for a discussion or a tour of facilities. In most cases, the administrators do not have a clear view of our mission and goals and the state of our facilities before they arrive, but they leave with a much better understanding and a much greater investment in our goals.

Because ours is a discipline that is consistently underrated and misunderstood, an ongoing education program is necessary to help administrators from foreign fields understand the breadth and depth of communication study. Administrators usually recognize the importance of communication in society, but frequently fail to appreciate its importance in the university. Upper level administrators welcome opportunities to interact with successful student projects and organizations. A perceptive department head can seize those moments when access is available and when the prospect for successful representation is at hand. For example, our board of trustees is still talking about a live teleconference we staged between them and our Hollywood Studies students in Los Angeles. Board members spent a fascinating hour via satellite talking with alumni sponsors and 60 students about their internships in Hollywood. No memo we could have produced would have equaled the singular emotional quality of that live interchange between governors and students.

Relationships cannot substitute for academic quality, but they can certainly enhance already positive relationships and provide a measure of goodwill in any difficult situation. It is rare to find a unit surprised by downsizing or realignment when a close and productive relationship exists between the unit head and higher administration. There is an element of trust and ownership surrounding a strong administrator–departmental relationship that has serious, positive implications for the health of the unit within the university.

REACHING OUT TO EXTERNAL CONSTITUENCIES

A strong and abiding advantage for many communication programs is their close relationship to the media professions. Quality programs will find a highly supportive ally among professionals because of closely linked internship programs, cooperation on placement, faculty with professional experience, and high professional standards in the curriculum.

Professional organizations are quick to come to the aid of programs that have a productive professional orientation, but the absence of strong relationships with industry professionals is a clear sign of vulnerability. Programs that have marginal professional ties will have difficulty fighting reorganization.

Communication programs naturally have stronger alumni relationships than most other nonprofessional units. Students with a strong, positive extracurricular experience on campus are more likely to have positive recollections about their department and college. Units that have alumni advisory boards are far better prepared to face downsizing or realignment than those with no such ongoing ties because alumni will already be informed about the quality of the program and be acquainted with senior administrators. Savvy department heads and deans will always arrange for alumni to meet with higher administrators when the grads are on campus. They will also ensure that their units participate actively in state and regional professional conventions and become partners with professional associations.

It also helps to have professionals involved in the wider life of the university. Department chairs and deans can help to position friends of the unit on presidential advisory boards, boards of regents, and development boards. There is no area of the university where supporters cannot help communication programs.

RESPONDING TO ADMINISTRATIVE CHANGE

Although the measures described previously can be helpful to prevent downsizing and realignment, units faced with this reality must develop a realistic plan for change and implement it successfully. Four recommendations are to: (a) assess proposals for downsizing or realignment objectively; (b) present a realistic, positive alternative that is sensitive to the administration's concerns; (c) build a coalition to support the alternative plan; and (d) implement an effective communication strategy for the plan.

Assess Proposals for Downsizing or Realignment Objectively

Before dismissing a plan for downsizing or realignment out of hand, the unit should make an objective assessment. One cannot assume that all change is bad. It is quite possible that the administration might have a clearer vision for the unit than its own faculty. Especially in the age of convergence, combining related or allied departments can be beneficial to the units. Departments can thrive in a new, broader, more integrated environment.

Wilson and Ross (1995) concluded after a national survey of programs where communications and journalism coexist that fears of reduced staff, budget, and facilities that occur when reorganizations are announced "are exacerbated when the two departments enjoy significantly different enrollment, facilities, or prestige—which was often the case" (p. 91). They also suggested that programs should not dwell only on what is being lost, but on the new internal growth that is possible by seizing on the combined strength of merged units.

In sweeping reorganization plans that involve the entire institution, the effect on communication must be assessed in a broader context. Communication may not have fared particularly well, but it may still have emerged stronger than other comparable units. It is important not to have a naysaying attitude in an environment that actually favors your unit. If the department is having a difficult time coming to grips objectively with a proposed downsizing or realignment, it might be helpful to engage a consultant who can advise the faculty and unit leadership on the best posture to take, especially when the initial reaction will set the stage for the entire unfolding scenario. It is important to know the real impetus for the plan and the persons advocating it. In some cases, a state board of higher education or another outside body may be forcing constraints on the institution. In others, it is those within the institution driving the entire proposed change. Units need to assess the merits of the change and the odds that it will be implemented.

The most common proposed change is combining two or more communication units into a single department, eliminating a certain degree of specialization and independence. In most cases, these recommendations are contained in a planning document that lays out a broad plan for downsizing and realignment. When a merger is proposed, the two or more units involved need to agree among themselves how to proceed. Ohio State University, when Journalism and Communication were asked to merge, there was no consensus. The School of Journalism agreed with the merger and wanted to remain in the College of Social and Behavioral Sciences. The Department of Communication argued for independence and a new home in the college of Business, Education, or Human Ecology. Journalism believed that it was much harder to argue for a new structure than to work within an existing one to build credibility and prestige. Communication saw only negatives in a merger and thought it was worth the fight to remain independent (Becker, 1995). When two departments cannot agree on a strategy, their bargaining power can be severely diminished.

There are also hazards to agreeing to mergers too early. At the University of Maine, Communication Studies and Journalism merged, only to find that the rest of the plan had fallen apart. Communicative Disorders, which was supposed to be merged with Nursing, became an independent department, negating any savings from the Communication Studies and Journalism mergers. Furthermore, the proposal to merge the College of Arts and Sciences with Social and Behavioral Sciences was abandoned, leaving the units within the colleges to pay for a combined budget reduction of $153,000 (Kelly & Weispfenning, 1995). The whole episode left the communication programs emotionally drained and feeling betrayed. Likewise, some faculty at Ohio State who initially supported the merger now feel betrayed by a lack of promises that have been fulfilled by the administration (Becker, personal communication, July 31, 1997).

A critical calculation needs to be made initially regarding the ability of the administration to carry out its plans, even though there is never sufficient evidence early on to make that kind of calculation expertly. Often, higher administrators' bold ideas collapse in the face of opposition. Rarely will every part of a plan be implemented. Thus, units should not give up if they believe they have a strong argument to make. On the other hand, units that do nothing, hoping to wait out the administration, may be making a bad mistake. In the Iowa State experience, Hale and Redmond (1995) explained that some colleagues argued for no proactive response based on the following assumptions:

> (1) the Department was operating from a position of strength rather than weakness; (2) there were no changes which the Department needed to undertake in order to improve the quality of the program; (3) the institutional evaluation of the Department would change with changes in institutional leadership. (p. 177)

All of these assumptions turned out to be flawed and the department's passivity meant lost opportunities.

Even when units agree with the thrust of a downsizing or realignment plan, it is important for them to negotiate from strength. The leadership should develop an implementation plan that protects the unit and postures it in the strongest possible position for the future. There should be rewards for units that support realignment and an opportunity to influence the course of that realignment. The goal is to enhance the long-term viability and productivity of the unit.

Present a Realistic, Positive Alternative
That Is Sensitive to Administration's Concerns

When units decide to oppose a downsizing or realignment plan, they must consider the odds of success and be prepared to offer a realistic alternative for change. Before making any response, the unit should mobilize to develop a plan. Any counterproposal should be especially sensitive to the administration's concerns and have a realistic chance of being adopted. Unless the plan answers the basic questions raised by the administration, it will have little chance of gaining acceptance regardless of how strongly it is pushed.

Information is a powerful weapon that can be singularly effective. When the University of Arizona administration recommended that the Department of Communication be restructured and lose its graduate program, the faculty were able to counter each of the administration's contentions with persuasive factual data. The indictment of the department contained several generalizations that all too often accompany assessment of communication programs. The dean's committee questioned the narrowness of its social science focus and its commitment to social science research and contended that much of its basic course content was not "oral" in nature and could therefore be absorbed by other social science departments. There were other contentions about the quality of graduate students and their placement (Crano, 1995).

Because several of the administration's assumptions were based on faulty data or misplaced generalizations, the department had ammunition with which to fight. It showed that it had been rated as one of the most productive research programs by a recent national survey, accepted graduate students with Graduate Record Examination scores among the very tops in the college in all three categories, admitted graduate students who made higher grades outside the department than within, admitted only 17% of applicants (compared to the 84% alleged by the administration), and secured $6.5 million in external funding (Crano, 1995). Indeed, the department seemed to be highly central to the college and university and had quality graduate students.

After the department presented its evidence, the provost's committee acknowledged that new data had resolved the issue of the graduate

program in the department's favor. The committee reaffirmed its recommendation that the undergraduate program be downsized, but it
was in a much more positive context dealing with the broader field of
information science. Department head William Crano (1995) observed,
"We won because we went to our strengths. We live and die by data
and its scientific analysis. In this case, the data were on our side, and
we were able to demonstrate the strength of our argument to responsible and conscientious people" (p. 188).

Developing a plan can often be a very positive experience for a unit.
When our College of Communications and Fine Arts at Southen Illinois
University was abolished in the early 1990s, the provost announced that
the "residue" units that did not go to the College of Liberal Arts should
find a home somewhere within the university (Stone, 1995). The "residue"
units (Cinema and Photography, Journalism, Radio–Television, Broadcasting Service) quickly formed a Phoenix Committee that carefully
crafted a bold and visionary alternative to the administration's proposal.
The proposed College of Mass Communication and Media Arts would
have an ambitious three core sequence featuring visual communication,
media and society, writing, and critical thinking, and would embody the
convergence that was sweeping the communications industries. There
would be an innovative new program for a multimedia degree, a plan for
a collegewide graduate program, and a closer integration of units for the
digital age. The work of the Phoenix Committee brought faculty together
who had hardly known each other and cemented strong relationships
among them. Proposals that had languished on the table for years suddenly found consensus support. Crisis had created opportunities to forge
new relationships and to put aside old controversies to work for the
common good. A carefully conceived plan also supplies a road map for
future strategies, providing faculty with a pathway to change.

Trying to forge a consensus plan can also reveal differences among
faculty that have not been always apparent. Hale and Redmond (1995)
recounted how a lack of cohesiveness among their faculty at Iowa State
precluded any kind of realistic plan from being developed: "Too often, the
effort which was expended was directed toward personal attacks rather
than creative problem solving, and to undercutting proposals rather than
helping to constructively examine and improve proposals" (p. 178). Without a cohesive plan, strong leadership, and a realistic chance of success,
opposing the administration can be a nightmare. Opposition not tightly

focused and effectively presented creates a more negative environment without improving the unit's bargaining position.

Build a Coalition to Support Alternative Plan

Rarely can a communication department, regardless of how well connected, influence the administration's policy singlehandedly. It must have friends from within and outside the university rally to its side. Like with any lobbying effort, a unit must build a coalition of those with a common interest in seeing an alternative plan move forward.

It is obviously easier for a well-integrated unit within the campus community to build coalitions. A major reason units become vulnerable is their isolation. In a crisis situation, it readily becomes apparent how well connected communication is to the heart and soul of the university.

Coalitions, by nature, are fragile enterprises often hanging together quite tenuously. Coalitions can be populated by strange bedfellows and the "enemy of my enemy is my friend" dictum sometimes applies. Department heads must be resourceful in building coalitions, seizing on faculty ties to other faculty and administrators, relationships with service enterprises, and student support. There can be both a base coalition of early supporters and an emerging coalition of partners who join once the public phase of the communication campaign has begun. Especially valuable are coalition partners who change camps to support the department's alternative.

Outside of the university, communication can have valuable allies in its alumni and friends in the mass media, provided that these groups have been cultivated previously. Even in situations in which the alumni and media are estranged, however, they may become supportive. Difficult situations provide opportunities to reengage alumni and media colleagues who have rarely been involved in the life of the department and can help build an ongoing commitment to the unit.

In mobilizing alumni and media groups, the department needs to develop a communications network to ensure that allies understand the facts of the situation, what the administration is proposing, how the department's alternative is better, and how they can make a difference. Mass media interests can be brought into the coalition singularly or through media organizations. Support from the state press association, for example, is usually a prerequisite for any successful effort to influence the administration on a journalism issue.

Academic organizations can also be valuable members of a coalition. When the University of Washington's mass communication programs were under siege, leaders of the Association for Education in Journalism and Mass Communication and other academic organizations made a persuasive case for keeping a program highly regarded within the field. It would be a mistake, however, for academic groups to inject themselves into every reorganization, downsizing, or realignment battle. Only when the arguments are clear cut and the academic standing of the program nationally is high will outside intervention be effective. Academic organizations, meanwhile, have a role to play in making a general argument for better consideration of communication programs in arts and sciences units.

Implement a Communication Strategy

Implementation of a successful communication strategy requires both a public and a private plan. In the public dimension, focal points should be created where the strengths of the alternative plan can be showcased. Departments have the burden of communicating the substance of their plan and building persuasive momentum. The communication is targeted to the committed who need to be reinforced, the opponents who need to be pacified, and the general population who need to be informed and persuaded.

Communication with coalition members is important to inform and energize them. They will have different professional ties and social relationships than communication faculty and can reach persons otherwise inaccessible. Persuasive communication targeted to major opinion leaders within the university is also an important part of the strategy. Some of this will be public, but most will be accomplished through back-channel communication.

There should be ongoing discussions with the administration behind the scene to keep them informed about the benefits of the alternative plan, the strength of the coalition, and the strategy for success. Administrators who have a trusted and ongoing dialogue with the department during fairly contentious times will be far more likely to compromise than those who are cut off from communication. Alumni who have a special relationship with top administrators can be highly valuable in this private communication, making headway where subordinate administrators cannot.

It is important not to back administrators into a corner, but to sustain them as active partners. One hopes that higher administrators would eventually invest themselves in an alternative plan and support its implementation. This will not occur if administrators lose face or are stampeded into action.

In the Southern Illinois University reorganization case, the provost went from being the chief opponent of creating a new college to being a strong supporter of creating a new College of Mass Communication and Media Arts. This transformation process took numerous meetings and sensitive negotiations over several months. Fortunately, the door to compromise was never closed by either side, allowing the growing momentum of the alternative plan to succeed. Because the provost eventually played a key role in creating the new college, he felt significant ownership and continued to provide the new college with exceptional support throughout his tenure.

A two-front assault is often necessary where an alumni "loose cannon" can ratchet up the pressure on the administration at the same time that very constructive private negotiations are continuing. Sometimes, administrators need to hear the unvarnished truth of the situation from an outside source and be confronted forcefully with the power equation. Department heads and deans must find the right mix of brute force and gentle diplomacy and know when to apply each.

There will be occasions where constructive back-channel communication with higher administrators will be impossible. The administrator is so wedded to his or her approach that no amount of communication will bring positive movement. Unfortunately, this environment is often a prescription for a lose–lose situation. Even if the department wins the battle, it may have to contend with a vindictive administrator with a long memory. In a totally hostile environment, the unit will have to let external forces lead the charge, using their power leverage to defeat the plan, remove the administrator who is fighting for it, or create inertia. Having a low probability of dealing rationally and constructively with an administrator is a major factor that should influence the decision whether or not to oppose the university's plan. Some units may accede to the administration's plan based totally on this sobering assessment. Others may use the intransigence and arrogance of the plan's major proponent as a springboard for an all-out assault.

Rather than make the final decision about the fate of a unit themselves, some higher administrators will delegate the judgment to a governing body like the faculty senate. Putting the question into this arena requires a traditional lobbying strategy where the arguments are made separately to each member of the governing body. Most of the footwork is done long before the governing body meets. Supporters have to be identified who can present the case for the departmental alternative and who can persuade other members. Each voting member has to be approached individually by faculty members with a common interest. Coalitions are vital to building a broad base of support. Members of these bodies usually come to the table with no strong preconceptions about the proposed changes and can be influenced by the merits of the arguments. It becomes more difficult, however, when the move affecting communications is part of a larger package because some members will be reluctant to break it apart or to open the door for an assault on their unit. (For a summary of suggestions, see the Appendix.)

CONCLUSION

Tip O'Neill's dictum that "all politics is local" also applies to the academic environment. Each downsizing and realignment situation is different at each university. Individual situations are influenced significantly by the campus' own leadership, political dynamic, academic quality, budgetary situation, and personal relationships. An isolated event in one university is not necessarily the harbinger of a national trend.

Yet, downsizing and realignment are facts of life in the modern university and certain broad tendencies are emerging. In an era of tight budgets and converging media, communication units have to be especially vigilant. The best preventive measures for communication administrators are to make their units more central to the mission of the university; to build close, productive relationships with higher administration; to reflect convergence in the curriculum; and to maximize relationships with internal and external constituencies.

Internal management has long been the primary focus of communication administrators, but they and their faculties should become aware of the important impact that administrators can make beyond the department. Effective representation is a prerequisite for effective leadership. Departments would be well served to emphasize the external role when they recommend leaders to represent them. Building strong relationships throughout the university and the professional world is one of the key roles that administrators can play to guard against realignment.

The growth of colleges of communication has provided a degree of protection to the field, provided that departments within those structures maintain quality and reach out effectively and proactively to other areas of the university. More vulnerable are communication programs within liberal arts or arts and sciences colleges that have been undervalued, misunderstood, and underappreciated. In some cases, units are under attack for superficial or stereotypical reasons that belie their quality and centrality within the university. The field must mount a defense of the discipline that transcends the peculiarities of a particular campus and insulates units from unwarranted assaults.

With information industries becoming increasingly important to the world economy, communication programs are in an excellent position to raise their status within the institution and to build firmer links to a brighter future. For this to happen, a new generation of frontline leaders will have to push their units closer to the mainstream of the university and be willing to alter their own structures to converge with a changing academic and professional marketplace.

APPENDIX: SUMMARY OF SUGGESTIONS TO FACE REALIGNMENT AND DOWNSIZING

1. Preventative measures

    (a) Develop a database that certifies academic and extracurricular quality.

    (b) Use interdisciplinary programs and initiatives to become more central in the university.

    (c) Choose leaders capable of positioning units more favorably within and outside the university.

    (d) Reach out to external constituencies.

2. Reactive measures

    (a) Assess proposals for downsizing or realignment objectively.

    (b) Present a realistic, positive alternative that is sensitive to administration's concerns.

    (c) Build and mobilize a wide-ranging coalition of support for an alternative plan.

    (d) Devise a multilevel communication strategy that deals systematically with every decision-making person or group affecting the future of the unit.

ACKNOWLEDGMENTS

I wish to thank Southern Illinois University journalism doctoral student
Cindy Price for her research and editorial assistance.

REFERENCES

Becker, L. B. (1995, September). Ohio State University's merger: Journalism and
    communication. *Journal of the Association for Communication Administration, 3*,
    153–157.
Crano, W. D. (1995, September). University of Arizona Phoenix in Tucson: Arizona's
    Department of Communication's campaign for fairness and survival. *Journal of
    the Association for Communication Administration, 3*, 180–189.
Hale, C. L., & Redmond, M. V. (1995, September). Speech communication at Iowa
    State University: A history of broken promises and shifting leadership. *Journal
    of the Association for Communication Administration, 3*, 169–179.
Kelly, C. M., & Weispfenning, J. (1995). *The rhetoric of downsizing at the University of
    Maine: A case study.* Otterbein College, Westerville, OH: Authors. (ERIC Docu-
    ment Reproduction Service No. ED 393–373).
Long, N. R. (1993, Fall). Anatomy of a continuing education downsizing. *Journal of
    Continuing Higher Education, 41*, 26–32.
Nelson, P. E. (1995, September). A summary of ideas for sustaining communication
    programs. *Journal of the Association for Communication Administration, 3*, 216–220.
Stone, G. (1995, September). Demise of the College of Communications and Fine
    Arts at SIUC. *Journal of the Association for Communication Administration, 3*,
    158–168.
Wilson, P., & Ross, S. D. (1995, May). The unification of journalism and communi-
    cation studies: The benefits of change. *Journal of the Association for Communication
    Administration, 2*, 82–93.

14

Intra-University Competition and Outside Stakeholders

Michael A. McGregor
Indiana University

Alison Alexander
University of Georgia

In this chapter we present a tale of two departments—departments of telecommunications with similar purposes, curricula, students, and faculty. But there the similarities end; one of the departments—at the University of Georgia (UGA)— is located within a School of Journalism and Mass Communication, and the other—at Indiana University (IU)— is rostered in a College of Arts and Sciences. As you will discover after reading this chapter, our mode of operation in dealing with intra-university competition and external stakeholders differs significantly, based largely on the place the departments occupy in the organization of the university (see Medsger, 1996; *Planning for Curricular Change*, 1987; *State of the Field*, 1994;).

In substance this chapter addresses important issues that arise outside the department: competition from other departments for courses and students, expectations of industry constituencies, and relationships with alumni and friends of the department. Clearly the issues arising from these external forces are increasingly important as we encounter ever-

259

dwindling resources. Campuses are turning more to rewarding schools and colleges based on the number of credit hours they generate, and industry friends as well as alumni are increasingly looked on as fiscal saviours for departments seeking additional resources. As you will see, the location of a department within the university structure often dictates the ways in which a department can respond to these challenges. Even more often, the university structure affects the outcomes.

CAMPUS STRUCTURES

The Bloomington campus of IU supports 10 major schools and colleges plus several smaller programs. The 10 major schools and colleges, in order of their size based on credit-hour generation, include the College of Arts & Sciences; the School of Business; the School of Health, Physical Education, and Recreation; the School of Education; the School of Music; the School of Public and Environmental Affairs; the School of Law; the School of Optometry; the School of Journalism; and the School of Library and Information Sciences. The Department of Telecommunications at IU is one of 60 departments and programs in the College of Arts & Sciences. The department has approximately 400 undergraduate majors, making it the fifth-largest major in the college; it generates nearly 4,500 credit hours per semester, ranking 20th in that category in the college. Faculty FTE equals 18.3, which, given the number of majors, gives the department the second-highest major-to-faculty ratio in the college. The graduate program enrolls approximately 45 students per year, 20 of which are funded by the department. The department has three full-time secretaries, one of whom serves as the graduate secretary and one of whom handles department budget and personnel matters. Also rostered in the department is a full-time professional advisor and a half-time administrative assistant who works mostly on alumni affairs and fundraising.

The undergraduate curriculum is divided into four areas of study: management and strategy; design and production; technology, economics, and policy; and society and culture. At the graduate level the department offers a masters of science focusing on media management or multimedia design, a master of arts and the PhD. Areas of emphasis for MA and PhD students include communications processes and effects, communications and culture, and law and policy.

The Athens campus of the UG supports 13 major schools and colleges including in order of number of student majors: Arts & Sciences, Education, Business, Agricultural and Environmental Science, Family and Consumer Science, Graduate School, Journalism, Law, Forest Resources, Social Work, Environmental Design, Pharmacy, and Veterinary Medicine. The Department of Telecommunications is one of three departments (along with Advertising/Public Relations and Journalism) within the Henry W. Grady College of Journalism and Mass Communication. The department has approximately 220 majors; the entire College of Journalism and Mass Communication has approximately 750 majors. The department employs 14 full-time faculty, a secretary, and an engineer. The Peabody Awards are housed within the Grady College and are physically located within the Telecommunications area. One of our faculty is the director; there are two full-time staff working in the Peabody area as well. The college, additionally, has a number of major resources including a department of student services, professional advisors, a graduate office, a business manager, a development director, an alumni director, a director of service activities, a faculty member serving as director of technology development, and other assorted staff.

The undergraduate curriculum at UGA is in transition as the university system moves from the quarter to the semester system. The new telecommunications curriculum will have one major with sequences in production, electronic media studies, management, and broadcast news. Areas of emphasis within the graduate program (MA or PhD) emerge through a combination of required course work and committee input into plans of study.

INTRA-UNIVERSITY COMPETITION

The Bloomington campus of IU is governed fiscally by a system known as responsibility centered management (RCM). Under this system, each school on campus is a responsibility center and the campus allocates money to the centers based on a number of factors, the most of important of which is credit-hour generation. Once an allocation is made to the schools, they then have complete control of their budgets. It is important to note that RCM does not filter down to the departments in the college, although the college does make many of its departmental allocations based on the number of credit hours a department generates.

Given this reality, schools and departments find it in their best economic interest to boost their credit hours as much as possible. This leads to a number of strategies employed to meet that goal; unfortunately, few of those strategies have the students' academic well-being in mind. For example, the Telecommunications Department, in response to calls from the campus to increase the writing component in freshman-level courses, developed a set of writing assignments for the introductory course. Graduate student associate instructors (AIs) are assigned to two sections of 25 students each, and much of their 20-hour-per-week workload is spent grading writing assignments. The college recently informed the department that henceforth AIs should be assigned to three sections of 30 students each, effectively raising their student load from 50 to 90. Obviously, the writing assignments bite the dust. Similarly, the department recently decided to drop the enrollment in all 300-level courses from 40 to 35—a modest step toward a higher quality classroom experience. However, the college now "suggests" that enrollments go back to 40. Notwithstanding the rhetoric of quality, it is clearly a numbers game.

Credit-hour generation at UGA is not the overwhelming concern that it is at IU. The Grady College is a small college with high admission standards and a campuswide perception of quality. Because it is viewed as a professional school, its budget is not totally based on credit hours generated. Both because of accreditation and the cost of upgrading facilities, the Grady College can successfully argue for money based on criteria that go beyond credit generation. There is, however, a downside in the area of credit generation for free-standing colleges. For example, none of our courses is listed in the arts and sciences core. Hence, students who enroll in our courses must usually count these among their limited hours of elective credit, effectively preventing us (and perhaps protecting us) from becoming a "service program."

Having a strong service component to a program can be a two-edged sword. Although offering courses required or recommended for core credit can generate many student credit hours, service courses do not offer the protection that many departments expect. Requirements can always be changed. Hence, upper level administrators may be unwilling to allocate new faculty to meet service course obligations. Perhaps more importantly for our purposes, though, service courses do very little to enhance the stature of a department. When a department is being evaluated by administrators, a primary focus is on the number of majors—not just the credit hours. It seems to us that numbers do not save departments that are under attack. Once that attack has been made, the only possible answers are ones that involve the issue of quality: majors, faculty, alumni, and influence (see Blanchard & Christ, 1993; Christ, 1994, 1997; Rowland, 1993).

Whatever the level of intra-university competition, a department should be strategic in bolstering its image and protecting itself. These strategies include convincingly defining the mission of the department, protecting against core curricular encroachment, seeking alliances with other programs when appropriate and beneficial, demonstrating excellence, and developing a good relationship with the dean. Department faculty must look and move forward while constantly peering over their shoulders.

Defining Your Unit on Campus

As the field of telecommunications becomes broader and more encompassing, defining the role of a telecommunications department becomes more difficult. Our departments were once called radio–TV–film (film was later dropped in both cases). The department at IU evolved from speech and drama programs; the department at UGA within the College of Journalism. Again, in both cases the department changed its name to Telecommunications in to better reflect its curriculum and constituency.

At present, both departments try to position themselves as the place on campus to study all manner of electronic media and its operations (with the exception, noted already, of radio–TV news at IU). Nonetheless, this is confusing to students, especially high school students, who see the wide array of communications-related departments on campus and do not understand the differences among them. In addition, the term *telecommunications* can have a wide variety of meanings in different contexts. Our departments use the word to apply to any electronic communication, but some only apply the word to traditional telephony environments. Accordingly, although the word accurately describes what we do, many of our constituencies do not understand.

This confusion can be both a blessing and a curse. It is a curse because faculty and staff are constantly having to explain to everyone on campus that we are *not* the campus phone company and we do not really know when their phone service will be turned on again. Although most of us have a very good idea why campus telephone rates are outrageously high, we do not share those opinions with callers trying to reach Communications Services. On the other hand, at least at IU, the college dean and his staff do not have much of a clue as to what telecommunications means either, and that gives us constant opportunities to educate them, and believe us, they need it.

The breadth of our departments is both a strength and a weakness in some ways. The strength lies in our ability to attract students with many varied interests, from station management to multimedia production, from research to voice and data network design, and from the study of television criticism to electronic media law. The weakness lies in the fact that our breadth necessarily creates overlap—and potential competition—with other departments and schools on the campus. More will be said about this particular issue in the next section on the effective use of campus curriculum procedures.

Defining your unit on campus can be difficult to accomplish. First, you must be able to articulate a clear and cogent rationale as to why your department is central to the mission of the university and the college. (For clarity, we use the term *college* to denote the immediate location of the department, for example the College of Journalism or the College of Arts and Science; we use *university* to refer to the entire institution.) Like an author ready to pitch a good script concept, a department chair needs a well-developed sentence, paragraph, and page description of why the department fits and what it uniquely contributes to the explicitly stated goals and missions of the university. Upper level administrators pay more attention to these statements than faculty tend to think. Perhaps we all need to borrow a page from the advice given to job applicants: Mimic as much as possible the mission statement, themes, goals, and so forth of your institution. If you do not know what they are, make it your job to find out. If they do not exist, look for the boilerplate rhetoric found on Web pages, at the beginning of course catalogs, or in speeches of your university president or campus provost (whatever their title). (See Christ & Blanchard, 1994; Christ & Hynes, 1997; Tucker, 1992.)

It is the job of department chair to be an articulate and effective advocate for the place of your department. It is even the job of chair to refute the sometimes outrageous slings and arrows of colleagues from other disciplines who find your group unimpressive. Be prepared. Previous chairs or more senior faculty can cue you into the common slurs in your location: You do not have any academic coherence, you are not central to the mission, you have no quality, or (my personal favorite) you are popular because you are so . . . (fill in the blank). In some cases, these arise from individuals within disciplines that are facing severe student shortages and are understandably hostile toward disciplines that attract large numbers of students. Some come from individuals who really do not understand what we do—frequently equating our activities with speech or drama performance courses, with technical training, or with the 1990s counterpart of encounter groups.

Of course, implicit within this advice is the assumption that your department has gone to the trouble of articulating a mission statement, and a set of responses in answer to the questions of where and how the department fits within the college and university. If you have not, get busy. This is not a mere formality but a strategic document that can be used to bolster your organizational status. (Note: Many departments have such a document even if not officially stated as a "mission." One place to look is in universitywide publications that describe your department, such as the undergraduate bulletin.)

Do not underestimate the importance of personally being able to answer questions about the aims and disciplinary status of the field, but to also offer evidence of quality in instruction, research, and service. It works like advertising: Sometimes repeating a catch phrase often enough penetrates even the most obdurate. And, by the way, it is worth your time to come up with these pithy phrases. Wait until the first time your university president describes your department as one internationally renowned for its innovative work in new technologies (or whatever).

If only arming the department head with reasonable answers to questions or attacks would solve these problems, life would be much simpler, but such is not the case. No matter how good your answers, some may not wish to be persuaded. So, beyond being a good advocate what can you do?

Protect Your Curriculum

In order to position itself on campus, and continue to take advantage of the benefits accruing from breadth of offerings, the department must carve out for itself a core curriculum that it and it alone offers on the campus. This becomes an important part of defining your department on campus. Let there be competition at the edges, but protect your core at all costs. Every department and its clone wants to offer multimedia design or Internet studies it seems, and so do we. But in the case of our departments it is easy to pinpoint large parts of our curricula that no one can offer but us, and that helps define us.

The design and production area of study at IU provides a good example. Production studios on campus in the Schools of Education and Journalism converted their production studios to other uses. Therefore, if a student is interested in studio production, our department is the only shop for it on campus. The same is true for video field production (with the exception of the Journalism School, which uses different equipment for its electronic newsgathering instruction) and audio production. These are high-demand courses that provide some of the character and reputation of the department.

On the Bloomington campus of IU the most obvious source of competition is the School of Journalism, but in reality there is generally little conflict. Similarly on the Athens campus of UG, the most obvious source of competition would be the Department of Communication, with similarly little conflict. Over the years the two units have carved out their own sequences and rarely does one unit encroach on the other. At IU, when the last broadcast news faculty member retired from the Telecommunications Department, we made the decision to leave that area to Journalism. At UGA, graduate students frequently take communications courses, and vice versa. On both our campuses, there is an understanding of role and responsibilities between the two units and a recognition that we should complement each other.

Defining your program involves offering something valuable to the campus and to your students that no other unit on campus can offer. There may be competition for students at the fringes, but that is to be expected. However, when some department begins to encroach on your core business, it is time to get tough. That is when knowledge and the effective use of campus curriculum procedures becomes crucial.

At IU, in addition to simply raising the number of students per class, College departments and the various other schools on campus seek to attract students by offering popular courses, and new courses are proposed constantly. Because the media are getting so much national attention, departments and schools try to find a way to cash in on that popularity. The Bloomington campus of IU, like most campuses, has elaborate procedures to approve new courses and modify old ones. The College of Arts and Sciences has its own process, similar but independent of the campus procedure. Effective use of these procedures is crucial to maintaining control over your curriculum and staving off intra-university competition.

Within the college, all curriculum changes are approved by a college curriculum committee and then sent on to the campus for approval at the campus level. Periodically the associate dean in charge of undergraduate affairs will send around a list of proposed course additions and amendments. It is important to peruse this list carefully—just reading the course titles is not always enough. When a conflict arises, that is, when another department proposes offering a course that we already offer, the associate dean is notified of the conflict and the two departments are asked to try to work it out if they can. Arguments concerning "duplication" can be effective at this level.

This is a beneficial first step because it allows the department chair to educate someone else in the college about what we do. When the Telecommunications Department proposed a new course entitled "Media and Politics," it was immediately challenged by the Political Science Department. In the process of discussing the conflict, we were able to show them that our course did in fact use some of the political science literature that they covered, but also included a great deal of communications literature that they never even knew existed. They dropped their challenge and we gained some respect.

On the other side of the coin, when the Sociology Department proposed a new course called "Media and Society," we objected. Our department has been teaching that for decades. But when the department chairs met to discuss the conflict, it again became clear that our focuses and content were much different. We dropped the challenge; they learned more about us and now they "owe" us one.

So, in general, if the English department wants to offer an occasional seminar in women and the media, let them. Your department may be able to take advantage of your accommodating behavior down the road by being treated similarly when you want to offer something that slightly conflicts with their curricula. It is a nice, two-way relationship where everyone wins, including the students.

However, let us say, just by way of example, that Fine Arts proposes a new series of courses on "video art" and it turns out those courses are really nothing more than a dressed-up attempt to offer field production classes. In this case the department would not back down and if Fine Arts pursued the courses, there would be a formal challenge at the college. Then the college curriculum committee would have to make a decision on the issue, and assuming they do their job correctly, those new courses would be rejected as a duplication of effort and a waste of valuable resources.

The same basic procedure supposedly takes place at the campus level, but the notification requirement is far less formalized. At UGA, where conflict would most likely occur outside the college, the dean receives all potential course conflict review requests. Rarely do we protest; most of our courses are filled with majors, and so unavailable campuswide. We were, nonetheless, surprised to see an interdisciplinary film studies major emerge from Arts and Sciences. On reflection, because we had dropped film courses long ago, we ventured no objections. This should provide an interesting venue for our students who are interested in working in film to broaden their knowledge. Once the dust has settled a bit from the semester transition, however, it will be interesting to see what new areas of curriculum conflict emerge.

Sometimes the process works and sometimes it does not. Regardless, departments like ours must be ever vigilant to protect our turf against course robbers. Fight like hell when you must, compromise when it is beneficial, and always grasp the opportunity to educate someone outside your department about what you do.

Develop Alliances With Other Programs and Schools

Another way to protect departments from intra-university competition is to seek mutually beneficial alliances with other programs on campus. This is more than a manipulative strategy; it is at the core of establishing your importance to the university. Such alliances can promote a sharing of ideas and students and can act as a way to gain notoriety and respect on campus. These alliances can be informal *ad hoc* affairs such as banding together with other programs to sponsor a visiting speaker or campus seminar. Or the alliances can be more formal, taking the form of special "minors," providing necessary courses for other programs, or even establishing joint degree programs with other schools. Telecommunications at IU and UGA pursue these options. Here are some examples that you might emulate.

All arts and sciences students at IU must complete a 15-hour minor area of study. Usually, this minor is taken within the college, as outside-college minors run the risk of violating college rules about how many hours of credit can be taken outside the college. Realizing the natural affinity between our management and strategy course work and some offerings in the School of Business, we proposed and received approval for a special 18-hour minor in business for our students. Most of our students focusing on the business side of telecommunications take the business minor. Although this alliance is mostly a one-way street—not many business students take that many of our courses—it nonetheless gives us a student presence in the Business School.

We are the beneficiaries of a similar program involving the School of Health, Physical Education and Recreation (HPER) and the School of Music. HPER's Department of Kinesiology offers a program in sports communication. Much of the curriculum involves learning how an athlete's body functions so that it can be explained to laymen. Students in this program must take a full measure of communications classes as well, in Journalism, Speech Communication, and Telecommunications. When our classes fill with our own majors, the HPER students are stranded. Often we can work out a deal to add more sections of courses the HPER students need. This serves the students and builds our enrollments. A similar situation involves some music students who must complete 30 hours outside of the school of music in one concentration area. We highly promote the department to those students, noting the natural affinity between music and the entertainment industries.

At UGA, two telecommunications "majors" are offered in other colleges. Consonant with the land-grant mission of the university, a major is offered in agricultural communications within the Agricultural and Environmental Sciences College. Students must take eight courses in journalism and mass communication. A similar program in consumer journalism requires students in the Family and Consumer Sciences to take six courses from our college. For the many other students who are interested in mass communication, but unable to major in our areas, the college also offers a minor that requires students to take six courses in the college.

At IU, we established a joint venture with the School of Library and Information Science (SLIS). This school only offers graduate degrees and does not generate significant credit hours. SLIS and the Director of Undergraduate Studies from telecommunications created a new 1-hour course for beginning telecommunications students, taught by SLIS faculty. The course dovetailed with our introductory survey course and provided library bibliography building training for sources most useful to telecommunications students. Our students benefitted from better library skills, their papers got better, and SLIS generated a few more credit hours.

Two new initiatives may prove IU's most exciting joint ventures yet. First we are developing a joint JD/MS degree with the law school. The program will allow students to complete two degrees that would normally take 5 years in a 4-year period. Such a program is especially salient on this campus because the law school has several noted communications and constitutional scholars on its faculty and the school publishes the *Federal Communications Law Journal*, on which a number of our students work. At UGA, an honors program option, one that is open only to students who are enrolled in the university honors program, allows students to complete a Bachelor of Arts in Journalism and an MBA in 5 years. Some of our best students are pursuing this admittedly difficult program of study.

The second new initiative at IU is the Masters in Immersive Mediated Environments MIME). This masters degree program is multidisciplinary in nature and pulls faculty from a number of schools and programs around the campus, including Business, Education, SLIS, Fine Arts, Computer Science, Psychology, Cognitive Science, and Telecommunications. When put in place, the program will provide students with in-depth theoretical and practical knowledge of multimedia design. At UGA, an interdisciplinary studies major in 3-D animation is becoming popular. Combining art, drama, and telecommunications, these undergraduates are pursing a highly specialized program in an area of great industry demand.

Obviously not all campuses will offer opportunities exactly like these, but there may be similar ones or quite different ones to pursue. Always be on the lookout for these beneficial alliances. The more people on campus who know who you are and what you do, the better off you will be.

Demonstrate Your Excellence

Use every opportunity to demonstrate to the university community the quality of your program, your alumni, your faculty, and your students. Any time you find your department ranked high among your peer institutions, make sure that information is conveyed to upper administrators—as often as possible. Also toot your horn widely when your faculty or students are singled our for prominent national awards and honors.

What do you have to offer that other programs may not? For many, it is highly visible alumni that might be lured back to speak at the university. It may be an ability to produce video materials for various university organizations through a student organization. One chair noted that his department has begun offering communication training to the state legislature.

One avenue to visibility that has been particularly successful at UGA involves bringing highly visible entertainment industry professionals to campus. The inevitable connections that accrue from our work within the profession, and at UGA the linkage with the Peabody awards, has meant that many famous individuals visit campus yearly. Our student honorary has a yearly award for distinguished service to broadcasting. One major criteria for getting this award is that the individuals appear at the banquet to accept the award and to deliver a speech. The university president and vice-presidents are always invited, as they are to the Peabody luncheon in New York City. Do not let these situations go unrecognized.

Another avenue to visibility is to receive universitywide grants and awards. Develop a facility in preparing proposals quickly. If your institution is like ours, it seems "opportunities" with a 2-day turn-around are always turning up. A good file of proposals, curricular needs, development ideas, faculty vita and letters of praise, symposia ideas, equipment lists, and collaborative proposals can be used to net institutional goodies. It is important to be a recipient; winning these grants and awards adds prestige to your program. Your name should frequently appear in the university press releases.

Similarly, encourage your best faculty to become involved in university governance. Foster an atmosphere in which service is expected and individuals are carefully chosen for important, relevant committees. You want your best out there impressing the university community.

Departments do not exist in isolation. The public perception of your department is vital in achieving appropriate recognition and receiving the resources you need. As an administrator, one must always be proactive in this arena.

Develop a Good Relationship With Your Dean

Although most chairs think of themselves as faculty, they are in an administrative position. The chair must reflect the concerns of upper administration, communicate policies, and implement required changes. Thus, a chair's relationship with the dean is an important component of effectiveness. Deans are increasingly spending their time fundraising, in addition to their other obligations of managing a multimillion-dollar budget, implementing their own goals and visions, being a public spokesperson for the college, listening to complaints, and being able to talk to anyone about something.

Deans and chairs must develop trust if they are to work together effectively. With the many activities just noted, it is easy for a dean to be only superficially informed about a department. Chairs should quickly determine how a dean prefers to communicate: e-mail, regular face-to-face discussions, or memos. Then keep the lines of communication open. Deans *will* hear about problems or issues. The worst thing you can do is be the kind of chair who only communicates with a dean when there is a crisis. A department head should be willing to be open and candid in discussion with deans. Be carefully prepared for your regular meetings and use these opportunities to explore ideas and options, discuss facing challenges, and—never to be missed—the successes of the department. For our purposes, a supportive dean—or failing that a dean who can be persuaded to value your department—is invaluable in bolstering your image in the upper levels of administration, in standing ground against competitive departments, and with outside stakeholders.

DEALING WITH OUTSIDE STAKEHOLDERS

Ever notice how all the big newspaper companies throw their money around to journalism schools? Everywhere you turn, the Gannett Foundation is giving millions to this school, the Knight-Ridder Foundation is giving millions to that school, and the Scripps-Howard Foundation is giving millions to another school. In fact, the Henry W. Grady College of Journalism and Mass Communication receives significant support from the James M. Cox, Jr. Foundation. However, if your department is located in a college of arts and sciences, you are clearly out of this loop. At IU, we approached the Tribune Foundation recently and learned that they only give grants to journalism programs, notwithstanding the fact that Tribune now has sizable holdings (and earnings) outside its journalistic enterprises.

So where do departments outside journalism schools look for the big bucks? The GE/NBC Foundation? The Westinghouse/CBS Foundation? Perhaps the Disney/ABC Foundation? To the best of my knowledge, if such foundations exist, they do not distribute money to academic programs the way large newspaper foundations do. We are left to seek support from alumni and industry in other ways, through small grants, in-kind gifts, and internship opportunities to name a few. Accordingly, cultivating these groups is increasingly important.

Dealing With Alumni

Alumni are among the most significant outside stakeholders. They feel a connection to their department and can often become even more supportive over time. It is important that strategies be in place to cultivate alumni.

Alumni like to feel that their degree has value. Communicating with them about the successes of old and new faculty, facilities, awards, and grants builds their pride and sense of attachment. They like to hear that current faculty and students are more able than ever, and they love to hear about other alumni. Your alums will get magazines from the college and the university, and if they are members of the alumni association, they will receive publications from that source as well. But unless you tell them about the department, nobody will. A semiannual department newsletter provides an excellent vehicle for staying in touch with your graduates.

If you do not already do this, newsletters need not be back breakers. There is probably an office on campus that will assist you: the alumni association, a publications office, perhaps even the college development office. Most of the newsletter can be filled with the comments of alums who have written in, although this takes a while if you are just starting. You can also ask a prominent alum to write a feature article on anything he or she wishes. This can lead to some very good copy with almost no effort on your part. Throw in a couple pictures, an article from the chair on the state of department, and that is about it. You will incur some production and printing costs, but those are small indeed compared to the goodwill you will generate among your alumni for giving them the feeling that they still belong to the department. Additionally, some departments and organizations are beginning to experiment with Web pages and online newsletters. With e-mail links to all faculty, alumni chat lines, and other variations that are emerging, these can brilliantly maintain links with alumni.

Although receiving information is important, alumni also like to feel personally engaged. One way is to involve them in the occasional committee or project: developing internships in a certain area, recruiting students, or promoting a departmental project. An excellent way to involve alumni is to invite them back to campus to speak to a class. They enjoy the nostalgia, and students benefit from hearing about the "real" world. Advisory and alumni boards can formalize many of these relationships. Remember that these alumni can represent the department in a variety of public and private forums beyond the university. On occasion, contact with alumni will produce a donation: a scholarship, a research fund, some unrestricted funds, or even an endowed chair. Work with your university development office to identify alums capable of such largess. But remember that the goodwill is invaluable in many ways that cannot be measured.

It can also be very good alumni relations to nominate distinguished alumni for college and campus honors. Such awards can be quite prestigious and an honor not only to the alum but to the sponsoring department as well. It never hurts to look at the wall in the distinguished alumni room and see the picture of one of your graduates right next to a Nobel prize winner in physics.

Alumni are much tougher to reach from a department in a large college. Almost all solicitations at the university are made on behalf of the various schools, not individual departments. Even getting lists of alumni addresses can be trying. Departments have a very difficult time getting the attention of the university's major fundraising organization, usually the university foundation. In large colleges, the college office of development works with individual departments on special projects, but its primary focus is to develop funding for the college.

The question arises then of how a department situated like this takes advantage of its industry and alumni constituencies despite the limitations of its location in a large liberal arts college. There are several strategies that can be utilized, and some are more successful than others. Almost all of these strategies rely on departmental personnel doing most of the work; department administrators must be aware that they must either take on much of this burden or assign the tasks to other faculty, most of whom already feel overworked.

Parents as an Outside Stakeholder

Although not alumni, parents are an external constituency to remember. One of the most successful activities at UGA is the graduation convocation. At the end of each term, students, faculty, and parents come together to individually recognize each graduate. Unlike the larger university graduation, each student walks across the stage as his or her name is announced, receives a small token (e.g., a paperweight) and shakes hands with the dean and the university president or vice president. A brief speech by the dean usually focuses on the importance of communications and journalism in our era and the responsibilities these graduates will assume, ably trained to meet these challenges by the Grady College. A reception after the half-hour ceremony allows parents to meet faculty. This convocation is often chosen by students over the university graduation ceremony. Departments in large colleges probably cannot conduct their own commencement ceremonies. However, at IU we have a reception for our graduates and their parents where many of the same activities can be conducted. The benefits in engaging parents and imparting a sense of commitment to students cannot be overestimated.

Industry Connections

Media industries are another significant outside stakeholder. They are, of course, concerned that our alumni are capable and eager. A department should promote that perception for the benefit of students and alumni. Additionally, the industry can be an excellent resource for insights, internships, co-ops, tours, and equipment donations.

As with alumni, engaging industry professionals in the department is the key to developing relationships. Many are eager to speak with students, and to "give back" in some way. Some would delight in appearing at job fairs—especially if you have minority students. In general, you will find individuals with a generally positive disposition toward education and students who enjoy the interaction with them. As with alumni, ask for their help with occasional projects. Because of their profession, they can frequently help build connections with others who have similar interests. Again, they can also represent the department within public and professional forums. What we find particularly sad are the number of professionals we meet who are eager to tour, to speak, to consider internships and whose comment is, "No one has ever asked me before." Do not be afraid to ask.

One word of caution is in order: Not all industry people are positively disposed to training in our field. Some came from disciplines other than ours and believe that is the better route. Others feel their own education failed them. Unfortunately, many have seen student interns or new hires who lack basic skills. There is no way to confront this directly; one can only hope that seeing your students, facilities, and faculty will over time erode that attitude.

About the only time local media leaders who are not our alumni take the initiative to contact departments is when they think we have done something wrong. During our time as department chairs, we received several calls from local station managers asking why our graduates did not know this or that particular piece of information. When this happens to you, use these as teachable moments. Invite the caller to the office, hear their complaints, and then use the opportunity to educate them about what you really do, as opposed to what they think you should be doing. Our guests always left impressed with what we were trying to accomplish, and asked how they could help the department. Although the initial contact may not be particularly pleasant, the outcome of such encounters can be quite positive.

Dealing with your outside constituencies—other departments on campus, partners in industry, and your alumni—represents one of the most important, yet least emphasized, things that a department administrator must attend to. Most department administrators understand how easy it is to get caught up in the bureaucratic minutia of the job, only lifting your head from the sea of paper and required signatures to prepare the next budget, supervise the next hire, build the next course schedule, or more likely, put out the latest fire that should never have been started in the first place. Given all that, it is still important to make time for these external constituencies. Spending some quality time on the issues we have addressed in this chapter can lead to a more respected, increasingly productive, and higher quality program.

REFERENCES

Blanchard, R. O., & Christ, W. G. (1993). *Media education and the liberal arts: A blueprint for the new professionalism*. Hillsdale, NJ: Lawrence Erlbaum Associates.

Christ, W. G. (Ed.). (1994). *Assessing communications education: A handbook for media, speech, and theatre educators*. Hillsdale, NJ: Lawrence Erlbaum Associates.

Christ, W. G. (Ed.). (1997). *Media education assessment handbook*. Mahwah, NJ: Lawrence Erlbaum Associates.

Christ, W. G., & Blanchard, R.O. (1994). Mission statements, outcomes, and the new liberal arts. In W. G. Christ (Ed.), *Assessing communication education: A handbook for media, speech, and theatre educators* (pp. 31–55). Hillsdale, NJ: Lawrence Erlbaum Associates.

Christ, W. G., & Hynes, T. (1997).The mission and purposes of journalism and mass communications education. *Journalism and Mass Communication Educator, 52*(2), 73–100.

Medsger, B. (1996). *Winds of change: Challenges confronting journalism education.* Arlington, VA: Freedom Forum.

Planning for curricular change in journalism education (2nd ed.). (1987). [Project on the Futurre of Journalism and Mass Communication Education]. Eugene: The Oregon Report.

Rowland, W. D., Jr. (1993). The traditions of communication research and their implications for telecommunications study. *Journal of Communication, 43*(3), 207–217.

State of the Field. (1994). Austin, TX: State of the Field Communication Conference.

Tucker, A. (1992). *Chairing the academic department* (3rd ed.) . New York: Macmillan.

15

Student Occupational Concerns in a Liberal Arts Program

Jeffrey McCall
DePauw University

It has surely always been the case that students attending a college or university have had expectations that a college degree eventually leads to greater employment success. However, trends in the 1990s seem to have increased the degree of this expectation. Corporate downsizing, and its related increase in job market competition from midcareer workers, has made college students fearful of what could be a very tight job market. In addition, recent pushes for more accountability in higher education have led to expectations that go beyond assuring that graduates have learned anything. As outcomes become important to college consumers, both students and their parents, perhaps the key outcome expected now is suitable employment after a course of study. Practically minded students of this era are clearly job-focused. It is common for prospective college students and their parents to spend more time considering a school's placement rate than the content of any academic program. Many colleges, in response to these "customer" demands, have expanded career services for students and made placement rates and alumni job networking part of the discussion in admissions and marketing materials.

WHAT STUDENTS SAY THEY WANT

One might figure that students attending liberal arts institutions would be more free from a preoccupation with jobs and careerism. After all, liberal arts institutions have long shunned vocationalism and prepro-fessional training in honor of long-standing traditional studies in the humanities, sciences, and the arts. However, recent data about student expectations at liberal arts institutions clearly contradict this notion that liberal arts students might be more noble and less concerned about the job world after graduation. The Office of Institutional Research at DePauw University (1995) summarized national findings of why students select a particular college or university. In these studies, 42% of students nationally indicated that they selected a school where they thought the graduates got good jobs. At selective, Protestant liberal arts schools, 60% of students chose the school in large part because they thought the graduates got good jobs. Even at an institution with a proud liberal arts tradition, DePauw University, 77% of incoming students reported that a major reason DePauw was chosen was because graduates get good jobs. This ironic phenomenon clearly suggests that even students at liberal arts institutions have been influenced by societal pressures for careerism. Students seek liberal arts institutions because of a perception that it will pay off, literally, in the career world, a motivation seldom noted in the missions of liberal arts schools. Given the high tuition expenses for attending a liberal arts institution, the pressure on these universities to produce for graduates entering the job market is enormous. Students, and their parents, are willing to invest more into what a liberal arts institution has to offer (smaller classes, more faculty interaction, cocurricular opportunities, etc.), but they clearly expect a bigger job bang for the extra tuition bucks they have committed.

There is nothing particularly wrong with students and parents being concerned about postgraduation job prospects. In this era, it would be senseless anyway for universities to try to convince students otherwise. Let them be career-minded. To try to convince them to the contrary would, of course, be a losing proposition. In addition, a vocal case against coming to college for career preparation could be interpreted that mere academic pursuits are not helpful in career development.

Instead, the key is to redefine for job-conscious students how they best prepare for the world of work.

THE NOTION OF LIBERAL EDUCATION

The liberal arts educational framework demands that students be given opportunities to learn how to think critically, to engage society as productive citizens, and to develop individualism. Kimball (1986) said the goal of liberal education is the "freeing of the mind to pursue truth" (p. 8). Thus, liberal education, unlike many industry professionals and even some accrediting agencies believe, is not merely general education. It is more than gathering information about a wide range of subjects, but rather an approach to learning about those subjects, communication included, that focuses on an individual's analytical search for truth. This vision of education is historically found in relatively small institutions that define themselves as liberal arts colleges. The approach and direction of the program, however, is the key to whether a student is liberally educated. A smaller program teaching mere practical skills would obviously be less "liberal" than a larger program focusing on critical thinking and individualism.

The goals of liberal education are not likely to be realized in programs of study or courses that merely impose on students the current industry-accepted standards and practices. That is not to say any study that is useful in preparing a student for an eventual profession is automatically illiberal. Students heading into communication-related careers need to be able to analyze and critically evaluate the processes and issues of the field. Students are well prepared for a communication career when they study the field within a liberating framework—they gain exposure to issues, concepts, and even practices of the communication process, but they gain the individual analytical understandings to analyze, evaluate, and change the field.

THE CHALLENGE OF CAREERISM

The challenge for liberal arts schools then becomes how to best accommodate demands for career preparation while adhering to their liberal arts heritage. It would be easy to sell out to the career pressures of the era and create preprofessional programs that just happen to be located on what were once liberal arts campuses. The temptation for this strategy is especially great for many communication departments at liberal arts institutions, particularly with regard to the study of mass media. Given the need to attract students and given that communication study has yet to enter the hallowed grounds of traditional liberal arts study (philosophy, sciences, history, literature, etc.), communication departments are easily tempted to heed calls for careerism at the expense of the study of content. The mistake of many departments is to too quickly assume that concerns about jobs translate into the need for more careerism in academic programs. Students (and their parents) want solid employment opportunities after graduation, and they likely have little concern about how the programs are structured that create these opportunities.

Pressures from the practitioner communication and media world have further complicated the situation. Practitioners have long criticized the academy for failing to adequately train students with entry-level skills for the workplace. The media industry made this point quite clear in its celebrated Roper Report (Roper Organization, 1987) of the late 1980s. That report, commissioned by the International Radio Television Society, the Radio–Television News Directors Association, and the National Association of Television Program Executives, profiled the practical media industry's dissatisfaction with media education at the nation's universities. This overall dissatisfaction theme has been continued in recent reports coming out of the Freedom Forum and the Society of Professional Journalists (SPJ). The Roper Report, among other things, concluded that media educators were out of touch with the "real world," and failed to train students sufficiently with practical skills (Roper Organization, 1987, pp. 4–5). The SPJ report (1996) similarly called for higher standards and more emphasis on "performance characteristics" (pp. 5–6). The Freedom Forum report also found much to criticize regarding the education of today's media students, and called for more focus on a "journalism culture" (Medsger, 1996, p. 66) to be delivered to campus by nonacademic industry practitioners. Continuing charges can be heard each year at various practitioner conventions and workshops. The practitioner world, thus, has created a false skills and training versus theory and understanding dichotomy that academicians have too quickly engaged for discussion.

Ultimately, the academy must withstand vocational pressures and commit to designing academic programs that stand for themselves in the career world. Those programs should be rooted in liberal study, as many scholars have indicated (see, e.g., Blanchard & Christ, 1993; Christ, 1997; McCall, 1992).

ANSWERING THE MYTH OF SKILLS
VERSUS UNDERSTANDING

A sensible academic program must not be sacrificed in the name of careerism. It is a myth to suggest that universities (and students) must choose between liberal-arts-based communication education or preprofessional career-based programs focusing on trainable skills, and that skills students get jobs and liberal arts students are unemployable. Academicians must clearly indicate to both students and the practitioner world that solid academic study is preparation for careers. This is where the academy must define the discussion on its own terms. Students are best prepared for careers by learning how to think critically, by improving their analytical abilities, and by becoming effective in both written and spoken expression. This is what happens at a university. The university context is virtually the last place for students to engage in such focused intellectual development for the rest of their lives. Further, it would seem to make sense, as well, that students who intend to pursue professional careers in communication would most benefit from developing their analytical competence and their self-expression abilities in the context of a program of study that focuses on the process of communication and its accompanying issues.

A number of leading media educators have helped to create an articulate case for resisting industry calls for occupationalism. In his spirited call for defending the university tradition, particularly in the area of media study, Carey (1978) said the focus of professionalism must be removed from academic programs:

> We must do that in order to reassert the university tradition, in order to reassert the general ethical and intellectual point of view against all the claims of specialism that would overwhelm it. We must recognize that we are not merely training people for a profession or for the current demands of professional practice but for membership in the public and for a future that transcends both the limitations of contemporary practice and contemporary politics. (p. 855)

Other scholars (Avery, 1995; Blanchard & Christ, 1993; Bliss, 1987; Carroll, 1987; McCall, 1992; McCloskey, 1994; Porter & Szolka, 1991) have lent their support to a vision of communication education that emphasizes critical understanding over training of specific skills.

Selling out to careerism and vocationalism in communication education creates several major problems. First, it is fundamentally not the best way for students to be educated for a life of work and individual challenges. Wood (1993) argued that society needs educated people who can "view the human dilemma from the broadest possible perspective," and "Nowhere is this need for the liberally trained generalist more obvious than in communications" (p. 3). Second, as has been expressed on a number of occasions, communication departments engaging in practitioner preparation reduce their own legitimacy in the academy (Blanchard & Christ 1993; McCall, 1995; Wartella, 1994; and others). This is dangerous in the current era of "back to basics" and overall accountability to the entire institution. Finally, caving in to calls for vocationalism from the industry basically allows the practical world to steal the academy's vision as a place for intellectual pursuits. Industry bashing of institutions of higher learning and industry calls for specific job training are counterproductive for both the academy's interests and the interests of students. It is also counterproductive for the media industry, although, sadly, too few practitioners recognize the benefits of new employees who can think critically as opposed to simply being able to execute skills. Such inappropriate industry criticism creates unnecessary confusion among students about what and how they should be studying in college.

IF NOT SKILLS AND OCCUPATIONAL COURSES, THEN WHAT?

Departments that do not cave in to calls for occupationalism, and instead adhere to their principles in offering a liberal-arts-based course of communication study, must be prepared to answer student questions about how what they will study can translate into job preparation. Too often, students expect that to be prepared for a career in advertising, they must take courses called "advertising." The same can be said for public relations, marketing, media production, and journalism. Given how many schools engage in course labeling based on job titles, it cannot be unexpected that students in the liberal arts context expect such courses to help them in their own career preparation. The basic problem with labeling courses with job titles is the assumption that one type of communication is here and another type of communication is there. Communication study must be conducted with a focus on understanding process (see Bohn, 1988). Understanding in the process of communication can be applied in many contexts of communication. Students need to understand that course work in interpersonal communication, organizational communication, media criticism, communication research, media effects, persuasion, argumentation, communication ethics, and so on, are indeed relevant and essential to understanding the processes of advertising, public relations, media sales, news reporting, and other related careers. Although none of these listed courses are connected to the title of a specific occupation, it can be easily noted that understanding of the content within those courses leads to more effective practice in professional communication jobs.

Industry professionals and some students may harp that they need more skills courses that show how to do a specific job, but what they really need is understanding of concepts and processes. Prospective advertising professionals are more "skilled" by understanding the processes of persuasion and interpersonal communication. Prospective reporters are more "skilled" when they understand the thinking of communication ethicists and the manner in which words generate meaning as found in the study of rhetorical theory. Studying how to do a particular job and understanding the underlying nuances of the process of that job are different things. (An auto mechanic knows the specific steps to take to fix an engine with a particular malfunction, but an engineer understands the physics behind why those steps correct the problem.) It can be argued that students might need a certain amount of "skill" to be employable in the communication professions, but this practice in skill should not come at the expense of conceptually based education. The career world needs the critical and analytical thinkers that can emerge from the classrooms providing a liberal education. Other avenues exist for students to gain practical skill while applying these conceptual understandings of communication. Such other avenues include student media outlets, internships, and even the early experiences of initial jobs, as is explained later in this chapter.

Again, the emphasis, as would be expected within the liberal arts context, is not merely on how to do a job (advertising, media production, public relations, etc.), but on why to do it, how to analyze it, and how to determine its effects. Dates (1990) confirmed this focus on theory as the appropriate guide for the communication curriculum. She said communication educators must educate students to be "people of intellectual competence and character," and that cannot be accomplished "by merely providing students with practical knowledge of the various professions" (p. 11). Wood (1993) believed providing students with theoretical perspectives is essential in the constantly changing environment of the professional communication world: "what we can give them (students) is the theoretical bases, the background and history, the communication principles that will be applicable tomorrow. If we are to be relevant, we must be theoretical—not faddish, not occupationally driven" (p. 3).

A recent study (Williamson & Iorio, 1996) concludes that communication curricula have, indeed, now accepted theoretical, historical, and philosophical approaches to the discipline, but that too little uniformity is found in terms of how the approaches are used in the various programs. The discipline's next step should be to solidify its commitment to such theoretical approaches and ensure the depth of these approaches throughout a curriculum. Surely, more work is needed to stabilize the theoretical foundation of communication study on college campuses.

STRATEGIES TO PROVIDE
CAREER PERSPECTIVES
IN THE LIBERAL ARTS CONTEXT

Protecting academic legitimacy, obviously, is a must, but that is not to say that universities ignore students' concerns for finding suitable employment after graduation. Those concerns need to be addressed, but in a parallel and secondary route that does not diminish or replace the substance or content of the academic program. With the proper focus and balance, students can be provided ample opportunity to engage the practitioner world and connect to the employment market while pursuing a legitimate and substantial program in communication.

Getting the Right Message to Students

The scheme of understanding communication processes within the liberal arts context must be articulated clearly to the students at every juncture of their educational journey, from the admissions process to the academic advising process and even into the actual course content.

Porter and Szolka (1991) affirmed the importance of directly explaining to students the nature of their liberal arts education in communication, and clarifying for them the distinction between a liberal arts program and a professional school: "If what our students are looking for is four years of 'hands-on' experience with television cameras and video editing machines and audio mixers then they belong elsewhere" (p. 20).

The admissions office personnel, too, must understand the liberal arts versus vocational distinctions so they can work at the outset to establish student visions. A communication department cannot assume, even if it has a clear mission in its own mind, that the admissions recruiters will understand or be able to disseminate that mission clearly to the prospective students. Admissions offices are subject to the same misconceptions about proper directions of communication education as are members of the public and the practical media industry. Further, in this era, admissions offices are keenly aware of public pressure for universities to deliver jobs to graduates. Thus, communication educators should take it on themselves to make sure admissions offices understand the rationale of a liberal-arts-based communication educational program and that the rationale is provided to students considering the particular institution. Two simple strategies can be implemented to make sure the admissions office understands the communication program's vision. First, department faculty can invite admissions officers for a meeting that explains the program rationale and defines the program thrust in contrast to other sorts of programs. Second, the department leadership should assert itself to take a role in devising the content of admissions materials that discuss the institution's communication educational program.

The Role of Advising in Career Matters

Just as faculty advise students with regard to courses and graduation requirements, advice needs to be provided on the career prospects in communication as well. Through individual advising sessions or department workshops, students can be made aware of their career options and the variety of information emerging about the importance of communication understanding in the professional world. Students need to be made aware of their employment options not only in traditional communication careers (electronic media, advertising, marketing, public relations, etc.), but also in communication-related careers (personnel, government service, law, education, business, etc.; see

Berko, Brooks, & Spielvogel, 1995; Sgambelluri & Huffer, 1994). This is an ideal occasion for students to get the message that a liberal arts based program in communication provides them more flexibility in the career world than a more vocationally driven program. Atkin (1993) said students need to be made aware of employment options beyond traditional broadcast communication jobs. He says students need "employment flexibility" to meet a "fluid job market" in which "conventional job descriptions" (p. 65) are less often seen.

Students can also be made more aware of the research findings regarding the communication job market. For example, Funkhouser and Savage (1987) indicated that student expectations of broadcast employment are not fully consistent with the perceptions of industry employers. Steinke (1993) gathered data indicating that broadcast managers prefer to hire new employees who have earned degrees in communication study. Schaffer (1996) wrote that students who are effective in speaking, listening, and writing (as communication majors should be) have opportunities in the field of new technologies, even without specific high-tech preparation. These are just a few examples, but it is clear that the information provided in these studies, and others, can be of use to students who will eventually leave the classroom and enter the world of work. Communication educators have a responsibility to see that students get access to this information.

Exposure to Industry Professionals

Students wanting to know about what happens in specific occupations should be exposed to the people who work in those occupations. There is nothing inconsistent with providing this exposure to industry practitioners even while operating a strong, liberal-arts-based academic program. Academics sometimes fear the industry practitioner who comes to campus and then bashes the academic approach to communication study, or even dismisses the relevance of studying communication as opposed to history, political science, or other supposedly more noble fields. This potential difficulty can be managed in several ways. First, faculty should take care to scout out the industry professionals they are considering inviting to campus. Invite those media spokespersons who have a sense of understanding (not necessarily a total endorsement) for the department's mission in communication education. Next, it is important for guest speakers to be given specific content areas to discuss in their presentations. This lets the speakers know precisely what insights they are being asked to share in the flow of a course, and hopefully avoids a more general discussion of whatever agenda the speaker would otherwise choose. Finally, students need to know the context in which a speaker is being brought to them. Faculty members should tell the students in advance about what topic the speaker will engage, why this speaker is able to address it, and how that fits within the course goals. The day following a practitioner's presentation, the professor should engage students in a discussion that gathers student reactions and clears up any questions or inconsistencies.

The key is that entire courses and programs not be centered around the presence of the visiting practitioners. There are many contexts where visiting industry spokespersons can impact students both inside and outside of the traditional classroom. These can include evening or luncheon talks, mock job interviews, weekend workshops, side-by-side work in student media organizations, and so forth, in addition to an occasional guest lecture in a particular class. However, academicians inviting practitioners to campus should make clear to the students and visitors the mission of such visits. The mission should not be to separate study from the practice of communication, but instead to demonstrate where these two paths merge. Faculty who bring industry pros to campus to show students the "real world" negate the very visions they should be creating in their classrooms—that the study of media is also "real" but done for understanding instead of application. Students should be encouraged to study the visiting professionals for the values, judgments, and cultures those professionals represent. Students who are supposedly being taught to become critical thinkers should not be lured into seeing every visiting practitioner as the appropriate industry model who drifts onto campus to "tell it like it is." Students can benefit from perspectives that tell it like it is, but they should be able to assess those perspectives from the standpoint of what should be.

Internship Programs

Internship programs can be justified within the context of a liberal arts institution. The key is to make certain that internship experiences blend within the overall thrust of the program's commitment to under-standing. Internships should not be viewed as replacing parts of the curriculum or merely as opportunities to learn what cannot be learned in the classroom. Internships should not be characterized as a separate place to learn job skills because the academic course work has no relevance to the workplace. Internships should be viewed as places for students to observe the professional culture and to determine if they see themselves fitting into that culture. Internships should be viewed as places where students can reflect on theoretical and critical assumptions formed in the classrooms. In this sense, the theoretical understandings gathered at the academy should follow the students into the practical setting. It is fine that students participate in internships to see how jobs are really done in the practitioner world, but the critical thinking skills they acquire on campus must be applied as they carefully assess the strengths and weaknesses of that practitioner world.

Internships can be conducted during summers when students break from the traditional academic calendar. Other internships can be coordinated during off-campus study programs on either the domestic or international level. Some schools make provisions for internship time during innovative academic calendars such as the 4-1-4 model or the 4-4-1 plan.

Although it is accepted practice that college credit accompany internship experiences, institutions should be careful about how much credit they give for those experiences. Internships should not be viewed as replacements for academic experiences, but rather as supplements for those academic initiatives. Whereas giving a course credit or two for internships would hardly diminish the overall strength of a program, awarding an entire semester's credit for an internship, as some universities do, suggests a message that practical experience can take the place of an academic semester. Students should also be expected to complete more academically related work as part of an internship experience. The internship work product alone should not generate academic credit. Reflective papers should be required as part of the internship to assure that students analyze their practical internship experiences in relationship to the theoretical and critical content of their academic study.

Co-Curricular Opportunities in Student Media

Student media outlets provide students with the opportunity to apply skills and develop expertise outside of the traditional classroom setting. Again, like the internship, student media activity should not be considered a replacement for classroom learning, but rather an enhancement of what is gained in the classroom. Ambitious students can use these student media avenues as a way to develop career-related qualities like leadership, creativity, collaboration, and responsibility—all traits fundamental to the liberal arts tradition and valued by industry professionals. Many student media organizations are structured in ways that closely approximate career duties in professional media—production, promotion, news, programming, and so on. Blanchard and Christ (1993) referred to such operations as media workshops. They distinguish this workshop concept from another viable avenue for student media opportunity—the media laboratory. The media laboratory is designed to provide a more experimental environment where students challenge and go beyond duplicating the standards and practices of the current professional media world. Blanchard and Christ contended, and quite appropriately so, that the laboratory approach is more consistent with the critical and analytical approach of liberal arts education. With either a workshop or laboratory approach, students can benefit from the experience of creating mediated messages in a nonclassroom setting. This experience should give students confidence as they move eventually from a university into a career setting.

Nonmedia student organizations can also provide opportunities for students interested in communication-related careers. Many student unions, student governments, volunteer associations, and so forth, have promotion or marketing departments that can make use of students wishing to apply their knowledge and gain practical experience.

Career Planning Offices

Most faculty do not have the time, resources, or background to run placement centers out of their offices. However, many have perspectives that can help the university placement centers work better for communication students seeking career opportunities. Career and placement centers have long been noted for directing most of their efforts toward students seeking employment in traditional business and sales, education, and technical areas. Communication faculty need to make sure that the career centers also have the background and interest to support students entering communication-related fields. The career planning staffers can be effective allies not only in placing communication students, but also in supporting visions of how the discipline is essential in the work world. The reassurance to students that can be found from placement staffers who are familiar with the career paths of communication graduates cannot be underestimated.

Communication faculty can work to build bridges with the career center through collaborating on projects of mutual benefit. Faculty can forward the names of communication alumni to the career center for use in an alumni clearinghouse of contacts that current students could use for internship leads, job leads, or career advice. Cosponsorship of an on-campus job fair, featuring the institution's communication alumni, is another avenue to explore.

In summary, students today are career-minded and it is fruitless to tell them they should not be. However, they can be reassured by a direct message that solid, liberal-arts-based academic preparation is an appropriate and effective way to prepare for a career. That academic preparation, combined with a structure that provides for analyzing, observing, and participating in the applied world, can lead a student to ample opportunities for success beyond the classroom. In this sense, students get the best of all possible worlds—an academic program of substance that positions them for a lifetime of personal and professional communication challenges, and an exposure to the avenues into their practical careers.

REFERENCES

Atkin, D. (1993). The influence of gender and area of specialty on salary for telecommunication graduates. *Journal of the Association for Communication Administration 1*, 59–66.

Avery, R. K. (1995). Mining the mother lode. *Western Journal of Communication, 59*(3), 246–251.

Berko, R., Brooks, M., & Spielvogel, J. C. (1995). *Pathways to careers in communication*. Annandale, VA: Speech Communication Association.

Blanchard, R. O., & Christ, W. G. (1993). *Media education and the liberal arts: A blueprint for the new professionalism*. Hillsdale, NJ: Lawrence Erlbaum Associates.

Bliss, E. (1987). What is needed in a broadcast journalism course. *Feedback, 28*(2), 3–6.

Bohn, T. W. (1988). Professional and liberal education. *ACA Bulletin, 64*, 16–23.

Carroll, R. (1987). No "middle ground": Professional broadcast education is liberal education. *Feedback, 28*(2), 7–10.

Carey, J. W. (1978). A plea for the university tradition. *Journalism Quarterly, 55*(4), 846–855.

Christ, W. G. (Ed.). (1997). *Media education assessment handbook*. Mahwah, NJ: Lawrence Erlbaum Associates.

Dates, J. L. (1990). The study of theory should guide the curriculum. *Feedback, 31*(3), 10–11.

Funkhouser, E., & Savage, A. L., Jr. (1987). College students' expectation for entry-level broadcast positions. *Communication Education, 36*(1), 23–27.

Kimball, B. A. (1986). *Orators and philosophers: A history of the idea of liberal education.* New York: Teachers College Press.

McCall, J. M. (1992). Mass communication education belongs to the university. *Journal of the Association for Communication Association, 82,* 33–38.

McCall, J. M. (1995, November). *Recapturing the role of communication arts and sciences in liberal education: Selling it to the academy.* Paper presented at the annual meeting of the Speech Communication Association, San Antonio, TX.

McCloskey, D. (1994). The neglected economics of talk. *Planning for Higher Education, 22,* 11–16.

Medsger, B. (1996). *Winds of change: Challenges confronting journalism education.* Arlington, VA: Freedom Forum.

Office of Institutional Research. (1995). *Report 3, CIRP Series.* Greencastle, IN: DePauw University.

Porter, M. J., & Szolka, P. (1991). Broadcasting students' perspectives on the liberal arts. *Feedback, 32*(2), 18–21.

The Roper Organization, Inc. (1987, December). *Electronic media career preparation study: Executive summary.* New York: International Radio & Television Society.

Schaffer, W. A. (1996). High tech jobs for low tech people: How to get paid for using liberal arts skills in the electronic world. In T. Lee (Ed.), *Managing your career* (pp. 18–29). Princeton, NJ: Dow Jones.

Sgambelluri, S., & Huffer, M. (1994). The liberal arts student's "roadmap" for career planning. In J. P. Downey (Ed.), *Choices and challenges: Job search strategies for liberal arts students* (pp. 1–23). Bloomington, IN: Tichenor.

Society of Professional Journalists. (1996). *Tomorrow's broadcast journalists.* Greencastle, IN: Author.

Steinke, G. (1993). Tennessee broadcasters prefer workers with college communications training. *Feedback, 34*(1), 8–9.

Wartella, E. (1994). *State of the field.* Austin: University of Texas, College of Communication.

Williamson, L. K., & Iorio, S. H. (1996). Communication curriculum reform, liberal arts components and administrative organization. *Journal of the Association for Communication Administration, 3,* 175–186.

Wood, D. N. (1993). Higher education and crap-detecting. *Feedback, 34*(2), 2–3.

16

Gender Issues

Terry Hynes
University of Florida

Concern about gender issues has been a major theme in U. S. cultural, political, and economic life since the explosion into the public realm of several simultaneously interrelated and divergent "movements" of the 1960s: the women's liberation movement, the civil rights movement, the anti-Vietnam war movement, and, by the end of that decade, the gay rights movement.

From the 1960s to present, the women's liberation and gay rights movements have generated considerable awareness of the inequities women, gays, and lesbians experience when they seek to participate fully in the political, economic, and cultural life of the United States. Awareness led to sometimes-passionate social action and some hard-won changes. Not surprisingly, however, because gender (like race) resonates against deeply held beliefs and fundamental values, gender issues continue to present significant challenges to our nation's willingness to offer genuinely equal opportunities to all its citizens.

Also not surprisingly, the gender challenges played out in the broader society are reflected in the microcosm of colleges and universities throughout the country. The "glass ceiling" and gender-based salary inequities are just two issues for which parallel scenarios have been played out in corporate, government, and university and college settings.

The mixture of progress and regress that has marked the broader social record on gender issues also is the hallmark of the gender record in universities. For example, more than 52% of the students in U. S. colleges and universities are women. Yet, only 25% of academic deans are women ("Does Gender Influence Campus Leadership Styles?" WIHE, 1996).

Across all types of U.S. institutions, the number of women faculty and women with tenure has changed little in the past 15 years: Just under one third of all faculty are women, compared to 27% in 1982. And 46% of women faculty have tenure, the same percentage with tenure as in 1975 ("Even the Ivy League Schools are Starting to 'Get It,'" WIHE, 1996).

The mixed record is true at major leadership levels also. In the past 20 years, for example, the number of women presidents of colleges and universities has more than tripled, from 148 in 1976 to 453 in 1996; yet women now comprise only 16% of the top leaders in U.S. higher education institutions ("Why Do Schools Choose Women as Leaders? Why Not?" WIHE, 1996).

The leadership picture in journalism and mass communication (JMC) education parallels the broader university picture: In 1985–1986, 92% of JMC administrators were men and only 8% were women. By 1990–1991 the percentage of men dropped to 84%, and the percentage of female administrators had doubled (16%). Relatively little gain for women occurred in the subsequent 5-year period, however: In 1995–1996, 81% of JMC administrators were men and 19% were women (ASJMC Faculty/Administrator Demographic Surveys, 1986, 1991, 1996).

This chapter deals with two broad categories of gender issues that affect communication and media administration: First it addresses some of the gender issues that all administrators, female and male, must deal with. Second it addresses some gender issues that are principally or solely dealt with by women or which women experience differently than men. This is not intended to be a comprehensive or exhaustive discussion of gender issues communication and media administrators are likely to confront. Nor does the discussion of even those issues that are included explore all nuances of these issues. There are simply too many issues and too many complexities for one chapter to adequately examine.

This chapter is, thus, an overview. It identifies and highlights a number of major, recurring gender issues that administrators need to be aware of and to deal with if they wish to create an environment in which all faculty, staff, students, and other administrators can do their best.

One outcome of the women's movement of the 1960s–1970s is that, through hard-fought battles, the study of women became a legitimate domain for university scholars. Specialized scholarship about women has resulted in a wealth of knowledge about, among other things, women's ways of learning and knowing, the feminization of the work force and women's ways of leading (e.g., Belenky, Clinchy, Goldberger, & Tarule, 1986; Bem, 1993; Goldberger, Tarule, Clinchy, & Belenky, 1996; Helgesen, 1990; cf. Creedon, 1993; Wood, 1994). Thus, this chapter draws from a substantial body of popular and research literature for a discussion of gender issues in communication and media administration.

In recent decades, especially, researchers have documented that women's ways of knowing, behaving, and leading differ in some significant ways from those of men. These differences are not necessarily the result of genetically based differences between the sexes. Rather, they are often the result of socialization and acculturation processes through which women and men learn, from their earliest years, to repeat behaviors that yield success, satisfaction, or other rewards as well as to avoid those behaviors that generate failure, dissatisfaction, or other punishments.

GENDER ISSUES THAT ALL ADMINISTRATORS DEAL WITH

All administrators deal with personnel, students, alumni, curricula and other administrative issues that have gender components. Awareness of the gender-related aspects of the broader issues can be a major asset in helping an administrator create an environment that is welcoming, supportive, and productive for everyone who is part of it. Creating such an atmosphere requires that an administrator be sensitive and responsive to gender-related issues.

Personnel: Recruitment and Retention

Gender components of personnel issues begin with the recruiting and hiring process. Assuring that the pool of applicants, candidates, and finalists for vacant positions includes women has become part of the culture of many campuses as the result of affirmative action policies and procedures. An administrator who indicates by word and action that equal opportunity is an important priority conveys a message that continues to be important for creating a hospitable environment for women (as well as other under-represented groups), and is perhaps even more important in a time when the value of affirmative action is being seriously challenged.

Successful recruitment of women can be helped by making sure the entire search process is as inclusive as possible. For example, women already on the faculty or staff should be included on faculty and staff search committees; female candidates should have ample opportunity to talk with women faculty and staff in order to better understand the opportunities they will have as well as the challenges they will face in the local culture.

Assigning committee responsibilities is another personnel-related area in which administrators can make a difference with respect to gender-related issues. Inviting women to participate in and appointing women to key committees both within the communication or JMC unit and elsewhere on campus can assist women in at least three important ways. First, participation on committees and other service activities help women understand and influence campus culture. Second, such service helps women gain experience and competence that will qualify them for administrative and other leadership positions in the future. Third, it enables women to develop a communication style that will be effective in the male-oriented political environment of most campuses.

Effective politics and effective communications are often inseparable. In a male-oriented political environment, one reason women may end up being ineffective is rooted in a communication style that is itself tied to their gender. That is, a key reason women and men do not communicate effectively or easily is gender based. It is important for both women and men to learn and understand the evidence related to this subject in order for each to be effective communicators and leaders (see, e.g., Tannen, 1994). Knowing and understand gender-related communications issues can assist all leaders—men and women—in overcoming one of the greatest obstacles to effective leadership.

Although it is important to protect newer faculty from too many service-related activities, it is also important to help all faculty understand how important it is for their own development as well as for long-term collegiality that they participate strategically and in meaningful ways in shaping policies within the communication or JMC unit, elsewhere on campus, and in the professional associations to which they belong.

Salary Equity

The Equal Pay Act of 1963 guarantees "equal pay for equal work." Exactly what constitutes "equal work" continues to be subject to varying interpretations. Some colleges and universities have consistently disadvantaged women in salary issues. Some colleges and universities have redressed this situation by developing procedures to surface emerging or continuing salary inequities. Communication and media administrators need to examine salaries of faculty and staff for inequities and use campus processes—or help develop them where they do not exist—to redress existing inequities.

Family-Friendly Workplace

Another gender component of personnel centers on family-related issues. Creating a "family-friendly" environment has implications for both women and men, of course. However, although we have come a long way in recognizing the need and ability of both sexes to share what was once regarded as women's work (e.g., providing primary care for children), there are still some realities that affect women differently than they affect men. Administrators can play a major role in constructing the supportive environment needed to accommodate these differences.

Women, first of all, are still the persons who become pregnant and give birth to children. The Family and Medical Leave Act of 1993 provides legal assurance that women and men may attend to fundamental family health and care issues without fear of losing their jobs, but the law does not necessarily fully accommodate the realities of difficult pregnancies, or the adjustments and exhaustion connected with a new infant who only slowly adapts to sleeping more than 4 hours at a time. Also, women who are the sole providers for their families may need a better accommodation to pregnancy and childbirth than the 12 weeks of unpaid leave the Family and Medical Leave Act provides for. Administrators can meet these gender-related needs by thoughtful and creative adaptation of schedules and assignments. For example, an administrator might assign a new mother who is the primary provider for her family independent studies, internships, or other appropriate responsibilities instead of a regularly scheduled class, in order to give the new mother the flexibility needed to stabilize her and her infant's schedules.

In addition, taking time out of a career to have a child usually means the mother, rather than the father, will take more time away from research and other scholarly and professional activities. Thus, the risk for women who have children during their early years as faculty members is that they will not be able to meet standards for tenure and promotion within the normal time frame. Many universities now enable women and men to stop the tenure clock in order to accommodate their biological clock. Administrators can play an important role by taking the initiative to help parents or prospective parents arrange for a leave of absence for a semester or year, for example, to meet family obligations. The leave would not be counted as service toward tenure.

Most commonly such leaves have been given to accommodate parents' responsibilities for their infants or young children. Increasingly, however, such leaves may be needed for children who are the caretakers for ill or elderly parents.

Concerns about child care can be very stressful for parents. Again, most often, this is not an equal opportunity stress. Mothers continue to be the primary parent dealing with child care issues in most families; and, children's needs are not always predictable. Infants and young children can become sick very suddenly. The primary parent may receive a call in the middle of a class to come and pick up a sick child from a child-care center or school. Administrators need to understand and help other faculty and staff understand that situations like these are normal, under the circumstances, and they can be accommodated in a family-friendly workplace. Some universities (e.g., Stanford) now offer child-care facilities on or near campus to assist parents in scheduling their lives. Appalachian State University in North Carolina has a holiday and snow day child-care program to assist employees in these situations. The Comfort Zone facility at Iowa State University cares for mildly ill children who cannot attend their regular child care site ("Family-Friendly Policies Earn Recogntion for 29 Campuses," WIHE, 1996). Creative communication and media administrators may think of additional ways in which their units or campus can help faculty, staff, and other administrators meet the challenges of child care.

When the women involved in family-related issues also happen to be administrators, their supervisors can make a difference by recognizing that women (and men) who have primary child-care or elder-care responsibilities may need a more flexible work schedule than the traditional 9 to 5. Corporations, in some instances, are already ahead of universities in this area.

Finally, regarding the administrator's role in creating a family-friendly workplace, most of what has already been said in this section also applies to staff employees, who are most frequently women. An administrator can make a significant difference by taking the initiative to work with all employees to provide flexible schedules or other appropriate accommodations that will meet the needs of both the workplace and the individual.

Students

Women comprise the majority of students in U.S. colleges and universities today. That has been true in communication and media programs for a relatively long time. For example, by 1977, the majority of students enrolled in JMC education programs were female. By 1990, about 60% of students enrolled in print and broadcast news, photo and magazine journalism, and advertising and public relations specialties were women, a figure that remained relatively constant through the mid-1990s (cf. Beasley & Theus, 1988; Creedon, 1993; Kosicki & Becker, 1992, 1996; Peterson, 1978).

The presence of women in large numbers, whether as students, faculty, or administrators, does not in itself, however, guarantee that a college or university will be a more hospitable place for women. Only slowly are colleges and universities being transformed into truly equal opportunity environments. Creating a welcoming, equitable, and fair environment for all persons begins even before students reach a campus. Brochures and other materials designed to recruit students should be welcoming to all students. At a minimum, the verbal elements should be nonsexist and the visual elements should fairly represent women as well as men.

Many students applying to journalism, communication, or media programs, as elsewhere on campus, are nontraditional students, and most nontraditional students are older women who either return to school after several years' absence to bear and raise children or, like increasing numbers of men, postpone attending college for several years after completing high school. Or they attend college part time while working full time, thus extending their education well beyond 4 years. Older women (and men) who have raised or are raising children or already have held responsible positions in a work environment may need a different kind of support system than do traditional-age students. Sometimes they are unwilling or just plain unable to work within the same routines as traditional students.

The new knowledge nontraditional students gain about themselves and the world around them may threaten their existing relationships with spouses, other family members, friends, and so on. (This may also be true for some traditional-age women students. For example, if a woman's family or racial and ethnic community does not value education for women, the very fact of her attending a university represents a challenge to family or community values. Such women may be marginalized at home or in their communities. To persevere to graduation, they may need special advising, and other attention.) Women students who are single or divorced and raising one or more children on their own may need to be connected to other women with similar circumstances, but they may not have the time to attend meetings, and other activities on campus. They may have child-care or elder-care responsibilities similar to those of faculty and staff, as described earlier, that affect their ability to take classes, and so on. Administrators need to be cognizant of all these variables and think creatively about the support they can provide or guide women students toward, either in the journalism, communication or media unit or from elsewhere on campus or in the community.

Administrators also can play a significant role in assuring that women students, whether traditional or nontraditional, have equitable opportunities to participate in student projects and organizations—and to participate in leadership positions in these activities. Women need a fair share of these curricular and extracurricular opportunities to develop and help others develop team-building, collaboration, conflict management, negotiation, and other skills that will be important to their success in future careers.

For administrators, a flip side to assuring women students equitable opportunities for themselves in curricular and extracurricular learning experiences is to help faculty value the experiences women bring to the learning environment. For example, administrators can help faculty recognize the importance of giving equal value to examples students use from work experience and those they use from the experience of raising children.

Advisory Boards, Alumni, and Alumnae

Advisory boards and former students are two other important groups administrators work with to create and maintain strong journalism, communication or media programs. Including women as members of advisory boards and keeping in touch with alumnae as well as alumni are obvious ways of using normal outreach activities to also remain updated on any new or continuing circumstances or opportunities that affect women professionals in journalism and other communication fields.

Curriculum

Curriculum is the special province of faculty, but administrators can provide leadership in raising awareness at two levels related to gender issues. One level concerns the content of the curriculum itself. Administrators can help faculty address questions like these: Is the curricular content adequate for instructing the next generation of professionals about gender-related issues in journalism and other communication fields? Are women and their accomplishments adequately and appropriately represented in courses throughout the curriculum? Where appropriate, administrators also can encourage faculty to develop a special course or courses focusing on women or gender-related journalism, communication, or media issues.

In addition to curricular content, instructional methods may offer administrators an opportunity to make a difference in creating a fair and equitable environment for women as well as men. Journalism, communication, and media administrators can take a leadership role in alerting faculty to the different ways in which women learn, as compared with their male counterparts. They can help assure that a variety of teaching methods is employed in the classroom to take advantage of how students learn best.

One common method used to help people learn, for example, is to teach by comparison or by citing examples. Making analogies, creating similes or metaphors, or using relevant instances can be very useful tools to aid instruction. However, comparisons and examples that rely solely or too heavily on sports or military terms or situations may leave women out of the loop.

Work done by researchers in recent years regarding women's ways of learning and knowing has yielded a wealth of literature about this subject (see, e.g., Belenky et al., 1986; Brown & Gilligan, 1992; Goldberger et al., 1996; Maher & Tetreault, 1994). At a minimum, administrators need to be sure faculty are aware of this information and can lead faculty in learning from this literature about the importance of praising, criticizing and coaching all students to the same degree, regardless of gender. This literature suggests also that competitive, hierarchical, and argumentative classroom environments are generally less hospitable to women than men (see, e.g., Goldberger et al., 1996; Maher & Tetreault, 1994). Women report that they tend to enjoy a collaborative learning environment. (See, e.g., Belenky et al., 1986, especially their discussion of the teacher as midwife. For examples of how other disciplines are adapting instructional methods to women's ways of learning, see, e.g., Rosser, 1995.)

Administrators also should inform faculty of their responsibility to assure their classroom environment does not include jokes or comments that contribute to a negative climate for women. Sexist jokes and comments reflect a fundamental lack of respect. They also may be construed as a form of sexual harassment, which can have serious legal consequences for individual faculty, administrators, and institutions if complaints are not dealt with.

Apparently neutral instructional methods may also have gender implications. For example, assigning, with little or no advance warning, a 24-hour take-home examination or coverage of night meetings to a class that includes women (or men) who are solely or primarily responsible for parenting (or for the care of elderly parents or other relatives) may exacerbate a student's problems unnecessarily. Administrators are in a key position to help faculty think outside of routine practices and develop alternative assignments or varied ways of developing and demonstrating competence in such skills as news writing, reporting, and so on.

Sexual Harassment

Sexual harassment is one of several forms of workplace harassment. (Other forms of employment discrimination may be related to race or religion, for example.) It is a serious issue that every administrator needs to be prepared to deal with. Sexual harassment is a form of sex discrimination referring to "the unwanted imposition of sexual requirements in the context of a relationship of unequal power" to the extent that the unwanted attention or behavior creates a hostile environment (MacKinnon, 1979; cf. Friedman, Boumil, & Taylor, 1992; MacKinnon, 1987, especially chaps. 2 and 9; Paludi, 1996, especially chaps. 1–2).

Although a very small percentage of sexual harassment situations occur because of women harassing men or same-sex harassment, the overwhelming number of sexual harassment situations occur with men harassing women. Thus, this discussion is articulated with the most common scenario as the standard. Sexual harassment law has grown out of Title VII, the Civil Rights Act of 1964. With respect to sexual harassment, a violation of a person's rights may occur if:

the person is subject to unwelcome harassment, based on sex; the harassment affected a condition of employment or a decision about academic perform-ance; the employer knew or *should have known* of the harassment and failed to take prompt remedial action; and the person being harassed acted reason-ably under the circumstances. (Greenawalt, 1995, p. 78, italics added)

Any of the following, for example, may be construed as sexual harassment: badgering a student or employee for a date after being refused initially; dating or having sex with a student or employee, especially if a work-related or course-related reward is a condition of dating or sexual activity; sharing sexually explicit material unrelated to a class with a student, class, or employee; making unwelcome, sexually related comments to a student or employee; or offering to reward a student or employee for sexual behavior.

Obviously, administrators need to avoid any of these behaviors themselves. In addition, administrators need to be prepared to deal immediately and decisively with complaints of sexual harassment, whether the complaints come from students, faculty, or staff and whether or not the complaints involve peer harassment (e.g., faculty to faculty) or harassment between persons in unequal power relationships (e.g., faculty to student). Administrators need to have a clear idea of campus policies regarding the handling of complaints about sexual harassment and follow them precisely.

Administrators also need to be clear and to help complainants un-derstand that administrators have a primary responsibility to follow campus policies, which usually include reporting any complaints to administrators assigned to handle them. Sometimes students, faculty, and staff who make a complaint of sexual harassment ask the person to whom they report the complaint to keep it confidential and not report it further. This happens sometimes because the complainant is still sorting through very complex feelings and reactions. Administrators (or others in supervisory positions) simply cannot withhold such com-plaints from appropriate campus personnel. Administrators need to inform victims early in conversations involving complaints of sexual harassment that they (the administrators) will have to follow campus policies regarding the handling of such complaints.

Administrators are in a position to be proactive in educating faculty, staff and students to issues of sexual harassment. They can make clear that sexual harassment is unacceptable behavior and will not be tolerated. Like others in positions of authority, administrators may need the wisdom of Solomon—or Solomon's sister or mother—to sort through complaints and determine when complaints of sexual harassment are supported by evidence. Again, two things can assist administrators in this regard: (a) following campus procedures, and (b) awareness of the research on this subject.

Campus policies generally help preserve due process rights, academic freedom, and constitutional rights of free speech for accuser and accused. In the most serious and complex cases, a college or university can become equally vulnerable to a lawsuit from the accuser for not treating accusations of harassment seriously enough to protect the victim or a lawsuit from the accused charging that the college or university's action in handling the complaint was so vigorous and unfair that the accused's civil rights were violated.

Most campus policies now alert faculty to the problems and complications inherent in romantic relationships with students (or to romantic relationships between supervisors and those they supervise in the workplace): These are fundamentally relationships between persons with unequal power. If the relationship sours, the fundamental inequality may become a factor in a sexual harassment complaint. Administrators need to be very judicious in sorting through evidence where highly charged emotions are involved.

Awareness of the research on sexual harassment can be very helpful to administrators. The research indicates, for example, that women are very reluctant to make complaints of sexual harassment and often do so only when the situation becomes intolerable (see, e.g., Dziech & Weiner, 1990; Paludi, 1996, especially chaps. 10 and 12). Their reluctance arises in part because of a "victim mentality" (they have been socialized to think they may have caused the behavior by "provocative" dress, etc.) or because they know how difficult it will be to make a successful, effective complaint against a powerful individual (e.g., a tenured professor).

Sexual harassment may occur through only one instance of the behavior constituting the harassment, but the effects of even one occasion can be very damaging and persistent for its victims, including feelings of guilt, failing grades, clinical depression, even attempted suicide among other results. An aware, effective leader needs to be cognizant of all possible ramifications of this behavior in order to minimize the damage to individuals involved and to take appropriate initiative to improve the environment.

Administrators need to keep abreast of the evolving law regarding sexual harassment. This is especially relevant for journalism, communication, or media administrators because some complaints of sexual harassment also may involve issues related to freedom of expression, one of the most fundamental values of our fields. For example, if a faculty member in advertising discusses incorporating sexual metaphors into the copy of product ads and a student perceives such discussion as creating a "hostile environment" for her, does an administrator have a right to ask the faculty member to restrict his or her language? Obviously, an administrator would need to look at all the circumstances and the full context and consult other appropriate campus administrators and legal counsel before taking any action. However, an administrator cannot simply ignore such complaints.

Administrators also need to be aware of policies that bring their campus into compliance under two related pieces of legislation, the 1990 Student's Right-to-Know and Campus Security Act and the 1994 Violence Against Women Act.

Sexual Orientation

Some men and women an administrator works with or is otherwise responsible for will live their lives in ways that are against the dominant gender scripts of the culture. Gay men, lesbians, and bisexuals, for example, by virtue of their sexual orientation, "challenge the presumed naturalness of the link between the sex of the body and the gender of the psyche" (Bem, 1993, p. 167). Persons who do not fit into the generally accepted social constructs about gender identity have a difficult enough time constructing a viable identity for themselves "in a society that insistently denies them any legitimacy" (Bem, 1993, p. 167) without also facing hostility or prejudice from college and university administrators, faculty, or staff. Administrators of journalism, communication, or media programs can ameliorate this situation by providing leadership in creating an environment that is appreciative and supportive of the diverse ways in which human beings legitimately exist in the world. College students, who are often at a particularly vulnerable stage of coming to grips with constructing their sexual identities, regardless of whether those identities are consistent with cultural definitions of male and female, are likely to be major beneficiaries of such a supportive environment.

GENDER ISSUES WOMEN EXPERIENCE

Administrators also can be more effective in their leadership roles if they understand gender issues that tend to be experienced solely or primarily by women themselves or that women experience very differently than men. Some of the gender issues women themselves experience are the same or mirror images of those already discussed in the previous section. For example, as employees, women know all too well from personal experience when their working environment is not "woman friendly." Child care is not just a woman's issue, but women continue to be the parent most commonly dealing with day-to-day stresses and strains of parenting. When administrators allow no flexibility in a work schedule or no accommodation or understanding of a parent's (usually the mother's) need to take care of a sick child or pick up a child at day care, women are usually the first to be disadvantaged.

Achieving Balance

Balancing professional and personal lives is a challenge for men and women in today's working world, but the reality is that women still are often expected to assume the primary role for parenting responsibilities or other family-related caregiving responsibilities. Many women resolve the potential conflicts between personal responsibilities and professional ambitions by foregoing professional advancement opportunities. It is still the case that women in higher administrative positions tend not to be married, for example, both in universities and in corporations. Many women in higher level administration admit they made a deliberate choice to forego marriage and family because professional advancement was their priority.

Administrators aware of and sensitive to this issue can, at the very least, be more empathetic to faculty and staff who are struggling with the tensions and pressures of balancing professional and personal lives. They may also find they lead and administer their programs more effectively if they work through the issues very consciously for themselves to achieve their own equilibrium.

Another kind of balance occurs in the daily aspects of administration itself. Women administrators still often believe they must work harder and smarter than men if they are to succeed over the long term. Just to survive as an administrator requires the ability to sort out priorities and devote time to issues, and so on, in relationship to where those issues fit among other compelling priorities. It is also helpful to decide beforehand which issues are absolutely central for one to take a stand on. When beginning a new administrative job, it is useful to make a list—a short list, even a list of one—of issues that you would be willing to take a stand on, even if it cost you your job. This is a first step to recognizing that many issues (everything not on your list) are negotiable at some level and not absolute values. The ability to negotiate effectively, which means being able to give as well as take, is important for effective, balanced leadership and administration.

Stereotypes

Gender stereotyping is not a new phenomenon. Stereotypes that associate men with hierarchical, autocratic practices have as long a history as those that identify women as natural nurturers and good communicators.

In many ways, the stereotypes have not changed. Rather, the stereotypes traditionally associated with women have now become socially acceptable, even preferred, in some situations. Women may want to take advantage of the newly privileged position these gender stereotypes hold, but no one should confuse the new positioning with a fundamental change in the stereotypes.

For example, one of the traditional stereotypes about women is they are more collaborative in their working relationships (see, e.g., Helgesen, 1990; Tanton, 1994). Business leaders and advisers—as well as leaders and advisers in universities and nonprofit organizations—recognize today that a collaborative work environment, in which employees have a chance to speak and be heard, is simply a more productive working environment. Businesses today value collaborative environments with employees working in teams and managing the workplace through horizontal (rather than hierarchical) reporting relationships chiefly because such an organizational structure is perceived to be better for company profitability.

One popular articulation of this view appears in Connie Glaser and Barbara Steinberg Smalley's (1995) *Swim with the Dolphins: How Women Can Succeed in Corporate America on Their Own Terms*. The trope on which their book is developed is the metaphor of women as democratic dolphins who are now able to nose out the sharks (men) in business. In this figure of speech, sharks, on the one hand, are tough taskmasters, aloof, manipulative, and task oriented. They emphasize competition, reject new ideas, and demand staff loyalty. Dolphins, on the other hand, are compassionate, visible, friendly, open, honest, and people-oriented as well as task oriented. They support collaboration and cooperation, welcome new ideas, and know they must earn staff loyalty.

Glaser and Steinberg Smalley (1995) and others build their theses from research evidence that indicates that women more so than men tend to develop collaborative skills—and attendant skills of good listening, strong communication, and team negotiation—as part of their acculturation. Women tend to develop a more participatory management style. They encourage teamwork and staff empowerment, numerous studies indicate, whereas the socialization process for men tends to reward and develop their competitive abilities (see, e.g., Cantor & Bernay, 1992; Helgesen, 1990; Tannen, 1994).

One manifestation of these different styles is reflected in a common scenario: It was not so long ago that women who chose not to stand toe to toe with their antagonists in a power struggle were regarded as too weak or soft to hold a leadership job. This bias still surfaces in some places and with some individuals. Women who become leaders or aspire to leadership need to understand the pervasiveness of stereotypes like this, and women and men need to be aware of the degree to which their impressions of leaders or candidates for leadership are formed by sometimes unconscious stereotypes.

Stereotypes are useful, as Lippmann suggested many years ago when he coined the term for the purpose it now serves. Stereotypes help us organize the "great booming buzzing confusion of the world" (Lippmann, 1922, p. 81). They help us categorize and understand what would otherwise be completely unintelligible and unmanageable. Stereotypes are, nonetheless, oversimplifications of reality.

Stereotypes, whether they are currently in vogue as is the case with women's perceived advantage in collaboration and related skills, are essentially reductive. Individuals and groups of women (and men) are far more complex than any set of stereotypical characteristics might suggest. Not all women are compassionate, friendly, people oriented, and so on. And some men are compassionate, people oriented, collaborative, and so on. Nor do women and men embody either of these sets of characteristics all of the time. (For suggestions about different ways of imagining human lives outside traditional stereotypes, see, e.g., Bem, 1993; Heilbrun, 1988; 1990.)

The jobs of leading and managing are also complex. There are times when collaboration—consulting, listening, negotiating—is exactly the right strategy for accomplishing a goal. But women administrators in journalism, communication, or media, as well as other fields, are likely to be more successful in their leadership positions if they recognize that the complexities of their jobs will require them, at times, to demonstrate the kind of decisiveness stereotypically associated with men if they are to assist faculty, staff, students, and others who have a vested interest in their unit in achieving their short- and long-term goals.

Double Binds

From the very first page of Heller's (1961) classic novel of World War II, the central character, Yossarian, finds himself continually in situations in which he cannot achieve a desired outcome or solution because of a set of inherently illogical rules or conditions. For example, in the crazy combat world of war, a soldier can be grounded if he is too crazy to be in a bomber. However, one of the rules is that he has to ask to be grounded. And if he asks to be grounded he cannot be judged crazy because he's *ipso facto* demonstrating the "process of a rational mind" by showing "a concern for one's own safety in the face of dangers that were real and immediate" (p. 55). Thus did the phrase *catch-22* enter common English usage as a shorthand description for a tricky or disadvantageous condition with no satisfactory outcome.

Psychologists use the phrase *double bind* to describe, in similar fashion, an impasse created when contradictory demands are made of an individual, so that no matter which directive the person follows, his or her response will be interpreted as incorrect.

Whether one calls them catch-22s or double binds, such punishing dilemmas can be among the most emotionally exhausting situations an administrator deals with. Men and women are both susceptible to them, although women tend to be more disadvantaged by the double binds they encounter as administrators, chiefly because the contextual administrative paradigm reflects male-dominated values and traditions.

To some extent, double binds or catch-22s derive from or are related to stereotypes, but they are different and more limiting because they offer no acceptable solution. For example, as Hon (1995a) noted in her research about women in public relations management, women administrators receive conflicting messages about acceptable managerial style:

> On the one hand, we expect leaders in organizations to be strong and aggressive. On the other hand, when women display these traits, they are often judged negatively because these attributes don't jibe with cultural expectations about female behavior. The Catch 22 [sic], though, is that if they were to display the softness people expect, this too would be perceived as inappropriate" (p. 23; see Hon, 1995b for a complete discussion of this research)

Double binds for women are numerous. For example, leaders are expected to speak up and to be articulate; but "nice" women who "know their place" are still often expected to be silent in public. Talkative women are still regarded as "silly," or "chatty." A variation on this is the view that women who speak like ladies are not assertive enough, and thus, not strong or authoritative enough to be leaders. However, if women speak up assertively, they are considered not nice, "unladylike," and thus even weird, unnatural, or too abnormal to be leaders.

Some men who have been socialized not to expect leadership of women have developed an interesting way of dealing with the dissonance they experience when a woman says something substantive, for example in a business meeting: They simply do not hear it. Many women have had the experience of being in a meeting where they offered a solution or suggested an idea or alternative way of dealing with a situation and were ignored or simply met with silence. Then, slightly later in the meeting, a male colleague offers the same solution, and, all of a sudden, it is heard and responded to.

Jamieson (1995) offered the most complete discussion of the major double binds women face, including the double binds she labeled womb-brain, silence-shame, sameness-difference, femininity-competence, and aging-invisibility. Jamieson's cogent and compelling discussion deserves to be read in its entirely, not least because of her realistically optimistic view of the progress women have made and continue to make as they surmount double binds, sometimes singularly, sometimes serially, but nearly always advancing to a new level where women are successful in changing legal and political structures and altering behaviors (Jamieson, 1995).

CONCLUSION

As noted at the outset, this chapter provides an overview of some of the gender-related issues which administrators of journalism, communication, and media programs face and may experience themselves. It identifies and highlights these gender-related issues but is not intended to be a comprehensive discussion or analysis.

Many of these issues are at least evolving, if not volatile. Thus, administrators who hope to lead and manage their units in an exemplary manner need to constantly monitor their environments and the scholarly and popular literature to assure that their knowledge of the issues is as current and complete as possible and that their behaviors, at a minimum, conform to legal and institutional standards and, optimally, are consistent with the goals of providing a supportive and inclusive environment for all.

REFERENCES

ASJMC Faculty/Administrator Demographic Survey. (1986). Columbia, SC: Association of Schools of Journalism and Mass Communication.
ASJMC Faculty/Administrator Demographic Survey. (1991). Columbia, SC: Association of Schools of Journalism and Mass Communication.
ASJMC Faculty/Administrator Demographic Survey. (1996). Columbia, SC: Association of Schools of Journalism and Mass Communication.
Beasley, M., & Theus, K. (1988). *The new majority.* Lanham, MD: University Press of America.
Belenky, M. F., Clinchy, B., Goldberger, N., & Tarule, J. (1986). *Women's ways of knowing.* New York: Basic Books.
Bem, S. L. (1993). *The lenses of gender.* New Haven, CT: Yale University Press.
Brown, L. M., & Gilligan, C. (1992). *Meeting at the crossroads: Women's psychology and girls' development.* Cambridge, MA: Harvard University Press.
Cantor, D., & Bernay, T. (1992). *Women in power: Secrets of leadership.* Boston: Houghton Mifflin.
Creedon, P. (Ed.). (1993). *Women in mass communication* (2nd ed.). Newbury Park, CA: Sage.
Does gender influence campus leadership styles? (1996, April). *Women in Higher Education* (WIHE). Madison, WI: The Wenniger Company.
Dziech, B. W., & Weiner, L. (1990). *The lecherous professor* (2nd ed.). Urbana: University of Illinois Press.
Even the Ivy League schools are starting to "get it." (1996, February). *Women in Higher Education* (WIHE). Madison, WI: The Wenniger Company.
Family-friendly policies earn recognition for 29 campuses. (1996, November). *Women in Higher Education* (WIHE). Madison, WI: The Wenniger Company.

Friedman, J., Boumil, M., & Taylor, B. (1992). *Sexual harassment*. Deerfield Beach, FL: Health Communications.

Glaser, C., & Smalley, B. S. (1995). *Swim with the dolphins: How women can succeed in corporate America on their own terms*. New York: Warner.

Goldberger, N., Tarule, J., Clinchy, B., & Belenky, M. (Eds.). (1996). *Knowledge, difference, and power*. New York: Basic Books.

Greenawalt, K. (1995). *Fighting words: Individuals, communities, and liberties of speech*. Princeton, NJ: Princeton University Press.

Heilbrun, C. (1988). *Writing a woman's life*. New York: Norton.

Heilbrun, C. (1990). *Hamlet's mother and other women*. New York: Ballantine.

Helgesen, S. (1990). *The female advantage: women's ways of leadership*. New York: Doubleday.

Heller, J. (1961). *Catch-22*. New York: Simon & Schuster.

Hon, L. (1995a). Feminism and public relations. *The Public Relations Strategist, 1*(2), 20–25.

Hon, L. (1995b). Toward a feminist theory of public relations. *Journal of Public Relations Research, 7*(1), 7–88.

Jamieson, K. H. (1995). *Beyond the double bind: Women and leadership*. New York: Oxford University Press.

Kosicki, G., & Becker, L. (1992). Annual census and analysis of enrollment and graduation. *Journalism Educator, 47*(3), 61–70.

Kosicki, G., & Becker, L. (1996). Annual survey of enrollment and degrees awarded. *Journalism Educator, 51*(3), 4–14.

Lippmann, W. (1922). *Public opinion*. New York: Harcourt Brace.

MacKinnon, C. (1979). *Sexual harassment of working women*. New Haven, CT: Yale University Press.

MacKinnon, C. (1987). *Feminism unmodified: Discourses on life and law*. Cambridge, MA: Harvard University Press.

Maher, F., & Tetreault, M. K. (1994). *The feminist classroom*. New York: Basic Books.

Paludi, M. (Ed.). (1996). *Sexual harassment on college campuses: Abusing the ivory power*. Albany: State University of New York Press.

Peterson, P. (1978). Journalism schools report record 65,962 enrollment. *Journalism Educator, 32*(4), 3–8.

Rosser, S. (Ed.). (1995). *Teaching the majority*. New York: Columbia University Teachers College Press.

Tannen, D. (1994). *Gender and discourse*. New York: Oxford University Press.

Tanton, M. (Ed.). (1994). *Women in management*. New York: Routledge.

Why do schools choose women as leaders? Why not? (1996, February). *Women in Higher Education (WIHE)*. Madison, WI: The Wenniger Company.

Wood, J. (1994). *Gendered lives: communication, gender, and culture*. Belmont, CA: Wadsworth.

17

Diversity and Multiculturalism

Jannette L. Dates
Carolyn A. Stroman
Howard University

There is no more comprehensive or far-reaching change in U.S. society in the 1990s than its growing multiculturalism and racial diversity. The result of the news media's tendency to bury their collective head in the sand on this point is that the "mainstream" news organizations in this country have abandoned their moral imperative to represent the society they serve. Simultaneously, they are losing their economic ability to survive in an increasingly diverse culture whose needs they fail to fulfill. The tasks of recruiting and retaining minority students and faculty, of infusing information about covering a multicultural society into our curricula, of pluralizing our student media, all present a substantial challenge to journalism educators. But, in the academy, as in the newsroom, the challenges of diversity must be met.

—Pease (1993, pp. 9,14)

Futurists predict that people of color will constitute one third of the U.S. population by the year 2000, as they also note that people of color and women are already more than half of the labor force, and that White men will constitute only 15% of the increase in the workforce in the coming years (Enoch, 1991; Hill, 1991).

Today, in the United States we already live in a multicultural world, where the popular culture has introduced us to others' foods, music, histories, customs, and more. Moreover, futurists predict that a multiplicity of infusions from culture to culture will continue unabated—and that we must develop respect for others if we are to be active, engaged participants in the new world order. Some believe that this diversity of people—with their cultures—enriches society, whereas some others hold the opposite view: that the United States and its system of higher education are diminished when "others" are embraced. These people seek to maintain the status quo or return to the way things were in a bygone era.

Because of the legacy of legally sanctioned unequal treatment of the descendants of U.S. slaves at nearly all levels in society, in the late 20th century many Americans found themselves giving careful scrutiny to concerns about how society functions, in attempts to see how to become more fair to all citizens. Race became an important issue on the national agenda, and with it, for some, came the issue of how to recognize and respect people from diverse racial and cultural backgrounds. Thus, a focus on multiculturalism emerged.

Multiculturalism may be defined as coming from many cultures. Specifically, it is the recognition that there are differences in perspectives and worldviews between racial and cultural groups in the United States. We argue in the following pages that acknowledging and embracing those differences and finding our commonalities enriches society.

By definition, multiculturalism leads to diversity, loosely defined here as the inclusion of a mixture of many perspectives and ways of knowing. More specifically, however, the focus on racial and cultural diversity is a means to an end; the end is the inclusion at all levels of the power, influence, and perspectives of all types of people, giving us a richer understanding of who we are as Americans and reaching beyond the boundaries that have traditionally separated people of one group from those of another.

Acrimonious debates about diversity and multicultural issues surfaced everywhere in the United States in recent years. The country seemed to be split along racial lines on numerous issues—particularly where race, power, and money were involved. Examples include the two O.J. Simpson trials and the debate on ebonics in the schools. As charges of racial discrimination mounted, corporate America and society at large have had to deal with racial discrimination issues. Despite the slick brochures and mission and goals statements that addressed fairness and equal opportunity, major corporations, such as Texaco, Inc. and Circuit City Stores, Inc., were forced to address accusations about unfairness in their practices, as relates to diversity and multicultural-ism. As part of a settlement agreement resulting from the well-publi-cized race discrimination lawsuit filed by African American employees at Texaco, Inc., an outside committee was appointed to oversee diversity efforts. Circuit City was court ordered to install a court-approved director of diversity management to oversee its hiring, training, and promotion practices (Walsh, 1997).

Of course, what is essentially at work is that diversity and multicul-turalism are direct, hard-hitting challenges to White cultural hegemony. The issue of hegemony is raised here because issues of power and equity undergird any understanding of multiculturalism. Schoem, Frankel, Zuniga, and Lewis (1993) wrote:

> One of the primary challenges of multicultural education is the need to recognize that the power of the dominant culture permeates our analytic frameworks and personal expectations, diminishes our critical awareness to examine the ways people of all cultures view one another and them-selves, and narrows our ability to think broadly and imaginatively. (p. 8)

Likewise, the issue of hegemony is raised by some who argue that even where some African Americans and other traditionally marginal-ized groups have established a place within the mainstream in increas-ingly more powerful roles, the hegemonic process limits possibilities for substantive systemic change. Cultural studies theorists such as Gramsci, Hall, and Gitlin describe the hegemonic process as the various means through which those who support the dominant ideology in a culture are continually able to reproduce that ideology in cultural institutions and products while gaining the tacit approval of those whom the ideology oppresses. According to this view, domination may be more than mere coercive force, and may include the creation of a reality that appears to make natural the reasonableness and inevitabil-ity of oppression. The dominant ideology is protected from radical change, they argue, as its proponents incorporate small amounts of oppositional ideology into the dominant media, attempting to neutral-ize the opposition, as they also achieve their goal: to avoid upsetting the "normal" balance (Dow, 1990) that retains dominant power and control in the same hands.

Using the concept of ideological hegemony to explain domination and subordination, Hall (1986) and Gramsci (1971) argued that ruling class alliances maintain power by cultivating a consensus among subordinate classes—ensuring the triumph of what is thought of as common sense among all sectors of society. However, they argued, cultural domination provokes its opposite, cultural resistance. Thus, ideological hegemony is an unstable equilibrium, a constant tug of war between opposing forces.

Many media industries recognized that sensitivity to issues of cultural diversity made good business sense. In the 1980s, the American Society of Newspaper Editors (ASNE) and the American Newspaper Publishers Association (ANPA) developed projects to increase cultural diversity in the workforce. Nonetheless, the newspaper industry was able to increase their "minority" workforce from a mere 4% in the late 1960s to only 9% more than 20 years later, far below the number in the nation's population and far below their set goal of parity by the year 2000 (Morgan, 1991). In the 1990s, merely 9% of all newspaper employees are people of color, and a majority of the nation's newspapers have no people of color in their professional ranks.

Media industries acknowledge that the future in circulation and reach and advertising and commercials lies in marketing strategies that focus on people of color and other traditionally underserved groups. Commitment to this change and a firm resolve to succeed are vital to the life and health of media organizations. In her column "From the Heart," however, Barbara Reynolds (1991), then of *USA Today*, noted in the early 1990s that the media willingly talk about diversity, but they fail to practice it.

Employment patterns demonstrate that most media workers—particularly decision makers—will remain White and male, and increasingly the audiences will be neither. Thus, White, mainstream men may continue to create the lenses through which the United States views race and itself—a distorted image, at best—unless more of a broad cross-section of people from all races, classes and cultures are included within the media's hierarchies.

If media gatekeepers are predominantly White and male, it is not so surprising that the messages they permit to pass through their media gates support their own view of the world, or that that view is based on a concept of White male supremacy that they, too, have been taught. It is also no surprise that these gatekeepers are not as likely to let pass alternative views of an African American or Latino, for example, or the perspectives that inform their worldviews. The results predictably are White supremacist images in the mass media that become interwoven in the fabric of popular culture—images that are instrumental in molding public opinion, influencing discussions about racial differences, and influencing actions.

We suggest that the commitment and resolve to reach the goal of greater diversity will occur most rapidly when the decision makers in key positions in media industries are themselves more culturally diverse and have broadened worldviews. In this regard academicians have a huge responsibility—for, these findings and predictions have implications for how we, in the academy, must shape the worldviews and educate the next generation of journalists and mass communicators who will be media industry leaders in the 21st century.

A number of factors have coalesced to force multiculturalism and diversity onto the higher education agenda. Notably among these factors were the establishment of ethnic studies and women's studies programs in the 1970s and an increase in the number of women, and African, Latino, Asian, and Native American (ALANA) students enrolled in institutions of higher learning. Both of these occurrences gave rise to serious challenges to the dominant canon—a canon that has been characterized as "Anglocentric, Eurocentric and male dominated" (Banks, 1991, p. 21). Emanating from opponents of the Eurocentric curriculum was the call for curriculum transformation; a salient feature of the challenges to the dominant worldview was the demand that content about women and various ethnic groups be included in the curriculum.

Efforts to institute a more inclusive curriculum, of course, were not without controversy and challenge; these attempts at curricula transfomation were met with a new movement: the political correctness (PC) movement. Proponents of this movement maintained that the traditional curriculum was objective and unassailable, and that the inclusive curriculum threatened academic excellence, among other things. Those aligned with the PC movement and other opponents of an integrated curriculum used " the rhetoric of objectivity and value-free standards of knowledge and excellence to attempt to make multiculturalism appear partisan, ideological, biased and subjective" (Schoem et al., 1993, p. 6).

In higher education, concomitant with the debate over the dominant canon and the resultant curriculum reform have come major, oftentimes bitter challenges to affirmative action efforts and the increasing diversity of U.S. colleges and universities. Beginning with the Supreme

Court's landmark ruling in *Regents of the University of California v. Bakke*, the legal challenges against affirmative action and increased diversity have continued to the present day. In 1974, Allan Bakke challenged affirmative action and diversity when he sued the University of California because of what he termed reverse discrimination, arguing that he had been denied admission to medical school while other less qualified minority candidates were admitted under a special program. In the 1978 *Bakke* decision, the attainment of a diverse student body was considered to be a constitutionally permissible goal for a university exercising its educational judgment, and race was recognized as one among a number of factors contributing to that diversity.

Several recent cases illustrate other challenges. In 1996, in *Hopwood v. Texas*, The University of Texas Law School was barred from using race as a factor in admissions and it was recently announced that the lawyers who were successful in the Texas case have filed a similar suit against the University of Washington's law school ("Suit Challenges Affirmative Action at U. of Wash.", 1997). Also, in *Podberesky v. Kirwan*, the University of Maryland's all-Black scholarship program was declared unconstitutional (Carter & Wilson, 1996). The University System of Georgia's affirmative action measures may experience a similar fate; a recently filed lawsuit seeks to bar the system from considering race in admissions, hiring, and other decisions (Healy, 1997).

THE ROLE OF ADMINISTRATORS

Mission statements, vision statements, core values, and goals at most institutions include support for a climate of civility, diversity, and freedom from oppression. In addition, even in an America that may become "post-affirmative action," we believe many will feel a deep commitment to multiculturalism and diversity as a major part of our responsibility as administrators. We believe we cannot afford to merely educate our students in climates of sameness—leaving them ill-prepared and vulnerable for the diverse, multicultural and multiracial world they will face in the 21st century.

Communications educators who are in the vanguard as leaders must step up to the plate. As we willingly examine our own backgrounds, biases, and experiences in preparation for and while helping students do the same, we might address the following types of questions:

1. How can we as a nation help young people find ways to live together better?
2. What are our core values?
3. Shall we teach our students to value themselves; to value each other; to value similarities, and to value differences?
4. Does valuing help us to respect each other? Does respect for others lead to a more civil society?
5. Do valuing and respect for others lead to inquiries about others' histories, customs, and lives?

In addition, if educational administrators believe in the previously noted premise—that hegemony is the core issue that underlies the ferment that the concept of race and power struggles engender—then we need to ask how we can fight against the domination of one group by another (hegemony), as we prepare students for participation in an increasingly multicultural world. As educators focus on such issues, we believe it will become self-evident that to establish and live up to our missions, visions, core values, and our professional responsibility, higher education must embrace multiculturalism and the diversity that it brings.

In the following pages we offer leaders in communication education information that will assist us if we wish to enfold multiculturalism and diversity within our academic worlds. We focus on issues that educators face in the academy; on useful strategies for infusing the curriculum with diversity and multiculturalism; and on strategies for bringing in persons from diverse groups for inclusion as faculty, students, and staff members. We also review the diversity found among mainstream communications programs in higher education and among the historically Black colleges and universities (For a list of the recommendations, see Appendix A).

STRATEGIES FOR ADMINISTRATORS' USE

Administrators can fight hegemony—the domination and subordination of one cultural and racial group by another—if, as we carry out our responsibilities, we engage in tenacious, daily struggles to live up to the mission, vision, and values of our institutions. Specifically, for example, administrators can:

- In hiring and recruitment, consciously seek out faculty, staff, and students of various cultural and racial groups.
- Fight to include members of this wider assortment of perspectives and worldviews in the decision-making processes and power levels in our institutions.
- Recognize, respect, and demonstrate that we value diversity.
- Encourage others, at all levels, to do the same.

The following strategies noted under the headings curriculum, students, and faculty and staff can be useful as well.

Curriculum

As vice presidents, deans, and department chairs help set policies for programs within their purviews, we need to understand ways in which we can give specific directions to faculties that are often resistant to change and which may be particularly resistant to inclusion and infusion strategies related to diversity. We might ask ourselves and our faculties questions such as the following:

1. How many courses in our program incorporate ALANA perspectives, and at what levels of integration (occasional mentions; a separate course; or as integral parts of many courses, including major and core courses)?
2. What other opportunities do we make available for our students to hear a balanced representation of perspectives and viewpoints?
3. What other opportunities do we make available for our students to participate with others (students, faculties) who are racially and culturally different from themselves?

The following ideas may be used by administrators as they influence faculties. Research shows that through the years, materials found in a majority of courses offered in journalism and mass communication programs have had a focus where nearly always the works of those of European ancestry were described and used as models for students. Although such descriptions and models have encouraged the general population, they have not, by and large, encouraged ALANA students, who rarely saw people who looked like themselves in textbooks or used as examples in courses. Moreover, at the same time that young ALANA students grew up alienated because of a general feeling of disrespect and denial by the larger society, young White Americans grew up with a distorted, inflated perception of White America's contributions to the world. Many White youngsters are totally unaware, for example, of the ALANA groups' persistent participation in society, despite the rebuffs that they so often experienced. Thus, most White Americans have been as much miseducated as the renowned African American educator Woodson (1990) contended the Negro had been miseducated, to believe Americans of European ancestry, alone, developed the industries—including the mass media systems—that developed and shaped United States.

Universities can assist in the development of cross-racial understanding and respect by balancing the nation's historical memory with more diverse viewpoints and perspectives. In this way, they can prepare all students to be more responsive to learning about other groups; to understand others' concerns; and to have a basis for interacting with people who differ from themselves and those with whom they are most familiar.

Students who have experienced multiculturally focused course work in college will be primed to lead media industries toward more diversity in their workforces and within their products. The development of respect for each others' contributions in colleges and across racial and ethnic lines will help Americans in general become less accepting of stereotyped representations in the media, and more responsive to the broad spectrum of storylines that may be developed from the experiences of those of ALANA, as well as European American origins, and across the genders.

All students need to see clear connections between the past and the present, and how history shapes current conditions in an evolving continuum. It is important for ALANA students to understand how some of their racial predecessors in media industries struggled to move past traditional gatekeepers to send their own messages to audiences and how media messages have been interpreted differently by those whose experiences differ from the "traditionally served" audiences.

Black, White, male, female, Latino, Asian, and Native American—all deserve to have their stories told and their experiences shared, in appropriate ways and at appropriate moments; a sizable body of literature is currently available on how to accomplish this. Martindale (1993), for example, offered good advice on how to infuse multiculturalism into the curriculum. She posed two fundamental questions that should serve as stimulants for both faculty and administrators desirous of making the curriculum more inclusive:

1. How many of the journalists whose writings we will study will be of the same racial or cultural groups as my students of color or—equally important—different from the majority of my students
2. How much does the content of my courses include and appreciate the contributions of persons from other racial and cultural groups (Martindale, 1993, p. 86).

Coward (1993), Cortes (1993), Marzolf (1993), Tan (1993), and Wilson (1993) provided additional perpectives on how to incorporate ALANAs and women into the communication curriculum. As an example, Marzolf (1993) suggested that instructors in any discipline can give assignments that require students to research gender- and race-related issues (e.g., gender and work, racial discrimination). Also, a sample syllabus for a course on ALANAs and mass communication is available in Subervi-Valez (1993).

In order to evolve to the point of being a multiculturally focused one, the curriculum must undergo the stages of curricular transformation from the exclusive curriculum, from which women and ALANAs are generally excluded, to the transformed curriculum, in which the voices and worldviews of women and ALANAs are focal points. As noted earlier, however, incorporating such knowledge into a curriculum that is perceived as sacrosanct involves a great deal of controversy and resistance. Nonetheless, area studies programs, including Afro-American Studies, American Studies, and women's studies programs have met the resistance, and, by and large, have contributed significantly to the muticulturally focused curriculum that has now evolved on some campuses. Administrators realize fully that curricular change most often is accompanied by resistance; a guiding principle for advocacy in this area by administrators might be that the curriculum must change as society changes. Therefore, we recommend the following strategies:

- Continuously monitor the curriculum for the infusion of information on the experiences and perspectives of ALANAs and women.
- Seek out and share with faculty the wealth of information that is available on programs that have successfully engaged in curricular transformation.

- Provide opportunities for faculty, especially faculty development seminars, to learn about cultures other than their own; this knowledge can be then incorporated into the curriculum.
- Provide incentives to faculty for curricula innovations pertaining to diversity and multiculturalism.

Students

Although ALANA students "color" U.S. campuses and journalism and mass communication units much more today than in previous decades, they still make up a small piece of the pie. Consequently, the problem of underrepresentation of ALANAs continues to exist, particularly in predominantly White 4-year colleges (Carter & Wilson, 1996).

Data from the 1995 survey of enrollment in journalism and mass communication programs indicate that there has been a decline in the enrollment of undergraduate ALANA students (Kosicki & Becker, 1996). As an example, the percentage of African Americans enrolled in journalism and mass communication units decreased from 13.5% in 1993 to 11.1% in 1995; in other communications programs, such as communication sciences, the low numbers remained low throughout the 1990s. Without a doubt, recruiting and retaining ALANA students continues to be a great challenge.

Several sources offer strategies for recruiting and retaining multiethnic students (see, e.g., Greenman, 1988; Hall, Hines, & Ruggles, 1989; Ruggles, 1993). Escalante (1993) recommended the Dow Jones Newspaper Fund, which has long been active in encouraging ALANAs to consider journalism as a career through its High School Jouralism Workshop for Minorities, as the "most logical resource" to which journalism departments can turn when they first decide to recruit potential ALANA journalists. Green (1989) made an important, although often overlooked suggestion: Provide the parents of potential students (as early as grade school) with information pertaining to opportunities in the communication field and ways that their children can access these opportunities.

Other strategies that can be used to recruit and retain ALANA students include the following:

- Establish contacts at both junior high schools and high schools with significant numbers of ALANA student enrollments.

- Develop articulation agreements with local community colleges that generally have a large proportion of ALANA students.
- Expand the pool of students by considering nontraditional students (e.g., working adults returning to college or enrolling for the first time); also consider enrolling average or marginal students, carefully monitoring their progress, and providing them with extra support, if necessary.

Once an academic unit has been successful in attracting ALANA students, priority must be placed on creating a comfortable environment, especially classroom climate, for both ALANAs and White students, who may be, for the first time in their lives, confronted with attending classes with people different from themselves. In particular, faculty and administrators should be aware that ALANAs may feel a sense of isolation or alienation on predominantly White campuses, and take steps to help alleviate the sense of isolation.

Although it is probably impossible for faculty and administrators in mainstream institutions to replicate the nurturance that exists at many historically Black colleges and universities (HBCU), they still must make special efforts to reach out to ALANA students and to personally encourage them to become a part of the campus. For example, when faculty members are advisors for an organization within your school or unit, administrators can encourage them to seek out ALANA students and invite them to join the organization. The point here is that some ALANA students may need extra support, and faculty who have demonstrated, by their words and actions, an open, supportive, caring attitude should be encouraged to provide guidance, encouragement, and positive feedback as well as constructive criticism to ALANA students. As an aside, administrators should develop ways to reward faculty who demonstrate a real interest in the needs and interests of students and who excel in nurturing all students.

We make the following recommedations for making ALANA students feel welcomed in the classroom:

- Seek advice and assistance from faculty at HBCUs on effective ways to reach out to ALANAs.
- Institute intercultural training programs for administrators, faculty, staff, and students to increase each culture's understanding of the perceptions and feelings of other cultures.

- Encourage faculty awareness and ability to assist ALANA students to face the special challenges they encounter on predominantly White campuses.
- Encourage faculty to create and maintain a climate of fairness and equity in the classroom and on campus.
- Encourage faculty to be aware of and respect different learning styles and to match their teaching style to the diverse learning styles of their students.

Administrative efforts to increase faculty awareness of how diversity affects the classroom climate can be aided enormously by personnel in student support services. Generally, these divisions have numerous time-tested strategies for easing the transition of all students into college life. Many of these strategies can be adapted to help ALANAs feel more at home on the campus and by extension in the classroom. For example, peer counseling is an effective way to assist students to confront academic and social problems; thus, administrators may facilitate ALANA students obtaining peer counseling.

Workshops that foster an appreciation of diversity and provide information on how to build on the various strengths of ALANAs are another channel that communication administrators should consider. Diversity consultants are widely available to provide such information and to assist in the development of new ways of enhancing cross-cultural understanding. A key notion that must undergird all attempts to enhance faculty awareness is that ALANAs bring to the classroom their own experiences, values, and worldviews and these differing realities must be recognized and adequately reflected in the curriculum, the classroom, and the entire university (Marchesani & Adams, 1992).

In order to sensitize faculty to some of the subliminal messages they may be unwittingly transmitting, we highlight a series of questions that faculty might consider and administrators might observe when White professors are teaching multiethnic classes. Do the professors

1. Call on ALANA students for class participation as frequently as they call on other students.
2. Ask them the same kinds of questions.
3. Pay the same attention to ALANA students when they speak.
4. Provide equally specific feedback on assignments.
5. Value students' papers addressing ethnic or racial issues as much as others (Green, 1989, pp. 115–116).

It is critical that faculty be encouraged to think about the diversity of students in relation to their own cultural beliefs and values. Faculty should also be encouraged to consider that learning styles vary from group to group and alternative pedagogical tools, such as role playing and group projects that involve student interaction, may be an appropriate way to address differences in learning styles and to provide alternative ways of learning.

Faculty and Staff

Along with the increase in the number of ALANA students on many U.S. campuses has come an increase in the ALANA faculty employed by these institutions. However, like the students, ALANA faculty are also greatly underrepresented (Carter & Wilson, 1996).

There are compelling reasons ALANA faculty and staff should be a part of the communication landscape. Of course, some ALANA students are uncomfortable about enrolling in communications programs in majority institutions. This reluctance may be partially explained by the fact that people of color are immensely underrepresented on the nation's communications faculties. Therefore department chairs and other administrators must increase their efforts to attract and retain ALANA faculty and staff.

Taylor (1993) provided numerous strategies for attracting ALANA faculty, including establishing personal relationships with ALANAs in professional organizations such as the Association for Education in Journalism and Mass Communication and advertising in publications that are geared toward ALANA audiences (e.g., *Black Issues in Higher Education*). We offer the following additional strategies that have been found to be effective by some administrators:

- Expand the pool of potential faculty by increasing the number of ALANA graduate students obtaining PhDs.
- Implement various nonpermanent configurations, including visiting scholars programs, short-term appointments or exchanges with ALANA faculty from HBCUs.
- Recruit qualified individuals who are currently not in the academy; possibly from corporations, the military, or the government.
- Exchange teaching tips with ALANA faculty and extend an invitation to ALANA faculty to collaborate on research projects.

- Where there are no ALANA faculty members readily available, be aggressive and firm about why this is so important and push to expand and extend searches.
- Ask senior-level faculty to serve as informal or formal mentors to ALANA faculty. Clearly, we hire persons who demonstrate potential, thus we are responsible for nurturing that potential. (For a list of faculty and student resources, see Appendix B.)

DIVERSITY WITHIN MAINSTREAM COMMUNICATIONS PROGRAMS

Because faculties often lack cultural diversity or prior exposure to others' cultures, they are usually unprepared to teach across cultural lines or to teach from a multicultural perspective. (See Marchesani and Adams, 1992, for an-depth discussion of techniques to facilitate learning and teaching in a multicultural college classroom.) The following additional strategies that address this issue have been effectively used by others:

1. Major faculty development activities (e.g., year-long interdisciplinary seminars) have been initiated to assist communications faculties in learning about the new communication scholarship on race, gender, and ethnicity and to infuse such knowledge throughout their courses.
2. One-course release time slots have been established to be rotated annually among different faculty members who use the time to redesign their courses, with multiculturalism and diversity integrally included.
3. Grants have been obtained from agencies such as the National Endowment for the Humanities, the Lilly Foundation, the Fund for the Improvement of Postsecondary Education, and the U.S. Department of Education for increasing multiculturalism and diversity in the classroom.

There are various teacher aides that can be used to prepare communications faculties to teach from a multicultural perspective. Using such aides, at recent national conferences some faculty members have presented papers and demonstrations about their experiences. *The Color of Fear*, a film about multicultural experiences as told through the eyes of various young people, was effectively used by some faculty members in communications programs. Focused on issues raised by faculties and students in mainstream universities as they struggled with issues of diversity and multiculturalism, the film assists teachers as they introduce sensitive issues in class. The panelists noted that discussions by students who viewed the film focused on comments by the White students in the film who made statements such as the following:

1. Racism is not my responsibility.
2. Affirmative action forces people to hire the unqualified.
3. Generation X does not have racism as one of its issues.

Panelists agreed that it was particularly important for students in intercultural and interpersonal courses to address and deal with these sensitive issues. Discussion flowed, as well, from the comments by other students in the film who focused on the lack of opportunities that many from marginalized groups endure. From such discussions, some faculty members noted that they were able to help students grasp, among other important understandings, that in a more fair world, equal opportunity for all is a major goal.

There are other ways in which programs can resourcefully focus attention on developing their diversity strategies. Some universities have forged alliances with historically Black colleges and universities. Ohio Dominican College developed a mentoring partnership between members of its faculty and faculty members from other universities with more experience at using multicultural perspectives in their course work. During academic year 1994–1995, Jim Schnell from Ohio Dominican and Jannette Dates from Howard University worked together on revising the curriculum and syllabi at Ohio Dominican to be more inclusive. They visited each others' campuses and published an article from this experience (Schnell & Dates, 1994).

Brigham Young University developed a partnership with Howard University that has yielded numerous faculty and student exchanges and, most recently, a cosponsored 2-hour video town meeting on issues related to communication and race. The town meeting aired on PBS affiliates. More such endeavors should be encouraged by individual universities and by national professional associations, such as the Broadcast Education Association, the Association for Education in Journalism and Mass Communication, and the National Communication Association.

DIVERSITY ISSUES AT HISTORICALLY
BLACK COLLEGES AND UNIVERSITIES

Significantly, if we communication educators are to produce African Americans for immediate placement in media and higher education occupations, we will need to go first to the historically Black colleges and universities to achieve that end. Currently, approximately 36 historically Black colleges and universities enroll about 50% of all African Americans studying journalism and mass communication. However, the media industries, foundations, and philanthropic organizations have not opened their coffers sufficiently to provide the support needed to allow these institutions to "acquire the necessary resources to enhance and guarantee quality education in communications" (Taylor, 1991). Indeed, a survey of media education at HBCUs made the following recommendations:

1. The communications industry should view HBCUs as playing a major role in its efforts to increase the cultural diversity of the industry, and a greater share of the industry's resources should be allocated for journalism and communication programs at HBCUs.
2. Foundations should fund media education at HBCUs at a level that is comparable to that provided to White institutions in order that HBCUs might reach parity with them (Stroman, 1991).

At Howard University, there is the largest concentration of African Americans studying communications in the United States. The Howard School of Communications has a current enrollment of approximately 1,000 undergraduate and graduate students. In a recent national survey, it was noted that Howard enrolled and graduated the largest number of African American students in journalism and mass communication of any institution in the nation (12% of the total enrollees and 15% of the total graduates). In addition to graduating the largest number of ALANA students, its PhD program in mass communication is currently one of the largest in the nation in terms of total student body (Kosicki & Becker, 1996). Its intercultural doctoral program was rated third in the nation by the National Communication Association in the fall of 1996. The Martin Luther King, Jr. Forensics Society/Mock Trial Debate Team won the American Mock Trial Association National Mock Trial Championship in 1997. Other large programs include Florida A&M,

Hampton, Grambling, Jackson State, Xavier, Morgan State, and Norfolk State Universities.

Like majority institutions, communication units at HBCUs are faced with the issue of addressing diversity and multiculturalism. Although most HBCUs have been able to recruit and maintain White faculty, they have not done as well in recruiting Latino, Asian, and Native American students. In order to do so, they must engage in many of the strategies suggested for academic units at other universities and colleges.

Faculty and administrators at HBCUs must ensure that their curricula reflect the worldviews of other students, and that Latina, Asian, White, and Native American students see reflections of their cultures. Faculty at HBCUs must be conscious of the learning styles of students from other cultures. Also, students from other cultures must be made to feel welcomed at HBCUs. As with other campuses, the campus climate at HBCUs must be hospitable to students from other cultures.

Finally, although there may be ethnic diversity among the faculty in communication programs, the recommended gender balance is not always met. In these cases, administrators at HBCUs must make strong efforts to increase the representation of women on their faculties.

SUMMARY AND CONCLUSIONS

In summary, these strategies have been aimed at communication administrators. Obviously, we consider these to be useful strategies, but we also recognize that every institution is different and that there is no pat formula that will guarantee success as we assume or continue the task of infusing and including multiculturalism and diversity in our institutions and programs. There are no easy resolutions to what is essentially one of the most challenging issues facing college and university administrators. However, we can draw your attention to some guiding principles that others have found to be successful. Programs that have successfully met the challenge of diversity and multiculturalism have some combination of the following:

- Comprehensive, strategic planning for diversity and multiculturalism, beginning at the highest levels in the institution where strong leadership is exhibited from the top down.
- Philosophical commitment to multiculturalism and diversity.
- Respect for cultural differences and diversity.

- Innovative approaches for teaching about diversity.
- Rewards or incentives for cultural diversity efforts.
- Faculty development activities that provide opportunities for education and training in the area of diversity and multiculturalism.

Perhaps the most important attribute that a college or university can embody is that the president and the board of trustees embrace multiculturalism and diversity and use their authority to provide an institutionwide, integrated approach to enhancing diversity and multiculturalism.

Infusing diversity and multiculturalism in its entirety may appear to be a colossal challenge for the academy as well as society at large. However, some colleges and universities have surmounted the myriad challenges and succeeded. Through a number of imaginative strategies, they have given more than lip service to the notion of diversity and multiculturalism; in effect, they have recruited, retained, and graduated ALANA students; they have recruited, mentored, and eventually tenured ALANA faculty; and they have transformed the curriculum with a diverse worldview. These institutions have embraced Asante's (1996) description of multiculturalism in education as "the quality of creating and sustaining curricula, academic activities, programs, and projects that actively enhance respect for all human cultures" (p. 1). In short, these colleges and universities have made a permanent transformation from a monocultural to a multicultural institution.

In conclusion, we note that one of the main problems facing U.S. citizens today is the breakdown in communications across the racial divide. Just as there is often a generation gap, and the concomitant lack of communications between generations in families, there is a racial and ethnic communications gap in our country today. Yet, for all of us, the United States is home. We must begin an open dialogue as we review and confront old wounds and then put them behind us.

Now is the time to begin the process of shaping a better, more culturally inclusive worldview within the academy. We must commit ourselves to such a process for the good of the students whose lives are in our hands. They will face a very different United States than the one we knew as we grew up. They look to us for leadership and guidance on this matter, and we must not let them down. We educators will want 21st-century leadership in communication industries and in higher education to be based on broad and deep understandings, conscientiously crafted, and grounded in a firm moral and ethical base, under-girded by sound philosophical reasonings, that we have helped tomorrow's leaders to acquire through their studies with us.

APPENDIX A: DIVERSITY
AND MULTICULTURALISM
RECOMMENDATIONS FOR COMMUNICATION
ADMINISTRATORS

1. Consciously seek out faculty, staff, and students of various cultural and racial groups.
2. Fight to include members of this wider assortment of perspectives and worldviews in the decision-making processes and power levels in our institutions.
3. Recognize, respect, and demonstrate that we value diversity.
4. Encourage others, at all levels, to do the same.

Curriculum

1. Continuously monitor the curriculum for the infusion of information on the experiences and perspectives of ALANAs and women.
2. Seek out and share with faculty the wealth of information that is available on programs that have successfully engaged in curricular transformation.
3. Provide opportunities for faculty, especially faculty development seminars, to learn about cultures other than their own; this knowledge can be then incorporated into the curriculum.
4. Provide incentives to faculty for curricula innovations pertaining to diversity and multiculturalism.

Students

1. Establish contacts at both junior high schools and high schools with significant numbers of ALANA student enrollment.
2. Develop articulation agreements with local community colleges that generally have a large porportion of ALANA students.

3. Expand the pool of students by considering nontraditional students (e.g., working adults returning to college or enrolling for the first time); also consider average or marginal students and carefully monitoring their progress, providing them with extra support, if necessary.

Faculty and Staff

1. Expand the pool of potential faculty by increasing the number of ALANA graduate students obtaining PhDs.
2. Implement various nonpermanent configurations, including visiting scholars programs, short-term appointments, or exchanges with ALANA faculty from HBCUs.
3. Recruit qualified individuals who are currently not in the academy; corporations, the military, or the government are all viable recruitment sources.
4. Exchange teaching tips with ALANA faculty and extend an invitation to ALANA faculty to collaborate on research projects.
5. Where there are no ALANA faculty members readily available, be aggressive and firm about why this is so important and push to expand and extend searches.

APPENDIX B: RECOMMENDED SOURCES FOR UNDERSTANDING DIVERSITY AND MULTICULTURALISM COMMUNICATION EDUCATION

Sources for Faculty

Adams, M., Bell, L. A., & Griffin, P. (Eds.). (1997). *Teaching for diversity and social justice: A sourcebook*. New York: Routledge.

Banks, J. A. (Ed.). (1995). *Handbook of research on multicultural education*. New York: Macmillan.

Banks, J. A. (1997). *Teaching strategies for ethnic studies* (6th ed.). Boston: Allyn & Bacon.

Banks, J. A., & Banks, C. A. M. (1997). *Multicultural education: Issues and perspectives*. Boston: Allyn & Bacon.

Border, L. L. B., & Chism, N. V. N. (Eds.). (1992). *Teaching for diversity*. San Francisco: Jossey-Bass.

Bramlett-Solomon, S. (1989). Bringing cultural sensitivity into reporting classrooms. *Journalism Educator, 44,* 28.

Cohen, J., Lombard, M., & Pierson, R. M. (1992). Developing a multiculturalism mass communication course. *Journalism Educator, 47,* 3–12.

Cohen, M. C., Richardson, S. L., & Hawkins, T. D. (1997). *Multicultural activities for the group communication classroom.* Boston: Houghton Mifflin.

Dates, J. L., & Stroman, C. A. (1996). African American women and mass communication research. In D. Allen, R. R. Rush, & S. J. Kaufman (Eds.), *Women transforming communications: Global intersections* (pp. 249–258). Thousand Oaks, CA: Sage.

de Uriate, M. L. (1993). Laying out pluralism: Laboratory publications practice for the future. In C. Martindale (Ed.), *Pluralizing journalism education: A multicultural handbook* (pp. 179–186). Westport, CT: Greenwood.

Jenkins, M. M. (1990). Teaching the new majority: Guidelines for cross-cultural communication between students and faculty. *Feminist Teacher, 5*(1), 8–14.

Jeter, J. P. (1993). Using the Black press as a teaching tool. In C. Martindale (Ed.), *Pluralizing journalism education: A multicultural handbook* (pp. 149–153). Westport, CT: Greenwood.

Kern-Foxworth, M. (1993). Selecting bias-free textbooks for journalism courses. In C. Martindale (Ed.), *Pluralizing journalism education: A multicultural handbook* (pp. 173–178). Westport, CT: Greenwood.

Lutzker, M. (1995). *Multiculturalism in the college curriculum: A handbook of strategies and resources for faculty.* Westport, CT: Greenwood.

Questions and responses on multicultural teaching and conflict in the classroom. (1993). In D. Schoem, L. Frankel, X. Zuniga, & E. A. Lewis (Eds.), *Multicultural teaching in the university* (pp. 293–311). Westport, CT: Praeger.

Rountable discussion: The insiders' critique of multicultural teaching. (1993). In D. Schoem, L. Frankel, X. Zuniga, & E. A. Lewis (Eds.), *Multicultural teaching in the university* (pp. 279–291). Westport, CT: Praeger.

Schmitz, B. (1992). Cultural pluralism and core curricula. In M. Adams (Ed.), *Promoting diversity in college classroms: Innovative responses for the curriculum, faculty, and institutions* (pp. 61–69). San Franscisco: Jossey-Bass.

Schoem, D., Frankel, L., Zuniga, X., & Lewis, E. A. (Eds.). (1993). *Multicultural teaching in the university.* Westport, CT: Praeger.

Weinstein, G., & Obear, K. (1992). Bias issues in the classroom: Encounters with the teaching self. In M. Adams (Ed.), *Promoting diversity in college classroms: Innovative responses for the curriculum, faculty, and institutions* (pp. 39–50). San Franscisco: Jossey-Bass.

Sources for Students

Allen, D., Rush, R. R., & Kaufman, S. J. (Eds.). (1996). *Women transforming communications: Global intersections.* Thousand Oaks, CA: Sage.

Berry, V. T., & Manning-Miller, C. L. (Eds.). (1996). *Mediated messages and African-American culture: Contemporary issues.* Thousand Oaks, CA: Sage.

Biagi, S., & Kern-Foxworth, M. (1997). *Facing difference: Race, gender, and mass media.* Thousand Oaks, CA: Pine Forge Press.

Dates, J. L., & Barlow, W. (Eds.). (1993). *Split image: African Americans in the mass media* (2nd ed.). Washington, DC: Howard University Press.

Dines, G., & Humez, J. M. (Eds.). (1995). *Gender, race, and class in media: A text-reader.* Thousand Oaks, CA: Sage.

Kern-Foxworth, M. (1994). *Aunt Jemima, Uncle Ben, and Rastus: Blacks in advertising, yesterday, today, and tomorrow.* Westport, CT: Greenwood.

Thernstrom, S. (Ed.). (1981). *Harvard encycopedia of American ethnic groups.* Cambridge, MA: Harvard University Press.

Wilson, C. C. (1991). *Black journalists in paradox: Historical perspective and current dilemmas.* Westport, CT: Greenwood Press.

Wilson, C. C., & Gutierrez, F. (1995). *Race, multiculturalism, and the media: From mass to class communication.* Thousand Oaks, CA: Sage.

REFERENCES

Asante, M. K. (1996, May/June). Multiculturalism. *ACADEME: Bulletin of the American Association of University Professors,* pp. 1–5.

Banks, J. A. (1991). *Teaching strategies for ethnic studies* (5th ed.) Boston: Allyn & Bacon.

Carter, D. J., & Wilson, R. (1996). *Fourteenth annual status report on minorities in higher education.* Washington, DC: American Council on Education.

Cortes, C. E. (1993). The Latino press in American journalism history. In C. Martindale (Ed.), *Pluralizing journalism education: A multicultural handbook* (pp. 103–111). Westport, CT: Greenwood.

Coward, J. M. (1993). Native Americans in journalism and mass communication education. In C. Martindale (Ed.), *Pluralizing journalism education: A multicultural handbook* (pp. 121–131). Westport, CT: Greenwood.

Dow, B. J. (1990). Hegemony, feminist criticism and the Mary Tyler Moore show. *Critical Studies in Mass Communication, 7*(3), 261–274.

Enoch, J. E. (1991, May/June). Gearing up. *Minorities and Women in Business,* pp. 20–21.

Escalante, V. (1993). Finding potential minority journalism students. In C. Martindale (Ed.), *Pluralizing journalism education: A multicultural handbook* (pp. 27–32.) Westport, CT: Greenwood.

Gramsci, A. (1971). *Selections from the prison notebooks.* New York: International Publishers.

Green, M. F. (Ed.). (1989) *Minorities on campus: A handbook for enhancing diversity.* Washington, DC: American Council on Education.

Greenman, J. (1988). *Recruiting and retention of minority students: A "how-to" guide for journalism schools* [A report of the ASNE Minorities Committee]. Washington, DC: American Society of Newspaper Editors (ASNE).

Hall, D., Hines, B., & Ruggles, R. M. (1989, July). *Recruiting and retaining Black students for journalism and mass communication education.* Special issue of *Insights.*

Hall, S. (1986). Gramsci's relevance for the study of race and ethnicity. *Journal of Communication Inquiry, 10,* 5–27.

Healy, P. (1997, March 14). A lawsuit against Georgia University System attacks a range of race-based policies. *The Chronicle of Higher Education*, pp. A25–26.

Hill, S. (1991, May/June). Sara Lee corporation: Celebrating diversity. *Minorities and Women in Business*, pp. 20–21.

Kosicki, G. M., & Becker, L. B. (1996). Annual survey of enrollment and degrees awarded. *Journalism & Mass Communication Educator, 51*(3), 4–14.

Marchesani, L. S., & Adams, M. (1992). Dynamics of diversity in the teaching–learning process: A faculty development model for analysis and actions. In M. Adams (Ed.), *Promoting diversity in college classrooms: Innovative responses for the curriculum, faculty, and institutions* (pp. 9–20). San Francisco: Jossey-Bass.

Martindale, C. (1993). Infusing multiculturalism information into the curriculum. In C. Martindale (Ed.), *Pluralizing journalism education: A multicultural handbook* (pp. 77–93). Westport, CT: Greenwood Press.

Marzolf, M. (1993). Including information about women. In C. Martindale (Ed.), *Pluralizing journalism education: A multicultural handbook* (pp. 133–142). Westport, CT: Greenwood.

Morgan, J. C. (1991, June). Philanthropy: A traditional key to journalism access challenged by today's economic woes. *Black Issues in Higher Education*, pp. 46–47.

Pease, T. (1993). Philosophical and economic arguments for media diversity. In C. Martindale (Ed.), *Pluralizing journalism education: A multicultural handbook* (pp. 7–15). Westport, CT: Greenwood.

Reynolds, B. (1991, July 26). From the heart: Press talks diversity but won't practice it. *USA Today*, p. 11A.

Ruggles, R. M. (1993). Recruiting students. In C. Martindale (Ed.), *Pluralizing journalism education: A multicultural handbook* (pp. 33–41). Westport, CT: Greenwood.

Schnell, J., & Dates, J. L. (1994). Multicultural curriculum development in communication arts. *STAM Journal, 24,* 45–50.

Schoem, D., Frankel, L., Zuniga, X., & Lewis, E. A. (Eds.). (1993). The meaning of multicultural teaching: An introduction. In D. Schoem, L. Frankel, X. Zuniga, & E. A. Lewis, (Eds.), *Multicultural teaching in the university* (pp. 1–12). Westport, CT: Praeger.

Stroman, C. A. (1991). *Survey of programs in journalism and mass communications at historically Black colleges and universities (HBCUs)* (Tech. Rep. for the Association of Black College Journalism and Mass Communications Programs). Washington, DC: Center for Communications Research, Howard University.

Subervi-Velez, F. A. (1993). Mass communication and ethnic minority groups: An overview course. In C. Martindale (Ed.), *Pluralizing journalism education: A multicultural handbook* (pp. 159–172). Westport, CT: Greenwood.

Suit challenges affirmative action at U. of Wash. (1997, March 14). *The Chronicle of Higher Education*, p. A27.

Tan, A. S. (1993). Asian Americans in the journalism curriculum. In C. Martindale (Ed.), *Pluralizing journalism education: A multicultural handbook* (pp. 113–119). Westport, CT: Greenwood.

Taylor, O. L. (1991). People of color and the mass media: An unfinished agenda. *Black Issues in Higher Education, 8,* 96.

Taylor, O. L. (1993). Strategies for enhancing cultural diversity on journalism and mass communication faculties. In C. Martindale (Ed.), *Pluralizing journalism education: A multicultural handbook* (pp. 49–60). Westport, CT: Greenwood.

Walsh, S. (1997, March 14). Court targets race bias at Circuit City. *Washington Post*, pp. A1, 24.

Wilson, C. C. , II. (1993). The African American heritage in journalism. In C. Martindale (Ed.), *Pluralizing journalism education: A multicultural handbook* (pp. 95–101). Westport, CT: Greenwood.

Woodson, C. G. (1990). *The miseducation of the Negro*. Trenton, NJ: Africa World Press. (Original work published 1933)

18

Promotion, Tenure, and the Evaluation of Faculty

Patricia D. Witherspoon
Mark L. Knapp
The University of Texas at Austin

Faculty evaluation is, first and foremost, a communication process. Whether its purpose is to assess an individual for a merit salary increase, the award of tenure, or promotion to full professor, the strength of the process depends on the quality of interaction among its participants. Administrators, faculty budget councils and committees, outside reviewers of credentials, and the candidates being evaluated bear responsibility for the acquisition and assessment of information through individual analysis and group discussion. The purpose of this chapter is to suggest ways to enhance faculty evaluation as a communication process, through the careful involvement of participants and the use of adequate methods and materials.

The processes a university uses to evaluate faculty are critical components of its culture, created through years of practice and multiple drafts of policies and procedures. The award of tenure has become inextricably associated with the protection of academic freedom within institutions of higher education. To some university constituencies both inside and outside academe, tenure is also synonymous with institutionalized protection of mediocre performance. Such has not always been the case.

Emperors, kings, and clerics in the Middle Ages offered scholars protection from attacks on their homes, exemption from military service, and even pardons from charges of heresy (Metzger, 1973). Such awards of privilege were bestowed because scholars were perceived as people of societal value. They interpreted canon and civil law, privately analyzed and publicly debated the elements of logic, and identified and presented cultural contributions from peoples outside of Europe. Additionally, scholars served their communities as advisers, mediators, and diplomats.

This chapter is based on the belief that our colleagues continue to be people of value and that faculty evaluation is the best way to foster an individual's personal development, as well as the improvement of the professoriate. It should seek to reward, offer constructive criticism, and sometimes advise faculty that their professional strengths are not suited to academe.

The first section of this chapter discusses the features critical to the success of a faculty evaluation process and suggests criteria and issues related to the assessment of teaching, research, and service. The second section focuses on components of the promotion and tenure process, the roles assumed by different participants in the process, the materials often used in these reviews, and issues faced by administrators during them. The components of, and issues germane to, posttenure review are discussed in the third section. The final section summarizes the chapter and offers suggestions for the faculty evaluation process as it is conducted in communication schools, colleges, and departments (see Appendix for resources).

FACULTY EVALUATION

Faculty members are evaluated by their students, their colleagues (on site and off), and university administrators. These three (or four) groups may share some of the same goals for their faculty evaluations, but different goals and objectives are present as well. No matter what kind of faculty evaluation is being conducted and no matter who is conducting it, the following features are critically important to the success of the evaluation process:

1. Faculty Participation. If faculty have a role in developing (or changing) a system designed to evaluate them, there is a greater likelihood that the system will succeed. Joint participation of the evaluators

and the evaluated necessitates the sharing of goals and intentions that profits both parties. Recognizing those goals shared by both parties and working to blend other goals into a workable system provides the kind of involvement necessary to a successful evaluation. There have been instances where teacher evaluation systems have been developed and implemented without input from students or faculty. The system's effectiveness then suffers from the lack of good ideas during the development stage as well as the lack of commitment to its use during the implementation stage.

2. Regular Implementation. Faculty evaluation, in order to become a well-known and valued part of the local culture, must occur on a regular and expected timetable. Sporadic implementation legitimately raises the questions of how important the process is and the strength of commitment by those who administer the evaluations. In our department we annually evaluate the faculty and these evaluations are used to distribute merit monies. In a year when there was no merit money, we did the evaluations anyway. It was important for faculty to know their work for that year did not go unnoticed and that when merit money was available we would have a record of their work during that year. The same principle applies to teacher evaluations. If student evaluations of teachers are considered important, they should be a planned and expected part of every course every year.

3. Clear Expectations. All parties involved in any evaluation should, to the fullest extent possible, enter into the endeavor with similar expectations. To accomplish this, the expectations associated with the evaluation should be clearly written and distributed. Even though general guidelines for promotion and faculty evaluation may be clear, they may still be in need of local interpretations and operational definitions. This does not mean effective evaluation systems specify exact (and inflexible) details for performance in their general guidelines. A promotion committee may not wish to say that tenure-track faculty members must have 12 publications to get promoted, but they can say something like: "In this area of study, the last two faculty members who were promoted averaged about two publications per year." To encourage quality publications, faculty seeking promotion may be told: "The publications we value the most are those in our field's most prestigious journals and we expect at least some of your work will appear in journals such as (name them)." In the case of a faculty member who is close to doing what is necessary for promotion to full professor

and a promotion committee feels specificity is possible and will serve a motivational purpose, it may wish to be very specific; for example, "By (date), finish and get good prepublication reviews of your book and get the article you are revising accepted in (name) journal and we'll consider you for promotion."

It is not uncommon for those being evaluated to want more specificity, whereas those doing the evaluation want less. It is important to talk about these needs and avoid both extremes. Evaluations inevitably involve a degree of subjectivity by the evaluators, but this should be far less of a problem if the evaluators and those being evaluated are engaged in an ongoing effort to maintain as much clarity as possible.

4. Timely Feedback. Faculty evaluations are driven by the desire to monitor behavior. The extent to which they will impact behavior is not solely dependent on timely feedback, but it is a critical factor. Student evaluations of a teacher are usually taken directly to a processing center where tabulations of statistical data are performed. Presumably, teachers can use these data to plan and adjust the courses they teach the following semester. However, if data on their teaching are not returned until they are well into the teaching of another course, they are not helpful in making timely adjustments. The same could be said for a tenure-track faculty member who only learns that this institution values articles in a certain journal during the last year of his or her probationary period.

5. Motivation to Achieve. Faculty members, like people in other professions, will utilize faculty evaluation systems to their fullest when they believe the evaluations are linked to desirable consequences. Whether it is a teaching award, a large increase in salary, a promotion, or the pleasure of comparing oneself favorably with one's colleagues, evaluations should be viewed in the context of faculty members' motivation to succeed. When achievements are evaluated and nothing happens, it surely will affect the achievement motivation negatively; when achievements are evaluated and the only consequences perceived are punitive, the motivation to succeed can be replaced by the motivation to beat the evaluation system.

6. Fair Application. Faculty evaluations must be perceived as fairly administered to all or their value is lost. Court cases are plentiful that highlight two faculty members with similar performance evaluations in which one is promoted and the other is denied promotion. Fairly administering faculty evaluations does not mean everyone will be

treated exactly the same. Administrators and promotion committees must be able to factor in the specific circumstances associated with each person being evaluated, simultaneously weighing the extent to which decisions about one person are fair to others.

When faculty evaluations have been forged with input from those involved; when they occur regularly and predictably, when they set forth clear expectations for what is to be evaluated and how the evaluation is to be used, when the parties involved receive timely feedback from the evaluation, when the consequences of the evaluation provide an increased motivation to achieve, and when the evaluation system is perceived as fairly applied to all those being evaluated, the system has the best chance to succeed.

What is typically evaluated? No matter what the type of faculty evaluation, there are standard categories for assessing faculty performance. These include teaching, research, and service. Faculty evaluations for teaching awards, promotions, annual reviews, and 3-year reviews normally include an up-to-date curriculum vitae accompanied by other requested documentation (e.g., teaching evaluations, course syllabi, reprints of published articles, etc.). Faculty who are evaluated should treat these evaluation processes as they would any communication transaction and arrange the materials so they communicate accurately, efficiently, clearly, and persuasively. Although we may sometimes wish otherwise, the presentation of the materials (e.g., neatness, page numbers, co-authors listed, charts, tables, readability) to be evaluated is a message to which evaluators pay attention. Sometimes carelessness is interpreted as more deliberate (with a correspondingly negative evaluation) as in the case where a faculty member fails to indicate that he or she is the editor of a volume, not the author. With these general ideas in mind, let us examine each of the familiar categories for evaluation.

1. Teaching. Teaching effectiveness is a complex activity and the more information available about a faculty member's teaching, the greater his or her chances of receiving an evaluation that adequately deals with that complexity. Therefore, faculty are often encouraged to develop and maintain a *teaching portfolio*. Common components of a teaching portfolio include: (a) course and instructor evaluations by students—including both written comments and numerical ratings; (b) course syllabi; (c) unsolicited letters from students; (d) peer evaluations;

(e) videotapes of the instructor teaching; (f) advising and mentoring activities at both graduate and undergraduate levels; (g) noncurricular teaching—for example, workshops, community talks; (h) new course development; (i) examples of instructor evaluations—for example, graded papers; (j) student products and awards; (k) teaching awards and (l) work with student organizations. Some colleges and universities also solicit *exit survey* information—that is, surveying students 6 months after graduation and asking them to indicate the teachers from whom they learned the most.

Evaluators of a professor's teaching commonly look for signs of quantitative and qualitative excellence. This may take the form of high student evaluations and innovative course developments or it may be evidence indicating one has gone to great lengths to improve his or her teaching. Extra credit is often given for high teaching evaluations without correspondingly high grades given to the students; teaching elective courses that draw students from across the campus; and a willingness to teach courses for which there is a high demand.

2. Scholarship. Normally, scholarship means the publication of one's research and the presentation of one's creative work. Published research is often given the most credit if it appears in print on a regular basis and is published in prestige journals or journals that have a high rejection rate. Books based on one's research are usually evaluated more highly than textbooks. If one's book is published by a publishing house revered for its publication of quality scholarship, evaluators consider this a plus. Obtaining a grant or grants to support one's research is also considered a sign of excellence in scholarship. Although many institutions do not reward the writing and submission of research and training grants that are not funded, some do. Whether these unfunded proposals are considered part of a faculty member's scholarship or not, grant writers should be fully informed how such material will be weighted and evaluated. Research that has not been published (including in press works) should have independent reviews and a letter from the editor or publisher verifying the date of publication accompanying them. Given the explosion of professional journals in recent years, a familiar attitude among evaluators is that virtually anything can get published. For those with this attitude, measures of quality are the preeminent concern.

When scholars with established reputations are asked to evaluate the work of a faculty member, the focus is almost always on scholarship and the questions are fairly predictable. Although the wording may be different from institution to institution, outside evaluators are asked to address: (a) their relationship with the person being evaluated, (b) their opinion of the contribution(s) made by the scholarly work of the person being evaluated, (c) how the person being evaluated compares with similar scholars in his or her growth as a scholar, and (d) what reputation the person being evaluated has in the relevant scholarly community. The magnitude of the external evaluator's reputation and his or her institution are also factored into the comments made.

Creative scholarship in communication takes many forms (e.g., screenwriting, photojournalism, advertising, stage performances, etc.). Some of these faculty members also publish in scholarly journals, but others do not. How should creative work be evaluated? In the College of Communication at the University of Texas, faculty from several different areas of communication scholarship proposed an evaluation process that relies on: (a) developing a reputation of excellence, (b)creating a system of peer review, and (c) developing a creative or artistic portfolio (similar to the teaching portfolio mentioned earlier) to document their work. Because creative endeavors may interface with non-academic markets as well as academic markets, this raises questions about how to weight the contribution. If, for example, a performance studies faculty member appears in a Broadway play and is paid for the work, to what extent is this tied to the knowledge base of this area and to what extent should the activity count toward merit pay or promotion? What weight should be given to films reaching a regional audience rather than a national or local one?

Issues related to the evaluation of creative work have prompted some institutions and scholarly organizations to consider the development of guidelines for such evaluations. The College Art Association, for instance, has adopted standards for the retention and tenure of visual arts faculty.

3. Service. In some colleges and universities, service is given equal weight with teaching and scholarship; in others it is given less weight. If evaluators give less weight to service, faculty should be informed. In our department, annual evaluations of faculty performance are weighted as follows: teaching, 36%; scholarship, 36%; and service 28%. Service is commonly thought of as administrative and committee work that serves one's professional associations, one's own institution (department, college, and university) and one's local community. If the types of service are valenced differently, faculty members should be informed. The aforementioned issue concerning payment for a creative

product or activity also raises its ugly head when evaluating service. This occurs when a faculty member serves as a consultant to a profit-making company and is paid for it. Should this activity then be given credit (and if so, how much) as community service when his or her university is evaluating faculty for merit money? From the standpoint of formal policy, the answer to this question in most communication departments is "no." Nevertheless, under certain circumstances paid consultancies may be considered as worthwhile service activities (e.g., when the consultancy brings recognition to the department and the field or when it is closely linked with the faculty member's research program).

PROMOTION AND TENURE

For many members of the professoriate, faculty evaluation is associated solely with the process of promotion and the award of tenure. Although we suggest in the next section that periodic evaluation of all faculty is an important component of faculty development, most of us began our careers linking evaluation with the watershed event in everyone's career: the attainment of tenure.

At many institutions of higher education, an evaluation of a faculty member's work in his or her third year of employment is a precursor to tenure review: A dossier of teaching evaluations, publications, and letters from outside reviewers is prepared and evaluated by the departmental promotion committee. This review is important because it forewarns the candidate if he or she is not on schedule for promotion, in accordance with university and departmental criteria, and because it reinforces productive behavior that will stand the individual in good stead at tenure time. It also reflects enough of the formal trappings of the tenure review so the candidate obtains a general understanding of how the process works before it occurs. In these ways, the promotion process for the award of tenure begins with the third-year review.

Purpose of Tenure

To individuals outside of academe, tenure appears to be a utopian state, characterized by a sealed guarantee of lifetime employment. According to one university president, however, tenure:

is a condition of employment under which a faculty member enjoys the prospect of continuing employment unless the institution can show good cause to terminate the employment. It is not a guarantee of a lifetime job. It is not analogous to tenure in the federal judiciary where impeachment is necessary to terminate the appointment. A tenured faculty member can be dismissed if the institution can show good cause under its rules and regulations. (Flawn, 1990, pp. 70–71)

For our purposes, the award of tenure is a significant commitment on the part of the institution, recognizing excellent and sustained contributions (and the prospect of them) to the university and the discipline in the areas of teaching, research, and service.

The Process and Its Participants

The formal relationship between the principals in this process may or may not be specified by the institution. In one culture, the department chair acts as a mentor—carefully guiding and advising the candidate at each stage in the promotion process and acting as the candidate's advocate. Under this system, some candidates may perceive they are not as carefully mentored as others. Another approach tries to replace the role of advocate with a system that attempts to provide each candidate with similar guidelines and more objective advising. The data, it is argued, will speak for the candidate. Mentoring faculty should be practiced and valued throughout a faculty member's career, but there are differing approaches to mentoring during the promotion process.

There are at least four stages in the evaluative process leading to the award of tenure:

1. Collection of materials. The candidate, in cooperation with the department chair, collects teaching evaluations, copies of publications, and other materials as discussed later in this chapter. Faculty members should begin collecting these materials during the first semester of their appointment, but all materials should be organized 3 to 6 months before they are reviewed by the departmental promotion committee, the chair of the department, and the dean because sometimes they are reviewed by a university committee, as well.

2. Contact of outside reviewers. At the beginning of the collection process, outside reviewers should be contacted by the chair, asking their willingness to review a candidate's dossier. The candidate may be allowed to identify three to four individuals he or she prefers for this task, and departmental promotion committee members may also offer

names. From this list the chair selects four or five names. Many institutions have standardized letters to send these individuals, identifying the criteria to be considered, the preferred topics to be discussed in the review, and the due date for the review. These letters also should inform the reviewer of the state's laws relating to the right to see materials in one's personnel file. Outside reviewers should not be a candidate's closest friends or departmental colleagues. Outstanding scholars at peer institutions who may know the individual's work are the evaluators a department chair should seek.

3. Preparation of the dossier. Prior to departmental review, a candidate's dossier is created in accordance with criteria established by the president's or provost's office, and in an order prescribed by that office. This order allows dossiers institutionwide to have some degree of commonality, at least in the presentation of information. Materials and summary evaluations of each section should follow the university's format and any suggested "tips" offered by the president's or provost's office.

4. Review of the dossier. Finally, the departmental promotion committee and the chair independently review the dossier and make a promotion recommendation. The number of votes for, against, and abstaining are recorded. The dossier and departmental recommendation are then sent to the dean or an advisory committee in the college or university for review and recommendation. Then the materials are considered by members of central administration, including the provost or vice president for academic affairs, the president, the graduate dean, and other university administrators deemed appropriate by the president or the board of trustees or regents.

Components of the Dossier

Earlier in this chapter we discussed the materials used in the ongoing process of faculty evaluation, whether its purpose is a merit increase, a teaching award, or promotion. This section specifically focuses on materials often included in the promotion and tenure document. There is, of course, variance among institutional requirements for what a tenure candidate's dossier should contain. The following listing describes the contents of a sample document, and is based on guidelines provided by the president's office at our institution. Many institutions have such guidelines for departmental use.

1. A curriculum vitae, which lists degrees, professional appointments, and a publications record that indicates the candidate's involvement in each entry (i.e., whether he or she is a co-author, first author, etc.). Forthcoming works, either in press, accepted, or under review, should be distinguished. The vitae also should include a listing of advising and related student service, university and professional service, and honors received in the department, the college, at the university level, or within discipline-specific scholarly organizations.

2. Annual reports of academic work that summarize an individual's teaching responsibilities in organized classes, the supervision of independent study students, or those conducting thesis and dissertation work.

3. Letters from journal or book editors indicating the status of works in press.

4. Additional or supplementary information included at the candidate's discretion (e.g., videotapes of performances, films, and other creative work). A listing of research leaves, or leaves without pay, also should be enclosed with the vitae.

5. A teaching portfolio, which may include a chart summarizing the candidate's instructional activities (e.g., courses taught, enrollments in all classes, a peer evaluation report, student evaluations, a summary sheet of instructor ratings and written comments, and a listing of the names of students whose theses and dissertations have been supervised). A teaching portfolio may also include sample syllabi, descriptions of curricular revisions the candidate has made, a statement of teaching philosophy, convention papers or journal articles on pedagogy, and unsolicited letters from former students.

6. Publications and other evidence of scholarship. Whereas all publications are listed in the vitae, only four or five publications, identified by the candidate as most significant to the field, may be included in the promotion document.

7. Evidence of academic advising and service to students that indicates the faculty member's participation in undergraduate and graduate advising, participation in department or university orientation programs, work with student organizations, assistance with internship placement, and involvement with formal career services programs. Service as an undergraduate or graduate adviser deserves particular mention in the dossier.

8. A listing of administrative and committee service to the department, college, and university with leadership positions identified specifically (e.g., chair of a curriculum review committee).

9. Evidence of public service to the discipline (e.g., the editorship of a journal or service as an elected officer in a scholarly organization). Relevant community service also may be noted (e.g., membership on boards or committees in the community).

10. A listing of honors, fellowships, grants, lectures and visiting teaching appointments at other universities.

11. Letters of reference and evaluation from outside reviewers should conclude the dossier—letters that address the accomplishments of the candidate and summarize his or her professional standing. Accompanying these letters should be descriptions of the evaluators—their institution, rank, area(s) of specialization and why they were selected as referees.

The critical components of the dossier are the *evaluations* of teaching, research, advising, service, and honors received by the candidate. An outstanding dossier is one that thoroughly presents sufficient information to justify the award of tenure. At the same time, the evaluations of academic activities and recognition should be succinct and clear. In other words, the case for tenure should be communicated with the audience in mind, and should include evidence and reasoning that build a prima facie case for promotion. The candidate, his or her colleagues, and the department chair should be actively concerned with this process. Indeed, a department develops a reputation on campus and in the discipline based in part on its ability to evaluate carefully, make hard decisions, and present strong cases for promotion. As a result, the process as well as the candidate is under review when recommendations for promotion and tenure are made to the dean and the president for approval. To enhance the credibility of the process, it is beneficial to review the work of assistant and associate professors annually. A general impression therefore may evolve within the departmental promotion committee that a faculty member is indeed qualified for promotion, culminating in a group decision that it is time to prepare the appropriate credentials.

As the dossier is completed within the department, and revised if necessary in the dean's office before transmittal to the president's office, a checklist should be prepared from institutional guidelines on the promotion process so that the department chair, the dean, and their staffs can check and recheck the components of the dossier for completeness and accuracy. The quality of the dossier should be a reflection of the quality of the candidate.

Postevaluation Recommendations

There are decisional options available at each stage of the tenure award process, although some stages allow more choices than others. For tenure-track faculty who are in their "up and out" year, the departmental promotion committee, the chair, the dean, and the executive officers will either vote to approve or deny promotion. If a candidate has had good reasons to attempt to receive tenure earlier than is the norm, the promotion committee may approve or deny tenure, or hold the dossier "without prejudice" until a later date. If the candidate is being considered for promotion to full professor, the promotion committee may approve the promotion, deny it, or decide to hold the dossier without prejudice until a later year. Under the latter circumstances, the committee may ask the chair to provide the candidate with a listing of criteria he or she should meet in order to receive a positive vote from them in the future. If the decision by the departmental promotion committee is a positive one, the college or university committee, the dean, and the executive officers may approve, deny, or hold without prejudice the candidate's credentials.

Preparing for Central Administration's
Review of Candidates

The dean or administrator who will be presenting promotion and tenure candidates at central administration's meeting to make final decisions is well-served by visiting with the chair of each department's candidates, and listening to the deliberations of the college or university promotion committee as part of the dossier review process. Such preparation will allow the dean to understand each candidate's strengths and weaknesses, and answer questions about his or her work as well as summarize it at the meeting with the president and other executive officers.

The dean may know a tenure decision at the end of this meeting—but be asked to keep it confidential until the candidate is notified in writing by the president. Although changes in status may not occur until they receive the imprimatur of the board of trustees or regents, candidates may be informed of the decision "pending trustee or regent approval." Administrators serve their departments, and individual faculty, best if tenure decisions are not reported via the rumor mill. Prematurely talking about a candidate's success or failure, even to your closest confidant on the faculty, abrogates a confidential decision-making process, may create embarrassment for the candidate, campus administrators, and the department, and unjustifiably increases public attention to a private matter. Consequently, an administrator should not contribute to the rumor mill about this or any other personnel issue. Candidates must remember that a promotion is not official until the governing board of the institution has approved it, and new titles should not be printed on business cards, etched into doors, or used in correspondence until the date when the promotion is officially in effect.

Promotion to Full Professor

An institutional decision to promote a faculty member to the rank of full professor communicates that the individual continues to make substantial contributions to his or her discipline and university through scholarly and creative productivity and teaching. If more specific criteria are used in the evaluation process, the candidate and the outside reviewers of the dossier should have written copies of those criteria. As we indicated in the previous section, the process for reviewing credentials for this type of promotion is generally the same as that for the award of tenure. The components of the dossier are also similar, although there should be increased evidence of scholarly productivity, visibility, and influence; evidence that the candidate continues to be an effective teacher; and evidence of more substantive service to the various audiences served by the candidate.

Occasionally, an individual will receive consistently superior annual evaluations, and will be recommended by his or her peers for early promotion to full professor. In general, an early promotion takes place before 6 years in rank have elapsed. Associate professors who have been in rank more than 6 years are recommended, at some point in their careers, for promotion to full professor if they can show evidence of a renewed scholarly or creative productivity for the preceding 3 to 5 years, which is considered a good yardstick for future contributions.

Given the foregoing attempts to create a process beneficial both to a candidate and his or her department, charges of unfairness from an unsuccessful candidate are not likely to occur. Additionally, annual faculty evaluations and third-year reviews should help counsel individuals about the likelihood of their success in academe, or the need for them to pursue other career possibilities in lieu of confronting ongoing problems in their teaching, research, or creative work. Nevertheless all communication administrators on a campus should know their institution's grievance policy and procedures related to the denial of promotion and tenure.

Post-Tenure Review

In 1989, the University of California at Berkeley developed a policy for terminating tenured teachers. That same year, the Arkansas legislature, under then-Governor Bill Clinton, voted to require the annual evaluation of all tenured faculty in the state's public higher education institutions, in part to identify those who should not be retained in their positions. During the 1990s colleges and universities throughout the country have discussed and debated proposals requiring mandatory evaluation of tenured faculty. Faculty governing bodies and boards of trustees have adopted a number of these proposals.

There are multiple and interrelated sources of pressure for post-tenure review, including: federal elimination of the mandatory retirement age, inadequate state appropriations for faculty salaries in public higher education institutions, and perceptions among legislators and some members of the public that there is a lack of accountability in a system that seems to protect the long-term economic security of individuals whose work and work schedules are not well-known or understood. Perceptions and legislation therefore have combined to force boards of trustees and university chancellors and presidents to consider carefully the evaluation of tenured faculty.

Whereas post-tenure review may be thought by some as a way to identify and eliminate "dead wood" on a faculty, others are emphasizing the ways it can enhance professional development. As the University of Texas System Board of Regents wrote in its "Guidelines for Periodic Evaluation of Tenured Faculty":

Periodic evaluation is intended to enhance and protect, not diminish, the important guarantees of tenure and academic freedom. The purpose of periodic evaluation is to provide guidance for continuing and meaningful faculty development; to assist faculty to enhance professional skills and goals; to refocus academic and professional efforts, when appropriate; and to assure that faculty members are meeting their responsibilities to the University and the State of Texas. (The University of Texas System Board of Regents, 1996)

Colleges and universities throughout the United States are implementing, or considering the implementation of, various policies and procedures for post-tenure reviews.

Components of a sample process include the following:

1. A required annual review for *all* faculty, conducted by a committee in each university department. The review may be conducted in connection with merit pay increase decisions. Materials reviewed include annual reports of academic activities (teaching, research, and service) and evidence of teaching quality (student evaluations).

2. Review of tenured faculty every 5 years by a departmental committee. The chair is responsible for notifying the faculty to be evaluated at least 6 months before the review. Each faculty member may meet with the committee at his or her request. The department chair communicates the result of the review to the faculty member and to the dean for appropriate action. Materials reviewed include curriculum vitae, student evaluations of teaching for the review period, annual reports for the review period, and any other materials a faculty member may wish to provide.

3. If the result of the review is a negative evaluation, the dean or the faculty member may request a more intensive review by a peer committee in the college or school in which the department is located. This committee is comprised of tenured faculty. If there are no colleges or schools in the administrative structure, the same departmental committee can continue the review, or a new committee can be appointed. The committee may request additional information from the faculty member. At his or her request, the faculty member may meet with this committee. The results of the second review are communicated in writing to the faculty member, the chair, and the dean.

4. Post-tenure reviews may be phased in on a campus. The process may begin with approximately 20% of the current tenured faculty in each department or equivalent unit under review. New tenured

faculty are reviewed 5 years after their promotion or date of initial appointment.

5. A campus faculty committee monitors the review process and reports its findings annually to the faculty governing body at the institution and to the central administration of the university.

6. If a faculty member's review is positive, he or she is eligible for merit raises, promotions, teaching awards, and other forms of recognition.

7. If a review is unsatisfactory, individuals are not eligible for merit raises. They also may be asked to work with staff in a teaching effectiveness program on campus or with a peer who may serve as a research mentor.

8. Some post-tenure review processes avoid the mention of dismissal as a possible result of these processes. Others provide for dismissal if the review committee finds continuing and substantial evidence of incompetence, unsatisfactory performance, or moral turpitude. In such cases, proceedings must include a listing of specific charges by the institutional president and an opportunity for a hearing before a faculty tribunal. The burden of proof is on the institution to show cause for dismissal, and a faculty member's rights of due process and academic freedom are to be protected.

Critics of post-tenure review are concerned about its possible infringement on academic freedom and its potential assault on the right of continuous employment for those who attain the requisite excellence in teaching, research, and service. However, if post-tenure review, as discussed here, is not instituted in a university, we recommend some type of periodic evaluation of all faculty members. Feedback elicited in such reviews can be a major source of information in academic programs committed to faculty development, and until the processes of post-tenure review are evaluated systematically over time, their worth, or danger, remains unknown.

CONCLUDING OBSERVATIONS

Faculty evaluation in general, and the processes that lead to promotion and the award of tenure specifically, should include the following components that befit this critical decisional process:

- Clearly articulated criteria that are written and widely distributed.
- Adequate information, covering a sufficient span of time, to identify a pattern of academic excellence.
- Continual communication between the candidate and the department chair as promotion materials are being prepared, among the communication administrators and relevant committees as the dossier is being evaluated, and among the dean's office and central administration as the dossier is being reviewed and discussed at that level.
- Sufficient feedback after the evaluation so that the candidate and others involved in the process understand the reasons for the decision(s).
- Members of the promotion committee are also members of the department and as such should serve as ongoing mentors to faculty as part of the evaluation and promotion processes.

If faculty evaluation is to be regarded as the preeminent component of faculty development, communication administrators must implement this process, whatever its ultimate purpose, with the same commitment to communication that they reflect in the classroom, the laboratory, and the field. In short, they must practice what they teach, illustrating that the process of evaluating faculty is one of the most important forms of human interaction within a university.

APPENDIX:
ADDITIONAL RESOURCES

Arreola, R. A. (1995). *Developing a comprehensive faculty evaluation system.* Bolton, MA: Anker.

Braskamp, L. A., & Ory, J. C. (1994). *Assessing faculty work.* San Francisco: Jossey-Bass.

Centra, J. A., Froh, R. C., Gray, P. J., & Lambert, L. M. (1987). *A guide to evaluating teaching for promotion and tenure.* Acton, MA: Copley.

Diamond, R. M. (1994). *Serving on promotion and tenure committees: a faculty guide.* Bolton, MA: Anker.

Diamond, R. M. (1995). *Preparing for promotion and tenure review: A faculty guide.* Bolton, MA: Anker.

Dilts, D. A., Haber, L. J., & Bialik, D. (1994). *Assessing what professors do.* Westport, CT: Greenwood.

Seldin, P., and Associates (Eds.). (1990). *How administrators can improve teaching: Moving from talk to action in higher education.* San Francisco: Jossey-Bass.

REFERENCES

Flawn, P. T. (1990). *A primer for university presidents*. Austin: University of Texas Press.

Metzger, W. P. (1973). Academic tenure in America: a historical essay. In W. R. Keast (Ed.), *Faculty tenure* (pp. 93–159). San Francisco: Jossey-Bass.

University of Texas System Board of Regents. (November 14, 1996). *UT System guidelines for periodic evaluation of tenured faculty*. Austin, TX: Author.

19

Federal Mandates

Annelle Zerbe Weymuth
Northwest Missouri State University

Almost everyone in academia has heard of federal mandates like Title IX, Title VII, EEOC, 504, ADA, and FERPA and can recall that they are associated with nondiscrimination, sexual harassment, persons with disabilities, and student privacy issues. Vague recollections, however, will not protect a department chair or the faculty members. As a chair or director of an administrative unit, one must have a clear under-standing of these federal mandates. It is important to recognize the significant impact they can have on you, your department, and your institution, especially when litigation today can have a major public relations as well as financial impact. The federal laws considered in this chapter were chosen because of their direct relevance to the duties of the chairperson or administrator of a department. It is the chairperson who sets the tone for nondiscrimination and confidentiality between and among the faculty and students. This means that you are respon-sible for establishing the acceptable standards of behavior within your department or unit. Lack of knowledge about these widely publicized federal mandates will not hold up as a defense in a court of law for any academic administrator.

To be successful as a faculty chair one must understand the federal mandates addressing nondiscrimination, sexual harassment, disability, and student privacy rights and your campus' policies that implement these mandates. If a university receives federal funding, and all do when they receive federal student financial aid, then there must be compliance with these mandates. Each university must designate a compliance officer to provide information and training regarding these mandates. The compliance officer is typically assigned to the president's office or the university legal counsel. In this chapter, several legal guidelines for each of the federal mandates are briefly described and followed by some bulleted information about compliance issues regarding the mandate that you need to be aware of as department chair. This information is to make you more aware of the guidelines and to help you in your role as department administrator. It is not intended to substitute for the advisement of your own campus compliance officer or legal counsel.

EQUAL EMPLOYMENT OPPORTUNITY (EEO)

The objectives of the EEO program are straightforward. First, all faculty and students in your department are to be given full and fair opportunity for success in their academic pursuits regardless of race, sex, color, age, national origin, handicap, or religion. (Some colleges and universities include sexual preference in this list, but it is not included by the federal government.) Second, your department is to provide nondiscriminatory treatment of all faculty and students in the course of carrying out its educational mission. Discrimination is defined here as making decisions based on some distinguishing factor—such as race, sex, color, age, national origin, handicap, or religion. It is a legitimate part of your position as head of an academic department to recognize outstanding performance; however, it is unlawful to discriminate against faculty and students based on factors that have been prohibited by law and regulation (EEOC Compliance Manual, 1992).

There are two kinds of EEO discrimination recognized by the courts: disparate treatment and disparate impact (Gilson, 1989). *Disparate treatment* is when a person claims that he or she was treated differently from others by a supervisor because of race, sex, color, age, national origin, handicap, or religion. To defend against an allegation of disparate treatment, the chair must show that there was a legitimate, nondiscriminatory reason to take a particular action. Disparate treatment most often focuses upon the individual and disparate impact focuses on the entire institution. *Disparate impact* most often focuses on the system of entrance examinations, hiring procedures, and promotion that appears to treat everyone alike, but has the effect of harming a particular group. To defend against a disparate impact claim is much more difficult and often involves statistical studies and complicated validation of the systems the university might use.

Whereas disparate treatment and impact are reactive, affirmative action is proactive. Rather than waiting until an unfair action, such as disparate treatment or disparate impact, has been filed with the Equal Employment Opportunity Commission (EEOC), affirmative action was mandated to bring the workforce into balance, thus incorporating nondiscriminatory hiring practices into any agency receiving federal funds. Because universities have accepted federal funds in the form of Pell Grants and other financial assistance programs to help their students pay for their education, they fell under these guidelines. Affirmative action is a conscious, deliberate effort to make certain that qualified under-represented minority employees (regardless of race, age, sex, color, national origin, handicap, or religion) are given a full and fair opportunity to be represented and progress in the workplace (Gilson, 1989).

Affirmative action is a key area in which organizations have been required by the federal government to reduce discrimination; however, controversies currently abound over the status of affirmative action in various states. Affirmative action has taken a high profile position in recent U.S. presidential elections as different parties take positions for and against it. Several California and Texas universities have abandoned their affirmative action plans in the area of student admission to their schools and specific programs. To date, federal funds have not been withheld from those institutions that are no longer in compliance with affirmative action guidelines; however, several key court cases have yet to be heard (Lederman, 1997). It is best to consult with your EEO compliance officer as to the position your college or university is taking on this issue. To decide not to follow a federal mandate is not a decision to be made alone by a department chair or unit administrator because of the potential legal implications.

Various steps can be taken within the hiring process to help avoid discrimination and encourage a well-diversified workforce. For example, a survey could be given to assess the number of faculty who are employed and students who are studying within a department. It may be determined that there is an underrepresented group. When a lack of diversity is evident, then several key steps can be followed to increase the numbers of that particular minority group.

- Plan ahead for vacancies within the department for both faculty and students. This allows time for careful review and planning strategies within the department.
- Talk with your employment specialists (personnel or human resources department, and vice president for academic affairs or provost) and the recruiters for your institution. Ask the specialists to advise you of your options in filling the positions, the recruiting resources, the lead time necessary, and possible restructuring options within the department.
- Think about EEO implications. Ask yourself if your department is balanced with minorities and nonminorities appropriate for your region. Review or ask about the university's affirmative action plan to determine whether it may be necessary to take additional steps to enlarge the candidate pool in order to attract qualified minorities, which includes women.
- Consider special programs. This could include rank and tenure decisions that may have long-range impact on the department, or special offerings for more at-risk students.
- Specific to hiring, follow all guidelines established by your university to properly select the faculty member, staff, or student employee. Typically there are different guidelines for each type of employee. It is important to objectively and fairly assess each candidate's qualifications. By recording each step of the established process you are protecting youself and the institution. If all minimal qualifications, which have been well defined early in the job search, are well met and a group is found to be underrepresented, there is the opportunity to hire the minority, which includes women.

SEXUAL HARASSMENT

Twenty to thirty percent of undergraduate women nationwide had experienced some form of sexual harassment according to Bernice R. Sandler (1990), Executive Director of the Project on the Status and Education of Women of the Association of American Colleges, after surveying several thousand students from 24 campuses. Among graduate students the rate was 30% to 40%. Sexual harassment is a type of sexual discrimination prohibited by Title VII of the Civil Rights Act of 1964 and Title IX of the Education Amendments of 1972. The most often quoted definition comes from the Supreme Court case of *Meritor Savings Bank v. Vinson* (1986) (Wishnietsky, 1992). The guidelines used in this court decision define sexual harassment as:

> Unwelcome sexual advances, requests for sexual favors, and other verbal or physical conduct of a sexual nature ... when (1) submission to such conduct is made either explicitly or implicitly a term or condition of an individual's employment, (quid pro quo harassment) (2) submission to or rejection of such conduct by an individual is used as the basis for employment decisions affecting such individual, (quid pro quo harassment) or (3) such conduct has the purpose or effect of unreasonably interfering with the individual's work performance or creating an intimidating, hostile or offensive working environment, (condition of work harassment). (Meritor Savings Bank v. Vinson,1986)

An example of quid pro quo sexual harassment in the academic environment could include but is not limited to suggesting an exchange of a grade or recommendation for a sexual favor. A student would have a legitimate case if a grade of A were lowered for refusing to have a sexual relationship with a faculty member. However, incidents of an "offensive or hostile environment" are more likely to be found in the academic workplace, including offices and classrooms, than the *quid pro quo* harassment. Examples of an offensive or hostile academic environment include, but are not limited to, the instructor's use of unnecessary sexual remarks, jokes, and innuendoes about women in class, or the use of sexually explicit materials. Use of physical contact and entering another's personal space are also inappropriate. Jokes, which were considered appropriate and funny during one era involving a minority group, such as women, are often found to be offensive and insensitive during another.

Faculty who date students, especially those in their classes, create a potential source of litigation. Arguably, there can never be a consensual relationship between a supervisor and a subordinate or a professor and a student because of the inherent power differential. There is a need to balance and reconcile the protection to be given a student with the couple's individual rights of privacy. Many universities have policies that do not allow student–faculty dating.

As a chair or an administrator, you are an agent of the university and are thus potentially responsible and liable for the learning environment in your department. In sexual harassment cases, ignorance of the law is not a defense. This is why you have probably noticed that there are information pieces and training sessions on this topic at your institution, as well as readily available brochures for faculty and staff that establish guidelines for compliance and reporting sexual harassment offenses. The institution is liable if the harassing faculty member's actions were so pervasive and continuous that the institution (i.e., chairperson and fellow faculty members) should have been aware of them. Almost all universities and schools have attempted to limit their liability by adopting grievance procedures that require prompt remedial action for acts of harassment, *quid pro quo* or hostile or offensive environment. However, the mere existence of a grievance policy does not protect the university against litigation if nothing is done about the incident. The Supreme Court's opinion in *Meritor Savings Bank v. Vinson* (1986) would indicate that in order to help insulate the institution from liability, the grievance procedure must not only be tailored especially toward ending sexual harassment, but must be well publicized to discourage grievances. This is done by requiring as the first step that the grievant be encouraged to confront the person alleged to be committing the harassment. If this confrontation does not change the behavior, the institution must have in place a process to promptly respond to the grievance brought forth in either an informal or formal manner.

The person being harassed, whether a student or an employee, may just want the behavior stopped and wish that their name and the details not be revealed. Unlike a criminal trial where the person must be aware of his or her accuser, harassment situations can be handled through a dialogue between a faculty chairperson and an accused faculty member, thus requesting a change in behavior without a formal complaint. For example, if a student said that a faculty member in your department was starting each class period with a joke about "blondes" and it was considered offensive, then, as the department chair, on hearing the complaint you should go directly to the faculty member and ask that it be stopped without disclosing the name of the student to the faculty member.

For the sake of argument, let us assume that the faculty member did not change the behavior giving the argument that it was his or her "right" to open lectures in any way that he or she felt appropriate. The instructor would be on shaky legal ground, because all it takes is one student feeling uncomfortable about the jokes or derogatory comments about women to make a case. Some instructors have tried to argue that there is the right of academic freedom which allows them to tell the jokes. The *American Association of University Professors Policy and Reports* (1990) definition of academic freedom states, "Teachers are entitled to freedom in the classroom in discussing their subject, but they should be careful not to introduce into their teaching controversial matter which has no relation to their subject" (p. 3).

No university desires the legal cost and publicity associated with being a test case. Although many situations may be handled internally there is always the option to file a complaint outside of the university setting. The EEO campus compliance officer may work to resolve internal situations, but the person being harassed may also go off campus directly to the closest regional or state EEOC to file a grievance for sexual harassment or any other claim of discrimination. Once the EEOC is involved, the investigation is no longer internal to the campus and may begin to involve legal and public relations issues. When a resolution can be achieved at the campus level it is preferred, because there will be less publicity and fewer legal costs. The EEOC is currently very backlogged with cases, so this recourse takes a longer period of time. If the party who has allegedly been harassed has a case rejected by the EEOC, that party may still seek private legal counsel and sue the institution (Gilson, 1989).

There are two separate federal antidiscrimination laws: Title IX of the Educational Amendments of 1972 and Title VII of the 1964 Civil Rights Act. Both laws require adopting policies on sexual harassment and establishing grievance mechanisms with prompt appropriate action on charges that are found to have merit. However, there are differences in compensation and punitive damages to victims of sexual harassment with each. Title VII provides a jury trial, reinstatement with back pay, and limited compensatory and punitive damages to victims, whereas under Title IX neither damages nor a jury trial are available. Under both, at an institution in which members are found guilty, the prohibited action must discontinue or the institution could face elimination of federal funding (Feery, 1994). Legally, state and campus guidelines may be more stringent than those that come through the federal mandates. Over the past few years ceilings have been lifted on financial settlements, and in some states tort law claims permit unlimited damage, which is a major reason these claims are often included along with a Title VII claim (Sexual Harassment Is Against the Law, 1997). Also, be aware that the faculty member accused of the harassment can be held financially responsible, as well as the chairperson, the dean, the provost, and those up the line of administration. If there are any questions about your legal position within the university, refer to the EEO compliance officer and legal counsel on campus.

If complaints are brought forth, you, as a chairperson, will need to act on them quickly, working with your designated EEO campus compliance officer, dean, vice president, or provost. It may be difficult to think that a faculty member within your department would be capable of the alleged harassment, so you might be tempted to ignore a complaint rather than deal with it, but this is not wise. The worst way to handle a complaint is to investigate the complaint and do nothing about it. It is far better to pursue options for handling the complaint with the university compliance officer or legal counsel rather than burying it. At this beginning point there is the greatest chance of resolving the situation quietly and effectively for all concerned, which most likely will not be the situation if the complaints continue to be ignored. If you do not deal with the complaint, students begin talking among themselves, and someone will eventually direct them to the campus compliance officer or legal counsel. College students today are very aware of their rights and responsibilities, so they usually will pursue a complaint. Because of your position as a chair or administrator, you should be well aware of this federal mandate. Legal counsel would have a very difficult time justifying your behavior of ignoring a complaint. You may find yourself in court.

It is important that all individuals involved in a complaint keep confidential information regarding the case, but this is often difficult, especially if it has not been handled quickly. The faculty member and the student's personal and professional reputations may be at stake. As a chairperson of a department, the key to avoiding litigation is to educate students and faculty about their rights and responsibilities to speak up when they observe violations and follow closely the procedural process set forth by the institution for dealing with sexual harassment or discrimination complaints. If you, as a chairperson, have kept confidential all materials involved in the alleged case, reported and dealt with the incident quickly, and documented carefully what has occurred with names and dates, legal counsel will be able to represent you and your departmental position well.

The following are some simple guidelines that, if followed, may protect a faculty member from sexual harassment charges and investigations.

- Never touch another person. Touching, even in the most caring of situations, can be misconstrued, if not by the person being touched, then by an onlooker.
- Never confer with a student behind closed doors unless another person is in the room. It is smart to leave your door open or be sure to have a window in the door where a person passing by may look into the room.
- Be wary of using jokes in or out of the classroom that could be interpreted differently than intended. What one person may think of as funny or cute, another may find offensive.
- Be careful about using generalizing characteristics or labels for groups or classes of people. Few of these generalizations hold up to scrutiny, especially in an academic setting.
- Do not date students. Whether your university has a consensual amorous relationship policy or not, dating a student could put your job in jeopardy.
- Be aware that what is written to colleagues and students utilizing print or electronic mail could also be held up for scrutiny and be misinterpreted.

AMERICANS WITH DISABILITIES ACT (ADA)

Transition to a college or university is frequently difficult for students with disabilities, but you can make it easier by understanding and interpreting the guidelines for your department or unit. Students come to a college or university after receiving services through their high schools where school districts are mandated by the Individuals with Disabilities Education Act (IDEA) of 1975 to provide students with accommodations. In higher education, however, procedures radically change for the student. Rather than the IDEA mandating the services, now the services are governed by the Rehabilitation Act of 1973, Section 504, and the Americans With Disabilities Act (ADA) of 1990. The responsibility shifts to the student to be responsible for self-identifying his or her needs for services. The student must find a service provider on campus and provide documentation of his or her disability if he or she wants to receive accommodations. The institution is then responsible for providing these services (*Section 504 Compliance Handbook*, 1992).

Universities have been under the 504 mandate for several decades previous to the ADA. The Section 504 states: " No otherwise qualified handicapped individual in the U.S. shall, solely by reason of his/her handicap, be excluded from the participation in, be denied benefits of, or be subjected to discrimination under any program of activity receiving federal financial assistance." Some implications specific to this law include:

1. No student can be excluded from any course, major or program solely on the basis of disability.
2. Certain accommodations are mandated, such as the provision of alternative testing and evaluation methods for measuring student mastery.
3. Modifications, substitutions, or waivers of a course, major or degree requirement may be an option to meet the needs of some students, but your institution should have established guidelines for such decisions (*Section 504 Compliance Handbook*, 1992).

The ADA signed on July 26, 1990, was seen as a declaration of independence for people with disabilities because it required all public establishments to eliminate barriers and make accommodations. The ADA expanded the scope of the 504 from only designated institutions to all public areas. This meant that for the first time local restaurants, hotels, stores, and so forth, had to be in compliance even if they were not receiving federal funds. The impact of ADA on higher education will more likely be felt in the increased number of students who choose to attend, as well as a renewed focus on the campus' facilities, programs, employment, and promotional issues. The ADA defines a person with a disability as "someone who has a physical or mental impairment that substantially limits that person in some major life activity, has a record of such impairment, or is regarded as having such impairment." The ADA requires all colleges and universities to complete a self-evaluation for ADA compliance. This self-evaluation must include a review of access to facilities as well as programs. It is discriminatory to restrict the range of career options for students with disabilities as compared to nondisabled students with similar interests and abilities, unless such advice is based on strict licensing or certification requirements that may constitute an obstacle. Changes that are necessary must be accomplished if they can be completed without "undue burden" to the institution, which is difficult for a college or university with a large operating budget to prove. Unlike Section 504, the ADA allows for people who feel they have been discriminated against to file lawsuits in the courts, and as a result the plaintiff can receive monetary awards if the court finds in their favor (Section 504 Compliance Handbook, 1992).

As a chair of a department or an administrator of a unit, you will need to be sure that the needs of those with documented disabilities are met. This would include faculty and staff members, as well as students. In the academic environment some instructors who have not taught students with disabilities, especially those with learning disabilities, could benefit by knowing that such a student often fails to let their instructor know their needs are not being met until an exam or two has already been taken. Students in higher education are trying hard to make it on their own and become independent, so voicing their disability even to the most understanding faculty member is often very difficult. For a successful university experience it would be most helpful if you would encourage your faculty and staff to offer a statement in the syllabus to encourage a dialogue about their needs. An example would be as follows: "If any student in this class has a need for special accommodations, please feel free to discuss this with me." Such an invitation in the syllabus can go a long way toward encouraging students with disabilities to approach the instructor early, which is highly desirable. Your institution probably has a brochure that outlines the process to receive accommodations, which could then be given to the student.

Not all students will use all the approved accommodations in every class. It is the student's responsibility to meet with the instructor to discuss his or her individual class needs. It would not be appropriate for the faculty member to probe into all of the reasons behind the disability. There has been a conscious effort not to list here all the appropriate accommodations for each disability, because each accommodation is unique to the individual with that particular disability.

The following general guidelines may be helpful for any department or unit members to remember when interacting with a student:

- Treat the person with the disability with the same consideration and respect you would anyone else.

- Do not let the disability blind you to the student's abilities. People with disabilities do not want to be pitied. They want to be accepted for who they are and what they can do.
- People with disabilities have the same goals as any other group of people. They are people first and disabled second.
- Most people with disabilities consider their disability as an inconvenience, not as a terrible tragedy.
- Just as the nondisabled have their own characteristics, talents, and personalities, so do those with disabilities. As many with disabilities like to say, "If the person with the disability was a jerk before their disability, they will be a jerk after their disability." Each person must be considered on their own merits and not on any preconceived myth, whether it is positive or negative.
- If you are not sure how to address or describe the individual with the disability, ask the person what descriptive term he or she prefers.

The ADA compliance officer on your campus is a good source of information regarding access and accommodation issues that you will need to address as the department chair or unit administrator.

FAMILY EDUCATIONAL RIGHTS
AND PRIVACY ACT 1974 (FERPA)

Each university must comply with FERPA (sometimes referred to as the Buckley Amendment), which provides guidelines on storage and releasing of student and former student records (*A Guide to Postsecondary Institutions*, 1976). Information remains confidential between the individual student and the university, and is not to be released to a third party without the written consent of the student. As a chair or administrator of a unit it is very important to make sure that faculty and staff are aware of the limitations in giving information that by this law is considered confidential. Information about the currently enrolled student, such as name, age, address, phone, e-mail address, place and date of birth, major, participation in activities and sports, weight and height (in the case of athletes), dates of attendance, degrees and awards received, and most recent educational institution attended, is considered public information and may be released. However, information about a student's grade or status can not be released without a signed waiver by the student. The dean of students, registrar, EEO officer, and legal counsel, which deal most frequently with such requests, can be used as resources whenever there is a question about whether information about a student's class grade or discipline records are requested by a third party or outside agency. Without a release from the student (this also pertains to employees within the institution), the following information according to FERPA guidelines could not be released to any relative, businesses, or future employer: financial records (e.g., financial aid application information, billings, etc.), confidential letters of recommendation written before January 1, 1975, personal records of educators (e.g., instructor's grade book, class grades), employee records, and medical or other professional records—unless a release has been signed.

The biggest pitfall in most academic units is when parents (who may be paying for the education of a son or daughter who is over 18 years of age) want to know about their child's grade in the class. Because parents are adamant and sincere, the information is given by the faculty member. This is not to be done. Under the FERPA mandate the request would have to be denied, unless the student is willing to sign a release form. Exceptions to this rule include information released to university officials, officials of other schools where the student is seeking admission, federal or state educational authorities, financial assistance officials in connection with the receipt of financial assistance, state law officials or subpoenaed requests, accrediting organizations, and parents of dependent children. There continues to be much discussion over the interpretations of FERPA (Shiels, 1997), so be sure to ask if there is any question about the release of personal information (see recommendation in the appendix).

CONCLUSION

As chairperson of a department, your task is to make sure that your university's policies are carried out effectively; thus, it is important to have a good working relationship with those who are responsible for federal compliance on your campus. Federal mandates are constantly being changed by legislative decisions and case law, so most campuses must rely on the compliance officers to keep up with the changes. Existing case law provides little guidance for institutions like colleges and universities; thus, an attempt needs to be made to adopt sexual harassment policies that allow universities to avoid imputed liability.

On the advice of my legal counsel there has been no attempt in this chapter to give legal references as one would find in a legal brief. The information in this chapter is generally accepted knowledge of those dealing with federal mandates within a higher education setting. Compliance officers must rely on journals and subscription services that give interpretations of the law as cases are heard throughout the country, such as *EEOC Compliance Manual* (1992), *Section 504 Compliance Handbook* (1992), and *Educator's Guide to Controlling Sexual Harassment* (1993), to mention a few that are listed in the reference section. Also, by attending conferences focusing on legal issues in higher education one can stay current on the legal interpretations of the federal mandates. Because this chapter is intended only to make a chair or an administrator of a unit aware of the potential impact these mandates may have, it is important to refer specific questions related to the federal mandates to your own legal counsel.

APPENDIX: FEDERAL MANDATE RECOMMENDATIONS

EEO

- Let everyone know that you are opposed to any type of discrimination, and let your actions show it.
- Treat all employees equally. Even though there are obvious differences between individuals, the rules should be applied the same way to all.
- Try to keep personal opinions on nonwork issues to yourself and encourage your faculty members to do the same.
- Avoid assumptions about entire groups of people, such as people of color, women, and so on.
- Do not patronize any particular group.
- Avoid labels or any pejorative terms reflecting an attitude that would be noticed and resented by employees.

ADA

- Although minor adjustments may need to be made in the physical layout of the classroom or accommodations need to be made addressing teaching methodology, many instructors have found that the abilities and productivity of students with disabilities meet or exceed that of the other students.
- Do not assume that a person with disabilities needs special assistance. Asking is the best way to know what the student needs.

FERPA

- Do not disclose to anyone—not even parents—anything about the student's status that could not be easily accessed in a general campus directory without a written release from the student.

REFERENCES

American Association of University Professors policy and reports (7th ed.). (1990). Washington, DC: American Association of University Professors.

Educator's guide to controlling sexual harassment (Vol. 1). (1993). Washington, DC: Thompson.

EEOC Compliance Manual.(1992). Washington, DC: The Bureau of National Affairs.

Feery, J. (1994). Team input shapes a college's sexual harassment policy. *Personnel Journal, 73*(7), 76.

Gilson, R. J. (1989). *The federal manager's guide to EEO.* Huntsville, AL: Federal Personnel Management Institution.

A guide to postsecondary institutions for implementation of the family educational rights and privacy act of 1974 as amended (Popularly known as the "Buckley Amendment". (1976). Washington, DC: American Association of Collegiate Registrars and Admissions Officers.

Lederman, D. (1997). Supreme court agrees to consider affirmative-action case. *The Chronicle of Higher Education, 43*(44), A28.

Meritor Savings Bank v. Vinson, 477 U.S. 57 (1986).

Sandler, B. R. (1990). Sexual harassment increasingly reported on campus. *Women's International Network News, 16*(1), 36–38.

Section 504 Compliance Handbook. (1992). Washington, DC: Thompson.

Sexual harassment is against the law. (1997, June 13). Available FTP: http://www.afscme.org/afscme/wrkplace/sexh_04.htm.

Shiels, B. (1997, June). *Current issues under the family educational rights and privacy act ("FERPA").* Paper presented at the 37th annual conference of the National Association of College and University Attorneys, Seattle, WA.

Wishnietsky, D. H. (Ed.). (1992) *Sexual harassment in the educational environment.* Bloomington, IN: Phi Delta Kappa.

20

Self-Studies, External Reviews, and Programmatic Assessment

William G. Christ
Trinity University

Peter Orlik
Central Michigan University

David Tucker
University of Toledo

Programmatic review or assessment is a fact of life for universities and colleges. There are at least four kinds of reviews that communication and journalism and mass communication (JMC) units normally might face. First, there are reviews that are linked to the periodic self-studies required as part of a school's regional accreditation in the Middle States, North Central, Northwest, Southern or Western Association of Colleges and States (see Allison, 1994). Second, within JMC, there are reviews required of those programs that desire accreditation from the Accrediting Council for Education in Journalism and Mass Communication (ACEJMC). There are also other quasi-accrediting bodies like the Public Relations Students Society of America that recommend curricula to programs. Third, there are reviews that are initiated and conducted by a unit in order to establish credibility for the unit within a larger administrative structure at either the divisional, school, college, or university level. Finally, there are unit reviews that are "forced" on a unit by an administration that wants to see change and feels the unit is intransigent. In all four kinds of reviews, outside reviewers are usually brought in to evaluate a unit's strengths and weaknesses.

THE SELF-STUDY

All reviews should start with a systematic, comprehensive self-study. This self-study might include one or more of what Haley and Jackson (1995) suggested as a four-level hierarchy of assessment: (a) evaluation of individual program components (peer teaching review and course evaluations); (b) perceptions and performance of graduating seniors (survey of seniors, senior essays, university comprehensives, departmental comprehensives, and campaigns course); (c) evaluations of key constituents (faculty surveys, employer surveys, university alumni surveys and department graduate surveys), and (d) comprehensive program evaluation (program review and accreditation) (see Christ, 1994, 1995, 1997; Christ & McCall, 1994).

Christ and Blanchard (1994) suggested that faculty should address both off- and on-campus challenges when reviewing their programs. Off-campus, three challenges were identified: (a) historical changes facing all colleges and universities in the mid 1990s (e.g., downsizing and calls for general education), (b) emergent and converging communication technologies (e.g., linkages between the computer, programming, and traditional delivery systems), and (c) the philosophical and theoretical ferment within the communication discipline (e.g., linkages between intrapersonal, interpersonal, interactive, and mass communication). (For a more complete discussion of these "forces" see Blanchard & Christ, 1993.)

On campus, Christ and Blanchard (1994) suggested that faculty should ask (a) How and where their program fits within the university—how its mission, and curriculum fit the mission, philosophy, and anticipated outcomes of the university; (b) what outcomes are appropriate for the program as a whole; (c) what courses are appropriate to match those outcomes; (d) what outcomes are appropriate within a course (see also, Galvin, 1992). Buzza (1992) suggested four main areas that might be included in a self-study:

- Appropriateness and contributions of the program.
- Program effectiveness and quality.
- Data on enrollments and other aspects of the department, especially compared to similar departments and to the institution as a whole, and demographic data on faculty, students, and in some cases alumni/ae.
- Consideration of future directions for the department, including a discussion of departmental strengths, weaknesses, and aspirations (p. 27).

Besides these recommendations, there are at least six points that your program needs to address when developing the self-study:

1. You need to be clear about who will read the self-study and how it will be used. Some self-studies seem like acts of futility because they are written and never acted or reflected on. This leads to the second point.

2. Use the self-study to your advantage. Self-studies can be used to make a case for urgent needs and even if not followed provide a paper trail for future requests. It is important to establish the strengths and weaknesses of a program. Be prepared to follow up the self-study with specific recommendations.

3. Programmatic review and assessment are processes that take time. Thorough self-studies might take a year or more. If you do not have that kind of time for your self-study, deal with the big issues first. Be sure that the program's mission is linked to the university mission; that requests for resources are linked back to institutional missions; that problems that might haunt you are clearly articulated so they can be referred back to in future discussions.

4. Self-studies can pull a faculty together or break them apart because they require faculty to focus on areas that are sometimes left unresolved. Be aware that self-studies have their downside and that there are often multiple interpretations of the same historical events. Focusing on areas of agreement while acknowledging areas of disagreement is a prudent approach. This leads to the fifth point.

5. Do not use the self-study to get back at someone or to air dirty laundry. The self-study, which is going to be seen by outside reviewers, is not the place to get back at an administrator you do not like. Outside reviewers usually will be able to pick up on personality conflicts and vendettas. These conflicts might provide interesting background and

explanation, but usually get in the way of trying to move forward with a program.

6.   Self-studies allow a program to be visionary! They give a program the opportunity to define its field to upper level administrators who might not know anything about the area. They can be used as educational tools.

THE REVIEWERS

When a communication educator is called in to conduct an external review of another campus, it is often a trip into a tension zone. Perhaps the unit being reviewed is anxious to receive or retain accreditation. Or upper administration is exploring "reorganization options" that might combine and compress existing departments. A resource shortage within the unit or institution as a whole has prompted a reappraisal of allocation patterns. Or the campus mission statement has been revised and each department is being called on to demonstrate its centrality to this statement in some quantifiable manner.

The external reviewers must anticipate that anxiety will be present and recognize that they face the difficult task of meeting two distinct and sometimes antagonist expectations. Communication colleagues on the campus rely on the reviewers to defend–even save–their programs or sequences from marauding upper administrators. Those upper administrators, in contrast, count on the reviewers for expert and unbiased judgment as to the strengths and weaknesses of a department they seldom understand and that may be engaged in what they perceive as an untidy mix of liberal arts and preprofessional instruction.

Under such circumstances, it is essential that reviewers and programs understand each others' expectations before the physical visit begins. The following discussion is broken into three parts. First are questions reviewers normally ask themselves about the visit. Second are examples of benchmarks reviewers use to gauge the "health" of a program. Last are the responsibilities that programs should address as they begin their review.

The Reviewer's Thoughts

Reviewers face the challenge of balancing the needs of the unit and the administration. There are at least four questions that outside reviewers should ask themselves when going to a school:

1. Who requested/hired me?
2. What am I being asked to do?
3. What surprise awaits me?
4. How can I make this a win–win situation?

Who Requested or Hired Me?

Ideally, a reviewer has been selected by either the unit, the unit and administration together, or as in the case of accreditation, by an accrediting body that knows "the fit" between the reviewer and the program. A reviewer that is hired solely by the administration usually will not have the necessary credibility with the unit. The reviewer could be perceived as a "hatchet person" for the administration. If the reviewer has been selected solely by the unit, with neither the acknowledgment nor the blessing of the key administration, then credibility is also an issue. Reviewers ask, "Who requested me?" in order to understand part of the context in which they will operate.

What Am I Being Asked to Do?

Reviewers need to try and establish the agenda, hidden or otherwise. What is fascinating is that usually there are multiple agendas, especially if there is contentiousness among faculty or between the faculty and the administration. Behind the rhetoric normally lurk things that the different factions involved in the review want done. An administrator may want a chair fired or the curriculum revised. Some faculty may be looking for support in their request for more resources, whereas others may be looking for validation for their program. As reviewers discover what they are really being asked to do, normally there is one or more surprises. This leads to the third question.

What Surprises Await Me?

Usually there are one or more unanticipated revelations that help to explain departmental or administrative behavior: Someone felt that someone else stabbed them in the back. Resources were given at one time and were squandered. Perhaps there is a feeling of betrayal or bad blood. Often, these surprises are quickly communicated to reviewers (sometimes on the ride from the airport to the school). Sometimes these surprises are articulated by people outside the unit. It is often useful for reviewers to talk with not only the unit's faculty, administrators, and students, but with external faculty as well. These outside faculty, if selected carefully, can give reviewers a perspective not always available to the unit's own staff.

How Can I Make This a Win–Win Situation?

Departments usually are not monolithic. In fact, in troubled situations part of the issue is determining who the factions are: (a) senior, tenured faculty against new hires; (b) some tenured faculty against other tenured faculty with each side trying to recruit new hires; (c) faculty in different disciplinary areas: speech against theater against mass communication, broadcasting against print, and so forth; and (d) coalitions that change depending on the issue. And then, of course, there are the situations when faculty find themselves pitted against upper administration. Ideally, reviewers will look for solutions that allow each faction to believe that they will win something. Sometimes, however, this is impossible and some faction needs to be prepared for losing.

WHAT THE REVIEWER WILL LOOK FOR: PROGRAMMATIC BENCHMARKS

Dollar availability is a central issue on most campuses and is of special importance in facility-intensive programs such as electronic media. One can never stray too far from resource issues. In fact, it is those very resource aspects (or concerns or downright terrors) that often motivate the external review in the first place. Nevertheless, it is the responsibility of the reviewer to circumvent the dollar sign fixation by focusing instead on the programmatic attributes and mechanisms that currently exist. If these are soundly derived, the unit's case becomes much more compelling. If they are absent or poorly conceived, they may suggest that even the current level of resource support is in some ways being wasted.

The following are nine programmatic benchmarks. It may be argued that some of these yardsticks are of less import than others or that other significant questions are missing. However, it is the contention here that these nine elements accommodate the breadth of communication unit concerns in a focused and concise inventory that is understandable to—and digestible by—administrators from outside the field. Of course, for regional or "professional" accreditation, there will be other guidelines that must be followed as well. Regional guidelines are available from each of the regional offices, and ACEJMC guidelines are available from Executive Director, Association for Education in Journalism and Mass Communication, University of South Carolina, Columbia, South Carolina, 29208–0251.

Clear Sense of Programmatic Ownership

Each professor in the unit should have specific courses, research areas, or laboratory activities for which they are responsible. Each, therefore, can take responsibility for, and pride in, the direction and further refinement of those program elements that have been entrusted to their care. Similarly, every staff member should be vested with one responsibility that is clearly *developmental*—that requires them to improve their own knowledge, skills, and experiential base in order to advance that part of the unit's collective enterprise.

This process is often a function of position profiling via which each person knows what role they are expected to fulfill within the department. Certainly, many faculty will share in the teaching of multisection courses, but each of these faculty should also have an area for which they are uniquely responsible and that they have the latitude to shape and redirect as the discipline changes. "What am I here for?" should be a question to which each staff member has a ready and personally gratifying answer.

Up-to-Date and "Formatically" Unified
Course Syllabi

Regardless of the sequence of which it is part, every course offered by the unit should have a contemporary master syllabus on file. These should be designed to a standard pattern that requires the same components and sets them forth in the same order. For clarity and consistency, all individual instructor syllabi should flow from these masters and mirror the same explicit statements of student evaluation criteria. All master syllabi should be on file in the main department office with their last date of review prominently displayed. If each course has been reviewed by the collective faculty no more than 5 years ago, it is much easier to infer that the curriculum has been kept current, overlapping courses have been pruned, and outmoded classes have been deleted.

Operating Mechanisms for Continuous
Communication with Alumni and the Profession

Although all academic departments like to keep in contact with their graduates (if for no other reason than fundraising), such contact is mandatory for communication programs. A significant part of what many communication programs do is preprofessional preparation. Maintaining linkages with alumni not only provides feedback on the quality of that preparation but also spins an ever-widening web of industry contacts.

Similarly, the presence of an industry advisory board (see Limburg, 1994) formalizes this feedback and networking. Such a body may include graduates of the program as well as other prominent professionals who are in a position to monitor the industry on the department's behalf and offer valuable counsel on qualities their companies seek in new hires. If continuously solicited, this advice helps keep the unit responsive to real-world needs and signifies a program that is positioned to accommodate change. Thus, an active advisory group is one indication of a department that is dynamic and outward-looking instead of sedentary and parochial.

Internships are another key facet of this outreach, of course, and can be ideal vehicles for simultaneous interaction among students, professionals, and faculty. The availability of carefully prestructured internships is another indicator of faculty commitment to narrowing the gap between the campus and the industry.

Active and Curricularly Supportive
Student Organizations

By its very nature, a communication department is concerned with, and preparing students for, group-generated producing and decision-making situations. However, because course work offers instruction and insights in necessarily segmented modules, it is the cocurricular activities that should help provide the integrative experiences through which classroom knowledge can be field-tested and refined. Departments that facilitate continuously operative student organizations in each curricular area for which they are responsible (i.e., debate teams, university theater companies, radio stations, teleproduction units, and chapters of professional societies) demonstrate a willingness and capability to move beyond the predictability of the classroom and into the challenging and uncertain world of public display. As risky as this display might be for all concerned, such enterprises are hallmarks of a conscientious curriculum that takes itself and its students' needs seriously.

Balance Between Collegial Decision-Making and Executive Authority

The multifaceted nature of most communication units demands the equitable input of faculty representing all phases of the program. Except in the very smallest and narrow-focused programs, no one professor can be truly knowledgeable in all subject matter covered by the unit. Determinations within and between sequences must be the product of shared insight. Yet, such programmatic breadth can create fragmentation and disconnection if a coordinating hand is lacking.

Well-organized communication departments should be able to show the outside reviewer written procedures that (a) guarantee participation by all professors in program direction while (b) vesting clear authority and implementative responsibility in a unit director. These written policies should also set forth the process in which substantive faculty input should be explicitly guaranteed. Although this balance is difficult to achieve, the written recognition of its importance indicates to the reviewer that the department and institution are actively seeking to maximize the expertise that resides in their existing human resources.

Mechanisms for Encouraging and Monitoring Staff and Student Diversification

Unlike many of the other benchmarks, which the department itself must be primarily responsible for meeting, this element's attainment is a cooperative venture with other campus units. Most communication programs can count on their institution's affirmative action office to assist in attaining staff diversity and in their enrollment management office to serve a like function in the recruitment of students. Nonetheless, given the powerful societal role played by the profession for which we are preparing our majors, a communication department should be able to demonstrate to an outside reviewer how it is *building on* the efforts of such campuswide offices to enhance diversification efforts.

Systematic activities such as minority workshops, outreach media career days, guest lecture series featuring professionals from varied ethnic backgrounds, and class modules dedicated to the exploration of diversification issues are a few of the ways in which a department can demonstrate its commitment to sensitizing future professional communicators to their special responsibilities and opportunities.

Service Experiences Designed for the Broadest Campus Constituency

There is a temptation in many preprofessional programs to concentrate exclusively on the training of their own majors and largely ignore the campus as a whole. Not only does such an approach demean the importance of critical communication skills in the personal development of all students, it also isolates the communication unit from the rest of the university, making it difficult to create the kind of broad-based support necessary for the sustenance of our own costly facilities.

A communication program worthy of significant institutional nurturing will have identified ways in which it can serve the needs of students from other departments. This might be course work in basic oral communication, mass media theory or literacy, film appreciation, or organizational communication. It might also consist of dramatic productions chosen and mounted in consultation with other disciplines (such as English, music, and foreign languages), electronic showcases for the work of students and staff in other departments, and cosponsorship of lecture series. The communication unit that truly believes communication skills are essential in modern society should evidence this belief through the outreach activities it has undertaken on its own campus.

Logical, Competency-Relevant Major Entrance Requirements

Whether in business, teaching, music, law, medicine, or communication, professional programs of study should not be automatically open to any student admitted to the institution. Each of these professional programs requires certain enhanced competencies on the part of its prospective practitioners; ability skews that are not necessarily present in every student capable of college-level work. Program entrance requirements that go beyond those required for institutional admission help spotlight the competencies that a faculty believe are particularly important to success in their field. In addition, because our preprofessional programs are among the more expensive to operate, carefully derived entrance qualifications demonstrate a fiscal prudence in which program size is being qualitatively controlled. Selectivity, desirability, and respectability tend to be mutually supportive attributes.

Explicit Standards for Faculty Evaluation

Unlike the scholars in the history department and the performers on the applied music faculty, teaching in a communication program seldom exhibits a singular thrust. Instead, an appointment in our field often entails a variegated blend of creative, scholarly, pedagogical and service endeavors. Consequently, the criteria by which communication faculty are measured should specify the expectation construct for each position.

An outside reviewer will have great difficulty evaluating a faculty if that faculty lacks its own vision of the evaluation criteria it believes to be most valid. The broader the curriculum, the more likely it is that all professors should not be judged by the same proportional standard. What is the comparative importance of teaching, research, and creative output, and professional service in evaluating a member of the communication faculty? Does this proportional importance vary from position to position (from the communication theorist to the radio station supervisor)? Are these expectations established in written form and have they been agreed to by upper administration? In a well-defined program, the answers to these queries are clear, unequivocal, widely known, and widely supported.

As these nine benchmarks indicate, external reviewers bring no magical insights to the evaluation process. Instead, competent reviewers seek systematically to apply several intuitive yardsticks as a means of assessing whether or not the unit has a clear sense of its own mission and has taken all the steps of which it is capable to meet the requirements of this mission. The external review is of the greatest value when its comprehensive *description* provides the raw material from which the communication unit itself can fashion the most appropriate *prescription* for enhanced programmatic performance within its particular campus environment.

Besides these nine programmatic benchmarks, Buzza (1992) suggested a number of associated questions that reviewers might be expected to consider including: "formal organization of the department and staff," "informal structure of the department," "informal relationships within the department," "relationship between the department and central administration," "control the department has over budgets, personnel, curriculum, facilities, etc.," "department's remaining abreast of issues and trends in the discipline," "service (and extracurricular) demands placed on the department," "level of faculty morale; cohesiveness," "adequacy of the department in planning for the future," "innovativeness of the department," and "meeting needs of minority or international students, women, or students with special needs" (pp. 27–28).

THE UNIT

The Unit's Responsibility

Reviews are expensive in terms of time, money, and emotions. Because no program is perfect, even faculty in the best programs know that outside reviewers might overemphasize a weakness in their report while missing key successes. Following are 12 "tips" that should help a program prepare for the review process.

Be Careful Who You Pick for the Review Team. If possible, programs should help to pick reviewers of their program. They should be sympathetic to your area, have a reputation in the field, and care about curriculum and the diversity that makes up our field. If you are a mass communication department you will want a mass communication person represented. If you are a speech department, you will need someone who understands your field. It is wise to either choose people from programs like the one being reviewed, or "illustrious experts" who might give credibility or prestige to the program being reviewed. The wrong person on the review team can cause immense problems for a unit. Their biases might work against the program and its vision of the future.

Give Yourself Time. Self-evaluation is like a production or research. Anticipate how much time it will take and then double the time to be safe. Start early with the self-study. Programs need to involve all the faculty and remind them that what is said in the self-study will be taken seriously by the review team and used as a basis for asking questions. Ideally, the self-study will sound like one voice. Different faculty might be asked to take the lead in different sections, but ideally, there should be one "master" tone that characterizes the document. A schizophrenic self-study connotes to the reviewers a department that needs work. The self-study should be a cohesive and consistent explanation of the unit to the outside world.

Be Clear What You Want From the Review Team. As a unit, are you looking for accreditation? Are you looking for support for asking for more resources? Are you looking for people who will help you fire the chair? Are you looking for credibility? People in the unit need to talk to the review team about what they want from the team. In a nutshell, the unit's agenda should be clear and explicit.

Tell the Review Team What You Would Like to See. Do not expect the review team to read your mind. Tell them your side of the story. Each person interviewed should be able to clearly and succinctly tell the review team what they want out of the review process. In contentious departments there may be a number of wants that are articulated. But even then, the more a unit can speak from one prioritized agenda, the easier it will be for the reviewers to make the process a win–win situation.

Have Your Documentation Ready. Self-studies should be clear, accurate, and persuasive. Review teams look for balance in the self-study. The expectation is that all key documents should be delivered to the review team members weeks before the visit so that the team can read the material. Again, the self-study should be a reflection of the best of the unit. Besides the obvious need for content, style does matter. There should be a table of contents, clear headings and subheadings, and the report should be in the same font throughout. You want the reviewers to be able to locate different parts of the report easily. Misspellings, incorrect grammar, and sloppy prose all communicate the wrong message.

Do Not Try to Hide Your Problems, Challenges, or Weaknesses. Problems, secrets, hidden agendas, and weaknesses are usually communicated to the reviewers very quickly in the review process. All programs have weaknesses. What a unit wants to be able to do in its self-study is provide a context for the weaknesses. If resources are a problem because the upper administration does not trust the unit, then a history of the conflict would help explain the challenge. Reviewers are less concerned about conflicts and more concerned with understanding if there is any win–win way out of the conflict. Explanations of problems that are clear, insightful, and balanced are appreciated.

Expect Other Stakeholders to Be Interviewed. You can expect the review team to want to talk with the unit's faculty, several administrators, faculty from other departments, and students (majors and nonmajors). Do not be surprised if the review team asks to speak to other faculty from around the campus in order to get a handle on how the department is perceived.

Be Prepared to Find More Documentation. Do not be surprised if the review team asks for material you have not provided. Reviewing programs is like putting together a puzzle: All the pieces are not always presented in the initial self-study. Asking for more information does not necessarily mean that the reviewers think there is a problem. Enhanced information helps provide a context for understanding the lived experience of the unit.

Be Prepared to Answer Tough Questions. Good reviewers will be polite but persistent in their questions. They may ask units about funding, resources, faculty (including faculty governance, teaching loads, scholarship, and advising), curriculum, and the unit's relationship to other faculty and the administration. They will probably want to see syllabi, memoranda dealing with key requests, or grading patterns.

Try to Anticipate the Review Team's Questions. What this chapter has tried to do is to help administrators anticipate questions that the review team might ask. In regional and ACEJMC accreditation there are very explicit requirements that need to be addressed. Normally, questions from the review team will deal with factual data and the interpretation of those data.

You Can Expect the Review Team's Report To Be Balanced. Do not expect the report to be simply a reflection of your unit's position.

Such reports would be dismissed out of hand by administrators. No matter what the report says, it is important that you respond to it. This is especially true if you feel the reviewers missed the mark.

Be Prepared to Respond to the Reviewers' Report. Realize that reports, even those that seem to be corroborating your point of view, can be used against you. For example, even when a report says you are doing a good job in a certain area, it is possible for those in upper administration to read the same report and suggest that you are spending too many of your resources in that particular area. Reports can bring together or split departments. Try to anticipate the review team's recommendations. It is possible at times that the reviewers will, by the questions they ask or the answers they give to your questions, give you some idea about how they are viewing your program. Prepare and mobilize your faculty to be ready to respond. Even if the review is favorable, be sure to write a cover letter for the report to the upper administration that reemphasizes the points in the report on which you want the upper administration to concentrate.

CASE STUDY

In Spring 1995, the University of Toledo's Department of Communication found itself in a position best described by Christ and Blanchard (1994): "If communication education programs are seen as fragmented, peripheral, or even nonessential to the overall university mission by on-campus committees, then they are more susceptible to being downsized or eliminated" (p. 31). To say the department was in trouble would have qualified as a major understatement.

An umbrella department, it contained broadcasting, journalism, public relations, general communication, and communication disorders as concentrations. Each had its own set of requirements. The department had been undergoing an internal program review, similar to those described earlier in the chapter, for almost 2 years when the issue of maintaining or eliminating the department came to a head. The review process had, to that point, involved a self-study, an in-house study by a university panel, a dean's report, and an evaluation by a university-wide committee (the Academic Program Advisory Committee, or APAC). A recommendation by the Vice President for Academic Affairs to the Board of Trustees was yet to be written.

All University of Toledo departments undergo such a review once every 5 years. The self-study by the department had found that it was serving more students than feasible given the number of full-time faculty. (The number of majors was approximately 600 and the number of full-time faculty was 12.) Some students were getting to their senior year without having taken a course from a full-time faculty member. The unit's study also showed that it was being used as a cash cow by the College of Arts and Sciences and that it should get more of that money back for equipment and full-time faculty. The University panel found essentially the same thing. That three-member committee concluded in May 1994 by writing, "The faculty of the Department of Communication has worked hard to provide an effective program under extremely difficult conditions. Morale is at a low point. A reasonable level of University support must be provided to improve and assure teaching and research effectiveness. The University should make meeting the needs of this Department a high priority. If it does so, there is every reason to expect that the quality of the results will be gratifying in all respects" (personal communication, 1994).

The Dean of the College of Arts and Sciences was not impressed with either the department's self-study or the University review. In a memo dated May 29, 1994 (sent to the Office of Academic Affairs and to the University-wide Program Review Committee, but never to the department), the Dean blasted both reports, the department, and its faculty: "Let me say at the outset that I am very disappointed by the Committee's report. Committee members appear to have exhibited no independence of judgment by treating the assertions of the faculty as though they were fact" (personal communication, 1994). The Dean, of course, placed the blame squarely on the shoulders of the Department.

In January 1995, the University committee overseeing the program review (APAC) chose to take a middle ground. It recommended bringing in an outside consultant to "bring the Department together, to help it come to strong agreement about mission, goals, a plan of action and leadership and help it sort out problems and devise solutions using existing resources and strengths of the department" (personal communication, 1995).

The University committee also suggested four options:

- Focusing the program in majors (concentrations) for which the department is strong.

- Transferring academic programs of the department to other departments where the academic programs could be better supported.
- Dropping or phasing out weaker programs.
- Converting part-time positions to full-time or adjunct faculty positions.

The Vice President for Academic Affairs concurred with APAC, and moved to bring in outside consultants. The department was very concerned. The review, begun in the summer of 1993, was now 18 months old and the faculty believed that everything had been said. Why bring in outsiders?

There were several possibilities that occurred to the faculty. First, the Vice President would bring a handpicked team to do a hatchet job on the department. This would result in the department being disbanded with the various classes being taught by other departments across the University. Second, she might use the review against particular faculty. For instance, the head of the faculty union was a department member. Third, such an outside group might recommend downsizing the department through the elimination of expensive programs such as broadcasting and journalism.

Some of these fears were put aside when, in a meeting with the faculty, the Vice President asked for input on possible reviewers. This meant that the department was not under an immediate threat. It did not alleviate the possibility that the reviewers it picked might still not come to a negative conclusion, but at least the department was not terminated. Three reviewers were chosen and sent as much documentation about the department as possible. They received all reports and memos detailing the department review up to March 1995. They received copies of the catalog as well as curriculum vitae from all department faculty. The consultants arrived in early April. During their stay, they met with department faculty, administrators, and students. They also toured the facilities. Their 2 day visit generated a final report of 26 single-spaced pages.

There were four major recommendations made by the consulting team.

- Support and develop the strengths of this teaching faculty. Increase the number of full-time faculty over the next 3 years.

- Revise the undergraduate curriculum with a focus on integrating the various programs. With only 12 faculty and over 600 majors, it is impossible to retain the current curricular structure of five separate programs. This faculty is overburdened with attempts to meet the service needs of the university in general as well as the needs of their majors for sequenced courses offered in a timely and systematic rotation.
- Revitalize the faculty governance structure in the department. Given the size and complexity of the department, the department has been well-managed. It is time, however, to change the leadership and governance structure of the department to spearhead the changes needed to reinvigorate the department.
- Increase resources in the departmental budget. The report then went on to describe exactly what was meant by these recommendations.

A report of this nature can, in and of itself, represent some danger to a department. This was true in this case as well. There was the possibility that the university might say it would cost too much to implement these recommendations and disband the department. In this case, that did not happen.

Taking the recommendations one at a time, the University allocated two more full-time faculty slots to the department. One of these was to be in general communication, the other in TV production and new technologies. In addition, the department expanded its use of adjunct faculty, thus reducing its reliance on part-timers.

The second recommendation addressed the state of the department's curriculum. As stated earlier, the department was really a collection of various programs with no common core or thread running through it. Starting in the summer of 1995, the department began to revise its curriculum. The first step, however, was to revise the department's mission statement. It decided it must know who it thought it was before deciding what it thought it was going to teach. Once the mission statement was revised, it was easier to begin the examination of the curriculum (see Christ & Blanchard, 1994; Christ & Hynes, 1997).

The department opted for what has been referred to in the literature as convergence. It developed a common core, which was called "Requirements in Common." This was followed by a group of courses titled, "Applied Communication" and another titled, "Conceptual Communication." A senior portfolio class was added for assessment purposes. (For a complete copy of both old and new curricula, contact the Department of Communication, University of Toledo.) No longer was the unit separate little entities with a common chair. Instead it was now one integrated department.

As for the third recommendation, the department changed its chair as well as adding an associate chair. It has become the associate chair's job to guide and evaluate part-time faculty. The change in leadership has seemed to benefit the department in that the new chair is not saddled with old problems and relationships.

The fourth recommendation was to increase the resources available to the department. This has also been done. There is now an equipment budget as well as increased travel funds and office support.

SUMMARY

The Department of Communication at the University of Toledo benefited greatly from the overall review process. However, outside review under any circumstances may be a double-edged sword. It can be used to validate a department's request for resources or turned against the department, even if the conclusions of the outside evaluators are favorable, and it is not a given that such conclusions will be favorable.

Most faculty members, if asked, will say they are overburdened, overworked, underappreciated, and underpaid, and that their department is underfinanced. If the outside review team concludes otherwise, the faculty may be devastated. It is possible for a review team to conclude that the faculty is nonproductive, that research is a foreign term to these faculty, and that the university would be better off without this department. That is exactly why periodic reviews by the department itself (described earlier in this chapter) are essential to the overall well-being of the department. If a department examines itself in an objective fashion, it is possible to identify problems before they become debilitating. It is possible to use the review to make improvements to a department. When it gets to the point where the vice president is calling for an outside review, it should be apparent to one and all that there are major problems. Ideally, it would never get to that point.

APPENDIX A: UNIT CHECKLIST

Reviewers' Questions

- Who requested or hired me?
- What am I being asked to do?
- What surprises await me?
- How can I make this a win–win situation?

Programmatic Benchmarks

- Clear sense of programmatic ownership.
- Up-to-date and formatically unified course syllabi.
- Operating mechanisms for continuous communication with alumni and the profession.
- Active and curricularly supportive student organizations.
- Balance between collegial decision making and executive authority.
- Mechanisms for encouraging and monitoring staff and student diversification.
- Service experiences designed for the broadest campus constituency.
- Logical, competency-relevant major entrance requirements.
- Explicit standards for faculty evaluation.

The Unit's Responsibility

- Be careful who you pick for the review team.
- Give yourself time.
- Be clear what you want from the review team.
- Tell the review team what you would like to see.
- Have your documentation ready.
- Do not try to hide your problems, challenges, or weaknesses.
- Be prepared to find more documentation.
- Expect the review team to want to talk with the unit's faculty, several administrators, faculty from other departments, and students (majors and nonmajors).
- Be prepared to answer tough questions.
- Try to anticipate the review team's questions.
- Expect the review team's report to be balanced.
- Be prepared to respond to the reviewer's report.

REFERENCES

Allison, T. (1994). Regional association requirements and the development of outcomes statements. In W. G. Christ (Ed.), *Assessing communication education: A handbook for media, speech, and theatre educators* (pp. 57–86). Hillsdale, NJ: Lawrence Erlbaum Associates.

Blanchard, R. O., & Christ, W. G. (1993). *Media education and the liberal arts: A blueprint for the new professionalism*. Hillsdale, NJ: Lawrence Erlbaum Associates.

Buzza, B. W. (1992). External program review: The reviewer's perspective. In E. A. Hay (Ed.), *Program assessment in speech communication* (pp. 25–29). Annandale, VA: Speech Communication Association.

Christ, W. G. (Ed.). (1994). *Assessing communication education: A handbook for media, speech, and theatre educators*. Hillsdale, NJ: Lawrence Erlbaum Associates.

Christ, W. G. (1995, Winter). J/MC agenda for the 90's the role of journalism and mass communication in the university of the future. *Insights*, pp. 1–5.

Christ, W. G. (Ed.). (1997). *Media education assessment handbook*. Mahwah, NJ: Lawrence Erlbaum Associates.

Christ, W. G., & Blanchard, R. O. (1994). Mission statements, outcomes, and the new liberal arts. In W. G. Christ (Ed.), *Assessing communication education: A handbook for media, speech, and theatre educators* (pp. 31–55). Hillsdale, NJ: Lawrence Erlbaum Associates.

Christ, W. G., & Hynes, T. (1997). The missions and purposes of journalism and mass communication education, *Journalism and Mass Communication Educator, 52*(2), 73–92.

Christ, W. G., & McCall, J. (1994). Assessing "the what" of media education. In S. Morreale & M. Brooks (Eds.), *1994 SCA Summer Conference Proceedings and Prepared Remarks* (pp. 477–493). Annandale, VA: Speech Communication Association.

Galvin, K. N. (1992). Foundation for assessment: The mission, goals and objectives. In E. A. Hay (Ed.), *Program assessment in speech communication* (pp. 21–24), Annandale, VA: Speech Communication Association.

Haley, E., & Jackson, D. (1995). A conceptualization of assessment for mass communication programs. *Journalism & Mass Communication Educator, 50*(1), 26–34.

Limburg, V. E. (1994). Internships, exit interviews, and advisory boards. In W. G. Christ (Ed.), *Assessing communication education* (pp.181–200). Hillsdale, NJ: Lawrence Erlbaum Associates.

Criteria for the Assessment of Oral Communication

National Communication Association
formerly Speech Communication Association

A National Context

Assessment has received increasing attention throughout the 1970s and into the 1990s. Initially appearing in the standards developed by state departments of education, by 1980 over half of the states had adopted statewide student-testing programs. In *Educational Standards in the 50 States: 1990*, the Educational Testing Service reported that, by 1985, over 40 states had adopted such programs, and between 1985 and 1990, an additional five states initiated statewide student-testing programs, bringing the number of such programs to 47.

During the 1970s and 1980s, the number of different subjects and skills tested has also consistently increased, with additional attention devoted to how assessments are executed. Moreover, during this period, organizations, such as the National

Assessment of Educational Progress, intensified and expanded the scope of their assessment procedures as well as publicized the results of their findings nationally and annually.

By the end of 1989, the public recognized the significance of national educational assessments. In the *Phi Delta Kappan*–Gallup poll reported in the September issue of *Phi Delta Kappan*, 77 percent of the respondents favored "requiring the public schools in this community to use standardized national testing programs to measure academic achievement of students" and 70 percent favored "requiring the public schools in this community to conform to national achievement standards and goals."

Likewise, towards the end of the 1980s, colleges and universities began to realize that formal assessment issues were to affect them. For example, in its 1989–1990 *Criteria for Accredita-*

tion, the Southern Association of Colleges and Schools—which provides institutional certification for over 800 colleges and universities in the South—held that "complete requirements for an associate or baccalaureate degree must include competence in reading, writing, oral communications and fundamental mathematical skills." They also held that the general education core of colleges and universities "must provide components designed to ensure competence in reading, writing, oral communication and fundamental mathematical skills."

In 1990, a series of reports appeared which suggested that systematic and comprehensive assessment should become a national educational objective. In February 1990, for example, the National Governors' Association, in the context of President Bush's set of six educational goals, argued that, "National education goals will be meaningless unless progress toward meeting them is measured accurately and adequately, and reported to the American people." The nation's Governors argued that "doing a good job of assessment" requires that "what students need to know must be defined," "it must be determined whether they know it," and "measurements must be accurate, comparable, appropriate, and constructive." In July 1990, President Bush reinforced this line of reasoning in *The National Education Goals: A Report to the Nation's Governors*. And, in September 1990, the National Governors' Association extended and elaborated its commitment to assessment in *Educating America: State Strategies for Achieving the National Education Goals: Report of the Task Force on Education*.

Additionally, in 1990, in their report From *Gatekeeper to Gateway: Transforming Testing in America*, the National Commission on Testing and Public Policy recommended eight standards for assessment, arguing for more humane and multicultural assessment systems. Among other considerations, they particularly maintained that "testing policies and practices must be reoriented to promote the development of all human talent," that "test scores should be used only when they differentiate on the basis of characteristics relevant to the opportunities being allocated," and that "the more test scores disproportionately deny opportunities to minorities, the greater the need to show that the tests measure characteristics relevant to the opportunities being allocated."

NCA Assessment Activities

The evaluation and assessment of public address has been of central concern to the discipline of communication since its inception and to the National Communication Association (formerly Speech Communication Association) when it was organized in 1914. In 1970, NCA formalized its commitment to assessment when it created the Committee on Assessment and Testing (now known by the acronym CAT) for "NCA members interested in gathering, analyzing and disseminating information about the testing of speech communication skills." CAT has been one of the most active, consistent, and productive of NCA's various committees and task forces.

Under the guidance of CAT, NCA has published several volumes exploring formal methods for assessing oral communication. These publications began to appear in the 1970s and have continued into the 1990s. In 1978, for example, the National Communication Association published *Assessing Functional Communication*, which was followed in 1984 by two other major publications, *Large Scale Assessment of Oral Communication Skills: Kindergarten through Grade 12* and *Oral Communication Assessment Procedures and Instrument Development in Higher Education.*

In 1979, in *Standards for Effective Oral Communication Programs*, NCA adopted its first set of "standards" for "assessment and evaluation." The first standards called for "school-wide assessment of speaking and listening needs of students," "qualified personnel" to "utilize appropriate evaluation tools," a "variety of data" and "instruments" which "encourage" "students desire to communicate."

In 1986, in *Criteria for Evaluating Instruments and Procedures for Assessing Speaking and Listening*, NCA adopted an additional 15 "content" and "technical considerations" dealing "primarily with the substance of speaking and listening instruments" and "matters such as reliability, validity and information on administration." These criteria included the importance of focusing on "demonstrated" speaking skills rather than "reading and writing ability," adopting "assessment instruments and procedures" which are "free of sexual, cultural, racial, and ethnic content and/or stereotyping," employing "familiar situations" which are "important for various communication settings" in test questions, using instruments which "permit a range of acceptable responses" and generate "reliable" outcomes, employing assessments which are consistent with other "results" and have "content validity," and employing "standardized" procedures which "approximate the recognized stress level of oral communication" which are also "practical in terms of cost and time" and "suitable for the developmental level of the individual being tested."

In 1987, at the association's Wingspread Conference, "conference participants recommended that the chosen instrument conform to NCA guidelines for assessment instruments," and they specifically suggested that "strategies for assessing speaking skills" should be directly linked to the content of oral communication performances and student speaking competencies. Prescribed communication practices were to determine the choice of assessment strategies, with the following content standards guiding formal evaluations: "determine the purpose of oral discourse;" "choose a topic and restrict it according to the purpose and the audience;" "fulfill the purpose" by "formulating a thesis statement," "providing adequate support material," "selecting a suitable organization," "demonstrating careful choice of words," "providing effective transitions," "demonstrating suitable interpersonal skills;" employing "vocal variety in rate, pitch, and intensity;" "articulate clearly;" "employ the level of American English appropriate to the designated audience;" and "demonstrate nonverbal behavior that supports the verbal message." Additionally, the Wingspread Conference participants considered strategies for assessing listening and for training assessors (see: *Communication Is Life: Essential College Sophomore Speaking and Listening Competencies*, Annandale, VA: National Communication Association, 1990, pp. 51–74).

In 1988, the association's Flagstaff Conference generated a series of resolutions calling for a "national conference" and "task force on assessment" because "previous experience in developing standardized assessment has met with problems of validity, reliability, feasibility, ethics, and cultural bias" (in *The Future of Speech Communication Education: Proceedings of the 1988 National Communication Association Flagstaff Conference*, ed. by Pamela J. Cooper and Kathleen M. Galvin, Annandale, VA: National Communication Association, 1989, p. 80).

In July 1990, a National Conference on Assessment was sponsored by NCA, the NCA Committee on Assessment and Testing or CAT, and the NCA Educational Policies Board (EPB). The Conference generated several resolutions regarding assessment. Some of these resolutions reaffirmed existing NCA oral communication assessment policies. Others provided criteria for resolving new issues in assessment. Still others sought to integrate and establish a more coherent relationship among the criteria governing oral communication assessment. The recommended assessment criteria are detailed immediately below.

General Criteria

1. Assessment of oral communication should view competence in oral communication as a gestalt of several interacting dimensions. At a minimum, all assessments of oral communication should include an assessment of knowledge (understanding communication process, comprehension of the elements, rules, and dynamics of a communication event, awareness of what is appropriate in a communication situation), an assessment of skills (the possession of a repertoire of skills and the actual performance of skills), and an evaluation of the individual's attitude toward communication (e.g., value placed on oral communication, apprehension, reticence, willingness to communicate, readiness to communicate).

2. Because oral communication is an interactive and social process, assessment should consider the judgment of a trained assessor as well as the impressions of others involved in the communication act (audience, interviewer, other group members, conversant), and may include the self report of the individual being assessed.

3. Assessment of oral communication should clearly distinguish speaking and listening from reading and writing. While some parts of the assessment process may include reading and writing, a major portion of the assessment of oral communication should require speaking and listening. Directions from the assessor and responses by the individual being assessed should be in the oral/aural mode.

4. Assessment of oral communication should be sensitive to the effects of relevant physical and psychological disabilities on the assessment of competence. (e.g., with appropriate aids in signal reception, a hearing im-

paired person can be a competent empathic listener.)

5. Assessment of oral communication should be based in part on atomistic/analytic data collected and on a holistic impression.

5. Criteria for the Content of Assessment

1. Assessment of oral communication for all students should include assessment of both verbal and nonverbal aspects of communication and should consider competence in more than one communication setting. As a minimum assessment should occur in the one-to-many setting (e.g., public speaking, practical small group discussion) and in the one-to-one setting (e.g., interviews, interpersonal relations).

2. Assessment of speech majors and other oral communication specialists could include in addition assessment in specialized fields appropriate to the course of study followed or the specialty of the person being assessed.

2. Criteria for Assessment Instruments

1. The method of assessment should be consistent with the dimension of oral communication being assessed. While knowledge and attitude may be assessed in part through paper and pencil instruments, speaking and listening skills must be assessed through actual performance in social settings (speaking before an audience, undergoing an interview, participating in a group discussion, etc.) appropriate to the skill(s) being assessed.

2. Instruments for assessing oral communication should describe degrees of competence. Either/or descriptions such as "competent" or "incompetent" should be avoided as should attempts to diagnose reasons why individuals demonstrate or fail to demonstrate particular degrees of competence.

3. Instruments for assessing each dimension of oral communication competence should clearly identify the range of responses which could constitute various degrees of competence. Examples of such responses should be provided as anchors.

4. Assessment instruments should have an acceptable level of reliability, e.g. test/retest reliability, split-half reliability, alternative forms reliability, inter-rater reliability, and internal consistency.

5. Assessment instruments should have appropriate validity: content validity, predictive validity, and concurrent validity.

6. Assessment instruments must meet acceptable standards for freedom from cultural, sexual, ethical, racial, age, and developmental bias.

7. Assessment instruments should be suitable for the developmental level of the individual being assessed.

8. Assessment instruments should be standardized and detailed enough so that individual responses will not be affected by an administrator's skill in administering the procedures.

8. Criteria for Assessment Procedures and Administration

1. Assessment procedures should protect the rights of those being assessed in the following ways: administration of assessment instruments and assessment and the uses of assessment results should be kept confiden-

tial and be released only to an appropriate institution office, to the individual assessed, or if a minor, to his or her parent or legal guardian.

2. Use of competence assessment as a basis for procedural decisions concerning an individual should, when feasible, be based on multiple sources of information, including especially a) direct evidence of actual communication performance in school and/or other contexts, b) results of formal competence assessment, and c) measures of individual attitudes toward communication (e.g., value placed on oral communication, apprehension, reticence, willingness to communicate, and readiness to communicate).

3. Individuals administering assessment procedures for oral communication should have received sufficient training by speech communication professionals to make their assessment reliable. Scoring of some standardized assessment instruments in speaking and listening may require specialized training in oral communication on the part of the assessor.

3. Criteria for Assessment Frequency

Periodic assessment of oral communication competency should occur annually during the educational careers of students. An effective systematic assessment program minimally should occur at educational levels K, 4, 8, 12, 14, and 16.

Criteria for the Use of Assessment Results

The results of student oral communication competency assessment should be used in an ethical, non-discriminatory manner for such purposes as:

1. Diagnosing student strengths and weaknesses;

2. Planning instructional strategies to address student strengths and weaknesses;

3. Certification of student readiness for entry into and exit from programs and institutions;

4. Evaluating and describing overall student achievement;

5. Screening students for programs designed for special populations;

6. Counseling students for academic and career options; and

7. Evaluating the effectiveness of instructional programs.

No single assessment instrument is likely to support all these purposes. Moreover, instruments appropriate to various or multiple purposes typically vary in length, breadth/depth of content, technical rigor, and format.

The criteria contained in this document were originally adopted as resolutions at the NCA Conference on Assessment in Denver, Colorado, in July of 1990. Several of the criteria were authored by the Committee on Assessment and Testing Subcommittee on Criteria for Content, Procedures, and Guidelines for Oral Communication Competencies composed of Jim Crocker-Lakness (Subcommittee Chair), Sandra Manheimer, and Tom Scott. The introductory sections entitled "A National Context" and "NCA's Assessment Activities" were authored by James W. Chesebro, NCA Director of Education Services.

For further information on the assessment of communication, contact the National Communication Association, 5105 Backlick Rd. #F, Annandale, VA 22003; 703-750-0533; http://www.natcom.org

Author Index

Subject Index

411